Get the eBook FREE!

(PDF, ePub, Kindle, and liveBook all included)

We believe that once you buy a book from us, you should be able to read it in any format we have available. To get electronic versions of this book at no additional cost to you, purchase and then register this book at the Manning website.

Go to https://www.manning.com/freebook and follow the instructions to complete your pBook registration.

That's it!
Thanks from Manning!

Machine Learning Algorithms in Depth

Machine Learning Algorithms in Depth

VADIM SMOLYAKOV

MANNING
SHELTER ISLAND

For online information and ordering of this and other Manning books, please visit www.manning.com. The publisher offers discounts on this book when ordered in quantity. For more information, please contact

> Special Sales Department
> Manning Publications Co.
> 20 Baldwin Road
> PO Box 761
> Shelter Island, NY 11964
> Email: orders@manning.com

Manning Publications Co.	Development editor: Elesha Hyde
20 Baldwin Road	Technical editor: Junpeng Lao
PO Box 761	Review editor: Aleksandar Dragosavljević
Shelter Island, NY 11964	Production editor: Kathy Rossland
	Copy editor: Christian Berk
	Proofreader: Jason Everett
	Technical proofreader: Bin Hu
	Typesetter: Gordan Salinovic
	Cover designer: Marija Tudor

ISBN 9781633439214
Printed in the United States of America

To my parents, Sergey and Valeriya, for their constant love and support.

To my partner, Kelly, I love you infinitely.

brief contents

contents

preface

Welcome to *Machine Learning Algorithms in Depth*! The idea of writing this book came to me during my graduate school years. At the time, I was switching majors from wireless communications to machine learning and found that one constant during this transition was my fascination with algorithms. I wanted to study this subject in depth and really understand how to derive, implement, and analyze algorithms from the first principles. I was fortunate to have found a research home in the Sensing, Learning, and Inference group at MIT CSAIL, where I was exposed to a wide variety of machine learning applications centered on Bayesian inference. At the same time, the field of deep learning was rapidly evolving, and I found myself training and experimenting with a variety of neural network models for computer vision and natural language processing.

I've always been fascinated with the complementary strengths of probabilistic graphical models and deep learning models, and pondered ways in which the two can be combined. Throughout my graduate school journey, I was exposed to a variety of applications and developed a library of algorithms I implemented from scratch. I read many machine learning texts and was a technical editor for others, which lead me to finding a gap in the existing literature: a from-scratch approach to machine learning algorithms. This was my "aha!" moment, and it fueled my dream of writing a book. *Machine Learning Algorithms in Depth* takes the reader on a journey from mathematical derivation to software implementation of some of the most intriguing algorithms in ML. My goal in writing this book is to distill the science of ML and present it in a way that will convey intuition and inspire the reader to self-learn, innovate, and advance the field. Thank you for your interest, and welcome to the world of ML algorithms!

acknowledgments

I want to thank the people at Manning who made this book possible: publisher Marjan Bace and everyone on the editorial and production teams, including Patrick Barb, Elesha Hyde, and many others who worked behind the scenes.

Many thanks go to the technical peer reviewers, led by Aleksandar Dragosavljević—Abhilash Babu, Allan Makura, Ariel Gamiño, Bin Hu, Christian Sutton, Fernando García Sedano, Harsh Raval, James J. Byleckie, Japneet Singh, Johnny Hopkins, Jordan Samek, Kai Gellien, Khai Win, Kumar Abhishek, Madhav Ayyagari, Maria Ana, Marvin Schwarze, Maxim Volgin, Morteza Kiadi, Or Golan, Ravi Kiran Bamidi, Sadhana Ganapathiraju, Sanket Naik, Shreyas B. G., Sleiman Salameh, Sriram Macharla, Sumit Bhattacharyya, Vatsal Desai, and Walter Alexander Mata Lopez—as well as the forum contributors. The reviewers provided section-by-section feedback on everything from contents to figures to code implementation, and they played an important role in shaping the manuscript.

On the technical side, special thanks go to Junpeng Lao, who served as the book's technical editor. Junpeng Lao is a senior data scientist at Google. He earned his PhD and worked as a postdoc in cognitive neuroscience. He developed a fondness for Bayesian statistics and generative modeling after working primarily with bootstrapping and permutation testing during his academic life. He is also a core contributor to Blackjax, PyMC, and TensorFlow Probability. Many thanks also to Hubin Keio, who served as the book's technical proofreader. I was truly amazed at the level of detail and helpfulness of their feedback while writing the book.

Finally, I'd like to express gratitude to my partner, Kelly, for being very supportive throughout the process of writing this book.

about this book

This book dives into the design of ML algorithms from scratch. Throughout the book, you will develop mathematical intuition for classic and modern ML algorithms and learn the fundamentals of Bayesian inference and deep learning as well as data structures and algorithmic paradigms in ML.

Understanding ML algorithms from scratch will help you choose the right algorithm for the task, explain the results, troubleshoot advanced problems, extend algorithms to new applications, and improve the performance of existing algorithms.

What makes this book stand out from the crowd is its from-scratch analysis that discusses how and why ML algorithms work in significant depth, a carefully selected set of algorithms that I found most useful and impactful in my experience as a PhD student in machine learning, fully worked out derivations and implementations of ML algorithms explained in the text, as well as some other topics less commonly found in other ML texts.

After reading this book, you'll have a solid mathematical intuition for classic and modern ML algorithms in the areas of supervised and unsupervised learning, and will have gained experience in the domains of core ML, natural language processing, computer vision, optimization, computational biology, and finance.

Who should read this book

This book was written for anyone interested in exploring machine learning algorithms in depth. It may prove invaluable to many different types of readers, including the following:

- Aspiring data scientists
- Entry- to principal-level data scientists
- Software developers seeking to transition to data science
- Data engineers seeking to deepen their knowledge of ML models
- Graduate students with research interests in ML
- Undergraduate students interested in ML

The prerequisites for reading this book include a basic level of programming skills in Python, and an intermediate level of understanding of linear algebra, applied probability, and multivariable calculus.

How this book is organized

This book is structured in four parts. It is recommended that you read the chapters in sequence if the topic is new to you. However, feel free to reference a particular algorithm if you are more familiar with the subject. Each chapter is followed by a few exercises to help you practice some of the tools taught in the chapter, and you are welcome to reference appendix B for solutions to these exercises. Also, included at the end of each part is a machine learning research section with the purpose of reviewing state-of-the-art work and encouraging the reader to stay on top of a rapidly changing field.

Part 1 reviews different types of ML algorithms, motivates implementation from first principles, and introduces two main camps of Bayesian inference—Markov chain Monte Carlo and variational inference:

- Chapter 1 introduces the subject of Bayesian inference and deep learning as well as algorithmic paradigms and data structures used in the software implementation of machine learning algorithms.
- Chapter 2 introduces key Bayesian concepts and motivates Markov chain Monte Carlo via a series of examples, ranging from stock price estimation to Metropolis-Hastings sampling of a multivariate Gaussian mixture.
- Chapter 3 focuses on variational inference and, in particular, mean-field approximation in application to image denoising in the Ising model.
- Chapter 4 discusses linear, nonlinear, and probabilistic data structures as well as four algorithmic paradigms: complete search, greedy, divide and conquer, and dynamic programming.

Part 2 reviews supervised learning algorithms. Supervised learning algorithms contain labeled examples as part of the training dataset and consist of two main classes—classification and regression:

- Chapter 5 focuses on classification algorithms. We'll derive several classic algorithms, including the perceptron, SVM, logistic regression, naive Bayes, and decision trees.

- Chapter 6 highlights four intriguing regression algorithms: Bayesian linear regression, hierarchical Bayesian regression, KNN regression, and Gaussian process regression.
- Chapter 7 presents a selected set of supervised learning algorithms, including Markov models, such as page rank algorithms and hidden Markov models; imbalanced learning strategies; active learning; Bayesian optimization for hyperparameter selection; and ensemble methods.

Part 3 reviews unsupervised learning algorithms. Unsupervised learning takes place when no training labels are available. In the case of unsupervised learning, we are often interested in discovering patterns in data and learning data representations.

- Chapter 8 starts by looking at the Bayesian nonparametric extension of the K-means algorithm followed by the EM algorithm for Gaussian mixture models. We will then proceed with two different dimensionality reduction techniques—namely, PCA and t-SNE—in application to learning an image manifold.
- Chapter 9 continues the discussion of selected unsupervised learning algorithms. We'll start by looking at latent Dirichlet allocation for learning topic models, followed by density estimators and structure learning algorithms, and concluding with simulated annealing and genetic algorithms.

Part 4 reviews deep learning algorithms. Deep learning algorithms revolutionized the field of machine learning and enabled many research and business applications that were previously thought to be out of reach of classic ML algorithms.

- Chapter 10 begins with deep learning algorithm fundamentals, such as multi-layer perceptron and the LeNet convolutional model for MNIST digit classification, followed by more advanced applications, such as image search based on the ResNet50 convolutional neural network. We will dive into recurrent neural networks applied to sequence classification using LSTMs and implement a multi-input model from scratch for sequence similarity. Finally, we'll conduct a comparative study of different optimization algorithms used for training deep neural networks.
- Chapter 11 presents more advanced deep learning algorithms. We will investigate generative models based on variational autoencoders and implement an anomaly detector from scratch for time-series data. We'll study an intriguing combination of neural networks and probabilistic graphical models, and implement a mixture density network from scratch. Next, we'll describe the powerful transformer architecture and apply it to text classification. Finally, we'll examine graph neural networks and use one to classify nodes in a citation graph.

About the code

This book contains many examples of source code both in numbered listings and in line with normal text. In both cases, source code is formatted in a `fixed-width font` `like this` to separate it from ordinary text.

In many cases, the original source code has been reformatted; we've added line breaks and reworked indentation to accommodate the available page space in the book. In rare cases, even this was not enough, and listings include line-continuation markers (➥). Additionally, comments in the source code have often been removed from the listings when the code is described in the text. Code annotations accompany many of the listings, highlighting important concepts.

You can get executable snippets of code from the liveBook (online) version of this book at https://livebook.manning.com/book/machine-learning-algorithms-in-depth. All code examples are available for download from the book's website: https://www.manning.com/books/machine-learning-algorithms-in-depth and on GitHub: https://github.com/vsmolyakov/ml_algo_in_depth.

liveBook discussion forum

Purchase of *Machine Learning Algorithms in Depth* includes free access to liveBook, Manning's online reading platform. Using liveBook's exclusive discussion features, you can attach comments to the book globally or to specific sections or paragraphs. It's a snap to make notes for yourself, ask and answer technical questions, and receive help from the author and other users. To access the forum, go to https://livebook .manning.com/book/machine-learning-algorithms-in-depth/discussion. You can also learn more about Manning's forums and the rules of conduct at https://livebook .manning.com/discussion.

Manning's commitment to our readers is to provide a venue where a meaningful dialogue between individual readers and between readers and the author can take place. It is not a commitment to any specific amount of participation on the part of the author, whose contribution to the forum remains voluntary (and unpaid). We suggest you try asking the author some challenging questions lest his interest stray! The forum and the archives of previous discussions will be accessible from the publisher's website as long as the book is in print.

about the author

VADIM SMOLYAKOV is a data scientist in the Enterprise & Security DI research and development team at Microsoft. He is a former PhD student in AI at MIT CSAIL, with research interests in Bayesian inference and deep learning. Prior to joining Microsoft, Vadim developed machine learning solutions in the e-commerce space. In his current role, he is interested in developing AI products at scale and leading diverse teams.

about the cover illustration

The figure on the cover of *Machine Learning Algorithms in Depth*, titled "Maraichere," or "Vegetable Grower," is taken from a book by Louis Curmer published in 1841. Each illustration is finely drawn and colored by hand.

In those days, it was easy to identify where people lived and what their trade or station in life was just by their dress. Manning celebrates the inventiveness and initiative of the computer business with book covers based on the rich diversity of regional culture centuries ago, brought back to life by pictures from collections such as this one.

Part 1

Introducing ML algorithms

Welcome to *Machine Learning Algorithms in Depth*. In the first part of the book, we will discuss different types of ML algorithms, motivate their implementation from first principles, and introduce two main camps of Bayesian inference: Markov chain Monte Carlo and variational inference.

In chapter 1, we'll give reasons why we want to learn ML algorithms from scratch, introduce the subject of Bayesian inference and deep learning, and discuss algorithmic paradigms and data structures used in the software implementation of machine learning algorithms.

In chapter 2, we'll introduce key Bayesian concepts and motivate MCMC via a series of examples, ranging from stock price estimation to Metropolis-Hastings sampling of multivariate Gaussian mixtures.

In chapter 3, we'll focus on variational inference and, in particular, mean-field approximation applied to image denoising in the Ising model. We'll learn to approximate the full posterior distribution using KL divergence and maximize the evidence lower bound.

In chapter 4, we'll discuss linear, nonlinear, and probabilistic data structures as well as four algorithmic paradigms: complete search, greedy, divide and conquer, and dynamic programming. We'll examine a few examples in each area and conclude with ML research in sampling methods and variational inference.

Machine learning algorithms 1

An *algorithm* is a sequence of steps required to achieve a particular task. An algorithm takes an input, performs a sequence of operations, and produces a desired output. The simplest example of an algorithm is *sorting*, where given a list of integers, we perform a sequence of operations to produce a sorted list. A sorted list enables us to organize information better and find answers in our data.

Two popular questions to ask about an algorithm are how fast it runs (run-time complexity) and how much memory it takes (memory or space complexity) for an input of size n. For example, a comparison-based sort, as we'll see later, has $O(n \log n)$ run-time complexity and requires $O(n)$ memory storage.

There are many approaches to sorting, and in each case, in the classic algorithmic paradigm, the algorithm designer creates a set of instructions. Imagine a world where you can *learn* the instructions based on a sequence of input and output examples available to you. This is a setting of the ML algorithmic paradigm. Like a human brain learns when one plays a connect-the-dots game or sketches a natural landscape, we compare the desired output with what we have at each step and fill in the gaps. This, in broad strokes, is what (supervised) machine learning (ML) algorithms do. During training, ML algorithms learn the rules (e.g., classification boundaries) based on training examples by optimizing an objective function. During testing, ML algorithms apply previously learned rules to new input data points and provide a prediction, as shown in figure 1.1.

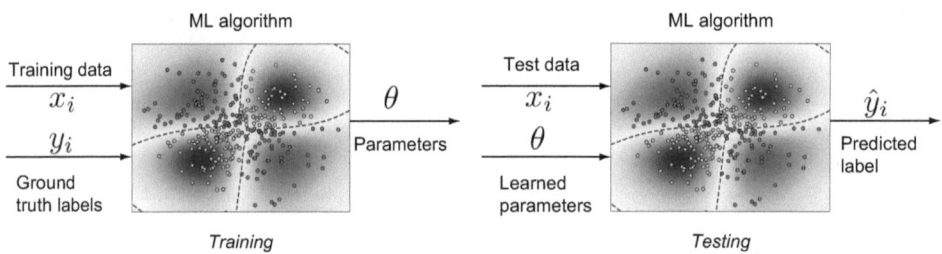

Figure 1.1   Supervised learning: training (left) and testing (right)

1.1 Types of ML algorithms

Let's unpack the previous paragraph a little bit and introduce some notation. This book focuses on ML algorithms that can be grouped together into the following categories: supervised learning, unsupervised learning, and deep learning. In *supervised learning*, the task is to learn a mapping f from inputs x to outputs y given a training dataset $D = \{(x_1, y_1), \ldots, (x_n, y_n)\}$ of n input–output pairs. In other words, we are given n examples of what the output should look like given the input. The output y is also often referred to as the *label*, and it is the supervisory signal that tells our algorithm what the correct answer is.

Supervised learning can be subdivided into *classification* and *regression*, depending on the quantity we are trying to predict. If our output y is a discrete quantity (e.g., K distinct classes), we have a classification problem. On the other hand, if our output y is a continuous quantity (e.g., a real number, such as stock price) we have a regression problem.

Thus, the nature of the problem changes based on the quantity y we are trying to predict. We want to get as close as possible to the ground truth value of y.

A common way to measure performance or closeness to ground truth is via the *loss function*. The loss function computes a distance between the prediction and the true label. Let $y = f(x, \theta)$ be our ML algorithm that maps input examples x to output labels y, parameterized by θ, where θ captures all the learnable parameters of our ML algorithm.

Then, we can define the classification loss function as the number of misclassified samples, as represented by equation 1.1.

$$L(\theta) = \frac{1}{n} \sum_{i=1}^{n} 1\,[y_i \neq f(x_i; \theta)] \qquad (1.1)$$

Here, $1[\,]$ is an indicator function that is equal to 1 when the argument inside is true and 0 otherwise. The expression in equation 1.1 denotes that we are adding up all the instances in which our prediction $f(x_i; \theta)$ did not match the ground truth label y_i and dividing by the total number of examples n. In other words, we are computing an average misclassification rate. Our goal is to minimize the loss function (i.e., find a set of parameters θ that make the misclassification rate as close to zero as possible). Note that there are many alternative loss functions for classification, such as cross-entropy, which we will examine in later chapters.

For continuous labels or response variables, a common loss function is the *mean squared error* (MSE). The MSE measures how far away our estimate is from the ground truth, as illustrated in equation 1.2.

$$L(\theta) = \frac{1}{n} \sum_{i=1}^{n} [y_i - f(x_i; \theta)]^2 \qquad (1.2)$$

As we can see from the equation, we subtract our prediction from the ground truth label, square it, and average the result over the data points. By taking the square we eliminate the negative sign and penalize large deviations from the ground truth.

One of the central goals of ML is to be able to generalize to unseen examples. We want to achieve high accuracy (low loss) on not just the training data (which is already labeled) but on new, unseen, test data examples. This generalization ability is what makes ML so attractive: if we can design ML algorithms that can see outside their training box, we'll be one step closer to artificial general intelligence (AGI).

In *unsupervised learning*, we are not given the label y, nor are we learning the mapping between input and output examples; instead, we are interested in making sense of the data itself. Usually, that implies discovering patterns in data. It's often easier to discover patterns if we project high-dimensional data into a lower-dimensional space as shown in figure 1.2. Therefore, in the case of unsupervised learning, our training dataset consists of $D = \{x_1, \ldots, x_n\}$ of n input examples, without any corresponding labels y. The simplest example of unsupervised learning is finding clusters within data. Intuitively, we know that data points that belong to the same cluster have similar characteristics. In fact, data points within a cluster can be represented by the cluster center as an exemplar and used as part of a data compression algorithm. Alternatively, we can look at the distances between clusters in a projected lower-dimensional space to understand the interrelation between different groups. Additionally, a point that's far away from all the existing clusters can be considered an anomaly, leading to an anomaly detection algorithm. As you can see, there's an infinite number of interesting use cases that arise from unsupervised learning, and throughout this book, we'll be learning some of the most intriguing algorithms in that space from scratch.

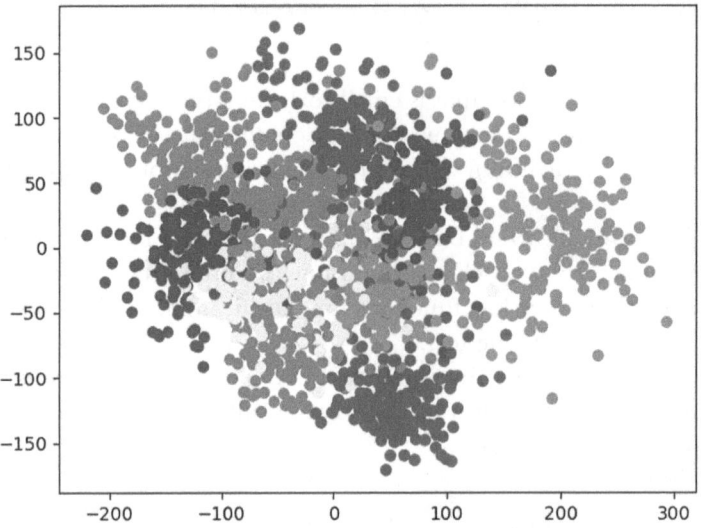

Figure 1.2   **Unsupervised learning: clusters of data points projected onto 2-dimensional space**

Another very important area of modern machine algorithms is *deep learning*. The name comes from a stack of computational layers forming a computational graph together. The depth of this graph refers to sequential computation and the breadth to parallel computation.

As we'll see, deep learning models gradually refine their parameters through a backpropagation algorithm until they meet the objective function. Deep learning models have permeated the industry due to their ability to solve complex problems with high accuracy. For example, figure 1.3 shows a deep learning architecture for sentiment analysis. We'll learn more about what individual blocks represent in future chapters.

Figure 1.3   **Deep neural network (DNN) architecture for sentiment analysis**

Deep learning is a very active research area, and we'll be focusing on modern deep learning algorithms throughout this book. For example, in self-supervised learning, used in transformer models, we are using the context and structure of the natural language as a supervisory signal, thereby extracting the labels from the data itself. In addition to classic applications of deep learning in natural language processing (NLP) and computer vision (CV), we'll discuss generative models, learning how to predict time-series data and journey into relational graph data.

1.2 Why learn algorithms from scratch?

Understanding ML algorithms from scratch has several valuable outcomes for the reader. First, we will be able to choose the right algorithm for the task. By knowing the inner workings of an algorithm, we can understand its shortcomings, assumptions made in the derivation of the algorithm, as well as advantages in different data scenarios. This enables us to exercise judgment when selecting the right solution to a problem and save time by eliminating approaches that don't work.

Second, we will be able to explain the results of a given algorithm to stakeholders. Being able to interpret and present the results to the audience in industrial or academic settings is an important trait of an ML algorithm designer.

Third, we will be able to use intuition developed by reading this book to troubleshoot advanced ML problems. Breaking down a complex problem into smaller pieces and understanding where things went wrong often requires a strong sense of fundamentals and algorithmic intuition. This book will allow the reader to construct minimum working examples and build upon existing algorithms to develop and be able to debug more complex models.

Fourth, we will be able to extend an algorithm when a new situation arises in the real world—particularly, where the textbook algorithm or a library cannot be used as is. The in-depth understanding of ML algorithms that you will acquire in this book will help you modify existing algorithms to meet your needs.

Finally, we are often interested in improving the performance of existing models. The principles discussed in this book will enable the reader to accomplish that. In conclusion, understanding ML algorithms from scratch will help you choose the right algorithm for the task, explain the results, troubleshoot advanced problems, extend an algorithm to a new scenario, and improve the performance of existing algorithms.

1.3 Mathematical background

To learn ML algorithms from scratch, it's a good idea to review concepts from applied probability, calculus, and linear algebra. For a review of probability, the reader is encouraged to consult Dimitri Bertsekas and John Tsitsiklis's *Introduction to Probability* (Athena Scientific, 2002). The reader is expected to be familiar with continuous and discrete random variables, conditional and marginal distributions, the Bayes rule, Markov chains, and limit theorems.

For a review of calculus, I recommend James Stewart's *Calculus* (Thomson Brooks/Cole, 2007). The reader is expected to be familiar with the rules of differentiation and integration, sequences and series, vectors and the geometry of space, partial derivatives, and multidimensional integrals.

Finally, *Introduction to Linear Algebra* by Gilbert Strang (Wellesley-Cambridge Press, 2016) serves as a great introduction to linear algebra. The reader is expected to be familiar with vector spaces, matrices, eigenvalues and eigenvectors, matrix norms, matrix factorizations, positive definite and semidefinite matrices, and matrix calculus. In addition to the aforementioned texts, please see appendix A for recommended texts that can enrich your understanding of the algorithms presented in this book.

1.4   *Bayesian inference and deep learning*

Bayesian inference allows us to update our beliefs about the world given observed data. Our minds hold a variety of mental models explaining different aspects of the world, and by observing new data points, we can update our latent representation and improve our understanding of reality. Any *probabilistic model* is described by a set of parameters θ modeled as random variables, which control the behavior of the model, and associated data x.

The goal of Bayesian inference is to find the posterior distribution $p(\theta|x)$ (distribution over the parameters given the data) to capture a particular aspect of reality well. The posterior distribution is proportional to the product of the likelihood $p(x|\theta)$ (distribution over the data given the parameters) and the prior $p(\theta)$ (initial distribution over the parameters), which follows from the Bayes rule in equation 1.3.

$$p(\theta|x) = \underbrace{\frac{\overbrace{p(x|\theta)}^{\text{Likelihood}}\overbrace{p(\theta)}^{\text{Prior}}}{\underbrace{p(x)}_{\text{Evidence}}}}_{\text{Posterior}} = \frac{p(x|\theta)p(\theta)}{\underbrace{\int p(x|\theta)p(\theta)d\theta}_{\text{Partition function Z}}} \sim p(x|\theta)p(\theta) \tag{1.3}$$

The prior $p(\theta)$ is our initial belief and can be either noninformative (e.g., uniform over all possible states) or informative (e.g., based on experience in a particular domain). Moreover, our inference results depend on the prior we choose—not only the value of prior parameters but also on the functional form of the prior. We can imagine a chain of updates in which the prior becomes a posterior as more data is obtained in the form of a Bayes engine, as shown in figure 1.4. We can see how our prior is updated to a posterior via the Bayes rule as we observe more data.

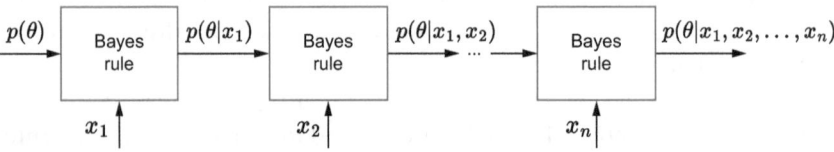

Figure 1.4   A Bayes engine showing the transformation of a prior to a posterior as more data is observed

Priors that have the same form as the posterior are known as *conjugate priors*, which are generally preferred, since they simplify computation by having closed-form updates. The denominator $Z = p(x) = \int p(x|\theta) p(\theta) d\theta$ is known as the *normalizing constant* or the *partition function* and is often intractable to compute, due to integration in high dimensional parameter space. In this book, we'll examine several techniques for estimating Z.

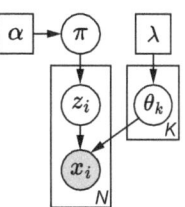

We can model relationships between different random variables in our model as a graph as shown in figure 1.5, giving rise to *probabilistic graphical models*. Each node in the graph represents a random variable (RV), and each edge represents a conditional dependency. The model parameters are represented by clear nodes, while shaded nodes represent the observed data, and rectangular plates denote a copy or a repetition of the random variable. The topology of the graph itself changes depending on the application you are interested in modeling. However, the goals of Bayesian inference remain the same: to find the posterior distribution over model parameters, given observed data.

Figure 1.5
A probabilistic graphical model (PGM) for a Gaussian mixture model

In contrast to PGMs, where the connections are specified by domain experts, *deep learning models* learn representations of the world automatically through the backpropagation algorithm that minimizes an objective function. *Deep neural networks* (DNNs) consist of multiple layers parameterized by weight matrices and bias parameters. Mathematically, DNNs can be expressed as a composition of individual layer functions, as in equation 1.4.

$$\text{DNN}(x; \theta) = f_L(f_{L-1}(\cdots(f_1(x; \theta_1))\cdots); \theta_L) \tag{1.4}$$

Here, $f_l(x) = f(x; \theta_l)$ is the function at layer l. The compositional form of the DNNs reminds us of the chain rule when it comes to differentiating parameters as part of stochastic gradient descent. Throughout this book, we'll look at several different kinds of DNNs, such as convolutional neural networks (CNNs), recurrent neural networks (RNNs), as well as transformers and graph neural networks (GNNs), with applications ranging from computer vision to finance.

1.4.1 Two main camps of Bayesian inference: MCMC and VI

Markov chain Monte Carlo (MCMC) is a methodology of sampling from high-dimensional parameter spaces to approximate the posterior distribution $p(\theta|x)$. In statistics, *sampling* refers to generating a random sample of values from a given probability distribution. There are many approaches to sampling in high-dimensional parameter spaces. As we'll see in later chapters, MCMC is based on constructing a Markov chain whose stationary distribution is the target density of interest (i.e., posterior distribution). By performing a random walk over the state space, the fraction of time we spend in each state θ will be proportional to $p(\theta|x)$. As a result, we can use Monte Carlo integration to derive the quantities of interest associated with our posterior distribution.

Before we discuss high-dimensional parameter spaces, let's examine how we can sample from low-dimensional spaces. The most popular method for sampling from univariate distributions is known as the *inverse cumulative density function* (CDF) *method;* it is defined as $\text{CDF}_X(x) = P(X \le x)$ (see figure 1.6).

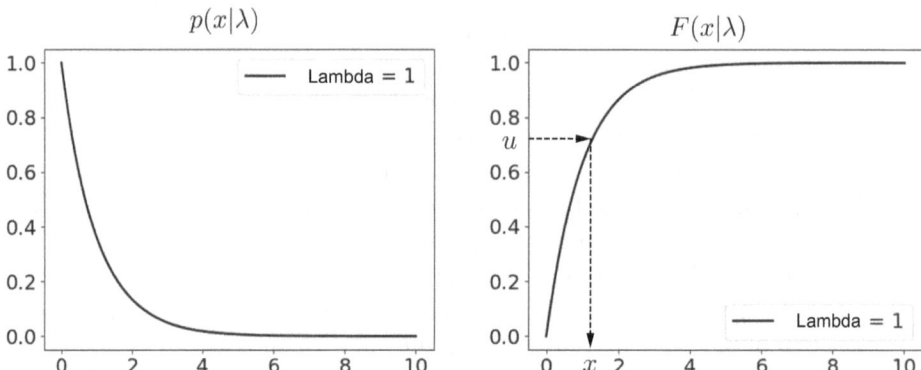

Figure 1.6 **Exponential RV probability density function (left) and cumulative density function (right)**

For example, let's examine an exponential RV with a probability density function (PDF) and CDF given by equation 1.5.

$$p(x|\lambda) = \lambda e^{-\lambda x}, x \ge 0 \quad F(x|\lambda) = \int_0^x p(x|\lambda)dx = 1 - e^{-\lambda x}, x \ge 0 \quad (1.5)$$

The inverse CDF can be found as shown in equation 1.6.

$$F^{-1}(u) = -\frac{\ln(1-u)}{\lambda} \quad (1.6)$$

Thus, to generate a sample from an exponential RV, we first need to generate a sample from uniform random variable $u \sim \text{Unif}(0, 1)$ and apply the transformation $-\ln(1-u)/\lambda$. By generating enough samples, we can achieve an arbitrary level of accuracy. One challenge of MCMC is determining how to *efficiently* generate samples from high-dimensional distributions. We'll look at two ways of doing that in this book: Gibbs sampling and Metropolis-Hastings (MH) sampling.

Variational inference (VI) is an optimization-based approach to approximating the posterior distribution $p(x)$. We simplify the notation here by assigning a generic distribution p(x) the meaning of a posterior distribution. The basic idea behind VI is to choose an approximate distribution $q(x)$ from a family of tractable distributions and then make this approximation as close as possible to the true posterior distribution $p(x)$. A *tractable distribution* simply refers to one that is easy to compute. As we will see in the mean-field section of the book, the approximate $q(x)$ can take on a fully factored representation of the joint posterior distribution. This factorization signifi-cantly speeds up computation.

Next, we introduce the Kullback-Leibler (KL) divergence and use it to measure the proximity of our approximate distribution to the true posterior. Figure 1.7 shows the two versions of KL divergence.

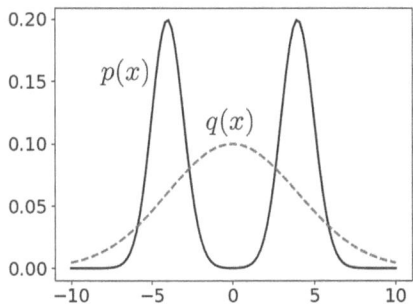 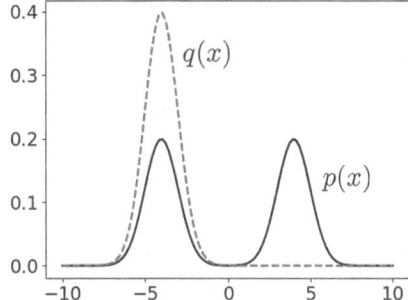

Figure 1.7   Forward KL (left) and reverse KL (right) approximate distribution q(x) fit to Gaussian mixture p(x)

The original distribution $p(x)$ is a bimodal Gaussian distribution (aka Gaussian mixture with two components), while the approximating distribution $q(x)$ is a unimodal Gaussian. As we can see from figure 1.7, we can approximate the distribution with two peaks either at the center with $q(x)$ that has high variance, to capture the support of the bimodal distribution, or at one of its modes, as shown on the right. This is a result of forward and reverse KL divergence definitions in equation 1.7. As we'll see in later chapters, by minimizing KL divergence, we effectively convert VI into an optimization problem.

$$KL(p\|q) = \sum p(x) \log \frac{p(x)}{q(x)} \qquad KL(q\|p) = \sum q(x) \log \frac{q(x)}{p(x)} \qquad (1.7)$$

1.4.2   Modern deep learning algorithms

Over the years, deep learning architecture has evolved from the basic building blocks of the LeNet CNN to visual transformer architectures. Certain architectural design themes, such as residual connections in the ResNet model, which became the stan-dard architectural choice of modern neural networks of arbitrary depth, began to emerge. In the later chapters of this book, we'll take a look at modern deep learning algorithms, including self-attention based transformers; generative models, such as variational autoencoders; and graph neural networks.

We will also discuss amortized variational inference, which is an interesting research area, as it combines the expressiveness and representation learning of deep neural net-works with domain knowledge of probabilistic graphical models. We will see one such application of mixture density networks, where we'll use a neural network to map from observation space to the parameters of the approximate posterior distribution.

Most deep learning models fall in the category of narrow AI showing high performance on a specific dataset. While it is a useful skill to be able to do well on a narrow set of tasks, we would like to generalize away from narrow AI and towards artificial general intelligence (AGI).

1.5   *Implementing algorithms*

A key part of learning algorithms from scratch is software implementation. It's important to write good code that is efficient both in its use of data structures and its low algorithmic complexity. Throughout this chapter, we'll be grouping the functional aspects of the code into classes and implementing different computational methods from scratch. Thus, you'll be exposed to a lot of object-oriented programming (OOP), which is common practice with popular ML libraries, such as scikit-learn. While the intention of this book is to write all code from scratch (without reliance on third-party libraries), we can still use ML libraries (e.g., scikit-learn, https://scikit-learn .org/stable/) to check the results of our implementation, if available. We'll be using the Python language throughout this book.

1.5.1   *Data structures*

A *data structure* is a way of storing and organizing data. Each data structure offers different performance tradeoffs, and some are more suitable for the task than others. We'll be using *linear data structures*, such as fixed-size arrays, primarily in our implementation of ML algorithms, since the time to access an element in the array is constant $O(1)$. We'll also frequently use dynamically resizable arrays (e.g., lists in Python) to keep track of data over multiple iterations.

Throughout the book, we'll be using *nonlinear data structures*, such as maps (dictionaries) and sets. We'll use these data structures because ordered dictionaries and ordered sets are built upon self-balanced binary search trees (BSTs) that guarantee $O(n\log n)$ insertion, search, and deletion operations. Finally, a hash table or unordered map is another commonly used, efficient data structure with $O(1)$ access time, assuming no collisions.

1.5.2   *Problem-solving paradigms*

Most of the ML algorithms in this book can be grouped into one of four problem-solving paradigms: complete search, greedy, divide and conquer, and dynamic programming. *Complete search* is a method for solving a problem by traversing the entire search space, looking for a solution. A machine learning example in which a complete search takes place is an exact inference by complete enumeration. During exact inference, we must completely specify a number of probability tables to carry out our calculations.

A *greedy algorithm* takes a locally optimum choice at each step, with the hope of eventually reaching a globally optimum solution. Greedy algorithms often rely on a greedy heuristic. A machine learning example of a greedy algorithm consists of sensor placement. For example, given a room and several temperature sensors, we would like to place the sensors in a way that maximizes room coverage.

Divide and conquer is a technique that divides the problem into smaller, independent sub-problems and then combines each of their solutions. A machine learning example that uses the divide and conquer paradigm can be found in the CART decision tree algorithm. As we'll see in a future chapter, in the CART algorithm, an optimum threshold for splitting a decision tree is found by optimizing a classification objective (e.g., Gini index). The same procedure is applied to a tree of depth one greater, resulting in a recursive algorithm.

Finally, *dynamic programming* (DP) is a technique that divides a problem into smaller, overlapping subproblems, computes a solution for each, and stores the solution in a DP table. A machine learning example that uses dynamic programming occurs in reinforcement learning (RL) when finding a solution to Bellman equations. For a small number of states, we can compute the Q-function in a tabular way using dynamic programming.

Summary

- An algorithm is a sequence of steps required to achieve a particular task. Machine learning algorithms can be grouped into one of the following categories: supervised learning, unsupervised learning, and deep learning.

- Understanding algorithms from scratch will help you choose the right algorithm for the task, explain the results, troubleshoot advanced problems, and improve the performance of existing models.

- Bayesian inference allows us to update our beliefs about the world given observed data, while deep learning models learn representations of the world through the algorithm of backpropagation that minimizes an objective function. There are two camps of Bayesian inference: Markov chain Monte Carlo (MCMC) and variational inference (VI). These camps focus on sampling and approximating the posterior distribution, respectively.

- It is important to write good code that is efficient both in its use of data structures and its low algorithmic complexity. Most of the ML algorithms in this book can be grouped into one of four problem-solving paradigms: complete search, greedy, divide and conquer, and dynamic programming.

Markov chain Monte Carlo

2

This chapter covers

- Introducing the Markov chain Monte Carlo
- Estimating pi via Monte Carlo integration
- Binomial tree model Monte Carlo simulation
- Self-avoiding random walk
- Gibbs sampling algorithm
- Metropolis-Hastings algorithm
- Importance sampling

In the previous chapter, we reviewed different types of ML algorithms and software implementation. Now, we will focus on a popular class of ML algorithms known as Markov chain Monte Carlo. Any probabilistic model that explains a part of reality exists in a high-dimensional parameter space because it is described by high dimensional model parameters. *Markov chain Monte Carlo* (MCMC) is a methodology of sampling from high-dimensional parameter spaces to approximate the posterior distribution $p(\theta|x)$. Originally developed by physicists, this method became popular in the Bayesian statistics community because it allows one to estimate high dimensional posterior distributions using sampling. The basic idea behind MCMC is to construct a Markov chain whose stationary distribution is equal to the target posterior $p(\theta|x)$.

In other words, if we perform a random walk across the parameter space, the fraction of time we spend in a particular state θ is proportional to $p(\theta|x)$.

We begin by introducing MCMC in the following section. We'll proceed with three warm-up Monte Carlo examples (estimating pi, binomial tree model, and self-avoiding random walk) before looking at three popular sampling algorithms (Gibbs sampling, Metropolis-Hastings, and importance sampling). The warm-up algorithms in this chapter are selected to give the reader an appropriate introduction to MCMC, and the sampling algorithms are selected for their wide application in sampling from probabilistic graphical models (PGMs).

2.1 Introduction to Markov chain Monte Carlo

Let's start by understanding high dimensional parameter spaces based on a simple example of classifying irises. An *iris* is a species of flowers consisting of three types: setosa, versicolor, and virginica. The flowers are characterized by their petal and sepal length and width, which can be used as features to determine the iris type. Figure 2.1 shows the iris pairplot.

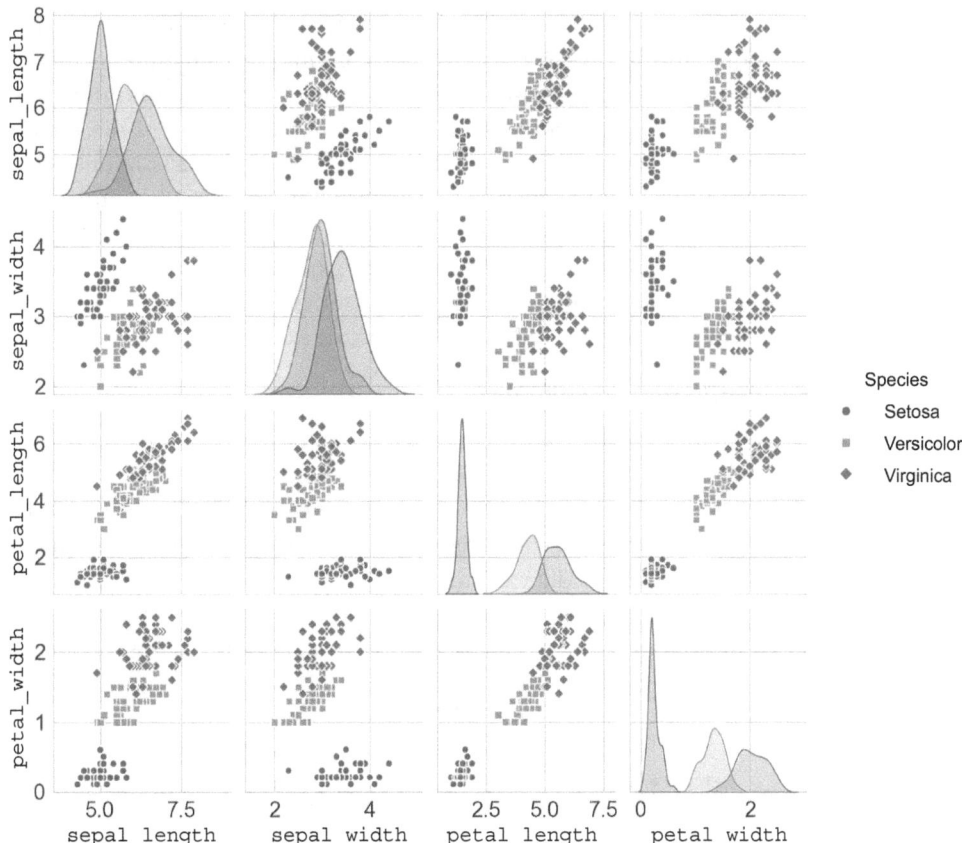

Figure 2.1 Iris pairplot: pairwise scatterplots color coded by iris species

A pairplot is a matrix of plots where off-diagonal entries contain a scatter plot of every feature (e.g., petal length) against every other feature, while the main diagonal entries contain plots of every feature against itself color-coded by the three iris species. The pairplot captures pairwise relationships in the iris dataset. Let's focus on the main diagonal entries and try to model the data we see. Since we have three types of Iris flowers, we can model the data as a mixture of three Gaussian distributions. A Gaussian mixture is a weighted sum of Gaussian probability distributions. Equation 2.1 captures this in mathematical terms.

Sum of K Gaussians

$$p(x|\theta) = \sum_{k=1}^{K} N\left(x; \mu_k, \sigma_k^2\right) \pi_k \tag{2.1}$$

Gaussian mixture   Gaussian RV   Mixture proportions

A mixture of Gaussians consists of K Gaussian RVs scaled by mixture proportions πk that are positive and add up to 1: $\sum \pi_k = 1$, $\pi_k > 0$. This is a high dimensional parameter problem because to fit the Gaussian mixture model, we need to find the values for the means μ_k, covariances σ_k^2, and mixture proportions π_k. In case of the iris dataset, we have K = 3, which means the number of parameters for the Gaussian mixture is equal to $9 - 1 = 8$ (i.e., we have 9 parameters in $\theta = \{\mu_k, \sigma_k^2, \pi_k\}_{k=1}^{3}$, and we subtract 1 because of the sum-to-one constraint for πk. In a later chapter, we'll look at how to find the Gaussian mixture parameters via the expectation-maximization (EM) algorithm. Now that we have an idea about parameter spaces, let's review our understanding of posterior distribution, using coin flips as an example.

2.1.1   *Posterior distribution of coin flips*

With MCMC algorithms, we attempt to approximate the posterior distribution through samples. In fact, most of the Bayesian inference is designed to efficiently approximate the posterior distribution. Let's understand what a posterior distribution is in a little more detail. Posterior arises when we have a model with parameters θ we are trying to fit to observed data x. Namely, it's the probability of parameters given the data $p(\theta|x)$. Consider an example of a sequence of coin flips where every coin is heads with probability θ and tails with probability $1-\theta$, as shown in figure 2.2.

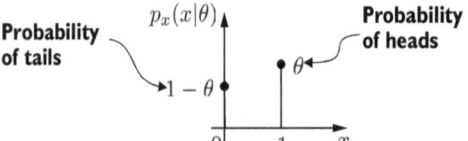

Figure 2.2   **Bernoulli random variable**

Figure 2.2 shows the probability mass function (PMF) of a Bernoulli RV modeling the coin flip. If θ = ½, we have a fair coin with an equal chance of heads (1) or tails (0); otherwise, we say that the coin is biased, with a bias equal to θ. We can write down the PMF of a Bernoulli RV as follows.

$$p_x(x|\theta) = \theta^x (1-\theta)^{1-x}, x \in \{0, 1\} \tag{2.2}$$

The mean of the Bernoulli RV is equal to $E[X] = \sum_x x p_x (x|\theta) = 0(1-\theta) + 1(\theta) = \theta$, while the variance is equal to $VAR(x) = E[x^2] - E[x]^2 = \theta - \theta^2 = \theta(1-\theta)$. Let's go back to our coin-tossing example. Let $D = \{x_1, ..., x_n\}$ be a sequence of independent and identically distributed (iid) coin flips. Then, we can compute the likelihood as follows.

$$
\begin{aligned}
p_x(D|\theta) &= p_x(x_1, \ldots, x_n|\theta) \\
&= \prod_{i=1}^{n} p(x_i|\theta) = \prod_{i=1}^{n} \theta^{x_i}(1-\theta)^{1-x_i} \\
&= \theta^{N_1}(1-\theta)^{N_0} \tag{2.3}
\end{aligned}
$$

Here, we assume $N_1 = \sum_{i=1}^{n} x_i$, or the total number of counts for which the coin landed heads, and $N_0 = n - N_1$, or the total number of counts for which the coin landed tails.

Equations 2.2 and 2.3 have the form $p(x|\theta)$, which is, by definition, the likelihood of data x, given the parameter θ. What if we have some prior information about the parameter θ; in other words, what if we know something about $p(\theta)$, such as the number of heads and tails we obtained in another experiment with the same coins? We can capture this prior information as follows.

$$\text{Beta}(\theta|a, b) \propto \theta^{a-1}(1-\theta)^{b-1} \tag{2.4}$$

Here, a is the number of heads and b is the number of tails in our previous experiment. When computing the posterior distribution, we are interested in computing $p(\theta|x)$. We can use the Bayes rule from chapter 1 to express the posterior distribution as proportional to the product of the likelihood and prior.

$$
\begin{aligned}
p(\theta|D) &\propto p(D|\theta)p(\theta) \\
&= \theta^{N_1}(1-\theta)^{N_0}\theta^{a-1}(1-\theta)^{b-1} = \theta^{N_1+a-1}(1-\theta)^{N_0+b-1} \\
&\propto \text{Beta}(\theta|N_1 + a, N_0 + b) \tag{2.5}
\end{aligned}
$$

Equation 2.5 computes the posterior distribution $p(\theta|D)$, which tells us the probability of heads for a sequence of coin flips. We can see that the posterior is distributed as a Beta random variable. Remember that our prior was also a Beta random variable; we say that the prior is "conjugate to the posterior." In other words, the posterior can be computed in closed form by updating the prior counts with observed data.

2.1.2 Markov chain for page rank

Before we dive into MCMC algorithms, we need to introduce the concept of a Markov chain. A *Markov chain* is a sequence of possible events, in which the probability of the current event depends only on the previous event. A first-order Markov chain can be written as shown in equation 2.6. Let $x_1,...,x_t$ be the samples from our posterior distribution; then, we can write the joint as follows.

$$
\begin{aligned}
p(x_1, \ldots, x_t) &= p(x_1)p(x_2|x_1)p(x_3|x_2)\cdots p(x_t|x_{t-1}) \\
&= p(x_1)\prod_{i=2}^{t} p(x_i|x_{i-1})
\end{aligned}
\tag{2.6}
$$

Notice how the joint factors as a product of conditional distributions, where the current state is conditioned only on the previous state. A Markov chain is characterized by the initial distribution over the states $p(x_1 = i)$ and a state transition matrix $A_{ij} = p(x_t = j|x_{t-1} = i)$ from state i to state j.

Let's motivate Markov chains via a Google page rank example. Google uses a page rank algorithm to rank billions of web pages. We can formulate a collection of n web pages as a graph G = (V, E). Let every node $v \in$ V represent a web page and every edge $e \in$ E represent a link from one page to another. Knowing how the pages are linked allows us to construct a giant, sparse transition matrix A, where A_{ij} is the probability of following a link from page i to page j, as shown in figure 2.3.

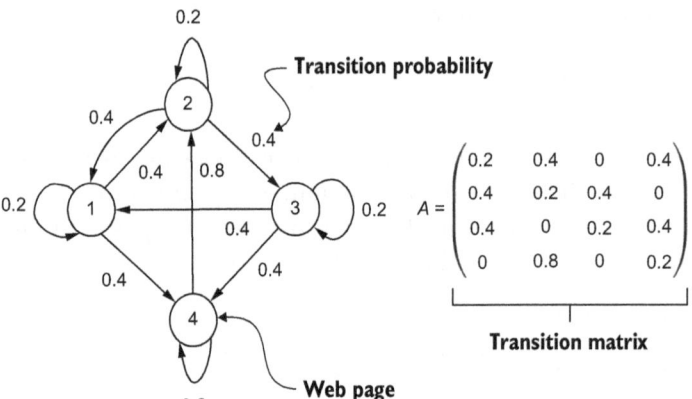

Figure 2.3 A graph of web pages with transition probabilities

Note that every row in the matrix A sums to 1 (i.e., $\sum_j A_{ij} = 1$). A matrix with this property is known as a *stochastic matrix*. Note that A_{ij} corresponds to transition probability from state i to state j. As we will see in a later chapter, page rank is a stationary distribution over the states of the Markov chain. To make it scale to billions of web pages, we'll derive from scratch and implement a power iteration algorithm. But for now, in the next few sections, we will look at different MCMC sampling algorithms: Gibbs sampling, Metropolis-Hastings, and importance sampling. Let's start with a couple of warm-up examples as our first exposure to Monte Carlo algorithms.

2.2 Estimating pi

The first example we will look at is estimating the value of π via Monte Carlo integration. *Monte Carlo* (MC) *integration* has an advantage over numerical integration (which evaluates a function at a fixed grid of points) in that the function is only evaluated in places where there is nonnegligible probability. Thus, MC integration scales better to high-dimensional problems.

Let's look at the expected value of some function $\mathbf{f}: \mathbb{R} \to \mathbb{R}$ of a random variable $Z = f(Y)$. We can approximate it by drawing samples y from the distribution $p(y)$ as follows.

$$E[f(Y)] = \int f(y)p(y)dy \approx \frac{1}{S}\sum_{s=1}^{S} f(y_s), \text{ where } y_s \sim p(y) \quad (2.7)$$

In other words, we are approximating the expected value $E[f(y)]$ with an average of $f(y_s)$, where y_s are samples drawn from the distribution $p(y)$. Let's now use the same idea but apply it to evaluating an integral $I = \int f(x)\,dx$. We can approximate the integral as follows.

$$
\begin{aligned}
I &= \int_a^b f(x)dx = \int_a^b w(x)p(x)dx = E_p[w(x)] \\
&= \frac{1}{n}\sum_{i=1}^{N} w(x_i), \text{ where } x_i \sim p(x)
\end{aligned}
\quad (2.8)
$$

Here, $p(x) \sim \text{Unif}(a, b) = 1/(b-a)$ is the PDF of a uniform random variable over the interval (a, b) and $w(x) = f(x)(b-a)$ is our scaled function $f(x)$.

As we increase the number of samples N, our empirical estimate of the mean becomes more accurate. In fact, the standard error is equal to $\sigma/\text{sqrt}(N)$, where σ is the empirical standard deviation.

$$\sigma^2 = \frac{1}{N-1}\sum_{i=1}^{N}(f(x_i) - I)^2 \quad (2.9)$$

Now that we have an idea of how Monte Carlo integration works, let's use it to estimate π. We know that the area of a circle with radius r is $I = \pi r^2$. Alternatively, the area of the circle can be computed as an integral.

$$I = \int_{-r}^{r} \int_{-r}^{r} 1[x^2 + y^2 \leq r^2] dx\, dy = E_{x,y}[w(x, y)] \qquad (2.10)$$

Here, $1[x^2 + y^2 \leq r^2]$ is an indicator function equal to 1 when a point is inside the circle of radius r and equal to 0 otherwise. Therefore, $\pi = I / r^2$. To compute I, note the following equation.

$$
\begin{aligned}
w(x, y) &= (b_x - a_x)(b_y - a_y)\, 1\left[x^2 + y^2 \leq r^2\right] \\
&= (2r)(2r) 1\left[x^2 + y^2 \leq r^2\right] \\
&= 4r^2 1\left[x^2 + y^2 \leq r^2\right] \qquad (2.11)
\end{aligned}
$$

We can summarize the pi estimation algorithm in the pseudo-code shown in figure 2.4.

```
1: function pi_est(R, N):
2: for i = 1 to N:
3:     X[i] ~ Unif(-R, R)  ┐→Uniform RVs
4:     Y[i] ~ Unif(-R, R)  ┘
5:     IN[i] = X[i]² + Y[i]² ≤ R²
6:     S[i] = (2R) × (2R) × IN[i]
7: end for
8: Î = 1/N Σᵢ₌₁ᴺ S[i]
9: π̂ = Î/R²  ←Pi estimate
10: π̂_se = σ_S/√N  ←Pi standard deviation
11: return π̂ ± π̂_se
```

8: $\hat{I} = \frac{1}{N} \sum_{i=1}^{N} S[i]$

9: $\hat{\pi} = \frac{\hat{I}}{R^2}$ ←Pi estimate

10: $\hat{\pi}_{se} = \frac{\sigma_S}{\sqrt{N}}$ ←Pi standard deviation

11: **return** $\hat{\pi} \pm \hat{\pi}_{se}$

Figure 2.4   Pi estimator pseudo-code

We generate N samples from a uniform distribution with support from $-R$ to R and compute a Boolean expression of whether our sample is inside or outside the circle. If the sample is inside, it factors into the integral computation. Once we have an estimate of the integral, we divide the result by R^2 to compute our estimate of pi. We are now ready to implement our pi estimator!

Listing 2.1   Pi estimator

```python
import numpy as np
import matplotlib.pyplot as plt

np.random.seed(42)          ⟵──── Fixes a seed for
                                  reproducible results

def pi_est(radius=1, num_iter=int(1e4)):   ⟵──── Experiments with a different
                                                 number of samples N

    X = np.random.uniform(-radius,+radius,num_iter)
    Y = np.random.uniform(-radius,+radius,num_iter)
```

```
R2 = X**2 + Y**2
inside = R2 < radius**2
outside = ~inside

samples = (2*radius)*(2*radius)*inside

I_hat = np.mean(samples)
pi_hat = I_hat/radius ** 2      ◁──── Pi estimate
pi_hat_se = np.std(samples)/np.sqrt(num_iter)     ◁────────┐  Pi standard
print("pi est: {} +/- {:f}".format(pi_hat, pi_hat_se))     │  deviation

plt.figure()
plt.scatter(X[inside],Y[inside], c='b', alpha=0.5)
plt.scatter(X[outside],Y[outside], c='r', alpha=0.5)
plt.show()

if __name__ == "__main__":

    pi_est()
```

If we execute the code, we get $\pi = 3.1348 \pm 0.0164$, which is a relatively good result (within the error bounds). Try experimenting with different numbers of samples N to see how fast we converge to π as a function of N. Figure 2.5 shows the accepted Monte Carlo samples in blue, corresponding to samples inside the circle, and the rejected samples in red, corresponding to samples outside the circle.

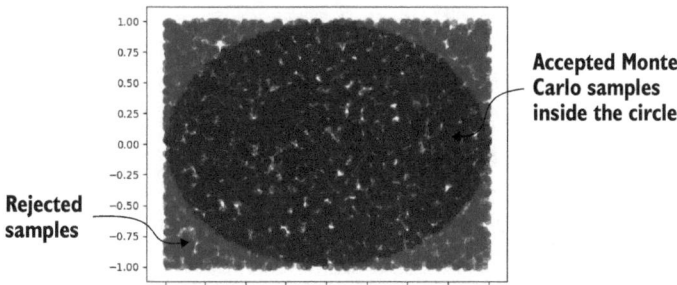

Accepted Monte Carlo samples inside the circle

Rejected samples

Figure 2.5   Monte Carlo samples used to estimate pi

In the preceding example, we assumed that samples came from a uniform distribution $X, Y \sim \text{Unif}(-R, R)$. In the following section, we will look at simulating a stock price over different time horizons using the binomial tree model.

2.3   Binomial tree model

Now, let's examine how Monte Carlo sampling can be used in finance. In a binomial tree model of a stock price, we assume that at each time step, the stock could be in either up or down states with unequal payoffs characteristic for a risky asset. Assuming the initial stock price at time $t = 0$ is \$1, at the next time step $t = 1$, the price is u in the up state and d in the down state, with up-state transition probability p. A binomial tree model for the first two timesteps is shown in figure 2.6. Note that the price in the next up (down) state is u (d) times the price of the previous state.

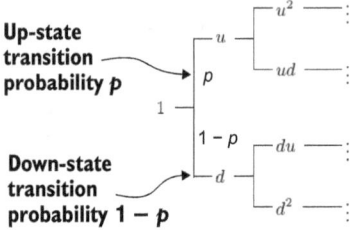

Up-state transition probability p

Down-state transition probability $1 - p$

Figure 2.6   Binomial tree model

We can use Monte Carlo to generate uncertainty estimates of the terminal stock price after some time horizon T. When using a binomial model to describe the price process of the stock, we can use the following calibration (the derivation of which is outside the scope of this book).

$$u = \exp\left(\sigma\sqrt{\frac{T}{n}}\right) = \frac{1}{d}$$

$$p = \frac{1}{2} + \frac{1}{2}\left(\frac{\mu}{\sigma}\right)\sqrt{\frac{T}{n}} \qquad (2.12)$$

Here, T is the length of the prediction horizon in years and n is the number of time steps. We assume 1 year equals 252 trading days, 1 month equals 21 days, 1 week equals 5 days, and 1 day equals 8 hours. Let's simulate the stock price using the binomial model with a daily time step for two different time horizons: 1 month from today and 1 year from today. We can summarize the algorithm in the pseudo-code shown in figure 2.7.

1: **function** binomial_tree(μ, σ, S_0, N, T, step):

2: $u = \exp\left(\sigma\sqrt{\frac{T}{n}}\right)$ ← **Up price**

3: $d = \frac{1}{u}$ ← **Down price**

4: $p = \frac{1}{2} + \frac{1}{2}\left(\frac{\mu}{\sigma}\right)\sqrt{\frac{T}{n}}$ ← **Up-state transition probability**

5: up_times = Binomial $\left(\frac{T}{step}, p, N\right)$

6: down_times = $\frac{T}{step}$ − up_times

7: $S_T = S_0 \times u^{up\_times} \times d^{down\_times}$

8: **return** S_T

Figure 2.7   Binomial tree pseudo-code

We begin by initializing up price u and down price d, along with up-state transition probability p. Next, we simulate all the up-state transitions by sampling from a Binomial random variable with the number of trials equal to T/step, the success probability p, and the number of Monte Carlo simulations equal to N. The down-state transitions are computed by complimenting up-state transitions. Finally, we compute the asset price by multiplying the initial price S_0 with the price of all the up-state transitions and all the down-state transitions.

Listing 2.2   Binomial tree stock price simulation

```
import numpy as np

import seaborn as sns
import matplotlib.pyplot as plt

np.random.seed(42)

def binomial_tree(mu, sigma, S0, N, T, step):

    #compute state price and probability
    u = np.exp(sigma * np.sqrt(step))    ◁──── Up-state price
    d = 1.0/u
    p = 0.5+0.5*(mu/sigma)*np.sqrt(step)    ◁──── Probability of up state

    #binomial tree simulation
    up_times = np.zeros((N, len(T)))
    down_times = np.zeros((N, len(T)))
    for idx in range(len(T)):
        up_times[:,idx] = np.random.binomial(T[idx]/step, p, N)
        down_times[:,idx] = T[idx]/step - up_times[:,idx]

    #compute terminal price
    ST = S0 * u**up_times * d**down_times

    #generate plots
    plt.figure()
    plt.plot(ST[:,0], color='b', alpha=0.5, label='1 month horizon')
    plt.plot(ST[:,1], color='r', alpha=0.5, label='1 year horizon')
    plt.xlabel('time step, day')
    plt.ylabel('price')
    plt.title('Binomial-Tree Stock Simulation')
    plt.legend()
    plt.show()

    plt.figure()
    plt.hist(ST[:,0], color='b', alpha=0.5, label='1 month horizon')
    plt.hist(ST[:,1], color='r', alpha=0.5, label='1 year horizon')
    plt.xlabel('price')
    plt.ylabel('count')
    plt.title('Binomial-Tree Stock Simulation')
    plt.legend()
    plt.show()

if __name__ == "__main__":

    #model parameters
    mu = 0.1
    sigma = 0.15    ◁──── Volatility
    S0 = 1    ◁───┐
                  │  Starting price
    N = 10000
    T = [21.0/252, 1.0]    ◁──── Time horizon, in years
    step = 1.0/252    ◁───┐
                          │  Time step, in years
    binomial_tree(mu, sigma, S0, N, T, step)
```

Down-state price ──▷ `d = 1.0/u`

Mean ──▷ `mu = 0.1`

Number of simulations ──▷ `N = 10000`

Figure 2.8 shows that our yearly estimates have higher volatility compared to the monthly estimates. This makes sense, as we expect to encounter more uncertainty over long time horizons. In the next section, we will learn how to use Monte Carlo to simulate self-avoiding random walks.

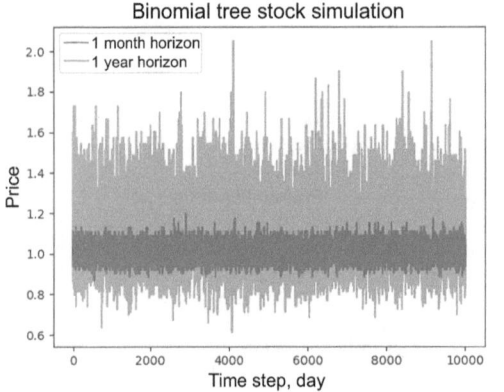
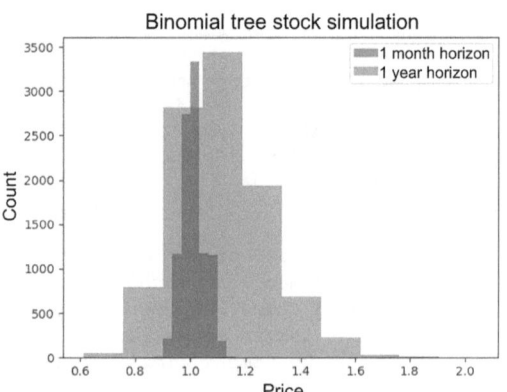

Figure 2.8   Binomial tree stock simulation

2.4   *Self-avoiding random walk*

Consider a random walk on a 2D grid. At each point on the grid, we take a random step with equal probability. This process forms a Markov chain $\{X_i\}_{i=1}^{n}$ on $\mathbb{Z} \times \mathbb{Z}$ with $X_0=(0, 0)$ and transition probabilities given by equation 2.13.

$$P(X_i = (k, l)|X_{i-1} = (i, j)) = \begin{cases} \frac{1}{4}, & \text{if } |k - i| + |l - j| = 1 \\ 0, & \text{otherwise} \end{cases} \qquad (2.13)$$

In other words, we have an equal probability of ¼ for transitioning from a point on the grid to any of the four—up, down, left, and right—neighbors. In addition, *self-avoiding* random walks are simply random walks that do not cross themselves. We can use Monte Carlo to simulate a self-avoiding random walk, as shown in the following pseudo-code (see figure 2.9).

We start by initializing the grid (lattice) to an all-zero matrix. We position the start of the random walk in the center of the grid, as represented by xx and xx. Notice that num_step is the number of steps in a random walk. We begin each iteration by computing the up, down, left, right values, which are equal to 1 if the grid is occupied and 0 otherwise. Therefore, we can compute available directions (neighbors) by computing 1 minus the direction. If the sum of neighbors is zero, there are no available directions (all the neighboring grid cells are occupied) and the random walk is self-intersecting, at which point we stop. Otherwise, we compute an importance weight as a product between the previous weight and the sum of neighbors. The importance weights are used to compute the weighted mean square distances of the random walk.

```
 1: function rand_walk(num_step, num_iter, moves):
 2: X, Y, lattice = 0, 0, 0
 3: weight = 1
 4: xx = num_step + 1 + X ← Middle of the x-axis
 5: yy = num_step + 1 + Y ← Middle of the y-axis
 6: lattice[xx, yy] = 1 ← Init grid position
 7: for i = 1 to num_step:
 8:     up = lattice[xx, yy+1]
 9:     down = lattice[xx, yy−1]
10:     left = lattice[xx−1, yy]
11:     right = lattice[xx+1, yy]
12:     neighbors = [1, 1, 1, 1] − [up, down, left, right] ← Available directions
13:     if sum(neighbors) == 0
14:         break ← Self-loop
15:     end if
16:     weight = weight × sum(neighbors) ← Computes importance weights
17:     direction ~ Cat ( neighbors / sum(neighbors) ) ← Samples a move direction
18:     X = X + moves[direction]
19:     Y = Y + moves[direction]
20:     // update grid coordinates
21:     xx = num_step + 1 + X
22:     yy = num_step + 1 + Y
23:     lattice[xx, yy] = 1
24: end for
25: return lattice
```

Figure 2.9 Random walk pseudo-code

Next, we sample a move direction from the available directions, represented by a sample from the categorical random variable. Since the neighbors array can only take the values of 0 and 1, we are sampling uniformly from the available directions.

Next, we update the grid coordinates xx and yy and mark the occupancy by setting `lattice[xx, yy]=1`. While only a single iteration is shown in the pseudo-code, the following code listing wraps the pseudo-code in an additional for loop over the number of iterations `num_iter`. Each iteration is an attempt or a trial to produce a nonintersecting (i.e., self-avoiding random walk). The square distance of the random walk and the importance weights are recorded in each trial. We are now ready to look at the self-avoid random walk code.

Listing 2.3 Self-avoiding random walk

```python
import numpy as np
import seaborn as sns
import matplotlib.pyplot as plt

np.random.seed(42)

def rand_walk(num_step, num_iter, moves):
```

```
#random walk stats
square_dist = np.zeros(num_iter)
weights = np.zeros(num_iter)

for it in range(num_iter):

    trial = 0
    i = 1
    while i != num_step-1:        <── Iterates until we have a
                                       noncrossing random walk

        #init
        X, Y = 0, 0
        weight = 1
        lattice = np.zeros((2*num_step+1, 2*num_step+1))
        lattice[num_step+1,num_step+1] = 1
        path = np.array([0, 0])
        xx = num_step + 1 + X
        yy = num_step + 1 + Y

        print("iter: %d, trial %d" %(it, trial))

        for i in range(num_step):

            up    = lattice[xx,yy+1]
            down  = lattice[xx,yy-1]
            left  = lattice[xx-1,yy]
            right = lattice[xx+1,yy]

            neighbors = np.array([1, 1, 1, 1]) -      Computes available
            ➥ np.array([up, down, left, right]) <──  directions

Avoids
self-loops  └──> if (np.sum(neighbors) == 0):
                     i = 1
                     break
                #end if
                                                      Computes
            weight = weight * np.sum(neighbors)  <──  importance weights

Samples a
move direction └──> direction = np.where(np.random.rand() <
                    ➥ np.cumsum(neighbors/float(sum(neighbors)))))

            X = X + moves[direction[0][0],0]
            Y = Y + moves[direction[0][0],1]

            path_new = np.array([X,Y])                Stores a
            path = np.vstack((path,path_new))  <──    sampled path

            #update grid coordinates
            xx = num_step + 1 + X
            yy = num_step + 1 + Y
            lattice[xx,yy] = 1
        #end for

        trial = trial + 1
```

```
        #end while
                                                    ┐ Computes square
        square_dist[it] = X**2 + Y**2     ←─────┘ extension

        weights[it] = weight
    #end for

    mean_square_dist = np.mean(weights * square_dist)/np.mean(weights)
    print("mean square dist: ", mean_square_dist)

    #generate plots
    plt.figure()
    for i in range(num_step-1):
        plt.plot(path[i,0], path[i,1], path[i+1,0], path[i+1,1], 'ob')
    plt.title('random walk with no overlaps')
    plt.xlabel('X')
    plt.ylabel('Y')
    plt.show()

    plt.figure()
    sns.displot(square_dist)
    plt.xlim(0,np.max(square_dist))
    plt.title('square distance of the random walk')
    plt.xlabel('square distance (X^2 + Y^2)')
    plt.show()

if __name__ == "__main__":
                                    Number of iterations
  ┌─> num_step = 150              for averaging results
  │   num_iter = 100     ←────────┘
  │   moves = np.array([[0, 1],[0, -1],[-1, 0],[1, 0]])  ←───── 2D moves
  │
  │   rand_walk(num_step, num_iter, moves)
```

Number of steps in a random walk

Figure 2.10 shows a self-avoiding random walk generated by the last iteration. There are 4^n possible random walks of length n on the 2D lattice, and for large n, it is very unlikely a random walk will be self-avoiding. The figure also shows a histogram of the

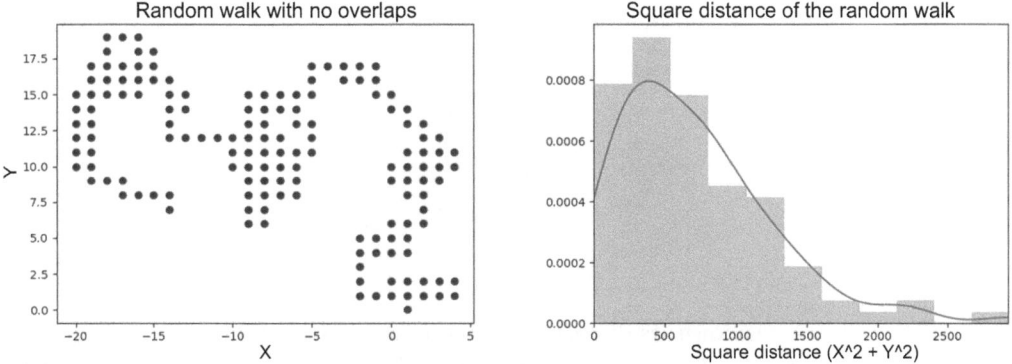

Figure 2.10 **Self-avoiding random walk (left) and random walk square distance (right)**

square distance computed for each random walk iteration. The histogram is positively skewed, showing a smaller probability of large-distance walks. In the next section, we will cover a popular sampling algorithm: Gibbs sampling.

2.5   Gibbs sampling

In this section, we introduce one of the fundamental MCMC algorithms, called *Gibbs sampling*. This form of sampling is based on the idea of sampling one variable at a time from a multidimensional distribution conditioned on the latest samples from all the other variables. For example, for a $d = 3$ dimensional distribution, given a starting sample $x^{\{k\}}$, we generate the next sample $x^{\{k+1\}}$ as follows.

$$x_1^{k+1} \sim p\left(x_1 | x_2^k, x_3^k\right)$$

$$x_2^{k+1} \sim p\left(x_2 | x_1^{k+1}, x_3^k\right)$$

$$x_3^{k+1} \sim p\left(x_3 | x_1^{k+1}, x_2^{k+1}\right) \tag{2.14}$$

The distributions in equation 2.14 are called *fully conditional distributions*. Also, notice that the naive Gibbs sampling algorithm is sequential (with the number of steps proportional to the dimensionality of the distribution) and it assumes we can easily sample from the fully conditional distributions. The Gibbs sampling algorithm is applicable to scenarios in which full conditional distributions in equation 2.14 are easy to compute.

One instance in which the fully conditional distributions are easy to compute is in the case of multivariate Gaussians with PDF, defined as follows.

$$\mathcal{N}(x; \mu, \Sigma) = \frac{1}{(2\pi)^{\frac{d}{2}} |\Sigma|^{\frac{1}{2}}} \exp\left[-\frac{1}{2}(x - \mu)^T \Sigma^{-1}(x - \mu)\right] \tag{2.15}$$

Let's partition the Gaussian vector into two sets $x\{1:D\} = (x_A, x_B)$ with the parameters shown in equation 2.16.

$$\mu = \begin{pmatrix} \mu_A \\ \mu_B \end{pmatrix}$$

$$\Sigma = \begin{pmatrix} \Sigma_{AA} & \Sigma_{AB} \\ \Sigma_{BA} & \Sigma_{BB} \end{pmatrix} \tag{2.16}$$

Then, it can be shown, as discussed in section 2.3 of Christopher M. Bishop's *Pattern Recognition and Machine Learning* (2006), that the full conditionals are given by equation 2.17.

$$p(x_A|x_B) = \mathcal{N}\left(x_A|\mu_{A|B}, \Sigma_{A|B}\right)$$

$$\mu_{A|B} = \mu_A + \Sigma_{AB}\Sigma_{BB}^{-1}(x_B - \mu_B)$$

$$\Sigma_{A|B} = \Sigma_{AA} - \Sigma_{AB}\Sigma_{BB}^{-1}\Sigma_{BA} \tag{2.17}$$

Let's understand the Gibbs sampling algorithm by looking at the pseudo-code in figure 2.11.

```
1: class gibbs_gauss
2: function gauss_conditional(mu, Sigma, setA, x):
3:   setU = set(range(len(mu)))  ← Universal set
4:   setB = setU\setA
5:   x_B, μ_A, μ_B = x[setB], mu[setA], mu[setB]
6:   μ_{A|B} = μ_A + Σ_{AB} Σ_{BB}^{-1}(x_B − μ_B)
7:   Σ_{A|B} = Σ_{AA} − Σ_{AB} Σ_{BB}^{-1} Σ_{BA}
8:   return μ_{A|B}, Σ_{A|B}
9: function sample(mu, Sigma, xinit, num_samples):
10:  x = xinit
11:  dim = len(mu)
12:  for s = 1 to num_samples:
13:    for d = 1 to dim:
14:      μ_{A|B}, Σ_{A|B} = gauss_conditional(mu, Sigma, set(d), x)
15:      x[d] ~ N(x; μ_{A|B}, Σ_{A|B})  ← Gibbs samples
16:    end for
17:    samples[s,:] = x
18:  end for
19:  return samples
```

Figure 2.11
Gibbs sampler pseudo-code

Our gibbs_gauss class contains two functions: gauss_conditional and sample. The gauss_conditional function computes the conditional Gaussian distribution $p(x_A|x_B)$ for any sets of variables setA and setB. setA is an input to the function, while setB is computed as a set difference between the universal set of dimension D and setA. Recall that in Gibbs sampling, we sample one dimension at a time, while conditioning the distribution on all the other dimensions. In other words, we cycle through available dimensions and compute the conditional distribution in each iteration. That's exactly what the sample function does. For each sample, we iterate over each dimension and compute the mean and covariance of the Gaussian conditional distribution, from which we then take and record a sample. We repeat this process until the maximum number of samples is reached. Let's see the Gibbs sampling algorithm in action for sampling from a 2D Gaussian distribution.

Listing 2.4 Gibbs sampling

```
import numpy as np
import matplotlib.pyplot as plt
```

```
import itertools
from numpy.linalg import inv
from scipy.stats import multivariate_normal

np.random.seed(42)

class gibbs_gauss:                                    ┌ Computes P(X_A | X_B = x) =
  def gauss_conditional(self, mu, Sigma, setA, x):  ◄─┘ N(mu_{A|B}, Sigma_{A|B})
      dim = len(mu)
      setU = set(range(dim))
      setB = setU.difference(setA)
      muA = np.array([mu[item] for item in setA]).reshape(-1,1)
      muB = np.array([mu[item] for item in setB]).reshape(-1,1)
      xB = np.array([x[item] for item in setB]).reshape(-1,1)

      Sigma_AA = []
      for (idx1, idx2) in itertools.product(setA, setA):
          Sigma_AA.append(Sigma[idx1][idx2])
      Sigma_AA = np.array(Sigma_AA).reshape(len(setA),len(setA))

      Sigma_AB = []
      for (idx1, idx2) in itertools.product(setA, setB):
          Sigma_AB.append(Sigma[idx1][idx2])
      Sigma_AB = np.array(Sigma_AB).reshape(len(setA),len(setB))

      Sigma_BB = []
      for (idx1, idx2) in itertools.product(setB, setB):
          Sigma_BB.append(Sigma[idx1][idx2])
      Sigma_BB = np.array(Sigma_BB).reshape(len(setB),len(setB))

      Sigma_BB_inv = inv(Sigma_BB)
      mu_AgivenB = muA + np.matmul(np.matmul(Sigma_AB, Sigma_BB_inv),
      ➡ xB - muB)
      Sigma_AgivenB = Sigma_AA - np.matmul(np.matmul(Sigma_AB,
      ➡ Sigma_BB_inv), np.transpose(Sigma_AB))

      return mu_AgivenB, Sigma_AgivenB

  def sample(self, mu, Sigma, xinit, num_samples):
      dim = len(mu)
      samples = np.zeros((num_samples, dim))
      x = xinit
      for s in range(num_samples):
          for d in range(dim):
              mu_AgivenB, Sigma_AgivenB = self.gauss_conditional(mu, Sigma,
              ➡ set([d]), x)
              x[d] = np.random.normal(mu_AgivenB, np.sqrt(Sigma_AgivenB))
          #end for
          samples[s,:] = np.transpose(x)
      #end for
      return samples

if __name__ == "__main__":

 num_samples = 2000
 mu = [1, 1]
```

```
Sigma = [[2,1], [1,1]]
xinit = np.random.rand(len(mu),1)
num_burnin = 1000

gg = gibbs_gauss()
gibbs_samples = gg.sample(mu, Sigma, xinit, num_samples)

scipy_samples =
⮕ multivariate_normal.rvs(mean=mu,cov=Sigma,size=num_samples,random_state=42)

plt.figure()
plt.scatter(gibbs_samples[num_burnin:,0], gibbs_samples[num_burnin:,1],
⮕ label='Gibbs Samples')
plt.grid(True); plt.legend(); plt.xlim([-4,5])
plt.title("Gibbs Sampling of Multivariate Gaussian"); plt.xlabel("X1");
⮕ plt.ylabel("X2")
plt.show()

plt.figure()
plt.scatter(scipy_samples[num_burnin:,0], scipy_samples[num_burnin:,1],
⮕ label='Ground Truth  Samples')
plt.grid(True); plt.legend(); plt.xlim([-4,5])
plt.title("Ground Truth Samples of Multivariate Gaussian");
⮕ plt.xlabel("X1");
plt.ylabel("X2")
plt.show()
```

From figure 2.12, we can see that Gibbs samples resemble the ground truth 2D Gaussian distribution samples parameterized by $\mu = [1, 1]^T$ and $\Sigma = [[2, 1], [1, 1]]$. In the next section, we will examine a more general MCMC sampling algorithm: Metropolis-Hastings sampling.

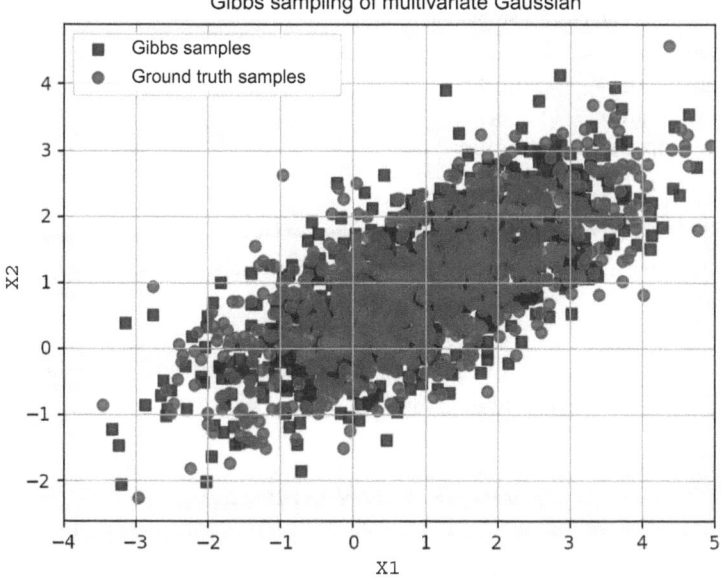

Figure 2.12
Gibbs samples of a
multivariate Gaussian

2.6   *Metropolis-Hastings sampling*

Let's look at a more general MCMC algorithm for sampling from distributions. Our goal is to construct a Markov chain whose stationary distribution is equal to our target distribution $p(x)$. The target distribution $p(x)$ is the distribution (typically a posterior $p(\theta|x)$ or a density function $p(\theta)$) we are interested in drawing samples from.

The basic idea in the Metropolis-Hastings (MH) algorithm is to propose a move from the current state x to a new state x' based on a proposal distribution $q(x'|x)$, and then either accept or reject the proposed state according to MH ratio that ensures that detailed balance is satisfied, as shown in equation 2.18.

$$p\left(x'\right) q\left(x|x'\right) = p(x)q\left(x'|x\right) \tag{2.18}$$

The detailed balance equation states that the probability of transitioning out of state x is equal to the probability of transitioning into state x. To derive the MH ratio, assume for a moment that the preceding detailed balanced equation is not satisfied, and then there must exist a correction factor $r(x'|x)$ such that the two sides are equal, and solving for it leads to the following MH ratio.

$$p\left(x'\right) q\left(x|x'\right) = r\left(x'|x\right) p(x)q\left(x'|x\right)$$
$$r\left(x'|x\right) = \min\left[1, \frac{p\left(x'\right) q\left(x|x'\right)}{p(x)q\left(x'|x\right)}\right] \tag{2.19}$$

We can summarize the Metropolis-Hastings algorithm as shown in figure 2.13.

Sample from the proposal distribution

1: Init x_0 at random
2: **for** $k = 0, 1, 2, \dots$ **do**
3:    propose a new state $x' \sim q(x'|x_k)$
4:    compute metropolis-hastings ratio:
5:    $r(x'|x) = \min\left[1, \frac{p(x')q(x|x')}{p(x)q(x'|x)}\right]$
6:    set $x_{k+1} = \begin{cases} x', \text{ with prob. } r(x'|x) \leftarrow \textbf{Accepts the sample} \\ x_k, \text{ with prob. } 1 - r(x'|x) \leftarrow \textbf{Rejects the sample} \end{cases}$
7: **end for**

Figure 2.13   Metropolis-Hastings pseudo-code

Let's implement the MH algorithm for a multivariate mixture of Gaussian target distribution and a Gaussian proposal distribution.

$$p(x) = \sum_{k=1}^{K} \pi(k)\mathcal{N}\left(x; \mu_k, \Sigma_k\right)$$
$$q\left(x'|x\right) = \mathcal{N}\left(x'|x, \Sigma\right) \tag{2.20}$$

Let's examine code listing 2.5. The `mh_gauss` class consists of the `target_pdf` function that defined the target distribution (in our case, the Gaussian mixture $p(x)$); the `proposal_pdf` function that defines the proposal distribution (a multivariate normal); and the `sample` function, which samples a new state from the proposal $q(x'|xk)$ conditioned on the previous state xk, computes the Metropolis-Hastings ratio, and either accepts the new sample with probability $r(x'|x)$ or rejects the sample with probability $1 - r(x'|x)$.

Listing 2.5   Metropolis-Hastings sampling

```python
import numpy as np
import matplotlib.pyplot as plt

from scipy.stats import uniform
from scipy.stats import multivariate_normal

np.random.seed(42)

class mh_gauss:
    def __init__(self, dim, K, num_samples, target_mu, target_sigma,
        target_pi, proposal_mu, proposal_sigma):
        self.dim = dim
        self.K = K
        self.num_samples = num_samples              # Target parameters:
        self.target_mu = target_mu                  # p(x) = \sum_k pi(k) N(x; mu_k, Sigma_k)
        self.target_sigma = target_sigma
        self.target_pi = target_pi

        self.proposal_mu = proposal_mu              # Proposal parameters:
        self.proposal_sigma = proposal_sigma        # q(x) = N(x; mu, Sigma)

        self.n_accept = 0
        self.alpha = np.zeros(self.num_samples)     # Sampling chain
        self.mh_samples = np.zeros((self.num_samples,   # params
            self.dim))

    def target_pdf(self, x):
        prob = 0
        for k in range(self.K):
            prob += self.target_pi[k]*\              # Target pdf: p(x) = \sum_k
                multivariate_normal.pdf(x,self       # pi(k) N(x; mu_k,Sigma_k)
                    .target_mu[:,k],self.target_sigma[:,:,k])
        #end for
        return prob

    def proposal_pdf(self, x):
        return multivariate_normal.pdf(x, self       # Proposal pdf:
            .proposal_mu, self.proposal_sigma)       # q(x) = N(x; mu, Sigma)

    def sample(self):
        x_init = multivariate_normal                 # Draws the initial sample
            .rvs(self.proposal_mu, self.proposal_sigma, 1)  # from the proposal.
        self.mh_samples[0,:] = x_init

        for i in range(self.num_samples-1):
            x_curr = self.mh_samples[i,:]
```

```
    x_new = multivariate_normal.rvs(x_curr, self
    ➥ .proposal_sigma, 1)

    self.alpha[i] = self.proposal_pdf(x_new) /
    ➥ self.proposal_pdf(x_curr)                          │   MH ratio
    self.alpha[i] = self.alpha[i] *                      │
    ➥ (self.target_pdf(x_new)/self.target_pdf(x_curr))  │

    r = min(1, self.alpha[i])        ◁────  MH acceptance probability
    u = uniform.rvs(loc=0, scale=1, size=1)
    if (u <= r):
        self.n_accept += 1
        self.mh_samples[i+1,:] = x_new    ◁────  Accept
    else:
        self.mh_samples[i+1,:] = x_curr   ◁────  Reject
#end for
print("MH acceptance ratio: ", self.n_accept/float(self.num_samples))

if __name__ == "__main__":

    dim = 2
    K = 2
    num_samples = 5000
    target_mu = np.zeros((dim, K))
    target_mu[:,0] = [4,0]
    target_mu[:,1] = [-4,0]
    target_sigma = np.zeros((dim, dim, K))
    target_sigma[:,:,0] = [[2,1],[1,1]]
    target_sigma[:,:,1] = [[1,0],[0,1]]
    target_pi = np.array([0.4, 0.6])

    proposal_mu = np.zeros((dim,1)).flatten()
    proposal_sigma = 10*np.eye(dim)


    mhg = mh_gauss(dim, K, num_samples, target_mu, target_sigma, target_pi,
    ➥ proposal_mu, proposal_sigma)
    mhg.sample()

    plt.figure()
    plt.scatter(mhg.mh_samples[:,0], mhg.mh_samples[:,1], label='MH samples')
    plt.grid(True); plt.legend()
    plt.title("Metropolis-Hastings Sampling of 2D Gaussian Mixture")
    plt.xlabel("X1"); plt.ylabel("X2")
    plt.show()
```

From figure 2.14, we can see that MH samples resemble the ground truth mixture of two 2D Gaussian distributions with means $\mu 1 = [4,0]$, $\mu 2 = [-4,0]$; covariances $\Sigma\_1 = [[2,1],[1,1]]$ and $\Sigma\_2 = [[1,0],[0,1]]$; and mixture proportions $\pi = [0.4,0.6]$.

Notice that we are free to choose any proposal distribution $q(x'|x)$ that makes the method flexible. A good choice of the proposal will result in a high sample acceptance rate.

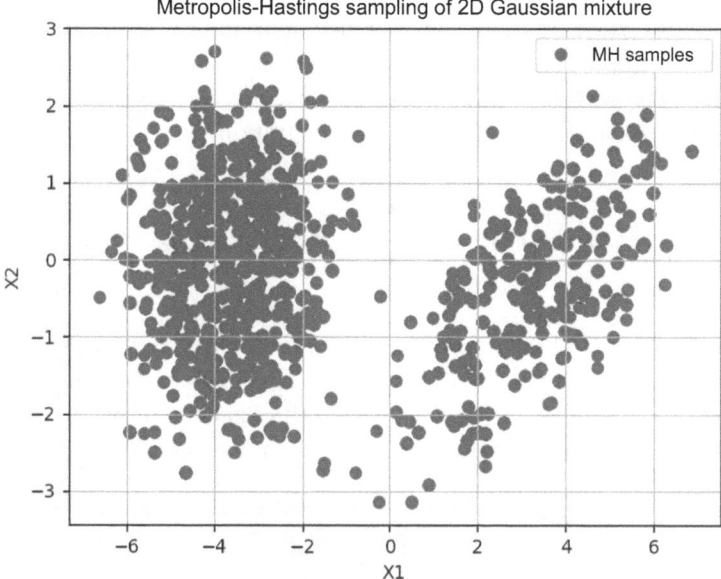

Figure 2.14   Metropolis-Hastings samples of a multivariate Gaussian mixture

In our implementation, we chose a symmetric Gaussian distribution centered on the current state shown in equation 2.21.

$$q\left(x'|x\right) = \mathcal{N}\left(x'|x, \Sigma\right) \tag{2.21}$$

This is known as a *random walk Metropolis algorithm*. If we use a proposal of the form $q(x'|x) = q(x')$, where the new state is independent of the old state, we get an independence sampler, which is similar to the importance sampling we will look at in the next section.

Also, notice that to compute the MH ratio, we don't need to know the normalization constants Z of our distributions, since the ratio and the Zs cancel out. There's a connection between the MH algorithm and Gibbs sampling: the Gibbs algorithm acceptance ratio is always 1.

2.7   Importance sampling

Importance sampling (IS) is a Monte Carlo algorithm for estimating integrals of the following form.

$$E[f(x)] = \int p(x)f(x)dx \tag{2.22}$$

The idea behind importance sampling is to draw samples in interesting regions (i.e., where both $p(x)$ and $|f(x)|$ are large). Importance sampling works by drawing samples from an easier-to-sample proposal distribution $q(x)$. Thus, we can compute the expected value of $f(x)$ with respect to the target distribution $p(x)$ by drawing samples from the proposal $q(x)$ and using Monte Carlo integration.

$$E[f(x)] = \int f(x)\frac{p(x)}{q(x)}q(x)dx \approx \frac{1}{N}\sum_{i=1}^{N} w(x_i)f(x_i), \text{ where } x_i \sim q(x) \quad (2.23)$$

In equation 2.23, we defined the importance weights as $w(x) = p(x)/q(x)$. Let's look at an example where we use importance sampling to approximate an expected value of $f(x) = 2\sin(\pi x/1.5)$, $x \geq 0$. We are asked to take the expectation with respect to an unnormalized Chi distribution parameterized by a noninteger degree of freedom (DoF) parameter k.

$$p(x) \sim x^{(k-1)} \exp\left\{-\frac{x^2}{2}\right\}, x \geq 0 \quad (2.24)$$

We will use an easier-to-sample from proposal distribution $q(x)$:

$$q(x) \sim N(x; 0.8, 1.5) \quad (2.25)$$

Let's look at the pseudo-code in figure 2.15.

```
1: class importance_sampler
2: function sample(N):
3:   for i = 1 to N:
4:     x_i ~ q(x) = N(x; μ, σ²) ←—Samples from the proposal
5:     w(x_i) = p(x_i)/q(x_i) ←—Computes importance weights
6:   end for
7:   E[f(x)] = 1/N Σ_{i=1}^{N} w(x_i)f(x_i)
8:   return w(x), E[f(x)]
```

Figure 2.15   Importance sampler pseudo-code

Our `importance_sampler` class contains a function called sample that takes the number of samples N as its input. Inside the sample function, we loop over the number of samples, and for each iteration, we sample from the proposal distribution $q(x)$ and compute the importance weight as the ratio of target distribution $p(x)$ to the proposal distribution $q(x)$. Finally, we compute the Monte Carlo integral by weighting our function of interest $f(x)$ by the importance weights, summing over all samples and dividing by N. Let's look at the following code listing, which captures all the details.

Listing 2.6 Importance sampling

```
import numpy as np
import matplotlib.pyplot as plt

from scipy.integrate import quad
from scipy.stats import multivariate_normal

np.random.seed(42)

class importance_sampler:

  def __init__(self, k=1.5, mu=0.8, sigma=np.sqrt(1.5), c=3):
      self.k = k              ⟵――┐ Target parameters p(x)

      self.mu = mu
      self.sigma = sigma       │ Proposal parameters q(x)
      self.c = c              ⟵――┐
                               │ Fixes c, s.t. p(x) < c q(x)
  def target_pdf(self, x):
      return (x**(self.k-1)) * np.exp(-x**2/2.0)  ⟵―― p(x) ~ Chi(k=1.5)

  def proposal_pdf(self, x):
      return self.c * 1.0/np.sqrt(2*np.pi*1.5) *
      ⟼ np.exp(-(x-self.mu)**2/(2*self.sigma**2))  ⟵―― q(x) ~ N(mu,sigma)

  def fx(self, x):
        return 2*np.sin((np.pi/1.5)*x)  ⟵―― Function of interest f(x), x >= 0

  def sample(self, num_samples):
      x = multivariate_normal.rvs(self.mu,
      ⟼ self.sigma, num_samples)        ⟵―― Sample from the proposal

      idx = np.where(x >= 0)   │ Discards negative samples, since
      x_pos = x[idx]           │ f(x) is defined for x >= 0

      isw = self.target_pdf(x_pos) /
      ⟼ self.proposal_pdf(x_pos)   ⟵―― Computes importance weights

      fw = (isw/np.sum(isw))*self.fx(x_pos)  │ Computes E[f(x)] = sum_i f(x_i)
      f_est = np.sum(fw)                     │ w(x_i), where x_i ~ q(x)

      return isw, f_est


if __name__ == "__main__":

  num_samples = [10, 100, 1000, 10000, 100000, 1000000]

  F_est_iter, IS_weights_var_iter = [], []
  for k in num_samples:
      IS = importance_sampler()
      IS_weights, F_est = IS.sample(k)
      IS_weights_var = np.var(IS_weights/np.sum(IS_weights))
      F_est_iter.append(F_est)
      IS_weights_var_iter.append(IS_weights_var)

  #ground truth (numerical integration)
  k = 1.5
```

```
I_gt, _ = quad(lambda x: 2.0*np.sin((np.pi/1.5)*x)*(x**(k-1))*np
⮕ .exp(-x**2/2.0), 0, 5)

#generate plots
plt.figure()
xx = np.linspace(0,8,100)
plt.plot(xx, IS.target_pdf(xx), '-r', label='target pdf p(x)')
plt.plot(xx, IS.proposal_pdf(xx), '-b', label='proposal pdf q(x)')
plt.plot(xx, IS.fx(xx) * IS.target_pdf(xx), '-k', label='p(x)f(x)
    integrand')
plt.grid(True); plt.legend(); plt.xlabel("X1"); plt.ylabel("X2")
plt.title("Importance Sampling Components")
plt.show()

plt.figure()
plt.hist(IS_weights, label = "IS weights")
plt.grid(True); plt.legend();
plt.title("Importance Weights Histogram")
plt.show()

plt.figure()
plt.semilogx(num_samples, F_est_iter, label = "IS Estimate of E[f(x)]")
plt.semilogx(num_samples, I_gt*np.ones(len(num_samples)), label = "Ground
⮕ Truth")
plt.grid(True); plt.legend(); plt.xlabel('iterations'); plt.ylabel("E[f(x)]
⮕ estimate")
plt.title("IS Estimate of E[f(x)]")
plt.show()
```

Figure 2.16 (left) shows the target pdf $p(x)$, the proposal pdf $q(x)$, and the integrand $p(x)f(x)$. Notice that we scaled the proposal pdf $q(x)$ by constant c, such that $p(x) < cq(x)$ for all $x \geq 0$. Furthermore, we restricted the samples from $q(x)$ to be positive (thus, sampling from a truncated Gaussian) to meet our constraint of $x \geq 0$ for $f(x)$. Figure 2.16 shows the improvement in the estimate of $E[f(x)]$ vs. the number of samples compared to the ground truth computed via numerical integration.

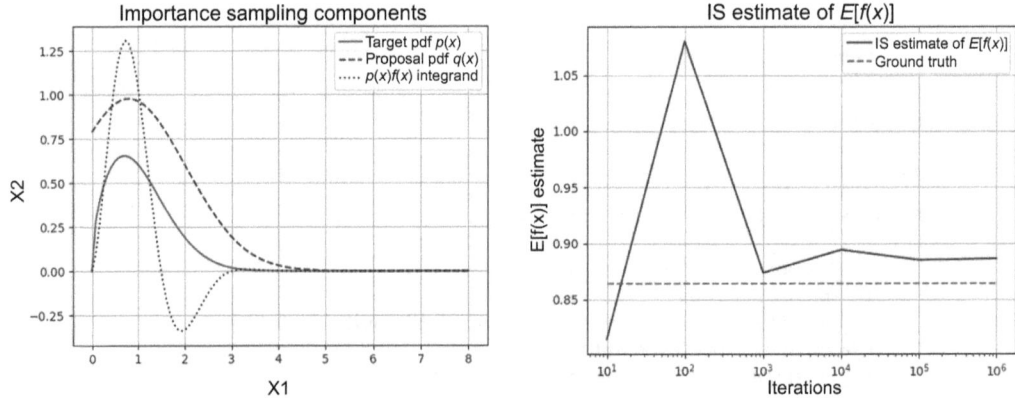

Figure 2.16   IS components (left) and IS estimate (right)

In the previous example, we used a normalized proposal distribution. However, for more complex distributions we often do not know the normalization constant (aka the partition function), since we are working with ratios of pdfs we'll see that the math holds for unnormalized distributions in addition we'll look at a way of estimating ratios of partition functions and discuss IS properties as an estimator.

Let's define a normalized PDF $p(x)$ and $q(x)$ as follows.

$$p(x) = \frac{1}{Z_p}\tilde{p}(x) \qquad q(x) = \frac{1}{Z_p}\tilde{q}(x) \tag{2.26}$$

Here, Z_p and Z_q are normalization constants of $p(x)$ and $q(x)$, respectively, and $\tilde{p}(x)$ and $\tilde{q}(x)$ are unnormalized distributions. We can write our estimate as follows.

$$
\begin{aligned}
E[f(x)] &= \int f(x)p(x)dx \\
&= \int f(x)\frac{q(x)}{q(x)}p(x)dx = \frac{Z_q}{Z_p}\int f(x)\frac{\tilde{p}(x)}{\tilde{q}(x)}q(x)dx \\
&\approx \frac{Z_q}{Z_p}\frac{1}{S}\sum_{s=1}^{S}\tilde{w}(s)f(s), \text{ where } s \sim q(x) \text{ and } \tilde{w}(s) = \frac{\tilde{p}(s)}{\tilde{q}(s)} \quad (2.27)
\end{aligned}
$$

Notice in equation 2.27, $\tilde{w}(s)$ are unnormalized importance weights. We can compute the ratio of normalizing constants as follows.

$$\frac{Z_p}{Z_q} = \frac{1}{Z_q}\int \tilde{p}(x)dx = \frac{1}{Z_q}\int \frac{\tilde{p}(x)}{q(x)}q(x)dx = \int \frac{\tilde{p}(x)}{\tilde{q}(x)}q(x)dx = \frac{1}{S}\sum_{s=1}^{S}\tilde{w}(s) \ (2.28)$$

Combining the two expressions above, we get the following.

$$E[f(x)] \approx \frac{Z_q}{Z_p}\frac{1}{S}\sum_{s=1}^{S}\tilde{w}(s)f(s) = \frac{\frac{1}{S}\sum_s \tilde{w}(s)f(s)}{\frac{1}{S}\sum_s \tilde{w}(s)} = \sum_{s=1}^{S}w(s)f(s) \tag{2.29}$$

Equation 2.29 justifies our computation in the code example for the estimate of $E[f(x)]$. Let's look at a few properties of IS estimator and compute quantities relevant to characterizing the performance of IS. The IS estimator can be defined as follows.

$$\hat{a} = E[a(x)] = \frac{\frac{1}{n}\sum_{i=1}^{n} \tilde{w}^i a(x_i)}{\frac{1}{n}\sum_{i=1}^{n} \tilde{w}^i} = \frac{1}{n}\sum_{i=1}^{n} w_*^i a(x_i),$$

$$\text{where } w_*^i = \frac{\tilde{w}^i}{\frac{1}{n}\sum_i \tilde{w}^i} \tag{2.30}$$

By the weak law of large numbers (WLLN), assuming independent samples x_i, we know that the average of iid samples converges in probability to the true mean.

$$a = E[w_* (X_i) a (X_i)] \rightarrow b(\hat{a}) = E[\hat{a}] - a = 0 \tag{2.31}$$

Here, X_i are assumed to be iid random variables distributed according to $q(x)$. As a result, IS is, in theory, an unbiased estimator. The variance of the IS estimator is given by the following.

$$\text{VAR}(\hat{a}) = \frac{\sigma^2}{n} = \frac{1}{n} \frac{\sum_{i=1}^{n} \left(\tilde{w}^i (a(x_i) - \hat{a}) \right)^2}{\left(\sum_{i=1}^{n} \tilde{w}^i \right)^2} \tag{2.32}$$

To check whether the IS estimate is consistent, we need to show that as we increase the number of samples n, the estimate converges to the true value in probability.

$$\lim_{n \to \infty} P\left(|\hat{a}_n - a| > \epsilon \right) = 0 \tag{2.33}$$

Using Chebyshev's inequality, we can bound the deviation as follows.

$$\lim_{n \to \infty} P\left(|\hat{a} - a| > \epsilon \right) \leq \frac{\text{VAR}(\hat{a})}{\epsilon^2} = \frac{\sigma^2}{n\epsilon^2} = 0 \tag{2.34}$$

As a result, the IS estimator is consistent; here, we didn't need to use an assumption that samples are independent, but we needed to assume that the variance of importance weights is finite. Thus, we expect the variance around the estimate to shrink as we add more samples. One factor that affects the variance of the estimator is the magnitude of importance weights. Since $w(x_i) = p(x_i)/q(x_i)$, the weights are small if $q(x_i)$ is similar to p(xi) and has heavy tails. This is the desired case that leads to a small variance in our estimate.

We would like to have a way of knowing when the importance weights are problematic (e.g., when only a couple of weights dominate the weighted sum). When samples are correlated, the variance is σ^2/n_{eff}, where n_{eff} is the effective sample size. To compute an expression for effective sample size, we set the variance of the weighted average equal to the variance of the unweighted average.

$$\text{VAR}\left(\frac{1}{n}\sum_{i=1}^{n}a(x_i)\right) = \frac{\sigma^2}{n_{eff}} = \text{VAR}\left(\frac{\frac{1}{n}\sum_{i=1}^{n}\tilde{w}^i a(x_i)}{\frac{1}{n}\sum_{i=1}^{n}\tilde{w}^i}\right)$$
$$\text{where } \text{VAR}(a(x_i)) = \sigma^2 \tag{2.35}$$

Solving for n_{eff}, we get the following equation.

$$n_{eff} = \frac{\left(\sum_{i=1}^{n}w_i\right)^2}{\sum_{i=1}^{n}w_i^2} = \frac{n}{1 + \text{VAR}\left(w_*^i\right)} \tag{2.36}$$

We can use n_{eff} as a kind of diagnostic for the importance sampler, where the target number n_{eff} depends on the application. The applications for importance sampling extend beyond approximating linear estimates, such as expectations and integrals as well as nonlinear estimates. In signal processing, importance sampling can be used for signal recovery, with fewer measurements.

2.8   Exercises

2.1   Derive full conditionals $p(x_A|x_B)$ for a multivariate Gaussian distribution where A and B are subsets of $x_1, x_2,..., x_n$ of jointly Gaussian random variables.

2.2   Derive marginals $p(x_A)$ and $p(x_B)$ for a multivariate Gaussian distribution where A and B are subsets of $x_1, x_2,..., x_n$ of jointly Gaussian random variables.

2.3   Let $y \sim N(\mu, \Sigma)$, where $\Sigma = LL^T$. Show that you can get samples y as follows: $x \sim N(0, I)$; $y = Lx + \mu$.

Summary

- Markov chain Monte Carlo (MCMC) is a methodology of sampling from high dimensional parameter spaces to approximate the posterior distribution $p(\theta|x)$.

- Monte Carlo (MC) integration has an advantage over numerical integration (which evaluates a function at a fixed grid of points), in that the function is only evaluated in places where there is a nonnegligible probability.

- In a binomial tree model of a stock price, we assume that at each time step, the stock could be in either up or down states with unequal payoffs characteristic of a risky asset.

- Self-avoiding random walks are simply random walks that do not cross themselves. We can use Monte Carlo integration to simulate a self-avoiding random walk.

- Gibbs sampling is based on the idea of sampling one variable at a time from a multidimensional distribution conditioned on the latest samples from all the other variables.

- The basic idea of the Metropolis-Hastings (MH) algorithm is to propose a move from the current state x to a new state x' based on a proposal distribution $q(x'|x)$ and then either accept or reject the proposed state according to MH ratio that ensures detailed balance is satisfied.

- The idea of importance sampling is to draw samples in interesting regions (i.e., where both $p(x)$ and $|f(x)|$ are large). Importance sampling works by drawing samples from an easier-to-sample proposal distribution $q(x)$.

Variational inference 3

In the previous chapter, we covered one of the two main camps of Bayesian inference: Markov chain Monte Carlo. We examined different sampling algorithms and approximated the posterior distribution using samples. In this chapter, we will discuss the second camp of Bayesian inference: variational inference. *Variational inference* (VI) is an important class of approximate inference algorithms; its basic idea is to choose an approximate distribution $q(x)$ from a family of tractable or easy-to-compute distributions with trainable parameters and then make this approximation as close as possible to the true posterior distribution $p(x)$.

As we will see in the mean-field section, the approximate $q(x)$ can take on a fully factored representation of the joint posterior distribution. This factorization significantly speeds up computation. We will introduce KL divergence and use it as a way to measure the closeness of our approximate distribution to the true posterior. By optimizing KL divergence, we will effectively convert VI into an optimization problem. In the following section, we will derive the evidence lower bound (ELBO) and interpret it in three different ways, which will become handy during our implementation of mean-field approximation for image denoising. The image denoising algorithm was selected because it illustrates the concepts discussed in this section via a visual example.

3.1 KL variational inference

We can use KL divergence to measure a distance between probability distributions. This is particularly useful when making an approximation to the target distribution, since we want to find out how close our approximation is. Let $q(x)$ be our approximating distribution and $p(x)$ be the target posterior distribution. Then, the reverse KL is defined as follows.

Approximating distribution

$$KL(q||p) = \sum_x q(x) \log \frac{q(x)}{p(x)} \tag{3.1}$$

Log ratio of approximate to actual

Consider a simple example, in which our target distribution is a standard univariate normal distribution $p(x) \sim N(0, 1)$ and our approximating distribution is a univariate normal with a mean μ and variance σ^2: $q(x) \sim N(\mu, \sigma^2)$. We can then compute $KL(q||p)$ as follows.

$$
\begin{aligned}
KL(q||p) &= \int q(x) \log \frac{q(x)}{p(x)} \\
&= -\int q(x) \log p(x) + \int q(x) \log q(x) \\
&= -\int q(x) \left[-\frac{1}{2} \log 2\pi - \frac{1}{2} x^2 \right] \\
&\quad + \int q(x) \left[-\frac{1}{2} \log 2\pi\sigma^2 - \frac{1}{2\sigma^2} (x - \mu)^2 \right] \\
&= \left[\frac{1}{2} \log 2\pi + \frac{1}{2} (\sigma^2 + \mu^2) \right] + \left[-\frac{1}{2} \log 2\pi\sigma^2 - \frac{1}{2} \right] \\
&= -\frac{1}{2} \left(1 + \log \sigma^2 - \mu^2 - \sigma^2 \right) \tag{3.2}
\end{aligned}
$$

We can visualize how $KL(q||p)$ changes as we vary the parameters of our approximate distribution $q(x)$. Let's fix $\sigma^2 = 4$ and vary the mean $\mu \in [-4, 4]$. We obtain figure 3.1.

Notice that the KL divergence is nonnegative and is smallest when $\mu = 0$ (i.e., the mean of the approximating distribution is equal to the mean of our target distribution $p(x) \sim N(0, 1)$). We can interpret KL divergence as a measure of distance between distributions.

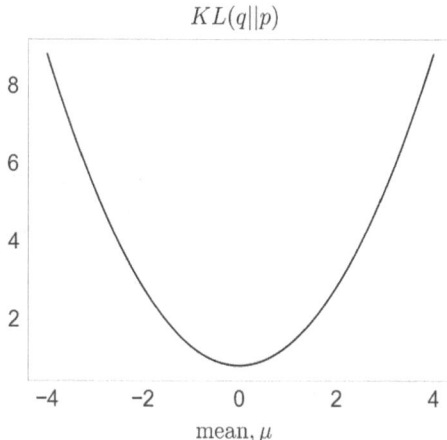

Figure 3.1 KL(q||p) for p(x)~N(0,1) and q(x)~N(μ,4)

Let $\tilde{p}(x) = p(x)Z$ be the unnormalized distribution, and then consider the following objective function.

$$
\begin{aligned}
J(q) &= KL(q||\tilde{p}) \\
&= \sum_x q(x) \log \frac{q(x)}{p(x)Z} = \sum_x q(x) \log \frac{q(x)}{p(x)} - \log Z \\
&= KL(q||p) - \log Z
\end{aligned}
\tag{3.3}
$$

Since KL divergence is nonnegative, $J(q)$ is an upper bound on the marginal likelihood.

$$
J(q) = KL(q||p) - \log Z \geq -\log Z = -\log p(D)
\tag{3.4}
$$

When $q(x)$ equals the true posterior $p(x)$, the KL divergence vanishes. The optimal value $J(q^*)$ equals the log partition function, and for all other values of q, it yields a bound. $J(q)$ is called the *variational free energy* and can be written as follows.

$$
\min_q J(q) = E_q[\log q(x)] + E_q[-\log \tilde{p}(x)] = -H(q) + E_q[E(x)]
\tag{3.5}
$$

The variational objective function in equation 3.5 is closely related to energy minimization in statistical physics. The first term acts as a regularizer by encouraging maximum entropy, while the second term is the expected energy and encourages the variational distribution q to explain the data.

The reverse KL that acts as a penalty term in the variational objective is also known as *information projection* or *I-projection*. In the reverse KL, $q(x)$ will typically underestimate the support of $p(x)$ and will lock onto one of its modes. This is due to $q(x) = 0$ whenever $p(x) = 0$ to ensure the KL divergence stays finite. On the other hand, the forward KL, known as *moment projection* or *M-projection* is zero avoiding $q(x)$ and will overestimate the support of $p(x)$, as shown in figure 3.2.

Figure 3.2   **Forward KL (left) $q(x)$ overestimates the support, while reverse KL (right) $q(x)$ locks onto a mode.**

Figure 3.2 shows samples from a 2D Gaussian mixture with 4 components $p(x)$) as well as density ellipses of approximating distribution $q(x)$. We can see that optimizing forward KL leads to $q(x)$ centered at zero (in the low-density region), as we over-estimate the support of $q(x)$. On the other hand, optimizing reverse KL leads to $q(x)$ centered at one of the four modes of the Gaussian mixture.

We can use Jensen's inequality to derive the ELBO, an objective that we can maximize to learn the variational parameters of our model. Let x be our data and z be the latent variables, and then we can derive our ELBO objective as follows.

$$
\begin{aligned}
\log p(x) &= \log \sum_z p(x, z) = \log \sum_z \frac{q(z)}{q(z)} p(x, z) \\
&= \log E_{q(z)}\left[\frac{p(x, z)}{q(z)}\right] \geq E_{q(z)}\left[\log \frac{p(x, z)}{q(z)}\right] \\
&= \underbrace{E_{q(z)}[\log p(x, z)]}_{\text{Energy term}} - \underbrace{E_{q(z)}[\log q(x)]}_{\text{Entropy term}} = \text{ELBO} \qquad (3.6)
\end{aligned}
$$

Notice that the first term is the average negative energy, and the second term is the entropy. Thus, a good posterior must assign most of its probability mass to regions of low energy (i.e., high joint probability density) while also maximizing the entropy of $q(z)$. Thus, variational inference, in contrast to the MAP estimator, prevents $q(z)$ from collapsing into an atom.

One form of ELBO emphasizes that the lower bound becomes tighter, as the variational distribution better approximates the posterior.

$$
\begin{aligned}
\text{ELBO} &= E_{q(z)}\left[\log \frac{p(x, z)}{q(z)}\right] = E_{q(z)}\left[\log \frac{p(z|x)p(x)}{q(z)}\right] \\
&= \underbrace{-KL(q(z)\|p(z|x))}_{\substack{\text{Distance between the approximating} \\ \text{q(z) and the posterior p(z|x)}}} + \log p(x) \qquad (3.7)
\end{aligned}
$$

Therefore, we can improve the ELBO by improving the model log evidence $\log p(x)$ through the prior $p(z)$ or the likelihood $p(z|x)$ or by improving the variational posterior approximation $q(z)$.

Finally, we can write the ELBO as follows.

Distance between the approximating
q(z) and the prior p(z) for sample i

$$\text{ELBO} = \frac{1}{n} \sum_{i=1}^{n} \left[\underbrace{E_{q(z)} \left[\log p(x_i|z_i) \right]}_{\text{Sample likelihood}} - \overbrace{KL(q(z_i)||p(z_i))} \right] \tag{3.8}$$

This version emphasizes a likelihood term for the i-th observation and KL divergence term between each approximating distribution and the prior. In all the preceding cases, the expectation with respect to $q(z)$ can be computed by sampling from our approximating distribution. Let's look at one of the most common variational approximations in the next section.

3.2   *Mean-field approximation*

One of the most popular forms of variational inference is the *mean-field approximation*, where we assume the posterior is a fully factorized approximation of the form.

$$q(x) = \prod_i q_i(x_i) \tag{3.9}$$

Here, we optimize over the parameters of each marginal distribution $q_i(x_i)$. We can visualize a fully factored distribution, as in figure 3.3.

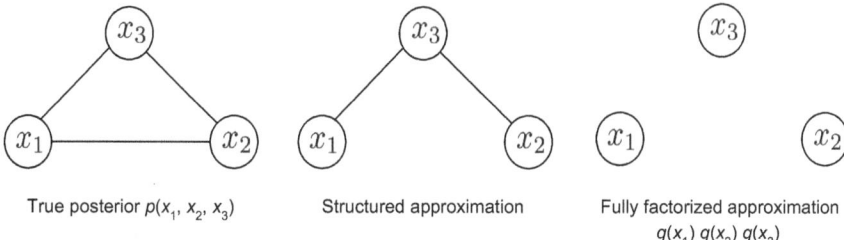

True posterior $p(x_1, x_2, x_3)$ Structured approximation   Fully factorized approximation
$q(x_1)\, q(x_2)\, q(x_3)$

Figure 3.3   True posterior (left), structured approximation (middle), and fully factored approximation (right)

For a distribution with three random variables, x_1, x_2, and x_3, we have the true posterior $p(x_1, x_2, x_3)$ that we are attempting to approximate by a fully factored distribution $q(x_1)\, q(x_2)\, q(x_3)$.

Our goal is to minimize variational free energy $J(q)$ or, equivalently, maximize the lower bound.

$$L(q) = -J(q) = \sum_x q(x) \log \frac{\tilde{p}(x)}{q(x)} \qquad (3.10)$$

We can rewrite the objective for each marginal distribution q_j, keeping the rest of the terms as constants, as demonstrated in section 21.3 of *Probabilistic Machine Learning* by Kevin Murphy (2012).

$$
\begin{aligned}
L(q_j) &= \sum_x \overbrace{\prod_i q_i(x_i)}^{\text{Mean-field approx}} \left[\log \tilde{p}(x) - \overbrace{\sum_k \log q_k(x_k)}^{\text{Mean-field approx}} \right] \\
&= \sum_{x_j} \sum_{x_{-j}} q_j(x_j) \prod_{i \neq j} q_i(x_i) \left[\log \tilde{p}(x) - \sum_k \log q_k(x_k) \right] \ \leftarrow \left|\begin{array}{l}\text{Factors}\\\text{out qj}\end{array}\right. \\
&= \sum_{x_j} q_j(x_j) \log f_j(x_j) \\
&\quad - \sum_{x_j} q_j(x_j) \sum_{x_{-j}} \prod_{i \neq j} q_i(x_i) \left[\sum_{k \neq j} \log q_k(x_k) + \log q_j(x_j) \right] \\
&= \sum_{x_j} q_j(x_j) \log f_j(x_j) - \sum_{x_j} q_j(x_j) \log q_j(x_j) + \text{const} \ \leftarrow \left|\begin{array}{l}\text{Treats non-qj}\\\text{terms as constant}\end{array}\right. \qquad (3.11)
\end{aligned}
$$

Here, we defined the following.

$$\log f_j(x_j) = \sum_{x_{-j}} \prod_{i \neq j} q_i(x_i) \log \tilde{p}(x) = E_{-q_j}[\log \tilde{p}(x)] \qquad (3.12)$$

Since we are replacing the values by their mean value, the method is known as the *mean field*. We can rewrite $L(q_j) = -KL(q_j \| f_j)$ and, therefore, maximize the objective by setting $q_j = f_j$ or, equivalently, equation 3.13.

$$\log q_j(x_j) = \log f_j(x_j) = E_{-q_j}[\log \tilde{p}(x)] \qquad (3.13)$$

Here, the functional form of q_j will be determined by the type of variables x_j and their probability model. We will use this result in the next section to derive the image denoising algorithm from scratch.

3.3   *Image denoising in an Ising model*

The Ising model is an example of a Markov random field (MRF) and has its origins in statistical physics. A Markov random field is a set of random variables with a Markov property described by an undirected graph, in which the nodes represent random variables and the edges encode conditional independence. The Ising model assumes we have a grid of nodes, where each node can be in one of two possible states. The state of each node depends on the neighboring nodes through interaction potentials. In the case of images, this translates to a smoothness constraint (i.e., a pixel prefers to be of the same color as the neighboring pixels). In the image denoising problem, we assume we have a 2D grid of noisy pixel observations of an underlying true image and we would like to recover the true image.

Let y_i be noisy observations of binary latent variables $x_i \in \{-1, +1\}$. We can write down the joint distribution as follows.

$$
\begin{aligned}
p(x, y) = p(x)p(y|x) &= \prod_{(s,t)\in E} \Psi_{st}(x_s, x_t) \prod_{i=1}^{n} p(y_i|x_i) \\
&= \prod_{(s,t)\in E} \exp\{x_s w_{st} x_t\} \prod_{i=1}^{n} N\left(y_i|x_i, \sigma^2\right) \quad (3.14)
\end{aligned}
$$

In equation 3.14, the interaction potentials are represented by Ψ_{st} for every pair of nodes x_s and x_t in a set of edges E, and the observations y_i are Gaussian with mean x_i and variance σ^2. Here, w_{st} is the coupling strength and assumed to be constant and equal to $J > 0$, indicating a preference for the same state as neighbors (i.e., the potential $\Psi(x_s, x_t) = \exp\{x_s J x_t\}$ is higher when x_s and x_t are both either +1 or -1).

To fit the model parameters using variational inference, we first need to maximize the ELBO.

$$
\begin{aligned}
\text{ELBO} &= E_{q(x)}\left[\log p(x, y)\right] - E_{q(x)}\left[\log q(x)\right] \\
&= E_{q(x)}\left[\sum_{(s,t)\in E} x_s w_{st} x_t + \sum_{i=1}^{n} \log N\left(x_i; \sigma^2\right)\right] \\
&\quad - \sum_{i=1}^{n} E_{q_i(x)}\left[\log q_i(x)\right] \quad (3.15)
\end{aligned}
$$

Here, we are using the mean-field assumption of a fully factored approximation $q(x)$.

$$
q(x) = \prod_{i=1}^{n} q(x_i; \mu_i) \quad (3.16)
$$

Using the result derived in equation 3.12, we state that $q(x_i; \mu_i)$, which minimizes the KL divergence, is given by the following.

$$q_i(x_i) = \frac{1}{Z_i} \exp\left[E_{-q_i}\{\log p(x)\}\right] \tag{3.17}$$

Here, E_{-q_i} denotes the expectation over every q_j except for $j = i$. To compute $q_i(x_i)$, we only care about the terms that involve x_i (i.e., we can isolate them as shown in equation 3.18).

$$
\begin{aligned}
E_{-q_i}\{\log p(x)\} &= E_{-q_i}\{x_i \sum_{j \in N(i)} w_{ij}x_j + \log N(x_i, \sigma^2) + \text{const}\} = \\
&= x_i \sum_{j \in N(i)} J \times \mu_j + \log N(x_i, \sigma^2) + \text{const}
\end{aligned}
\tag{3.18}
$$

Here, $N(i)$ denotes the neighbors of node i and μ_j is the mean of a binary random variable.

$$\mu_j = E_{q_j}[x_j] = q_j(x_j = +1) \times (+1) + q_j(x_j = -1) \times (-1) \tag{3.19}$$

Figure 3.4 shows the parametric form of our mean-field approximation for the Ising model.

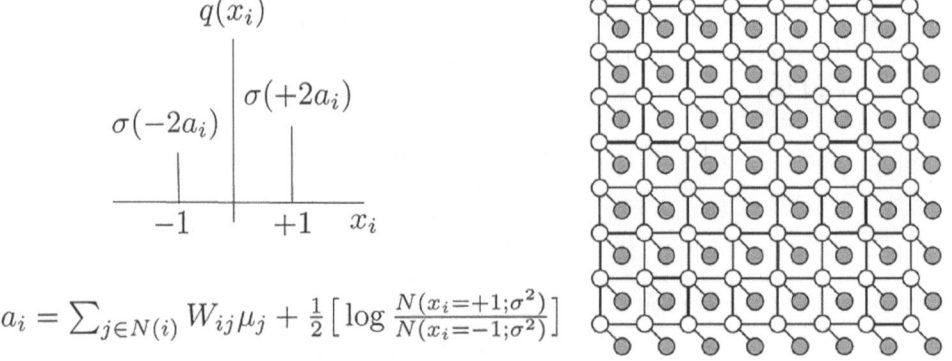

Figure 3.4   Ising model and its approximating distribution $q(x)$

To compute this mean, we need to know the values of $q_j(x_j = +1)$ and $q_j(x_j = -1)$. Let $m_i = \Sigma_{\{j \in N(i)\}} w_{ij} \mu_j$ be the mean value of neighbors and let $L_i^+ = N(x_i = +1, \sigma^2)$ and $L_i^- = N(x_i = -1, \sigma^2)$; then, we can compute the mean as follows.

$$q_i(x_i = +1) = \frac{\exp\left\{m_i + L_i^+\right\}}{\exp\left\{m_i + L_i^+\right\} + \exp\left\{-m_i + L_i^-\right\}}$$

$$= \frac{1}{1 + \exp\left\{-2m_i + L_i^- - L_i^+\right\}}$$

$$= \frac{1}{1 + \exp\left\{-2a_i\right\}} = \sigma(2a_i) \tag{3.20}$$

Here, $a_i = m_i + \frac{1}{2}(L_i^+ L_i^-)$ and $\sigma(x)$ is a sigmoid function. Since $q_i(x_i = -1) = 1 - q_i(x_i = +1) = 1 - \sigma(2a_i) = \sigma(-2a_i)$, we can write the mean of our variational approximation $q_i(x_i)$ as follows.

$$\mu_i = E_{q_i}[x_i] = \sigma(2a_i) - \sigma(-2a_i) = \tanh(a_i) \tag{3.21}$$

In other words, our mean-field updates of the variational parameters μ_i at iteration k are computed as follows.

$$\mu_i^{(k)} = \tanh\left(\sum_{j \in N(i)} w_{ij}\mu_j^{(k-1)} + \frac{1}{2}\left[\log \frac{N(x_i = +1, \sigma^2)}{N(x_i = -1, \sigma^2)}\right]\right)$$

$$\times \lambda + (1 - \lambda) \times \mu_i^{(k-1)} \tag{3.22}$$

Here, we added a learning rate parameter $\lambda \in (0, 1]$. We further note that we can simplify the computation of the ELBO term by term, as follows.

ELBO first term

$$\sum_{(s,t) \in E} E_{q(x)}[x_s w_{st} x_t]$$

By definition of expectation

$$= \frac{1}{2}\sum_{i=1}^{n}\sum_{j \in N(i)}\left(\sum_{x_i \in \{-1,+1\}}\sum_{x_j \in \{-1,+1\}} q_i(x_i)q_j(x_j)x_i J x_j\right)$$

$$= \frac{1}{2}\sum_{i=1}^{n}\sum_{j \in N(i)}\left(q_i(x_i = +1)JE[x_j] - q_i(x_i = -1)JE[x_j]\right)$$

After substitution of values for xi and xj

$$= \frac{1}{2}\sum_{i=1}^{n}\sum_{j \in N(i)} E[x_i] J E[x_j] \tag{3.23}$$

By definition of expectation

Equation 3.24 is similar.

ELBO second term

$$\underbrace{E_{q(x)}\left[\log N(x_i, \sigma^2)\right]}_{} = \sum_{i=1}^{n}\left[\overbrace{\sum_{x_i \in \{-1,+1\}} q_i(x_i)\log N(x_i, \sigma^2)}^{\text{By definition of expectation}}\right] =$$

$$\sum_{i=1}^{n}\left[\underbrace{\sigma(2a_i)\log N(x_i = +1, \sigma^2) + \sigma(-2a_i)\log N(x_i = -1, \sigma^2)}_{\text{After expanding the summation}}\right] \quad (3.24)$$

To better understand the algorithm, let's examine the pseudo-code in figure 3.5.

```
 1: class image_denoising
 2: function mean_field(σ, y, w, λ, max_iter):
 3: logp1 = log N(y; x_i = +1, σ²)
 4: logm1 = log N(y; x_i = −1, σ²)
 5: logodds = logp1 − logm1
 6: p1 = sigmoid(logodds) //init
 7: μ⁽⁰⁾ = 2 × p1 −1 //init
 8: for k = 1 to max_iter:
 9:     S̄_ij = ∑_{j∈N(i)} w_ij μ_j^(k−1)
10:     μ_i^(k) = tanh(S̄_ij + ½logodds) × λ + (1 − λ) × μ_i^(k−1)
11:     ELBO[k] = ELBO[k] + ½ (S̄_ij × μ_i^(k))
12:     a = μ^(k) + ½ logodds
13:     qxp1 = sigmoid(+2a)
14:     qxm1 = sigmoid(−2a)
15:     Hx = −qxm1 × log(qxm1) − qxp1 × log(qxp1)
16:     ELBO[k] = ELBO[k]+ ∑_{i=1}^{N} (qxp1[i]× logp1[i] + qxm1[i]× logm1[i])
          + ∑_{i=1}^{N} (Hx[i])
17: end for
18: return μ^(k)
```

Figure 3.5   Mean field VI for Ising model pseudo-code

In the `image_denoising` class, we have a single method called `mean_field`, which takes as input the noise level sigma, noisy binary image y, coupling strength w=J, learning rate lambda, and max number of iterations. We start by computing log-odds ratio (i.e., the probability of observing image pixel y under a Gaussian random variable with the means +1 and -1). We then compute the sigmoid function of the log-odds ratio and use the result to initialize the mean variable. Next, we iterate until we have the max number of iterations, and in each iteration, we compute the influence of the neighbors `sij`, which we include in the mean-field update equation. We then compute our objective function `ELBO` and mean entropy `Hx` to monitor the convergence of the algorithm.

We now have all the tools we need to implement the mean-field variational inference for the Ising model in application to image denoising! In the following listing, we will read in a noisy image and execute mean-field variational inference on a grid of pixels to denoise it.

Listing 3.1 Mean-field variational inference in an Ising model

```
import numpy as np
import pandas as pd

import seaborn as sns
import matplotlib.pyplot as plt

from PIL import Image
from tqdm import tqdm
from scipy.special import expit as sigmoid
from scipy.stats import multivariate_normal

np.random.seed(42)
sns.set_style('whitegrid')

class image_denoising:

    def __init__(self, img_binary, sigma=2, J=1):

        #mean-field parameters
        self.sigma  = sigma          Noise level
        self.y = img_binary + self.sigma*np.random
        .randn(M, N)                 y_i ~ N(x_i; sigma ^ 2);
        self.J = J       Coupling strength (wij)
        self.rate = 0.5              Smoothing rate update
        self.max_iter = 15
        self.ELBO = np.zeros(self.max_iter)
        self.Hx_mean = np.zeros(self.max_iter)

    def mean_field(self):

        #Mean-Field VI
        print("running mean-field variational inference...")
        logodds = multivariate_normal.logpdf(self.y.flatten(), mean=+1,
        cov=self.sigma**2) - \
                multivariate_normal.logpdf(self.y.flatten(), mean=-1,
                cov=self.sigma**2)
        logodds = np.reshape(logodds, (M, N))

        #init
        p1 = sigmoid(logodds)
        mu = 2*p1-1          Initial value of mu

        a = mu + 0.5 * logodds
        qxp1 = sigmoid(+2*a)  #q_i(x_i=+1)
        qxm1 = sigmoid(-2*a)  #q_i(x_i=-1)

        logp1 = np.reshape(multivariate_normal.logpdf(self.y.flatten(),
        mean=+1, cov=self.sigma**2), (M, N))
        logm1 = np.reshape(multivariate_normal.logpdf(self.y.flatten(),
```

```
⟿ mean=-1, cov=self.sigma**2), (M, N))

for i in tqdm(range(self.max_iter)):
    muNew = mu
    for ix in range(N):
        for iy in range(M):
            pos = iy + M*ix
            neighborhood = pos + np.array([-1,1,-M,M])
            boundary_idx = [iy!=0,iy!=M-1,ix!=0,ix!=N-1]
            neighborhood = neighborhood[np.where(boundary_idx)[0]]
            ⟿ xx, yy = np.unravel_index(pos, (M,N), order='F')
            nx, ny = np.unravel_index(neighborhood, (M,N), order='F')

            Sbar = self.J*np.sum(mu[nx,ny])
            muNew[xx,yy] = (1-self.rate)*muNew[xx,yy] +
            ⟿ self.rate*np.tanh(Sbar + 0.5*logodds[xx,yy])
            self.ELBO[i] = self.ELBO[i] + 0.5*(Sbar * muNew[xx,yy])
        #end for
    #end for
    mu = muNew

    a = mu + 0.5 * logodds
    qxp1 = sigmoid(+2*a) #q_i(x_i=+1)
    qxm1 = sigmoid(-2*a) #q_i(x_i=-1)
    Hx = -qxm1*np.log(qxm1+1e-10) - qxp1*np.log(qxp1+1e-10) #entropy

    self.ELBO[i] = self.ELBO[i] + np.sum(qxp1*logp1 + qxm1*logm1)
    ⟿ + np.sum(Hx)
    self.Hx_mean[i] = np.mean(Hx)
#end for
return mu

if __name__ == "__main__":

    #load data
    print("loading data...")
    data = Image.open('./figures/bayes.bmp')
    img = np.double(data)
    img_mean = np.mean(img)
    img_binary = +1*(img>img_mean) + -1*(img<img_mean)
    [M, N] = img_binary.shape

    mrf = image_denoising(img_binary, sigma=2, J=1)
    mu = mrf.mean_field()

    #generate plots
    plt.figure()
    plt.imshow(mrf.y)
    plt.title("observed noisy image")
    plt.show()

    plt.figure()
    plt.imshow(mu)
    plt.title("after %d mean-field iterations" %mrf.max_iter)
    plt.show()
```

```
plt.figure()
plt.plot(mrf.Hx_mean, color='b', lw=2.0, label='Avg Entropy')
plt.title('Variational Inference for Ising Model')
plt.xlabel('iterations'); plt.ylabel('average entropy')
plt.legend(loc='upper right')
plt.show()

plt.figure()
plt.plot(mrf.ELBO, color='b', lw=2.0, label='ELBO')
plt.title('Variational Inference for Ising Model')
plt.xlabel('iterations'); plt.ylabel('ELBO objective')
plt.legend(loc='upper left')
plt.show()
```

Figure 3.6 shows experimental results for binary image denoising via mean-field variational inference.

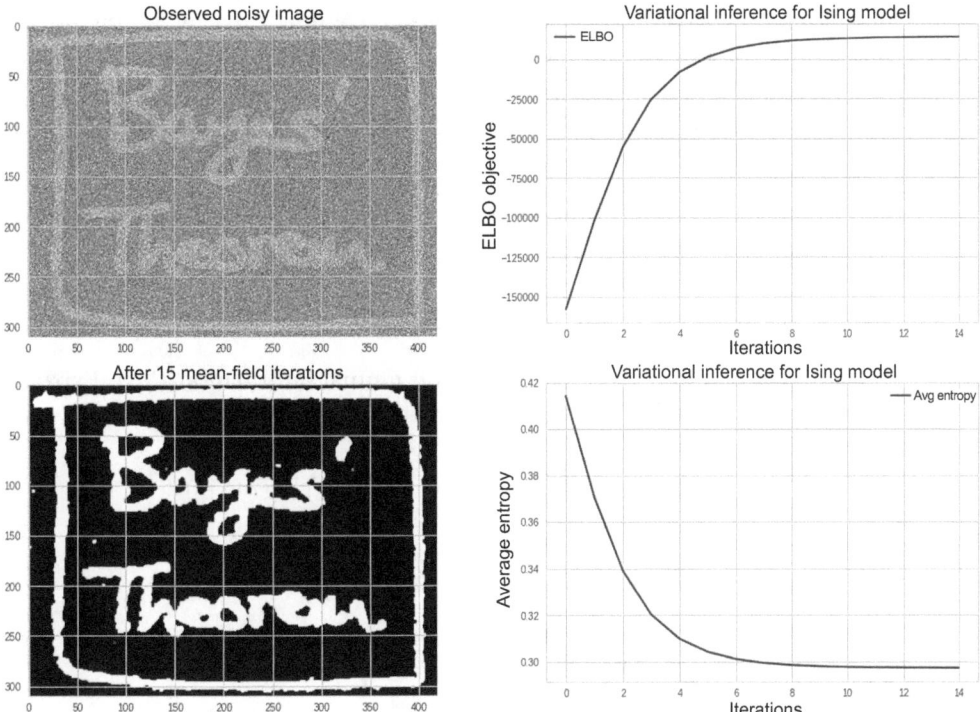

Figure 3.6   Mean-field variational inference for image denoising in an Ising model

The noisy observed image is shown in the top left and is obtained by adding Gaussian noise to each pixel and binarizing the image based on a mean threshold. We then set the variational inference parameters, such as the coupling strength $J=1$, noise level $\sigma=2$, smoothing rate $\lambda=0.5$, and max number of iterations of 15. The resulting denoised binary image is shown in the bottom-left corner of the figure. We can also see an increase in the ELBO objective (top right) and a decrease in the average entropy of our binary random variables $q_i(x_i)$ representing the value of each pixel (bottom right) as the number of mean-field iterations increases. The 2D Ising model can be extended in multiple ways (e.g., via 3D grids and κ-states per node [aka a Potts model]).

3.4 MI maximization

In this section, we look at mutual information (MI) maximization, which commonly occurs in information planning and data communications settings. Consider a wireless communications scenario, in which we transmit a signal $x \sim p_X(x)$, it passes through a multiple-input, multiple-output (MIMO) channel H. At the output, we receive our signal, $y = Hx + n$, where $n \sim N(0, \sigma^2 I)$ is an additive Gaussian noise. We would like to maximize the amount of information transmitted over the wireless channel. In other words, we would like to maximize the capacity or mutual information between the transmitted signal X and the received signal Y: $C = \max I(X;Y)$, where the maximization is taken over $p(x)$. To compute channel capacity, we discuss a general procedure based on KL divergence to approximately maximize mutual information.

$$I(X;Y) = H(X) - H(X|Y) = -E_{p(x)}\big[\log p(x)\big] - E_{p(x,y)}\big[\log p(x|y)\big] \quad (3.25)$$

Let $q(x)$ be an approximating distribution to $p(x)$, and then consider KL divergence between the posterior distributions of p and q, as shown in equation 3.26.

$$D_{KL}(p(x|y)||q(x|y)) \geq 0 \quad (3.26)$$

We would like to derive a lower bound on mutual information (MI). Expanding the expression in equation 3.26, we can proceed as shown in equation 3.27.

$$\sum_x p(x|y) \log p(x|y) - \sum_x p(x|y) \log q(x|y) \geq 0 \quad (3.27)$$

Multiplying both sides by $p(y)$, we get the following.

$$\sum_{x,y} p(y)p(x|y) \log p(x|y) \geq \sum_{x,y} p(x,y) \log q(x|y) \quad (3.28)$$

Recognizing the left-hand side as $-H(X|Y)$, we obtain the following MI lower bound.

$$I(X;Y) = H(X) - H(X|Y) \geq H(X) - E_{p(x,y)}\big[\log q(x|y)\big] = \tilde{I}(X;Y) \quad (3.29)$$

Using the preceding lower bound, we can describe MI maximization algorithm (see figure 3.7).

1: Choose approximating distribution family $Q(x; \theta)$
2: Initialize θ
3: **repeat**
4:    for a fixed $q(x|y; \theta)$, find
5:       $\theta^{new} = \text{argmax}_\theta \tilde{I}(X; Y)$
6:    for a fixed θ, find
7:       $q_{new}(x|y; \theta) = \text{argmax}_{q(x|y) \in Q} \tilde{I}(X; Y)$
8: **until** convergence

Figure 3.7   Mutual information maximization pseudo-code

The preceding algorithm alternates between finding a set of parameters that maximize the MI lower bound and finding the approximate distribution.

In this section, we saw how we can use the definitions of entropy, mutual information, and KL divergence to derive a lower bound that could then be iteratively maximized by updating our approximation distribution q. In the following chapter, we will look at ML from a computer science perspective and explore useful data structures and algorithmic paradigms.

3.5   *Exercises*

3.1 Compute KL divergence between two univariate Gaussians: $q(x) \sim N(\mu_1, \sigma_1^2)$ and $q(x) \sim N(\mu_2, \sigma_2^2)$.
3.2 Compute $E[X]$, $\text{Var}(X)$, and $H(X)$ for a Bernoulli distribution.
3.3 Derive the mean, mode, and variance of a Beta(a, b) distribution.

Summary

- The main idea of variational inference is to choose an approximate distribution $q(x)$ from a family of tractable distributions and then make this approximation as close as possible to the true posterior distribution $p(x)$.

- An evidence lower bound is an objective function that we seek to maximize to learn the variational parameters of our model.

- In mean-field approximation, we assume the approximate distribution $q(x)$ is fully factorized.

- Mutual information maximization can be carried out by deriving and maximizing the MI lower bound.

Software implementation 4

This chapter covers

- Data structures: linear, nonlinear, and probabilistic
- Problem-solving paradigms: complete search, greedy, divide and conquer, and dynamic programming
- ML research: sampling methods and variational inference

In the previous chapters, we looked at two main camps of Bayesian inference: Markov chain Monte Carlo and variational inference. In this chapter, we review computer science concepts required for implementing algorithms from scratch. To write high-quality code, it's important to have a good grasp of data structures and algorithm fundamentals. This chapter is designed to introduce common computational structures and problem-solving paradigms. Many of the concepts reviewed in this section are interactively visualized on the VisuAlgo website (https://visualgo.net/en).

4.1 Data structures

A *data structure* is a way of storing and organizing data. Data structures support several operations, such as insertion, search, deletion, and updates, and the right choice of data structure can simplify the runtime of an algorithm. Each data structure offers different performance tradeoffs. As a result, it's important to understand how data structures work.

4.1.1   Linear

A data structure is considered *linear* if its elements are arranged in a linear fashion. The simplest example of a linear data structure is a *fixed-size array* (where the size of the array may be specified as a constraint of the problem). The time it takes to access an element in an array is constant: $O(1)$. If the size of the array is not known ahead of time, it's best to use a *dynamically resizable array* (e.g., a List in Python or a Vector in C++), as these data structures are designed to handle resizing natively.

Two common operations applied to arrays are searching and sorting. The simplest search is a linear scan through all elements in $O(n)$ time. If the array is sorted, we can use binary search in $O(\log n)$ time, which is an example of a divide-and-conquer algorithm, which we will discuss soon. Naive array sorting algorithms, such as selection sort and insertion sort, have a complexity of $O(n^2)$ and are, therefore, only suitable for small inputs. In general, comparison-based sorts where elements are compared pairwise, such as merge, heap, or quicksort, have the runtime of $O(n \log n)$ because the time complexity can be thought of as traversing a complete binary tree, where each leaf represents one sorted ordering. In this representation, the height of the tree h is equal to the algorithm runtime. Since there are $n!$ possible orderings (leaf nodes), we can bound the runtime as follows.

$$
\begin{aligned}
h &= \log n! = \log n(n-1)(n-2) \times \cdots \times 1 \\
&= \log n + \log(n-1) + \cdots + \log 1 \\
&< \log n + \log n + \cdots + \log n = n \log n = O(n \log n)
\end{aligned}
\tag{4.1}
$$

If we add additional constraints on the input, we can construct linear-time $O(n)$ sorting algorithms, such as count sort, radix sort, and bucket sort. For example, count sort can be applied to integers in a small range, and radix sort works by applying count sort digit by digit, as discussed in *Competitive Programming* by Steven Halim (2010). Making algorithms distributed can further reduce runtime as described in *The Art of Multiprocessor Programming* by Mauice Herlihy and Nir Shavit (2012).

A *linked list* consists of nodes that store a value and a next pointer, starting from the head node. It's usually avoided due to its linear $O(n)$ search time. A *stack* allows $O(1)$ insertions (push) and $O(1)$ deletions (pop) in the last-in, first-out (LIFO) order. This is particularly useful in algorithms that are implemented recursively (e.g., bracket matching or topological sort). A *queue* allows $O(1)$ insertion (enqueue) from the back and $O(1)$ deletion (dequeue) from the front; thus, it follows the first-in, first-out (FIFO) model. It's a commonly used data structure in algorithms such as breadth-first search (BFS) and those based on BFS. In the next section, we will define and examine several examples of nonlinear data structures.

4.1.2   *Nonlinear*

A data structure is considered *nonlinear* if its elements do not follow a linear order. Examples of nonlinear data structures include a *map* (dictionary) and a *set*. This is because ordered dictionaries and ordered sets are built on self-balanced binary search trees (BST) that guarantee $O(n \log n)$ insertion, search, and deletion operations. BSTs have the property that the root node value is greater than its left child and less than its right child for every subtree. Self-balanced BSTs are typically implemented as Adelson-Velskii-Landis (AVL) or red–black (RB) trees (see *Introduction to Algorithms* by Thomas H. Cormen, Charles E. Leiserson, Ronald L. Rivest, and Clifford Stein [1990] for details). The difference between an ordered map (dictionary) and ordered set data structures is that the map stores (key–value) pairs, while the set only stores keys. A *heap* is another way to organize data in a tree representation. For example, an array $A = [2, 7, 26, 25, 19, 17, 1, 90, 3, 36]$ can be represented as a tree, as shown in figure 4.1.

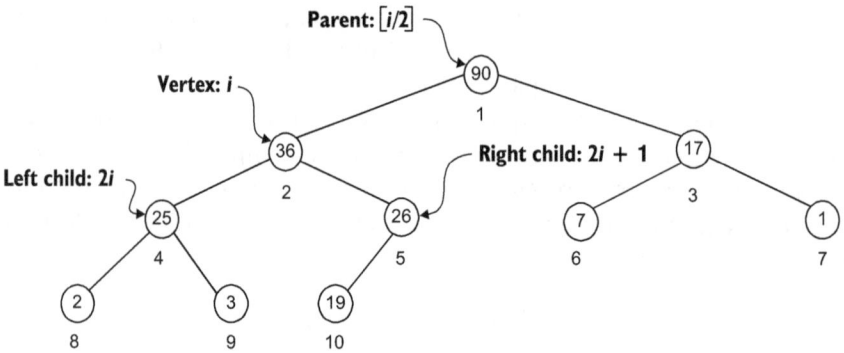

Figure 4.1   A binary heap

We can easily navigate the binary heap $A = [90, 36, 17, 25, 26, 7, 1, 2, 3, 19]$, starting with a vertex i and using the simple index arithmetic $2i$ to access the left child, $2i+1$ to access the right child, and $i/2$ to access the parent node. Instead of enforcing the binary search tree (BST) property, the (max) heap enforces the heap property: in each subtree rooted at x, items on the left and right subtrees of x are smaller than (or equal to) x. This property guarantees that the top of the (max) heap is always the maximum element. Thus, (max) heap allows for fast extraction of the maximum element. Indeed, extract max and insert operations are achieved in $O(\log n)$ tree traversal, performing swapping operations to maintain the heap property whenever necessary. A heap forms the basis for a *priority queue*, which is an important data structure in algorithms such as Prim and Kruskal minimum spanning trees (MST), Dijkstra's single-source shortest paths (SSSP), and the A* search. Finally, a *hash table* or unordered map is a very efficient data structure, with $O(1)$ access assuming no collisions. One commonly used class of hash tables is direct addressing (DA), where the keys themselves are the indices. The goal of a hash function is to uniformly distribute the elements in the table so as to minimize collisions. On the other hand, if you are looking to group similar items in the same bucket, locality-sensitive hashing (LSH) allows you to find nearest neighbors, as described in *Beyond Locality-Sensitive Hashing* by Alexandr Andoni Piotr Indyk, Huy Le Nguyen, and Ilya Razenshteyn (SODA, 2014).

4.1.3   *Probabilistic*

Probabilistic data structures are designed to handle big data. They provide probabilistic guarantees and result in drastic memory savings. Probabilistic data structures tackle the following common big data challenges:

- Membership querying: bloom filter, counting bloom filter, quotient filter, and cuckoo filter
- Cardinality: linear counting, probabilistic counting, LogLog, HyperLogLog, and HyperLogLog++
- Frequency: majority algorithm, frequent, count sketch, and count-min sketch
- Rank: random sampling, q-digest, and t-digest
- Similarity: LSH, MinHash, and SimHash

For a comprehensive discussion on probabilistic data structures, please refer to *Probabilistic Data Structures and Algorithms for Big Data Applications* by Andrii Gakhov (2022). In the next section, we will discuss four main algorithmic paradigms.

4.2   *Problem-solving paradigms*

There are four main algorithmic paradigms: complete search, greedy, divide and conquer, and dynamic programming. Depending on the problem at hand, the solution can often be found by recalling the algorithmic paradigms. In this section, we'll discuss each strategy and provide an example.

4.2.1   *Complete search*

Complete search (aka brute force) is a method for solving a problem by traversing the entire search space to find a solution. During the search, we can prune parts of the search space that we are sure do not lead to the required solution. For example, consider the problem of generating subsets. We can either use a recursive solution or an iterative one. In both cases, we terminate when we reach the required subset size. In the following listing, we will implement a complete search strategy based on an example of generating subsets.

Listing 4.1   Subset generation

```
def search(k, n):
    if (k == n):
        print(subset)        ⟵——— process subset
    else:
        search(k+1, n)
        subset.append(k)
```

```
        search(k+1, n)
        subset.pop()
    #end if

def bitseq(n):
    for b in range(1 << n):
        subset = []
        for i in range(n):
            if (b & 1 << i):
                subset.append(i)
        #end for
        print(subset)
    #end for

if __name__ == "__main__":
    n = 4
    subset = []
    search(0, n)      <────── recursive

    subset = []
    bitseq(n)     <────── iterative
```

A machine learning example where a complete search takes place is in exact inference by complete enumeration—for details, see chapter 21 of *Information Theory, Inference and Learning Algorithms* by David J. C. MacKay. Given a graphical model, we would like to factor a joint distribution according to conditional independence relations and use the Bayes rule to compute the posterior probability of certain events. In this case, we need to completely fill out the necessary probability tables to carry out our calculation.

4.2.2   Greedy

A greedy algorithm takes a locally optimum choice at each step, with the hope of eventually reaching a globally optimum solution. Greedy algorithms often rely on a greedy heuristic, and one can often find examples in which greedy algorithms fail to achieve the global optimum. For example, consider the problem of a fractional knapsack. The purpose of a greedy knapsack problem is to select items to place in a knapsack of limited capacity W so as to maximize the total value of knapsack items, where each item has an associated weight and value. We can define a greedy heuristic to be a ratio of item value to item weight (i.e., we would like to greedily choose items that are simultaneously of high value and low weight and sort the items based on this criteria). In the fractional knapsack problem, we are allowed to take fractions of an item (as opposed to 0–1 knapsack). In the following listing, we will implement a greedy strategy based on the fractional knapsack example.

Listing 4.2   Fractional knapsack

```
class Item:
    def __init__(self, wt, val, ind):
        self.wt = wt
```

```
            self.val = val
            self.ind = ind
            self.cost = val // wt

    def __lt__(self, other):
        return self.cost < other.cost

class FractionalKnapSack:
    def get_max_value(self, wt, val, capacity):

        item_list = []
        for i in range(len(wt)):
            item_list.append(Item(wt[i], val[i], i))

        # sorting items by cost heuristic
        item_list.sort(reverse = True)    #O(nlogn)

        total_value = 0
        for i in item_list:
            cur_wt = int(i.wt)
            cur_val = int(i.val)
            if capacity - cur_wt >= 0:
                capacity -= cur_wt
                total_value += cur_val
            else:
                fraction = capacity / cur_wt
                total_value += cur_val * fraction
                capacity = int(capacity - (cur_wt * fraction))
                break
        return total_value

if __name__ == "__main__":
    wt = [10, 20, 30]
    val = [60, 100, 120]
    capacity = 50

    fk = FractionalKnapSack()
    max_value = fk.get_max_value(wt, val, capacity)
    print("greedy fractional knapsack")
    print("maximum value: ", max_value)
```

Since sorting is the most expensive operation, the algorithm runs in $O(n \log n)$ time. We can see that the input items are sorted by decreasing ratio of value/cost; after greedily selecting items 1 and 2, we take a 2/3 fraction of item 3 for a total value of $60 + 100 + (2/3)120 = 240$.

A machine learning example of a greedy algorithm consists of sensor placement. Given a room and several temperature sensors, we would like to place the sensors in a way that maximizes room coverage. A simple greedy approach is to start with an empty set S0 and at iteration i add the sensor A that maximizes an increment function, such as mutual information $F_{MI}(A) = H(V \setminus A) - H(V \setminus A | A)$, where V is the set of all sensors. Here, we used the identity $I(X; Y) = H(X) - H(X|Y)$. It turns out that mutual information is *submodular* if observed variables are independent given the latent state, which leads to efficient greedy submodular optimization algorithms with performance guarantees (e.g., see the *Optimizing Sensing: Theory and Applications* PhD thesis by Andreas Kraus [2008]).

4.2.3   *Divide and conquer*

Divide and conquer is a technique that divides a problem into smaller, *independent* subproblems and then combines solutions to each of the subproblems. Examples of the divide and conquer technique include sorting algorithms, such as quick sort, merge sort, and heap sort, as well as binary search. A classic use of binary search is searching for a value in a sorted array. In this use case, we first check the middle of the array to see if it contains what we are looking for. If it does or there are no more items to consider, we stop. Otherwise, we decide whether the answer is to the left or right of the middle element and continue searching. As the size of the search space is halved after each check, the complexity of the algorithm is $O(\log n)$. In the following listing, we will implement a divide and conquer strategy based on a binary search example.

Listing 4.3   Binary search

```
def binary_search(arr, l, r, x):
    #assumes a sorted array
    if l <= r:
        mid = int(l + (r-l) / 2)

        if arr[mid] == x:
            return mid
        elif arr[mid] > x:
            return binary_search(arr, l, mid-1, x)
        else:
            return binary_search(arr, mid+1, r, x)
        #end if
    else:
        return -1

if __name__ == "__main__":

    x = 5
    arr = sorted([1, 7, 8, 3, 2, 5])

    print(arr)
    print("binary search:")
    result = binary_search(arr, 0, len(arr)-1, x)

    if result != -1:
        print("element {} is found at index {}.".format(x, result))
    else:
        print("element is not found.")
```

A machine learning example that uses the divide and conquer paradigm can be found in the CART decision tree algorithm, in which the threshold partitioning is done in a divide-and-conquer manner, and the nodes are split recursively until the maximum depth of the tree is reached. In CART algorithm, as we will see in the next chapter, an optimum threshold is found greedily by optimizing a classification objective (e.g., Gini index), and the same procedure is applied on a tree of one depth greater, resulting in a recursive algorithm.

4.2.4 *Dynamic programming*

Dynamic programming (DP) is a technique that divides a problem into smaller, *overlapping* subproblems, computes a solution for each subproblem, and stores it in a DP table. The final solution is read off the DP table. Key skills in mastering dynamic programming include the ability to determine the problem states (entries of the DP table) and the relationships or transitions between the states. Then, having defined base cases and recursive relationships, one can populate the DP table in a top-down or bottom-up fashion. In top-down DP, the table is populated recursively, as needed, starting from the top and going down to smaller subproblems. In bottom-up DP, the table is populated iteratively, starting from the smallest subproblems and using their solutions to build on and arrive at solutions to larger subproblems. In both cases, if we already encountered a subproblem, we can simply look up the solution in the table (as opposed to recomputing it from scratch). This dramatically reduces the computational cost.

We use binomial coefficients example to illustrate the use of top-down and bottom-up DP. The following code is based on the recursion for binomial coefficients with overlapping subproblems. Let $C(n, k)$ denote n choose k, and then, we have the following equation.

$$\text{Base case} \quad : \quad C(n, 0) = C(n, n) = 1$$
$$\text{Recursion} \quad : \quad C(n, k) = C(n - 1, k - 1) + C(n - 1, k) \tag{4.2}$$

Notice that we have multiple overlapping subproblems. For example, for $C(n=5, k=2)$, the recursion tree is as shown in figure 4.2. We can implement top-down and bottom-up DP as shown in listing 4.4.

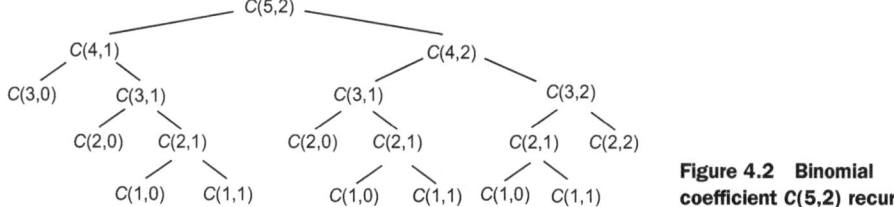

Figure 4.2 Binomial coefficient $C(5,2)$ recursion

Listing 4.4 Binomial coefficients

```
def binomial_coeffs1(n, k):
    #top down DP
    if (k == 0 or k == n):
```

```
        return 1
    if (memo[n][k] != -1):
        return memo[n][k]
    memo[n][k] = binomial_coeffs1(n-1, k-1) + binomial_coeffs1(n-1, k)
    return memo[n][k]

def binomial_coeffs2(n, k):
    #bottom up DP
    for i in range(n+1):
        for j in range(min(i,k)+1):
            if (j == 0 or j == i):
                memo[i][j] = 1
            else:
                memo[i][j] = memo[i-1][j-1] + memo[i-1][j]
            #end if
        #end for
    #end for
    return memo[n][k]
def print_array(memo):
    for i in range(len(memo)):
        print('\t'.join([str(x) for x in memo[i]]))

if __name__ == "__main__":
    n = 5
    k = 2
    print("top down DP")
    memo = [[-1 for i in range(6)] for j in range(6)]
    nCk = binomial_coeffs1(n, k)
    print_array(memo)
    print("C(n={}, k={}) = {}".format(n,k,nCk))

    print("bottom up DP")
    memo = [[-1 for i in range(6)] for j in range(6)]
    nCk = binomial_coeffs2(n, k)
    print_array(memo)
    print("C(n={}, k={}) = {}".format(n,k,nCk))
```

The time complexity is $O(nk)$, and the space complexity is $O(nk)$. In the case of top-down DP, solutions to subproblems are stored (memoized) as needed, whereas in bottom-up DP, the entire table is computed, starting from the base case.

A ML example that uses dynamic programming can be found in reinforcement learning (RL) when finding the solution to Bellman equations. We can write down the value of a state based on its reward at time t and the sum of future discounted rewards as shown in the following equation.

$$
\begin{aligned}
v_\pi(s) &= \Sigma_a \pi(a|s)\Sigma_{r,s'} p(r, s'|s, a)[r + \gamma v_\pi(s')] \\
&= E_\pi[R_t + \gamma v_\pi(S_{t+1})|S_t = s]
\end{aligned}
\tag{4.3}
$$

Equation 4.3 is known as the Bellman optimality equation for $v(s)$. We can recover the optimum policy by solving for an action that maximizes the state reward described by the Q-function.

$$\pi(s) = \arg\max_a q(s, a) \qquad (4.4)$$

For a small number of states and actions, we can compute the Q-function in a tabular way, using dynamic programming. In RL, we often want to balance exploration and exploitation—in which case, we take the preceding argmax with a probability of $1 - \epsilon$ and take a random action with probability ϵ.

4.3 ML research: Sampling methods and variational inference

In this section, we focus on ML research, which is a very important skill to have to be current in the field. We focus on the latest developments in the area of sampling methods and variational inference. As we observed in this chapter, many modern ML algorithms include clever algorithms to approximate hard-to-compute posterior densities as a result of intractable, high-dimensional integrals involved in the computation of the posterior.

It is worth spending time to briefly compare the differences between MCMC and variational inference. The advantages of variational inference include that for small to medium problems, it is usually faster, it is deterministic, it is easy to determine when to stop, and it often provides a lower bound on log likelihood. The advantages of sampling include that it is often simpler to implement, it is applicable to a broader range of problems (e.g., problems without nice conjugate priors), and sampling can be faster when applied to very large models or datasets. See chapter 24 of *Machine Learning: A Probabilistic Perspective* by Kevin P. Murphy for additional discussion on the topic.

In addition to the classic MCMC sampling algorithms we studied in previous chapters, a few others deserving attention are slice sampling (see Radford M. Neal's, "Slice Sampling," *Annals of Statistics*, 2003), the Hamiltonian Monte Carlo (HMC; see Radford M. Neal's, "MCMC Using Hamiltonian Dynamics," arXiv, 2012), and the no-U-turn sampler (NUTS; see Matthew D. Hoffman and Andrew Gelman's, "The No-U-Turn Sampler: Adaptively Setting Path Lengths in Hamiltonian Monte Carlo," *Journal of Machine Learning Research*, 2014). The state-of-the-art NUTS algorithm is commonly used as an MCMC inference method for probabilistic graphical models and is implemented in the PyMC3, Stan, TensorFlow Probability, and Pyro probabilistic programming libraries.

There have been several attempts to scale MCMC for big data, leading to Stochastic Monte Carlo methods that can be generally grouped into stochastic gradient based methods, methods using approximate Metropolis-Hastings with randomly sampled mini-batches, and data augmentation. Another popular class of MCMC algorithms is streaming Monte Carlo that approximates the posterior for online Bayesian inference. Sequential Monte Carlo (SMC) relies on resampling and propagating samples over time with a large number of particles.

Parallelizing Monte Carlo algorithms is another major area of research. If blocks of independent samples can be drawn from the posterior or a proposal distribution, the sampling algorithm can be parallelized by running multiple independent samplers on separate machines and then aggregating the results. Additional methods include divide-and-conquer and pre-fetching (see Jun Zhu, Jianfei Chen, and Wenbo Hu, Bo Zhang's, "Big Learning with Bayesian Methods," *National Science Review*, 2017).

Advances in variational inference (VI); span-scalable VI, which includes stochastic approximations; generic VI, which extends the applicability of VI to nonconjugate models; accurate VI, which includes variational models beyond mean-field approximation; and amortized VI, which implements the inference over local latent variables with inference networks (see Cheng Zhang, Judith Butepage, Hedvig Kjellstrom, and Stephan Mandt's, "Advances in Variational Inference," *IEEE Transactions on Pattern Analysis and Machine Intelligence*, 2019). Scalable VI includes stochastic variational inference (SVI), which applies stochastic optimization techniques of the variational objective. The efficiency of stochastic gradient descent (SGD) depends on the variance of gradient estimates (smaller gradient noise allows for larger learning rates and leads to faster convergence). Techniques such as adaptive learning rates and mini-batch size as well as variance reduction, such as control variates, nonuniform sampling, and other approaches, are used to speed up convergence.

In addition to stochastic optimization, leveraging model structure can help achieve the same objective. Examples include collapsed, sparse, parallel, and distributed inference. The collapsed VI relies on the idea of analytically integrating out certain model parameters. Sparse inference exploits either sparsely distributed parameters or datasets that can be summarized by a small number of representative points. In addition, structured VI examines variational distributions that are not fully factorized, leading to more accurate approximations.

Finally, amortized variational inference is an interesting research area that combines probabilistic graphical models and neural networks. The term *amortized* refers to utilizing inference from past computations to support future computations. Amortized inference became a popular tool for inference in deep latent variable models (DLVM), such as the variational autoencoder (VAE; see Diederik P. Kingma and Max Welling's, "Auto-Encoding Variational Bayes," arXiv, 2013). Similarly, neural networks can be used to learn the parameters of conditional distributions in directed probabilistic graphical models (PGM; see Diederik P. Kingma's, "Variational Inference and Deep Learning: A New Synthesis", PhD Thesis, 2017).

4.4   Exercises

4.1 Prove the following binomial identity: $C(n, k) = C(n-1, k-1) + C(n-1, k)$.

4.2 Derive the Gibbs inequality: $H(p, q) \geq H(q)$, where $H(p, q) = -\sum_x p(x) \log q(x)$ is the cross-entropy and $H(q) = -\sum q(x) \log q(x)$ is the entropy.

4.3 Use Jensen's inequality with $f(x) = \log(x)$ to prove the AM $\geq$ GM inequality.

4.4 Prove that $I(x; y) = H(x) - H(x|y) = H(y) - H(y|x)$.

Summary

- A data structure is a way of storing and organizing data. Data structures can be categorized into linear, nonlinear, and probabilistic.
- We looked at four algorithmic paradigms in this chapter: complete search, greedy, divide and conquer, and dynamic programming.
- Complete search (aka brute force) is a method for solving a problem by traversing the entire search space to find a solution. During the search, we can prune parts of the search space that we are sure do not lead to the required solution.
- A greedy algorithm takes a locally optimum choice at each step, with the hope of eventually reaching a globally optimum solution.
- Divide and conquer is a technique that divides a problem into smaller, independent subproblems and then combines solutions for each of the subproblems.
- Dynamic programming (DP) is a technique that divides a problem into smaller overlapping subproblems, computes a solution for each subproblem, and stores it in a DP table. The final solution is read off the DP table.
- Mastery of algorithms and software implementation can be achieved through the practice of competitive programming (see appendix A for resources).
- Machine learning mastery requires a solid understanding of fundamentals. See the recommended texts section in appendix A for ideas on how to increase the depth and breadth of your knowledge.
- The field of machine learning is rapidly evolving, and the best way to remain current is to read the latest research conference papers.

Part 2

Supervised learning

In the second part of the book, we will cover supervised learning algorithms. Supervised learning algorithms contain labeled examples as part of the training dataset and consist of two main classes, depending on the discrete or continuous nature of the quantity we are trying to predict: classification and regression. Supervised learning algorithms are widely used in machine learning, and we'll be deriving some of the most exciting algorithms from scratch, to build our experience with fundamentals and motivate the design of new ML algorithms.

In chapter 5, we'll focus on classification algorithms and derive several classic algorithms, including the perceptron, SVM, logistic regression, naive Bayes, and decision trees.

In chapter 6, we'll study four intriguing regression algorithms: Bayesian linear regression, hierarchical Bayesian regression, KNN regression, and Gaussian process regression. We'll derive all algorithms from the first principles and implement them using best practices.

In chapter 7, we'll investigate a selected set of supervised learning algorithms, including Markov models, such as page rank algorithms and hidden Markov models; imbalanced learning strategies; active learning; Bayesian optimization for hyperparameter selection; and ensemble methods. We'll conclude with ML research, focusing on supervised learning.

Classification algorithms

5

This chapter covers

- Introducing classification
- The perceptron algorithm
- The SVM algorithm
- SGD logistic regression
- The Bernoulli naive Bayes algorithm
- The decision tree (CART) algorithm

In the previous chapter, we looked at the computer science fundamentals required to implement ML algorithms from scratch. In this chapter, we focus on supervised learning algorithms. Classification is a fundamental class of algorithms and is widely used in machine learning. We will derive from scratch and implement several selected classification algorithms to build our experience with fundamentals and motivate the design of new ML algorithms. The algorithms in this chapter were selected because they illustrate important algorithmic concepts and expose the reader to progressively more complex scenarios that can be implemented from scratch. These concepts have wide application, including email spam detection, document classification, and customer segmentation.

5.1   Introduction to classification

In *supervised learning*, we are given a dataset $D=\{(x_1,y_1),\ldots,(x_n,y_n)\}$, consisting of tuples of data x and labels y. The goal of a *classification algorithm* is to learn a mapping from inputs x to outputs y, where y is a discrete quantity (i.e., $y\in\{1,\ldots,K\}$). If $K=2$, we have a binary classification problem, while for $K>2$, we have multiclass classification.

A classifier h can be viewed as a mapping between a d-dimensional feature vector $\varphi(x)$ and a k-dimensional label y (i.e., $h\colon \mathbf{R}^d\to\mathbf{R}^k$). We often have several models to choose from; let's call this set of classifier models H. Thus, for a given $h\in H$, we can obtain a prediction $y=h(\varphi(x))$. We are typically interested in predicting new or unseen data—in other words, our classifier h must be able to *generalize* to new data samples.

Finding the right classifier is known as *model selection*. We want to choose a model that has a sufficient number of parameters (degrees of freedom) to avoid underfitting or overfitting to training data, as shown in figure 5.1.

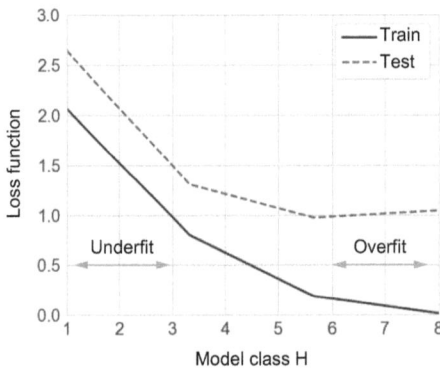

Figure 5.1   Model selection to avoid overfitting or underfitting to training data

For model classes $H=[1,2,3]$, training and test loss functions are both decreasing, which indicates that there's more capacity to learn; as a result, these models underfit the data. For model classes $H=[6,7,8]$, the training loss decreases while the test loss is starting to increase, which indicates that we are overfitting the data.

5.2   Perceptron

Let's start with the most basic classification model: a *linear classifier*. We'll be using the perceptron classifier on the iris dataset. We can define a linear classifier as shown in equation 5.1.

$$
\begin{aligned}
h(x;\theta) &= \operatorname{sign}(\theta_1 x_1 + \cdots + \theta_d x_d + \theta_0) \\
&= \operatorname{sign}(\theta \cdot x + \theta_0) = \begin{cases} +1 & \text{if } \theta \cdot x + \theta_0 \geq 0 \\ -1 & \text{if } \theta \cdot x + \theta_0 < 0 \end{cases}
\end{aligned}
\tag{5.1}
$$

Notice how the sign function of the inner product between the parameter θ and the feature input x maps to ± 1 labels. Geometrically, $\theta_x + \theta_0 = 0$ describes a hyperplane in d-dimensional space uniquely determined by the normal vector θ. Any point that lies on the same side as the normal θ is labeled $+1$, while any point on the opposite side is labeled -1. As a result, $\theta_x + \theta_0 = 0$ represents the *decision boundary*. Figure 5.2 illustrates these concepts in 2 dimensions.

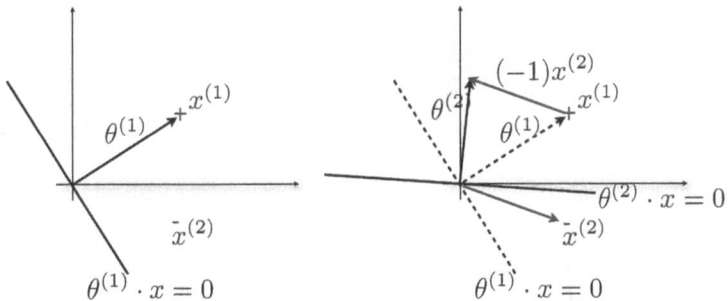

Figure 5.2   Linear classifier a decision boundary

How do we measure the performance of this classifier? One way is to count the number of mistakes it makes compared to ground truth labels y. We can count the number of mistakes as follows.

$$\mathcal{E}_n(\theta) = \frac{1}{n}\sum_{i=1}^{n}[[y_i \neq h(x_i; \theta)]] = \frac{1}{n}\sum_{i=1}^{n}[[y_i(\theta \cdot x_i + \theta_0) \leq 0]] \qquad (5.2)$$

Here, $[[\bullet]]$ is an indicator function, which is equal to 1 when the expression inside is true and 0 otherwise. Notice in equation 5.2, a mistake occurs whenever the label $y_i \in [+1, -1]$ disagrees with the prediction of the classifier $h(x_i; \theta) \in [+1, -1]$ (i.e., their product is negative).

Another way to measure the performance of a binary classifier is via a confusion matrix.

Figure 5.3 shows the table of errors called the *confusion matrix*. The prediction is correct when the predicted value matches the actual value, as in the case of true positive (TP) and true negative (TN). Similarly, the prediction is wrong when there is a mismatch between predicted and actual values, as in the case of false positive (FP) and false negative

		Actual	
		$y = 1$	$y = 0$
Predicted	$\hat{y} = 1$	TP	FP
	$\hat{y} = 0$	FN	TN

Figure 5.3   Confusion matrix for a binary classifier

(FN). As we vary the classification threshold, we get different values for TP, FP, FN, and TN. To better visualize the performance of the classifier under different classification thresholds, we can construct two additional figures: receiver operating characteristic (ROC) and precision-recall curve (see figure 5.4).

In the ROC plot on the left of figure 5.4, *TPR* stands for *true positive rate* and can be computed as follows: TPR = TP/(TP + FN). We can also compute the *false positive rate*

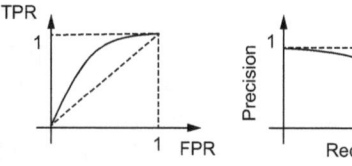

Figure 5.4   Receiver operating characteristic (ROC) plot (left) and precision-recall plot (right)

(FPR) as FPR = FP/(FP + TN). By varying our classification threshold, we get different points along the ROC curve. Perfect classification results in TPR = 1 and FPR = 0; in reality, the closer we are to the upper-left corner, the better the classifier will be. At the chance level, we get the diagonal TPR = FPR line. The quality of ROC curve is often summarized by a single number using the area under the curve or AUC. Higher AUC scores are better, with a maximum of AUC = 1.

In information retrieval, it is common to use a precision-recall plot, as shown on the right-hand side of figure 5.4. The precision is defined as Precision = TP/(TP + FP), and the recall is defined as Recall = TP/(TP + FN). A precision-recall curve is a plot of precision versus recall as we vary the classification threshold. The curve can be summarized by a single number using the mean precision by averaging over the recall values, which approximates the area under the curve. Additionally, for a fixed threshold, we can summarize performance in a single statistic, called the *F1 score*, which is the harmonic mean of precision and recall: F1 = 2PR/(P + R).

Perceptron is a mistake-driven algorithm: it starts with $\theta = 0$ and successively adjusts the parameter θ for each training example until there are no more classification mistakes, assuming the data is linearly separable. The perceptron update rule can be summarized as follows.

$$
\begin{aligned}
\text{if} \quad y_i \quad &\neq \quad h(x_i; \theta^{(k)}) \quad \text{then} \\
\theta^{(k+1)} \quad &= \quad \theta^{(k)} + y_i x_i \\
\theta_0^{(k+1)} \quad &= \quad \theta_0^{(k)} + y_i
\end{aligned}
\tag{5.3}
$$

Here, index k denotes the number of times the parameter updates (aka the number of mistakes). You can think of a θ_0 update as similar to a θ update but with $x = 1$. If the training examples are linearly separable, then the perceptron algorithm in equation 5.3 converges after a finite number of iterations. Notice that the order of input data points makes a difference in how parameter θ is learned; therefore, we can randomize (shuffle) the training dataset. In addition, we can introduce a learning rate to help with θ convergence—the properties of which we'll discuss following the implementation. The perceptron algorithm can be summarized in the pseudo-code in figure 5.5.

The code consists of `Perceptron` class with two functions: `fit` and `predict`. In the `fit` function, we take the training data X and labels y, and upon encountering an error (in which case, the `if` statement condition is `true`), we update the learning rate and update theta, as derived previously. Finally, in the `predict` function, we make a prediction for test data based on the sign of the decision boundary.

```
1: class perceptron
2: function fit(X, y):
3: k = 1
4: for epoch = 1, 2, . . . ,num_epochs
5:    for i = 1, 2, . . . , N
6:       if y_i(θ · x_i + θ_0) ≤ 0
7:          η = 1/(k+1)  ┐→ Updates the learning rate
8:          k+ = 1        ┘
9:          θ = θ + η y_i x_i  ┐→ Updates the theta
10:         θ_0 = θ_0 + η y_i    ┘
11:      end if
12:   end for
13: end for
14: return θ, θ_0
15: function predict(X):
16: ŷ = sign (θ · X + θ_0)
17: return ŷ
```

Figure 5.5 Perceptron algorithm pseudo-code

Lines 6–10 expressed in math:

$$k = 1$$

$$\text{if } y_i(\theta \cdot x_i + \theta_0) \le 0$$

$$\eta = \frac{1}{k+1}$$

$$k {+} = 1$$

$$\theta = \theta + \eta\, y_i x_i$$

$$\theta_0 = \theta_0 + \eta\, y_i$$

$$\hat{y} = \text{sign}\,(\theta \cdot X + \theta_0)$$

We now have all the tools to implement the perceptron algorithm from scratch! In the following code listing, we classify irises by training the perceptron algorithm on the training feature data and making a prediction based on the test data.

Listing 5.1 Perceptron algorithm

```python
import numpy as np
import seaborn as sns
import matplotlib.pyplot as plt

from scipy.stats import randint
from sklearn.datasets import load_iris
from sklearn.metrics import confusion_matrix
from sklearn.model_selection import train_test_split

class perceptron:
    def __init__(self, num_epochs, dim):
        self.num_epochs = num_epochs
        self.theta0 = 0
        self.theta = np.zeros(dim)

    def fit(self, X_train, y_train):
        n = X_train.shape[0]
        dim = X_train.shape[1]

        k = 1
        for epoch in range(self.num_epochs):
            for i in range(n):
                idx = randint.rvs(0, n-1, size=1)[0]      ◁──── Samples random point
                if (y_train[idx] * (np.dot(self.theta,
                    X_train[idx,:]) + self.theta0) <= 0):  ◁──── Hinge loss
                    eta = pow(k+1, -1)      ◁──┐
                    k += 1                      ┘ Updates learning rate
```

```
                    self.theta = self.theta + eta *
                  ⇒ y_train[idx] * X_train[idx, :]        Updates theta
                    self.theta0 = self.theta0 + eta *     and theta0
                  ⇒ y_train[idx]
                #end if

        print("epoch: ", epoch)
        print("theta: ", self.theta)
        print("theta0: ", self.theta0)
        #end for
    #end for

    def predict(self, X_test):
      n = X_test.shape[0]
      dim = X_test.shape[1]

      y_pred = np.zeros(n)
      for idx in range(n):
          y_pred[idx] = np.sign(np.dot(self.theta, X_test[idx,:]) +
          ⇒ self.theta0)
      #end for
      return y_pred

if __name__ == "__main__":

    iris = load_iris()       ◄——— Loads dataset
    X = iris.data[:100,:]
    y = 2*iris.target[:100] - 1    ◄——— Maps to {+1,-1} labels

    X_train, X_test, y_train, y_test = train_test_split(X, y, test_size=0.2,
    ⇒ random_state=42)

    #perceptron (binary) classifier
    clf = perceptron(num_epochs=5, dim=X.shape[1])
    clf.fit(X_train, y_train)
    y_pred = clf.predict(X_test)

    cmt = confusion_matrix(y_test, y_pred)
    acc = np.trace(cmt)/np.sum(np.sum(cmt))
    print("percepton accuracy: ", acc)

    #generate plots
    plt.figure()
    sns.heatmap(cmt, annot=True, fmt="d")
    plt.title("Confusion Matrix"); plt.xlabel("predicted");
     plt.ylabel("actual")
    plt.savefig("./figures/perceptron_acc.png")
    plt.show()
```

After running the algorithm, we get the classification accuracy results on the test dataset shown in figure 5.6.

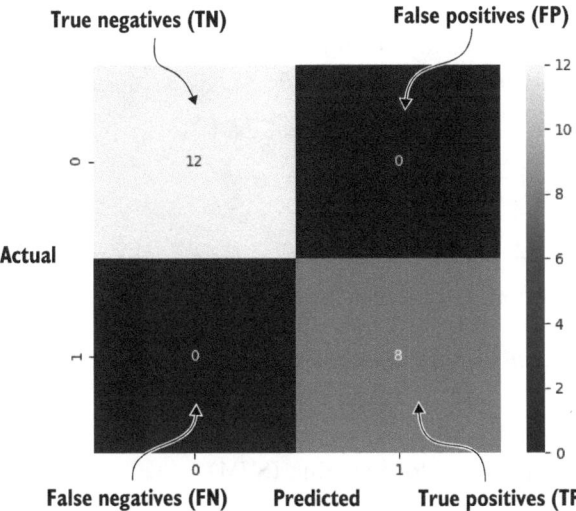

Figure 5.6   Perceptron binary classifier confusion matrix (iris dataset)

Let's take a second look at our implementation and understand it a little better. The perceptron algorithm can be formulated as stochastic gradient descent that minimizes a hinge loss function. Consider a loss function that penalizes the magnitude of disagreement $z_i = y_i(\theta \bullet x_i + \theta_0)$ between the label y_i and the prediction $h(x_i; \theta)$.

$$\text{Loss}_h(z) = \frac{1}{n} \sum_{i=1}^{n} \max\{1 - z_i, 0\} = \frac{1}{n} \sum_{i=1}^{n} \max\{1 - y_i(\theta \cdot x_i + \theta_0), 0\} \quad (5.4)$$

This is known as a hinge loss function, as illustrated in figure 5.7.

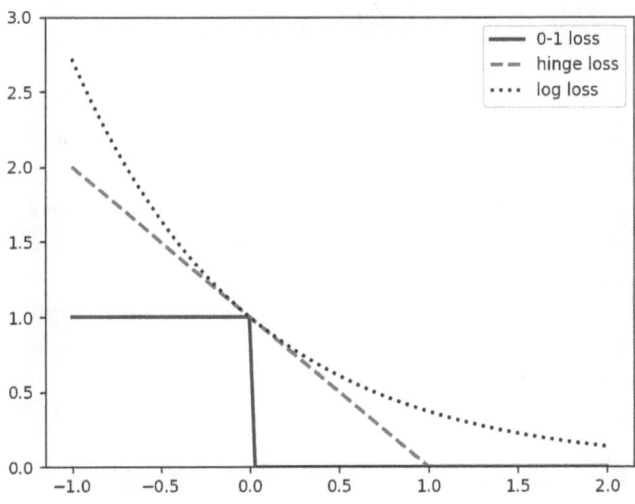

Figure 5.7   Hinge loss, 0–1 loss, and log-loss functions

The stochastic gradient descent attempts to minimize the hinge loss by taking a gradient with respect to θ. However, the max operator is not differentiable at $z_i = 1$. In fact, we have several possible gradients at that point, which are collectively known as *subdifferential*. Since hinge loss is a piecewise linear function, the gradient for $z_i > 1$ is equal to 0, while the gradient for $z_i \leq 1$ is equal to equation 5.5.

$$
\begin{aligned}
\nabla_\theta (1 - y_i(\theta \cdot x_i + \theta_0)) &= -y_i x_i \\
\nabla_{\theta_0} (1 - y_i(\theta \cdot x_i + \theta_0)) &= -y_i
\end{aligned}
\tag{5.5}
$$

Combining the expressions in equation 5.5 with a stochastic gradient descent update (where eta is the learning rate), we have equation 5.6.

$$
\theta^{(k+1)} = \theta^{(k)} - \eta_k \nabla_\theta \mathrm{Loss}_h (y_i(\theta \cdot x_i + \theta_0))
\tag{5.6}
$$

We get the perceptron algorithm! In the next section, we'll talk about another important classification algorithm: support vector machine (SVM).

5.3   *Support vector machine*

In the previous section, we evaluated the performance of our classifier by minimizing the expected loss function (aka empirical risk). One problem with the current formulation is there are multiple classifiers (multiple parameter values θ and θ_0) that can achieve the same empirical risk. So how do we choose the best model, and what does *best* mean?

One solution is to regularize the loss function to favor small parameter values, as shown in equation 5.7.

$$
L_n(\theta, \theta_0) = \frac{\lambda}{2} \|\theta\|^2 + \frac{1}{n} \sum_{i=1}^{n} \mathrm{Loss}(y_i(\theta \cdot x_i + \theta_0))
\tag{5.7}
$$

Here, the regularization applies to θ but not θ_0. The reason is because θ specifies the orientation of the decision boundary, whereas θ_0 is related to its offset from the origin, which is unknown at the start.

Let's try to understand the decision boundary better from a geometric point of view. It's desirable for the decision boundary, first, to classify all data points correctly and, second, to be maximally removed from all the training examples (i.e., to have the maximum margin). Suppose condition 1 is met and to optimize for condition 2, we need to compute and maximize the distance from every training example to the decision boundary. Geometrically, this distance is as follows.

$$
\gamma_i = \frac{y_i(\theta \cdot x_i + \theta_0)}{\|\theta\|}
\tag{5.8}
$$

Since we want to maximize the margin, we would like to maximize the minimum distance to the decision boundary across all data points (i.e., find `max[min_i yi]`). This can be formulated more simply as a quadratic program with linear constraints. A *quadratic program* is a type of mathematical optimization problem that involves optimizing a quadratic objective function subject to linear constraints on the variables.

$$\text{(primal)} \quad \min \frac{1}{2}\|\theta\|^2 \text{ subject to } y_i(\theta \cdot x_i + \theta_0) \geq 1, \quad i = 1, ..., n \qquad (5.9)$$

We are essentially minimizing the regularized loss function by choosing θ with a small l_2 norm subject to the constraints that every training example is correctly classified (see figure 5.8).

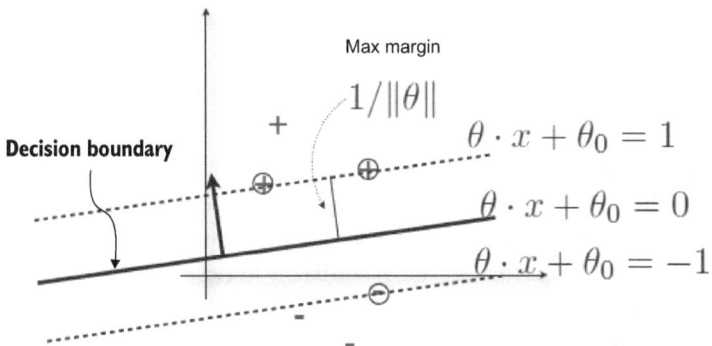

Figure 5.8 Max margin solution of SVM classifier

Notice that as we minimize $\|\theta\|^2$, we are effectively increasing the distance $\gamma_i \propto 1/\|\theta\|$ between the decision boundary and the training data points indexed by i. Geometrically, we are pushing the margin boundaries away from each other, as shown in figure 5.8. At some point, they cannot be pushed further without violating classification constraints. At this point, the margin boundaries lock into a unique maximum margin solution. The training data points that lie on the margin boundaries become *support vectors*. We only need a *subset* of training examples (support vectors) to fully learn SVM model parameters.

Let's see if we gain any advantages from solving the *dual* form of the quadratic program. Recall that if the primal is a minimization problem, then the dual is a maximization problem (and vice versa). Additionally, each variable of the original (primal) program becomes a constraint in the dual program, and each constraint in the primal program becomes a variable in the dual program.

We can obtain the dual form by writing out the Lagrangian (i.e., by adding constraints to the objective function with nonnegative Lagrange multipliers).

$$\max_{\alpha \geq 0} L(\theta, \theta_0; \alpha) = \frac{1}{2}\|\theta\|^2 - \sum_{i=1}^{n} \alpha_i [y_i(\theta \cdot x_i + \theta_0) - 1] \qquad (5.10)$$

We can now compute the gradient with respect to our parameters.

$$\nabla_\theta L(\theta, \theta_0; \alpha) \;=\; \theta - \sum_{i=1}^{n} \alpha_i y_i x_i = 0$$

$$\frac{d}{d\theta_0} L(\theta, \theta_0; \alpha) \;=\; -\sum_{i=1}^{n} \alpha_i y_i = 0 \tag{5.11}$$

By substituting the expression for θ back into our Lagrangian, we get the following.

$$\text{(dual)} \quad \max_{\alpha} \sum_{i=1}^{n} \alpha_i - \frac{1}{2}\sum_{i=1}^{n}\sum_{j=1}^{n} \alpha_i \alpha_j y_i y_j \left[x_i^T x_j\right]$$

$$\text{subject to} \quad \alpha_i \geq 0, \; \sum_{i=1}^{n} \alpha_i y_i = 0 \tag{5.12}$$

The most notable change in the dual formulation is that d-dimensional data points x_i and x_j interact via the inner product. This has significant computational advantages over the primal formulation (in addition to simpler constraints in the dual).

The inner product measures the degree of similarity between two vectors and can be generalized via the kernels $K(x_i, x_j)$. *Kernels* measure a degree of similarity between objects, without explicitly representing them as feature vectors. This is particularly advantageous when we don't have access to or choose not to look into the internals of our objects. Typically, a kernel function that compares two objects $x_i, x_j \in$ X is symmetric $K(x_i, x_j) = K(x_j, x_i)$ and nonnegative $K(x_i, x_j) \geq 0$. There is a wide variety of kernels, ranging from graph kernels that compute the similarity between graphs to string kernels and document kernels. One popular kernel example we will use in our SVM implementation is a radial basis function (RBF) kernel, shown in the following equation.

$$K(x_i, x_j) = \exp\left(-\frac{||x_i - x_j||^2}{2\sigma^2}\right) \tag{5.13}$$

We are now ready to implement a binary SVM classifier from scratch, using the CVXOPT optimization package. CVXOPT is a free software package for convex optimization based on Python programming language and can be downloaded at cvxopt.org.

The standard form of a quadratic program (QP) following CVXOPT notation is shown in the following equation.

$$\min_{x} \frac{1}{2} x^T P x + q^T x \quad \text{subject to} \quad Gx \leq h, \; Ax = b \tag{5.14}$$

Note that this objective function is convex if and only if matrix P is positive semidefinite. The CVXOPT QP expects the problem in the form of equation 5.14 parameterized by

(P, q, G, h, A, b). Let us convert our dual QP into this form. Let P be a matrix such that the following is true.

$$P_{ij} = y_i y_j \left[x_i^T x_j \right] \tag{5.15}$$

Then, the optimization program becomes the following.

$$\max_{\alpha} \sum_{i=1}^{n} \alpha_i - \frac{1}{2} \alpha^T P \alpha \quad \text{subject to} \quad \alpha_i \geq 0, \quad \sum_{i=1}^{n} \alpha_i y_i = 0 \tag{5.16}$$

We can further modify the QP by multiplying the objective and the constraint by −1, which turns this into a minimization problem and reverses the inequality. In addition, we can convert the sum over alphas into a vector form by multiplying the alpha vector by an all-ones vector.

$$\min_{\alpha} \frac{1}{2} \alpha^T P \alpha - 1^T \alpha \quad \text{subject to} \quad -\alpha_i \leq 0, \quad y^T \alpha = 0 \tag{5.17}$$

We can now use CVXOPT to solve our SVM quadratic program. Let's start by looking at the pseudo-code in figure 5.9.

```
1: class SupportVectorMachine
2: function fit(X, y):
3: P_ij = y_i y_j K(x_i, x_j)
4: q = −1
5: G_ij = −1         Formulates the SVM
6: h = 0             Quadratic Program
7: A = y
8: b = 0
9: sol = cvxopt.solvers.qp(P,q,G,h,A,b) ←Solves with CVXOPT
10: alphas = sol[x]
11: S = alphas > 1e − 11 ←Finds support vectors
12: θ = Σ_{i=1}^n y_i α_i x_i ←Finds the normal vector
13: θ_0 = y_s − Σ_{m∈s} α_m y_m [x_m^T x_s] ←Finds the intercept
14: return θ, θ_0
15: function predict(X, θ, θ_0):
16: ŷ = sign (θ^T X + θ_0) ← Makes a prediction
17: return ŷ
```

Figure 5.9 Support vector machine pseudo-code

The SVM class consists of two functions: fit and predict. In the fit function, we start off by formulating the quadratic problem to be solved by CVXOPT and defining all input parameters: (P, q, G, h, A, b). After calling the solver, we find the support vectors as alphas greater than 0 (up to a rounding error). Next, we compute the normal vector and the intercept, as discussed previously. In the `predict` function, we use the computed normal and intercept support vectors to make a label prediction on test data.

Listing 5.2   SVM algorithm

```
import cvxopt
import numpy as np

from sklearn.svm import SVC              ◄──── For comparison only
from sklearn.datasets import load_iris
from sklearn.metrics import accuracy_score
from sklearn.model_selection import train_test_split

def rbf_kernel(gamma, **kwargs):
    def f(x1, x2):
      distance = np.linalg.norm(x1 - x2) ** 2
      return np.exp(-gamma * distance)
    return f

class SupportVectorMachine(object):
  def __init__(self, C=1, kernel=rbf_kernel, power=4, gamma=None):
    self.C = C
    self.kernel = kernel
    self.power = power
    self.gamma = gamma
    self.lagr_multipliers = None
    self.support_vectors = None
    self.support_vector_labels = None
    self.intercept = None

  def fit(self, X, y):

    n_samples, n_features = np.shape(X)

    if not self.gamma:
        self.gamma = 1 / n_features

    self.kernel = self.kernel(
        power=self.power,
        gamma=self.gamma)

    kernel_matrix = np.zeros((n_samples, n_samples))
    for i in range(n_samples):
        for j in range(n_samples):
            kernel_matrix[i, j] = self.kernel(X[i],
            ➥ X[j])

    P = cvxopt.matrix(np.outer(y, y) * kernel_matrix,
    ➥ tc='d')
    q = cvxopt.matrix(np.ones(n_samples) * -1)
    A = cvxopt.matrix(y, (1, n_samples), tc='d')
    b = cvxopt.matrix(0, tc='d')
```

Regularization constant → `self.C = C`

Kernel parameters

Initializes the kernel method with parameters

Calculates the kernel matrix

Defines the quadratic optimization problem

```
        if not self.C: #if its empty
            G = cvxopt.matrix(np.identity(n_samples) * -1)
            h = cvxopt.matrix(np.zeros(n_samples))
        else:
            G_max = np.identity(n_samples) * -1
            G_min = np.identity(n_samples)
            G = cvxopt.matrix(np.vstack((G_max, G_min)))
            h_max = cvxopt.matrix(np.zeros(n_samples))
            h_min = cvxopt.matrix(np.ones(n_samples) * self.C)
            h = cvxopt.matrix(np.vstack((h_max, h_min)))

        minimization = cvxopt.solvers
            .qp(P, q, G, h, A, b)

        lagr_mult = np.ravel(minimization['x'])

        # Get indexes of non-zero lagr. multipiers
        idx = lagr_mult > 1e-11
        # Get the corresponding lagr. multipliers
        self.lagr_multipliers = lagr_mult[idx]
        # Get the samples that will act as support
          vectors
        self.support_vectors = X[idx]
        # Get the corresponding labels
        self.support_vector_labels = y[idx]

        self.intercept = self.support_vector_labels[0]
        for i in range(len(self.lagr_multipliers)):
            self.intercept -= self.lagr_multipliers[i] *
        self.support_vector_labels[
            i] * self.kernel(self.support_vectors[i], self.support_vectors[0])


    def predict(self, X):
        y_pred = []
        for sample in X:
            prediction = 0
            # Determine the label of the sample by the support vectors
            for i in range(len(self.lagr_multipliers)):
                prediction += self.lagr_multipliers[i] *
                  self.support_vector_labels[
                    i] * self.kernel(self.support_vectors[i], sample)
            prediction += self.intercept
            y_pred.append(np.sign(prediction))
        return np.array(y_pred)

def main():

    #load dataset
    iris = load_iris()
    X = iris.data[:100,:]
    y = 2*iris.target[:100] - 1
```

Solves the quadratic optimization problem, using cvxopt

Lagrange multipliers

Extracts support vectors

Calculates the intercept with the first support vector

Iterates through list of samples and makes predictions

Maps to {+1,-1} labels

```
X_train, X_test, y_train, y_test = train_test_split(X, y, test_size=0.4)
clf = SupportVectorMachine(kernel=rbf_kernel, gamma = 1)
clf.fit(X_train, y_train)
y_pred = clf.predict(X_test)
accuracy = accuracy_score(y_test, y_pred)
print ("Accuracy (scratch):", accuracy)

clf_sklearn = SVC(gamma = 'auto')
clf_sklearn.fit(X_train, y_train)
y_pred2 = clf_sklearn.predict(X_test)
accuracy = accuracy_score(y_test, y_pred2)
print ("Accuracy :", accuracy)

if __name__ == "__main__":
    main()
```

We can see that SVM classification accuracy based on our implementation matches the accuracy of sklearn model!

5.4   *Logistic regression*

Logistic regression is a classification algorithm. Let's dive into some of the theory behind logistic regression before implementing it from scratch! In a probabilistic view of classification, we are interested in computing $p(C_k|x)$ the probability of class label C_k, given the input data x. Consider two classes C_1 and C_2; we can use Bayes rule to compute our posterior probability.

$$p(C_1|x) = \frac{p(x|C_1)p(C_1)}{p(x|C_1)p(C_1) + p(x|C_2)p(C_2)} \tag{5.18}$$

Here, $p(C_k)$ are prior class probabilities. We can divide the right-hand side by the numerator and obtain the following.

$$p(C_1|x) = \frac{1}{1 + \frac{p(x|C_2)p(C_2)}{p(x|C_1)p(C_1)}} = \frac{1}{1 + \exp(-a)} = \sigma(a) \tag{5.19}$$

Here, we defined the following.

$$a = \ln \frac{p(x|C_1)p(C_1)}{p(x|C_2)p(C_2)} \tag{5.20}$$

In the multiclass scenario $(K > 2)$, we have the following.

$$p(C_k|x) = \frac{p(x|C_k)p(C_k)}{\sum_i p(x|C_i)p(C_i)} = \frac{\exp(a_k)}{\sum_i \exp(a_i)} \tag{5.21}$$

In equation 5.21, $a_k = \ln p(x|C_k)p(C_k)$. This expression is also known as a *softmax* function. The softmax function takes a vector of K real values and transforms it into a vector of K real values that sum up to 1. Therefore, the output of the softmax function can be interpreted as a probability distribution. Now, it's a matter of choosing conditional densities that model the data well. In the case of binary logistic regression parameterized by θ and with class label $y = C_k$, we have the following equation.

$$p(C_k|x) = p(y|x, \theta) = \text{Ber}\left(y|\sigma\left(\theta^T x\right)\right) \tag{5.22}$$

We can compute the joint distribution as follows.

$$p(x_i, y_i|\theta) = p(y_i|x_i, \theta)p(x_i|\theta) = \text{Ber}\left(y|\sigma\left(\theta^T x\right)\right)p(x_i|\theta) \tag{5.23}$$

Since we are not modeling the distribution of data $p(x_i|\theta) = p(x_i)$, we can write the log likelihood as follows.

$$
\begin{aligned}
\log p(D|\theta) &= \log \prod_{i=1}^{n} p(x_i, y_i|\theta) = \sum_{i=1}^{n} \log p(x_i, y_i|\theta) \\
&= \sum_{i=1}^{n} \log \text{Ber}\left(y|\sigma\left(\theta^T x\right)\right) \\
&= \sum_{i=1}^{n} \log\left[\sigma\left(\theta^T x_i\right)^{y_i}\left(1 - \sigma\left(\theta^T x_i\right)\right)^{1-y_i}\right] \\
&= \sum_{i=1}^{n}\left[y_i \log \sigma\left(\theta^T x_i\right) + (1 - y_i)\log\left(1 - \sigma\left(\theta^T x_i\right)\right)\right] \tag{5.24}
\end{aligned}
$$

Note that we are interested in maximizing the log likelihood or, equivalently, minimizing the loss or the negative log likelihood (NLL).

$$\min_{\theta} \text{Loss}(\theta) = \min_{\theta} \text{NLL}(\theta) = \max_{\theta} \log p(D|\theta) \tag{5.25}$$

We are planning on minimizing the logistic regression loss via stochastic gradient descent (SGD), which can be written as follows.

$$\theta_{k+1} = \theta_k - \eta_k g_k \tag{5.26}$$

Here, g_k is the gradient and η_k is the step size. To guarantee the convergence of SGD, the conditions expressed in the following equation, known as *Robbins-Monro conditions*, on the learning rate must be satisfied.

$$\sum_{k=1}^{\infty} \eta_k \;=\; \infty$$

$$\sum_{k=1}^{\infty} \eta_k^2 \;<\; \infty \tag{5.27}$$

We can use the following learning rate schedule, which satisfies the conditions in equation 5.27.

$$\eta_k = (\tau_0 + k)^{-\kappa} \tag{5.28}$$

Here, $\tau_0 \geq 0$ slows down early iterations of the algorithm and $\kappa \in (0.5, 1]$ controls the rate at which old values are forgotten. To compute the steepest descent direction g_k, we need to differentiate our loss function NLL(θ).

$$
\begin{aligned}
\frac{d}{d\theta} \log p(D|\theta) &= \sum_{i=1}^{n} [y_i \frac{d}{d\theta} \log \sigma \left(\theta^T x_i\right) \\
&\quad + (1 - y_i) \frac{d}{d\theta} \log \left(1 - \sigma \left(\theta^T x_i\right)\right)] \\
&= \sum_{i=1}^{n} [y_i \frac{\sigma \left(\theta^T x_i\right) \left(1 - \sigma \left(\theta^T x_i\right)\right)}{\sigma \left(\theta^T x_i\right)} x_i \\
&\quad + (1 - y_i) \frac{\sigma \left(\theta^T x_i\right) \left(1 - \sigma \left(\theta^T x_i\right)\right)}{1 - \sigma \left(\theta^T x_i\right)} (-x_i)] \\
&= \sum_{i=1}^{n} \left[y_i x_i \left(1 - \sigma \left(\theta^T x_i\right)\right) - (1 - y_i) x_i \sigma \left(\theta^T x_i\right) \right] \\
&= \sum_{i=1}^{n} \left[y_i - \sigma \left(\theta^T x_i\right) \right] x_i \\
&= \sum_{i=1}^{n} [y_i - \mu_i] x_i = -X^T (\mu - y)
\end{aligned} \tag{5.29}
$$

In equation 5.29, we used the fact that $d/dx\, \sigma(x) = (1 - \sigma(x))\sigma(x)$ and the mean of the Bernoulli distribution $\mu_i = \sigma(\theta^T x_i)$. Note that there exist a number of autograd libraries to avoid deriving the gradients by hand. Furthermore, we can add regularization to control parameter size. Our regularized objective and the gradient become the following.

$$
\begin{aligned}
\min_{\theta} \text{Loss}(\theta) &= \min_{\theta} [\text{NLL}(\theta) + \lambda \theta^T \theta] \\
g_k &= X^T (\mu - y) + 2\lambda\theta
\end{aligned} \tag{5.30}
$$

We are now ready to implement SGD for logistic regression. Let's start with the following pseudo-code, as shown in figure 5.10.

1: **class** sgdlr
2: **function** lr_objective(θ, X, y, λ)
3: $\quad \mu_i = \text{sigmoid}(\theta^T X_i)$
4: $\quad \text{cost} = -\sum_{i=1}^{n} [y_i \log \mu_i + (1 - y_i) \log (1 - \mu_i)] + \lambda \theta^T \theta$
5: $\quad \text{grad} = X^T (\mu - y) + 2\lambda \theta$ ← **Computes the gradient**
6: **return** cost, grad
7: **function** fit(X, y):
8: $\quad \eta_i = (\tau + i)^{-\kappa}$ ← **Sets the learning rate**
9: **for** $i = 1, 2, \ldots$ num_iter
10: $\quad\quad$ cost, grad = lr_objective(θ, X, y, λ)
11: $\quad\quad \theta = \theta - \eta_i$ grad ← **Updates the theta**
12: **end for**
13: **return** θ
14: **function** predict(X, θ):
15: $\quad \hat{y} = \text{sigmoid}(\theta^T X)$ ← **Makes a prediction**
16: **return** $\hat{y}$

Figure 5.10 Logistic regression algorithm pseudo-code

The sgdlr class consists of three main functions: lr_objective, fit, and predict. In the lr_objective function, we compute the regularized objective function and the gradient of the objective as discussed in the text. In the fit function, we first set the learning rate, and for each iteration, we update the theta parameters in the direction opposite to the gradient. Finally, in the predict function, we make a binary prediction of the label based on test data. In the following code listing, we use a synthetic Gaussian mixture dataset to train the logistic regression model.

Listing 5.3 SGD Logistic regression

```
import numpy as np
import matplotlib.pyplot as plt

def generate_data():

 n = 1000
 mu1 = np.array([1,1])
 mu2 = np.array([-1,-1])
 pik = np.array([0.4,0.6])

 X = np.zeros((n,2))
 y = np.zeros((n,1))

 for i in range(1,n):
     u = np.random.rand()
     idx = np.where(u < np.cumsum(pik))[0]
```

```
            if (len(idx)==1):
                X[i,:] = np.random.randn(1,2) + mu1
                y[i] = 1
            else:
                X[i,:] = np.random.randn(1,2) + mu2
                y[i] = -1
    return X, y

class sgdlr:

    def __init__(self):

        self.num_iter = 100
        self.lmbda = 1e-9

        self.tau0 = 10
        self.kappa = 1
        self.eta = np.zeros(self.num_iter)

        self.batch_size = 200
        self.eps = np.finfo(float).eps


    def fit(self, X, y):

        theta = np.random.randn(X.shape[1],1)      ⟵───  Random init

        for i in range(self.num_iter):
            self.eta[i] = (self.tau0+i)**(-self.kappa)

        batch_data, batch_labels = self.make_batches(
          X,y,self.batch_size)                      ⟵─── Divides data into batches
        num_batches = batch_data.shape[0]
        num_updates = 0

        J_hist = np.zeros((self.num_iter * num_batches,1))
        t_hist = np.zeros((self.num_iter * num_batches,1))

        for itr in range(self.num_iter):
            for b in range(num_batches):
                Xb = batch_data[b]
                yb = batch_labels[b]

                J_cost, J_grad = self.lr_objective(theta, Xb, yb, self.lmbda)
                theta = theta - self.eta[itr]*(num_batches*J_grad)

                J_hist[num_updates] = J_cost
                t_hist[num_updates] = np.linalg.norm(theta,2)
                num_updates = num_updates + 1
            print("iteration %d, cost: %f" %(itr, J_cost))

        y_pred = 2*(self.sigmoid(X.dot(theta)) > 0.5) - 1
        y_err = np.size(np.where(y_pred - y)[0])/float(y.shape[0])
        print("classification error:", y_err)
```

Learning rate schedule

```
        self.generate_plots(X, J_hist, t_hist, theta)
        return theta

def make_batches(self, X, y, batch_size):
    n = X.shape[0]
    d = X.shape[1]
    num_batches = int(np.ceil(n/batch_size))

    groups = np.tile(range(num_batches),batch_size)
    batch_data=np.zeros((num_batches,batch_size,d))
    batch_labels=np.zeros((num_batches,batch_size,1))

    for i in range(num_batches):
        batch_data[i,:,:] = X[groups==i,:]
        batch_labels[i,:] = y[groups==i]

    return batch_data, batch_labels

def lr_objective(self, theta, X, y, lmbda):        ◁───── Computes the objective

    n = y.shape[0]
    y01 = (y+1)/2.0

    mu = self.sigmoid(X.dot(theta))

    mu = np.maximum(mu,self.eps)      │ Bounds away from
    mu = np.minimum(mu,1-self.eps)    │ zero and one

    cost = -(1/n)*np.sum(y01*np.log(mu)+
    ↪ (1-y01)*np.log(1-mu))+np.sum(lmbda*theta*theta)      ◁───── Computes cost

    grad = X.T.dot(mu-y01) + 2*lmbda*theta      ◁──┐ Computes the gradient
                                                   │ of the lr objective
    #compute the Hessian of the lr objective
    #H = X.T.dot(np.diag(np.diag( mu*(1-mu) ))).dot(X) +
    ↪ 2*lmbda*np.eye(np.size(theta))

    return cost, grad

def sigmoid(self, a):
    return 1/(1+np.exp(-a))

def generate_plots(self, X, J_hist, t_hist, theta):

    plt.figure()
    plt.plot(J_hist)
    plt.title("logistic regression")
    plt.xlabel('iterations')
    plt.ylabel('cost')
    #plt.savefig('./figures/lrsgd_loss.png')
    plt.show()

    plt.figure()
    plt.plot(t_hist)
```

```
        plt.title("LR theta l2 norm")
        plt.xlabel('iterations')
        plt.ylabel('theta l2 norm')
        #plt.savefig('./figures/lrsgd_theta_norm.png')
        plt.show()

        plt.figure()
        plt.plot(self.eta)
        plt.title("LR learning rate")
        plt.xlabel('iterations')
        plt.ylabel('learning rate')
        #plt.savefig('./figures/lrsgd_learning_rate.png')
        plt.show()

        plt.figure()
        x1 = np.linspace(np.min(X[:,0])-1,np.max(X[:,0])+1,10)
        plt.scatter(X[:,0], X[:,1])
        plt.plot(x1, -(theta[0]/theta[1])*x1)
        plt.title('LR decision boundary')
        plt.grid(True)
        plt.xlabel('X1')
        plt.ylabel('X2')
        #plt.savefig('./figures/lrsgd_clf.png')
        plt.show()

if __name__ == "__main__":

    X, y = generate_data()
    sgd = sgdlr()
    theta = sgd.fit(X,y)
```

Figure 5.11 shows the stochastic nature of the loss function that decreases with the number of iterations as well as the decision boundary learned by our binary logistic regression.

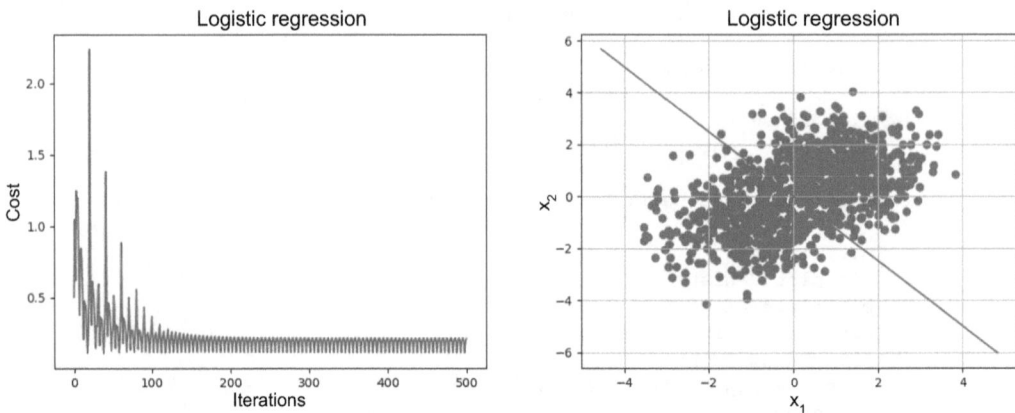

Figure 5.11   SGD logistic regression: Cost (left) and decision boundary (right)

A natural extension to the binary logistic regression is a multinomial logistic regression that handles more than 2 classes.

5.5 Naive Bayes

This section focuses on understanding, deriving, and implementing the naive Bayes algorithm. The fundamental (naive) assumption of the algorithm is that the features are conditionally independent, given the class label. This allows us to write the class conditional density as a product of one-dimensional densities.

$$p(x_i|y = c, \theta) = \prod_{j=1}^{D} p(x_{ij}|y = c, \theta_{jc}) \tag{5.31}$$

The model is called naive because we don't expect the features to be conditionally independent. However, even if the assumption is false, the model performs well in many scenarios. Here, we will focus on Bernoulli Naive Bayes for document classification, with the graphical model shown in figure 5.12. Note the shaded nodes represent the observed variables.

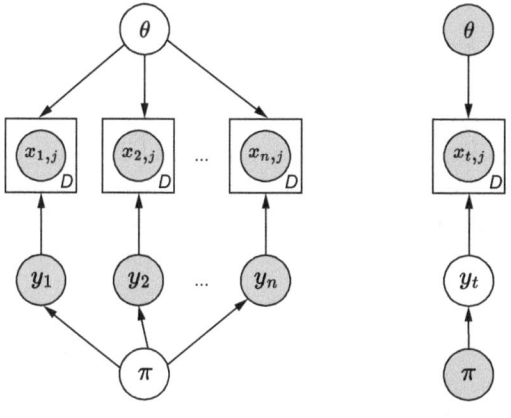

Naïve Bayes (train)   **Naïve Bayes (test)**   **Figure 5.12 Naive Bayes probabilistic graphical model**

The choice of class conditional density $p(x|y=c,\theta)$ determines the type of Naive Bayes classifier, such as Gaussian, Bernoulli, or multinomial. In this section, we focus on Bernoulli naive Bayes, due to its high performance in classifying documents.

Let x_{ij} be Bernoulli random variables indicating the presence ($x_{ij}=1$) or absence ($x_{ij}=0$) of a word $j \in \{1,...,D\}$ for document $i \in \{1,...,N\}$, parameterized by θ_{jc} for a given class label $y = c \in \{1, ..., C\}$. In addition, let π be a Dirichlet distribution representing the prior over the class labels. Thus, the total number of learnable parameters is $|\theta|+|\pi|=O(DC)+O(C)$ $= O(DC)$, where D is the dictionary size and C is the number of classes. Due to the small number of parameters, the Naive Bayes model is immune to overfitting.

We can write down the class conditional density as shown in equation 5.32.

$$p(x|y = c, \theta) = \prod_{i=1}^{n} \prod_{j=1}^{D} p(x_{ij}|y = c, \theta_{jc}) = \prod_{i=1}^{n} \prod_{j=1}^{D} \text{Bernoulli}(\theta_{jc}) \qquad (5.32)$$

We can derive the Naive Bayes inference algorithm by maximizing the log likelihood. Consider words x_i in a single document i.

$$p(x_i, y_i|\theta) = p(y_i|\pi) \prod_{j=1}^{D} p(x_{ij}|y_i, \theta)$$

$$= \prod_{c=1}^{C} \pi_c^{1[y_i=c]} \prod_{j=1}^{D} \prod_{c=1}^{C} p(x_{ij}|\theta_{jc})^{1[y_i=c]} \qquad (5.33)$$

Using the Naive Bayes assumption, we can compute the log likelihood objective.

$$\log p(D|\theta) = \log \prod_{i=1}^{n} p(x_i, y_i|\theta) = \sum_{i=1}^{n} \log p(x_i, y_i|\theta)$$

$$= \sum_{c=1}^{C} N_c \log \pi_c + \sum_{j=1}^{D} \sum_{c=1}^{C} \sum_{i:y_i=c} \log p(x_{ij}|\theta_{jc}) \qquad (5.34)$$

Note this is a constrained optimization program, since the probabilities of class labels must sum to one: $\sum \pi_c = 1$. We can solve the optimization problem in equation 5.34 using a Lagrangian by including the constraint in the objective function and setting the gradient of the Lagrangian $L(\theta, \lambda)$ with respect to (wrt) model parameters to zero.

$$L(\theta, \lambda) = \log p(D|\theta) + \lambda \left(1 - \sum_c \pi_c\right) \qquad (5.35)$$

Differentiating wrt π_c, we get the following.

$$\frac{d}{d\pi_c} L(\theta, \lambda) = \frac{d}{d\pi_c} \log p(D|\theta) - \lambda = N_c \frac{1}{\pi_c} - \lambda = 0 \qquad (5.36)$$

This gives us an expression for π_c in terms of λ: $\pi_c = (1/\lambda) N_c$. To solve for λ, we use our sum to one constraint.

$$\sum_c \pi_c = 1 \rightarrow \sum_c \frac{1}{\lambda} N_c = 1 \rightarrow \lambda = \sum_c N_c \qquad (5.37)$$

Substituting λ back into expression for π_c, we get $\pi_c = N_c / \sum N_c = N_c / N_{tot}$. Similarly, we can compute the optimum θ_{jc} parameters by setting the gradient of objective wrt θ_{jc} to zero.

$$\frac{d}{d\theta_{jc}} \log p(D|\theta) = \frac{d}{d\theta_{jc}} \sum_{i:y_i=c} [x_{ij} \log(\theta_{jc})$$

$$+ (1 - x_{ij}) \log(1 - \theta_{jc})] = 0$$

$$= \sum_{i:y_i=c} \left[\frac{x_{ij}}{\theta_{jc}} - \frac{1 - x_{ij}}{1 - \theta_{jc}} \right] = 0$$

$$\rightarrow \frac{N_{jc}}{\theta_{jc}} = \frac{1}{1 - \theta_{jc}} [N_c - N_{jc}] \rightarrow N_{jc} = N_c \theta_{jc} \qquad (5.38)$$

As a result, the optimum maximum likelihood estimate (MLE) value of $\theta_{jc} = N_{jc}/N_c$, where $N_c = \sum 1[y_i = c]$, which makes intuitive sense as a ratio of counts. Note that it's straightforward to add a Beta conjugate prior for the Bernoulli random variables and a Dirichlet conjugate prior for the class density to smooth the MLE counts.

$$p(\pi|D) = \text{Dir}(N_1 + \alpha_1, ..., N_c + \alpha_c)$$

$$p(\theta_{jc}|D) = \text{Beta}([N_c - N_{jc}] + \beta_0, N_{jc} + \beta_1) \qquad (5.39)$$

Here, we use *conjugate prior* for computational convenience, since the posterior and prior have the same form, which enables closed-form updates.

During test time, we would like to predict the class label y given the training data D and the learned model parameters. Applying the Bayes rule, we get the following.

$$p(y = c|x_{i,1}, ..., x_{i,D}, D) \propto p(y = c|D)p(x_{i,1}, ..., x_{i,D}|y = c, D)$$

$$= p(y = c|D) \prod_{j=1}^{D} p(x_{ij}|y = c, D) \qquad (5.40)$$

Substituting the distributions for $p(y = c|D)$ and $p(x_{ij}|y = c, D)$ and taking the log, we get the following.

$$\log p(y = c|x, D) \propto \log \hat{\pi}_c + \sum_{j=1}^{D} \left(1[x_{ij} = 1] \log \hat{\theta}_{jc} \right.$$

$$+ 1 [x_{ij} = 0] \log (1 - \hat{\theta}_{jc}) \Big) \qquad (5.41)$$

Here, π_c and θ_{jc} are the MLE estimates obtained during training. The Naive Bayes algorithm is summarized in the pseudo-code shown in figure 5.13.

The runtime complexity of MLE inference during training is $O(ND)$, where N is the number of training documents and D is the dictionary size. The runtime complexity during test time is $O(TCD)$, where T is the number of test documents, C is the number

1: Training:
2: $N_c = 0$, $N_{jc} = 0$
3: **for** $i = 1, 2, \ldots, n$ **do**
4:    $c = y_i$ //class label for ith example
5:    $N_c = N_c + 1$
6:    **for** $j = 1, \ldots, D$ **do**
7:       **if** $x_{ij} = 1$ **then**
8:          $N_{jc} = N_{jc} + 1$
9:    **end for**
10: **end for**
11: $\hat{\pi}_c = \frac{N_c}{N}$, $\hat{\theta}_{jc} = \frac{N_{jc}}{N}$
12: **return** $\hat{\pi}_c$, $\hat{\theta}_c$
13: Testing (for a single test document):
14: **for** $c = 1, 2, \ldots, C$ **do**
15:    $\log p[c] = \log \pi_c$
16:    **for** $j = 1, 2, \ldots, D$ **do**
17:       **if** $x_j = 1$ **then**
18:          $\log p[c]+ = \log \hat{\theta}_{jc}$
19:       **else**
20:          $\log p[c]+ = \log \left(1 - \hat{\theta}_{jc}\right)$
21:    **end for**
22: **end for**
23: $c = \arg \max_c \log p[c]$ **Figure 5.13   Naive Bayes**
24: **return** c   **algorithm pseudo-code**

of classes, and D is the dictionary size. Similarly, space complexity is the size of arrays required to store model parameters that grow as $O(DC)$. We are now ready to implement the Bernoulli Naive Bayes algorithm in the following listing!

Listing 5.4   Bernoulli naive Bayes algorithm

```python
import numpy as np
import seaborn as sns
import matplotlib.pyplot as plt

from time import time
from nltk.corpus import stopwords
from nltk.tokenize import RegexpTokenizer

from sklearn.metrics import accuracy_score
from sklearn.datasets import fetch_20newsgroups
from sklearn.model_selection import train_test_split
from sklearn.feature_extraction.text import CountVectorizer

sns.set_style("whitegrid")
tokenizer = RegexpTokenizer(r'\w+')
stop_words = set(stopwords.words('english'))
stop_words.update(['s','t','m','1','2'])
```

```
class naive_bayes:
    def __init__(self, K, D):
        self.K = K              ⟵── Number of classes
        self.D = D              ⟵┐
                                  │ Dictionary size
        self.pi = np.ones(K)
        self.theta = np.ones((self.D, self.K))   ⟵── Bernoulli parameters

    def fit(self, X_train, y_train):

        num_docs = X_train.shape[0]
        for doc in range(num_docs):

            label = y_train[doc]
            self.pi[label] += 1

            for word in range(self.D):
                if (X_train[doc][word] > 0):
                    self.theta[word][label] += 1
                #end if
            #end for
        #end for

        #normalize pi and theta
        self.pi = self.pi/np.sum(self.pi)
        self.theta = self.theta/np.sum(self.theta, axis=0)

    def predict(self, X_test):

        num_docs = X_test.shape[0]
        logp = np.zeros((num_docs,self.K))
        for doc in range(num_docs):
            for kk in range(self.K):
                logp[doc][kk] = np.log(self.pi[kk])
                for word in range(self.D):
                    if (X_test[doc][word] > 0):
                        logp[doc][kk] += np.log(self.theta[word][kk])
                    else:
                        logp[doc][kk] += np.log(1-self.theta[word][kk])
                    #end if
                #end for
            #end for
        #end for
        return np.argmax(logp, axis=1)

if __name__ == "__main__":

    import nltk
    nltk.download('stopwords')

    #load data
    print("loading 20 newsgroups dataset...")
    tic = time()
    classes = ['sci.space', 'comp.graphics', 'rec.autos', 'rec.sport.hockey']
```

The labels **Class priors** point to `self.pi = np.ones(K)`.

```
dataset = fetch_20newsgroups(shuffle=True, random_state=0,
    remove=('headers','footers','quotes'), categories=classes)
X_train, X_test, y_train, y_test = train_test_split(dataset.data,
    dataset.target, test_size=0.5, random_state=0)
toc = time()
print("elapsed time: %.4f sec" %(toc - tic))
print("number of training docs: ", len(X_train))
print("number of test docs: ", len(X_test))

print("vectorizing input data...")
cnt_vec = CountVectorizer(tokenizer=tokenizer.tokenize, analyzer='word',
    ngram_range=(1,1), max_df=0.8, min_df=2, max_features=1000,
    stop_words=stop_words)
cnt_vec.fit(X_train)
toc = time()
print("elapsed time: %.2f sec" %(toc - tic))
vocab = cnt_vec.vocabulary_
idx2word = {val: key for (key, val) in vocab.items()}
print("vocab size: ", len(vocab))

X_train_vec = cnt_vec.transform(X_train).toarray()
X_test_vec = cnt_vec.transform(X_test).toarray()

print("naive bayes model MLE inference...")
K = len(set(y_train)) #number of classes
D = len(vocab) #dictionary size
nb_clf = naive_bayes(K, D)
nb_clf.fit(X_train_vec, y_train)

print("naive bayes prediction...")
y_pred = nb_clf.predict(X_test_vec)
nb_clf_acc = accuracy_score(y_test, y_pred)
print("test set accuracy: ", nb_clf_acc)
```

As we can see from the output, we achieve 82% accuracy on the 20 newsgroups test dataset.

5.6   *Decision tree (CART)*

This section focuses on the classification and regression trees (CART) algorithm. Tree-based algorithms partition the input space into axis parallel regions such that each leaf represents a region. They can then be used to either classify the region by taking a majority vote or regress the region by computing the expected value. Tree-based models are interpretable and provide insight into feature importance. They are based on a greedy, recursive algorithm, since the optimum partitioning of space is NP complete.

In tree-based models during training, we are interested in constructing a binary tree in a way that optimizes an objective function and does not lead to underfitting or overfitting. A key determinant in growing a decision tree is the choice of the feature and the threshold to use when classifying the data points. Consider an input data matrix $X_{n \times d}$ with n data points of dimension (feature size) d. We would like to find the optimum feature and threshold for that feature that results in the split of data with minimum cost. Let $j \in \{1, ..., d\}$ represent feature dimension and $t \in \tau_j$ represent a threshold for feature j out of all possible thresholds τ_j (constructed by taking midpoints of our data x_{ij}). Then, we would like to compute the following.

$$j^*, t^* = \arg \min_{j \in \{1, ..., d\}} \min_{t \in \tau_j} \mathrm{cost}(\{x_i, y_i : x_{ij} \le t\})$$
$$+ \mathrm{cost}(\{x_i, y_i : x_{ij} > t\}) \tag{5.42}$$

Before we look at an example, let's look at potential costs we can use for optimizing the tree for classification. Our goal in defining a cost function is to evaluate how good our data partition is. We would like the leaf nodes to be pure (i.e., contain data from the same class and still be able to generalize to test data). In other words, we would like to limit the depth of the tree (to prevent overfitting) while minimizing impurity. One notion of impurity is the Gini index.

$$\sum_{k=1}^{K} \pi_k (1 - \pi_k) = \sum_k \pi_k - \sum_k \pi_k^2 = 1 - \sum_k \pi_k^2 \tag{5.43}$$

Here, π_k is a fraction of points in the region that belongs to cluster k.

$$\pi_k = \frac{1}{|D|} \sum_{i \in D} 1[y_i = k] \tag{5.44}$$

Notice that since π_k is the probability of a random point in the leaf belonging to class k and $1 - \pi_k$ is the error rate, the Gini index is the expected error rate. If the leaf cluster is pure ($\pi_k = 1$), then the Gini index is zero. Thus, we are interested in minimizing the Gini index.

An alternative objective is entropy, as shown in the following equation.

$$H(\pi) = - \sum_{k=1}^{K} \pi_k \log \pi_k \tag{5.45}$$

Entropy measures the amount of uncertainty. If we are certain that the leaf cluster is pure (i.e., $\pi_k = 1$), then the entropy is zero. Thus, we are interested in minimizing entropy when it comes to CART.

Let's look at a one-dimensional example of choosing the optimum splitting feature and its threshold. Let $X = [1.5, 1.7, 2.3, 2.7, 2.7]$ and class label $y = [1, 1, 2, 2, 3]$. Since the data is one-dimensional, our task is to find a threshold that will split X in a way that minimizes the Gini index. If we choose a threshold $t_1 = 2$ as a midpoint between 1.7 and 2.3 and compute the resulting Gini index, we get the following equation.

$$G = \frac{2}{5}G_{left} + \frac{3}{5}G_{right} = \frac{2}{5} \times 0 + \frac{3}{5} \times \left(1 - \frac{2^2}{3} - \frac{1^2}{3}\right) = 0.27 \qquad (5.46)$$

Here, G_{left} is the Gini index of $\{x_i, y_i: x_{ij} \leq 2\}$ and is equal to zero, since both class labels are equal to 1 (i.e., a pure leaf cluster) and G_{right} is the Gini index of $\{x_i, y_i: x_{ij} > 2\}$ and contains a mix of class labels $y_{right} = [2,2,3]$.

The key to CART algorithm is finding the optimal feature and threshold such that the cost (e.g., Gini index) is minimized. During training, we'll need to iterate through every feature one by one and compute the Gini cost for all possible thresholds for that feature. But how do we compute τ_j, a set of all possible thresholds for feature j? We can sort the training data $X[:, j]$ in $O(\log n)$ time and consider all midpoints between two adjacent data values. Next, we'll need to compute the Gini index for each threshold that can be done as shown in equation 5.47. Let m be the size of the node and m_k be the number of points in the node that belong to class k.

$$G = 1 - \sum_{k=1}^{K} \pi_k^2 = 1 - \sum_{k=1}^{k} \left(\frac{m_k}{m}\right)^2 \qquad (5.47)$$

We can iterate through the sorted thresholds τ_j in $O(n)$ time and compute the Gini index that would result in applying that threshold in each iteration. For i-th threshold, we get the following.

$$\begin{aligned} G_i &= \frac{i}{m}G_i^{left} + \frac{m-i}{m}G_i^{right} \\[2mm] G_i^{left} &= 1 - \sum_k \left(\frac{m_k^{left}}{i}\right)^2 \\[2mm] G_i^{right} &= 1 - \sum_k \left(\frac{m_k^{right}}{m-i}\right)^2 \end{aligned} \qquad (5.48)$$

Having found the optimum feature and threshold, we split each node recursively until the maximum depth is reached. Once we've constructed a tree during training, given test data, we simply traverse the tree from root to leaf, which stores our class label. We can summarize the CART algorithm in the pseudo-code in figure 5.14.

As we can see from the definition of `TreeNode`, it stores the predicted class label, id of the feature to split on and the best threshold to split on, pointers to the left and right subtrees, as well as the Gini cost and size of the node. We can grow the decision tree recursively by calling the `grow_tree` function, as long as the depth of the tree is less than the maximum depth determined ahead of time. First, we compute the class

```
1: class TreeNode(gini, num_samples, num_samples_class, class_label):
2:   self.gini = gini // gini cost
3:   self.num_samples = num_samples // size of node
4:   self.num_samples_class = num_samples_class //number of pts with label k
5:   self.class_label = class_label //predicted class label
6:   self.feature_idx = 0 //idx of feature to split on
7:   self.threshold = 0 //best threshold to split on
8:   self.left = None //left subtree pointer
9:   self.right = None //right subtree pointer
10: function grow_tree(X_train, y_train, depth)
11:   class_label = majority_vote(y_train)
12:   gini = compute_gini(y_train)
13:   node = new TreeNode(gini, class_label)
14:   //split recursively until max depth is reached
15:   if depth < max_depth
16:      idx, threshold = best_split(X_train, y_train)
17:      if idx is not None:
18:         indices_left = X_train[:,idx] < threshold
19:         node.feature_index = idx
20:         node.left = grow_tree(X_left, y_left, depth + 1)
21:         node.right = grow_tree(X_right, y_right, depth +1)
22: return node
```

Figure 5.14   CART decision tree algorithm pseudo-code

label via majority vote and the Gini index for training labels. Next, we determine the best split by iterating over all features and over all possible splitting thresholds. Once we determine the best feature idx and feature threshold to split on, we initialize left and right pointers of the current node with new TreeNode objects that contain data less than the splitting threshold and greater than the splitting threshold, respectively. We iterate in this fashion until reaching the maximum tree depth. We are now ready to implement the CART algorithm.

Listing 5.5   CART decision tree algorithm

```
import numpy as np
import matplotlib.pyplot as plt

from sklearn.datasets import load_iris
from sklearn.metrics import accuracy_score
from sklearn.model_selection import train_test_split

class TreeNode():
    def __init__(self, gini, num_samples, num_samples_class, class_label):
        self.gini = gini                               <— Gini cost
        self.num_samples = num_samples                 <— Size of the node
        self.num_samples_class = num_samples_class
        self.class_label = class_label                 <— Predicted class label
```

Number of node points with the label k

```
              self.feature_idx = 0        ◄────┐  idx of the feature to split on
Best      ┌─► self.treshold = 0                │
threshold │   self.left = None    ◄──── Left subtree pointer
to split on │  self.right = None   ◄────┐
          └                             │  Right subtree pointer

        class DecisionTreeClassifier():
         def __init__(self, max_depth = None):
              self.max_depth = max_depth

         def best_split(self, X_train, y_train):
              m = y_train.size
              if (m <= 1):
                   return None, None
Number of
points of
class k    ┌─►  mk = [np.sum(y_train == k) for k in range(self
           └─►     .num_classes)]
                                                              ┌── Gini of the
              best_gini = 1.0 - sum((n / m) ** 2 for n in mk)  ◄──┘  current node
              best_idx, best_thr = None, None

              #iterate over all features
              for idx in range(self.num_features):

                   thresholds, classes = zip(*sorted(zip(X[:,
Sorts data ┌─►       idx], y)))
along a    │
selected   │       num_left = [0]*self.num_classes
feature    └       num_right = mk.copy()

                   for i in range(1, m):    ◄────┐ Iterate over all
                                                 │ possible split positions
                        k = classes[i-1]

                        num_left[k] += 1
                        num_right[k] -= 1

                        gini_left = 1.0 - sum(
                             (num_left[x] / i) ** 2 for x in range(self.num_classes)
                        )

                        gini_right = 1.0 - sum(
                             (num_right[x] / (m - i)) ** 2 for x in
                             ► range(self.num_classes)
                        )

                        gini = (i * gini_left + (m - i) * gini_right) / m

                        if thresholds[i] == thresholds[i - 1]:
                             continue

                        if (gini < best_gini):
                             best_gini = gini
                             best_idx = idx
                             best_thr = (thresholds[i] +
                             ► thresholds[i - 1]) / 2  ◄──── Midpoint
```

```
                #end if
            #end for
        #end for
        return best_idx, best_thr

    def gini(self, y_train):
        m = y_train.size
        return 1.0 - sum((np.sum(y_train == k) / m) ** 2 for k in
        ➥ range(self.num_classes))

    def fit(self, X_train, y_train):
        self.num_classes = len(set(y_train))
        self.num_features = X_train.shape[1]
        self.tree = self.grow_tree(X_train, y_train)

    def grow_tree(self, X_train, y_train, depth=0):

        num_samples_class = [np.sum(y_train == k) for k in
        ➥ range(self.num_classes)]
        class_label = np.argmax(num_samples_class)

        node = TreeNode(
            gini=self.gini(y_train),
            num_samples=y_train.size,
            num_samples_class=num_samples_class,
            class_label=class_label,
        )
        if depth < self.max_depth:   ◄──┐  Split recursively until the
            idx, thr = self.best_split(X_train, y_train)   maximum depth is reached
            if idx is not None:
                indices_left = X_train[:, idx] < thr
                X_left, y_left = X_train[indices_left], y_train[indices_left]
                X_right, y_right = X_train[~indices_left],
        y_train[~indices_left]
                node.feature_index = idx
                node.threshold = thr
                node.left = self.grow_tree(X_left, y_left, depth + 1)
                node.right = self.grow_tree(X_right, y_right, depth + 1)

        return node

    def predict(self, X_test):
        return [self.predict_helper(x_test) for x_test in X_test]

    def predict_helper(self, x_test):
        node = self.tree
        while node.left:
            if x_test[node.feature_index] < node.threshold:
                node = node.left
            else:
                node = node.right
        return node.class_label
```

```
if __name__ == "__main__":

    #load data
    iris = load_iris()
    X = iris.data[:, [2,3]]
    y = iris.target

    X_train, X_test, y_train, y_test = train_test_split(X, y, test_size=0.2,
    ↪ random_state=42)

    print("decision tree classifier...")
    tree_clf = DecisionTreeClassifier(max_depth = 3)
    tree_clf.fit(X_train, y_train)

    print("prediction...")
    y_pred = tree_clf.predict(X_test)

    tree_clf_acc = accuracy_score(y_test, y_pred)
    print("test set accuracy: ", tree_clf_acc)
```

As we can see from the output, we achieve the test classification accuracy of 80% on the iris dataset.

5.7   Exercises

5.1 Given a data point $y \in R^d$ and a hyperplane $\theta \cdot x + \theta_0 = 0$, compute the Euclidean distance from the point to the hyperplane.

5.2 Given a primal linear program (LP) $\min c^T x$ subject to $Ax <= b$, $x >= 0$, write down the dual version of the LP.

5.3 Show that the radial basis function (RBF) kernel is equivalent to computing similarity between two infinite dimensional feature vectors.

5.4 Verify that the learning rate schedule $\eta_k = (\tau_0 + k)^{-\kappa}$ satisfies Robbins-Monro conditions.

5.5 Compute the derivative of the sigmoid function $\sigma(a) = [1 + \exp(-a)]^{-1}$.

5.6 Compute the runtime and memory complexity of the Bernoulli naive Bayes algorithm.

Summary

- The goal of a classification algorithm is to learn a mapping from inputs x to outputs y, where y is a discrete quantity.
- Perceptron is a classification algorithm that updates the decision boundary until there are no more classification mistakes.
- SVM is a max-margin classifier. The training data points that lie on the margin boundaries become support vectors.
- Logistic regression is a classification algorithm that computes class conditional density based on a softmax function.

- The naive Bayes algorithm assumes features are conditionally independent, given the class label. It is commonly used in document classification.
- The CART decision tree is a greedy, recursive algorithm that finds the optimum feature splits by minimizing an objective function, such as the Gini index.

Regression algorithms

6

In the previous chapter, we looked at supervised algorithms for classification. In this chapter, we will focus on supervised learning, in which we are trying to predict a continuous quantity. We will study four intriguing regression algorithms, which we will derive from the first principles: Bayesian linear regression, hierarchical Bayesian regression, KNN regression, and Gaussian process regression. These algorithms were selected because they span several important applications and illustrate diverse mathematical concepts. Regression algorithms are useful in a variety of applications. For example, they can be used to predict the price of financial assets or predict CO_2 levels in the atmosphere. Let's begin by reviewing the fundamentals of regression.

6.1   Introduction to regression

In supervised learning, we are given a dataset $D = \{(x_1, y_1), ..., (x_n, y_n)\}$ consisting of tuples of data x and labels y. The goal of a regression algorithm is to learn a mapping from inputs x to outputs y, where y is a continuous quantity (i.e., $y \in R$).

A regressor f can be viewed as a mapping between a d-dimensional feature vector $\varphi(x)$ and a label y (i.e., $f: R^d \to R$). Regression problems are typically harder (to achieve higher accuracy) compared to classification problems because we are trying to predict a *continuous* quantity. Moreover, we are often interested in predicting *future* response variable y based on past training data.

One of the most widely used models for regression is *linear regression*, which models the response variable y as a linear combination of input feature vectors $\varphi(x)$.

$$\underset{\text{Regression weights}}{y(x) = \underbrace{w^T} \underbrace{\phi(x)}_{\text{Features}} + \underbrace{\epsilon}_{\text{Gaussian noise}}} = \sum_{d=1}^{D} w_d \phi(x_d) + \epsilon \tag{6.1}$$

Here, ϵ is the residual error between our linear predictions and the true response. We can characterize the quality of our regressor based on the mean squared error (MSE).

$$\text{MSE}(w) = E\left[(y - \underbrace{f(x; w)}_{\text{Prediction}})^2\right] = \frac{1}{N} \sum_{i=1}^{N} \left(y_i - w^T \phi(x_i)\right)^2 \tag{6.2}$$

In this chapter, we will look at several important regression models, starting with Bayesian and KNN regression, and their extensions to hierarchical regression models, and concluding with Gaussian process (GP) regression. We'll focus on both the theory and implementation of each model from scratch.

6.2   Bayesian linear regression

Recall that we can write the linear regression as $y(x) = w^T x + \epsilon$. If we assume that $\epsilon \sim N(0, \sigma^2)$ is a zero-mean Gaussian RV with a variance σ^2, then we can formulate linear regression as follows.

$$p(y|x, \theta) = N\left(y|w^T x, \sigma^2\right) \tag{6.3}$$

Here, w are regression coefficients. To fit a linear regression model to data, we minimize the negative log likelihood.

$$
\begin{aligned}
\text{NLL}(w, \sigma^2) &= -\log p(y|x, \theta) \;\;\leftarrow\!\!\boxed{\substack{\text{Definition} \\ \text{of NLL}}} \\[2mm]
&= -\log \prod_{n=1}^{N} \left[\frac{1}{\sqrt{2\pi\sigma^2}} \exp\left[-\frac{1}{2\sigma^2}\left(y_n - w^T x\right)^2 \right] \right] \\[2mm]
&= -\sum_{n=1}^{N} \log\left(\frac{1}{\sqrt{2\pi\sigma^2}}\right) + \sum_{n=1}^{N} \frac{1}{2\sigma^2}\left(y_n - w^T x\right)^2 \\[2mm]
&= \frac{1}{2\sigma^2}\sum_{n=1}^{N}\left(y_n - w^T x\right)^2 + \frac{N}{2}\log\left(2\pi\sigma^2\right)
\end{aligned}
\tag{6.4}
$$

Keeping σ^2 fixed and differentiating with respect to w, we get the following equation.

$$
2X^T X w - 2X^T y + 2\lambda w = 0
\tag{6.5}
$$

From equation 6.5, we can write the following.

$$
\hat{w} = \left(X^T X + \lambda I\right)^{-1} X^T y
\tag{6.6}
$$

One problem with the estimation in equation 6.6 is that it can result in overfitting. To make the Bayesian linear regression robust against overfitting, we can encourage the parameters to be small by placing a zero-mean Gaussian prior.

$$
p(w) = \prod_{d} N\left(w_d | 0, \tau^2\right)
\tag{6.7}
$$

Thus, we can rewrite our regularized objective as follows.

$$
\min_w \text{NLL}\left(w, \sigma^2\right) + \lambda \|w\|_2^2
\tag{6.8}
$$

Solving for w as before, we get the following coefficients.

$$
\hat{w}_{ridge} = \left(X^T X + \lambda I\right)^{-1} X^T y
\tag{6.9}
$$

We can learn the parameters w using gradient descent! Let's look at the pseudo-code in figure 6.1.

1: **class** ridge_reg:
2: **function** fit(X, y)
3: **for** $i = 1, 2, \ldots,$ num_iter
4:     $\hat{y} = w^T X$
5:     $grad = -(y - \hat{y})^T X + \lambda w$
6:     $w = w - \eta_i \, grad$ ←**Update regression weights**
7: **end for**
8: **return** w
9: **function** predict(w, X)
10: $\hat{y} = w^T X$ ←**Make a prediction**
11: **return** $\hat{y}$

Figure 6.1   Bayesian linear regression pseudo-code

The `ridge_reg` class consists of the `fit` and `predict` functions. In the `fit` function, we compute the gradient of the objective function wrt `w` and update the weight parameters. In the `predict` function, we use the learned regression weights to make a prediction on test data.

Listing 6.1   Bayesian linear regression

```python
import math
import numpy as np
import pandas as pd

import matplotlib.pyplot as plt
from sklearn.datasets import fetch_california_housing

class ridge_reg():

    def __init__(self, n_iter=20, learning_rate=1e-3, lmbda=0.1):
        self.n_iter = n_iter
        self.learning_rate = learning_rate
        self.lmbda = lmbda

    def fit(self, X, y):
        X = np.insert(X, 0, 1, axis=1)          ← Inserts const 1 for
                                                    the bias term

        self.loss = []
        self.w = np.random.rand(X.shape[1])

        for i in range(self.n_iter):
            y_pred = X.dot(self.w)
            mse = np.mean(0.5*(y - y_pred)**2 +
                0.5*self.lmbda*self.w.T.dot(self.w))
            self.loss.append(mse)
            print(" %d iter, mse: %.4f" %(i, mse))
            grad_w = - (y - y_pred).dot(X) + self
                .lmbda*self.w
            self.w -= self.learning_rate * grad_w    ← Updates the
                                                        weights

    def predict(self, X):
```

Computes the gradient of NLL(w) wrt w →

```
        X = np.insert(X, 0, 1, axis=1)          Inserts const 1 for
        y_pred = X.dot(self.w)                   the bias term
        return y_pred

    if __name__ == "__main__":

        X, y = fetch_california_housing(return_X_y=True)
        X_reg = X[:,2].reshape(-1,1)
        X_std = (X_reg - X_reg.mean())/X.std()    Standard scaling
        y_std = (y - y.mean())/y.std()

        X_std = X_std[:200,:]
        y_std = y_std[:200]

        rr = ridge_reg()
        rr.fit(X_std, y_std)
        y_pred = rr.predict(X_std)

        print(rr.w)

        plt.figure()
        plt.plot(rr.loss)
        plt.xlabel('Epoch')
        plt.ylabel('Loss')
        plt.tight_layout()
        plt.show()

        plt.figure()
        plt.scatter(X_std, y_std)
        plt.plot(np.linspace(-1,1), rr.w[1]*np.linspace(-1,1)+rr.w[0], c='red')
        plt.xlim([-0.01,0.01])
        plt.xlabel("scaled avg num of rooms")
        plt.ylabel("scaled house price")
        plt.show()
```

Average number of rooms → (annotation pointing to `X_reg = X[:,2].reshape(-1,1)`)

Figure 6.2 shows the output of Bayesian linear regression algorithm.

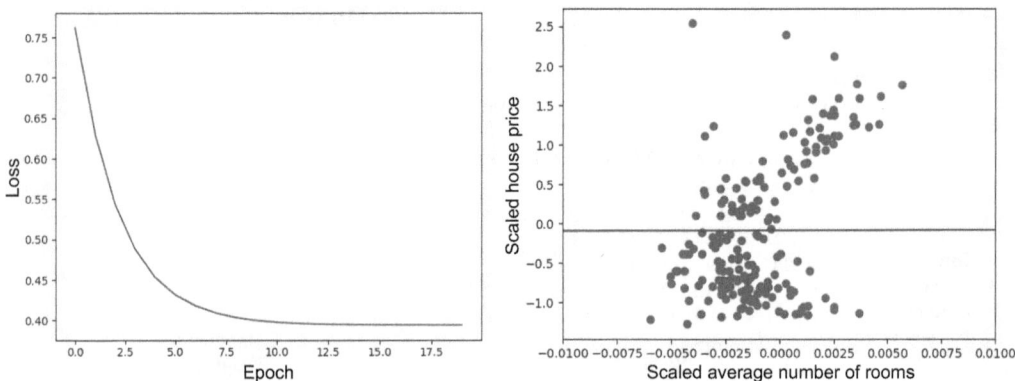

Figure 6.2   **Bayesian linear regression loss function (left) and plot (right)**

We can see the decrease in loss function over epochs on the left and a fit with the California house pricing dataset projection on the right. Note that both axes are standardized. The Bayesian linear regression successfully captures the trend of increasing house prices with the average number of rooms. In the next section, we will examine the benefits of a hierarchical model of linear regression.

6.3   *Hierarchical Bayesian regression*

Hierarchical models enable the sharing of features among groups. The parameters of the model are assumed to be sampled from a common distribution that models similarity between groups. Figure 6.3 shows three scenarios that illustrate the benefit of hierarchical modeling. In the figure on the left, we have a single set of parameters θ that model the entire sequence of observations, referred to as a *pooled model*. Here, any variation in data is not modeled explicitly, since we are assuming a common set of parameters that give rise to the data. On the other hand, we have an *unpooled model* scenario, in which we model a different set of parameters for each observation. In the unpooled case, we assume there is no sharing of parameters between groups of observations and each parameter is independent. The hierarchical model combines the best of both worlds: it assumes there is a common distribution from which individual parameters are sampled and, therefore, captures similarities between groups.

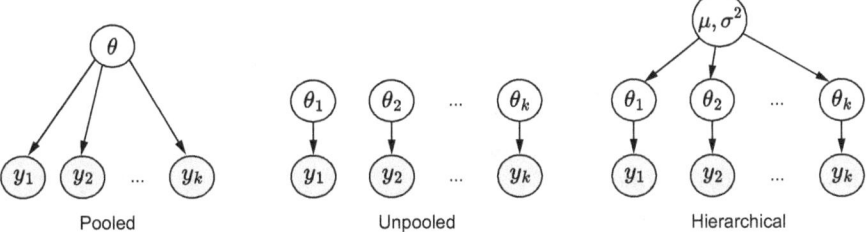

Figure 6.3   Pooled, unpooled, and hierarchical graphical models

In Bayesian hierarchical regression, we can assign priors on model parameters and use MCMC sampling to infer posterior distributions. We use the radon dataset to regress radon gas levels in houses of different counties, based on the floor number (in particular, whether or not there is a basement). Thus, our regression model looks like the following.

$$\alpha_c \; \sim \; N\left(\mu_a, \sigma_a^2\right)$$

$$\beta_c \; \sim \; N\left(\mu_\beta, \sigma_\beta^2\right)$$

$$\text{radon}_c \; = \; \alpha_c + \beta_c \times \text{floor}_{i,c} + \epsilon_c \qquad (6.10)$$

Notice that subscript c indicates a county; thus, we are learning an intercept and a slope for each county sampled from a shared Gaussian distribution. Thus, we are assuming a hierarchical model in which our parameters (α_c and β_c) are sampled from common distributions. In code listing 6.2, we will define probability distributions over regression coefficients and model the data likelihood as the normal distribution with uniform standard deviation. Having specified the graphical model, we can run inference using the no-U-turn sampler (NUTS), with the help of the PyMC library. PyMC is a probabilistic programming library in Python that can be downloaded at https://docs.pymc.io/. It is an excellent tool for Bayesian modeling and can be considered from scratch, since we are defining the probabilistic graphical model from scratch and then using off-the-shelf tools for sampling the posterior distribution. If this is your first exposure to probabilistic programming languages, I highly recommend completing the PyMC online examples to learn more about its capabilities.

Let's examine the pseudo-code in figure 6.4.

```
 1: function main(X, y):
 2: with pymc3.Model() as hierarchical_model:
 3:     μ_a ~ N(0, 100²)  ┐
 4:     σ_a ~ Unif[0, 100] │ → Hyperpriors
 5:     μ_b ~ N(0, 100²)  │
 6:     σ_b ~ Unif[0, 100] ┘
 7:     a ~ N (μ_a, σ_a²)  ← Intercept model
 8:     b ~ N (μ_b, σ_b²)  ← Slope model
 9:     ε ~ Unif[0, 100]  ← Error model
10:     y_exp = a + b × X  ← Expected value
11:     y_lh ~ N (X; y_exp, ε²)  ← Data likelihood
12: with hierarchical_model:
13:     mu, sds, elbo = pymc3.variational.advi(n = 100000) ┐
14:     step = pymc3.NUTS(scaling = sds², is_cov =True)   │ → PyMC inference
15:     trace = pymc3.sample(5000, step, start = mu)      ┘
16: return trace
```

Figure 6.4   Hierarchical Bayesian regression pseudo-code

The code consists of a single `main` function. In the first section of the code, we define the probabilistic model, and in the second section, we are using PyMC3 library for variational inference. First, we set the hyperpriors for the mean and variance of the regression intercept and slope models. Next, we define the intercept and slope model as the Gaussian RVs and define the error model as a uniform RV. Finally, we compute the regression expression and set it as a mean in the data likelihood model. We then proceed with NUTS inference implemented in PyMC.

Listing 6.2   Hierarchical Bayesian regression

```python
import numpy as np
import pandas as pd

import seaborn as sns
import matplotlib.pyplot as plt

import pymc3 as pm

def main():

 data = pd.read_csv('./data/radon.txt')      ◁────── Load data

 county_names = data.county.unique()
 county_idx = data['county_code'].values

 with pm.Model() as hierarchical_model:

     mu_a = pm.Normal('mu_alpha', mu=0., sd=100**2)
     sigma_a = pm.Uniform('sigma_alpha', lower=0,
     ➥ upper=100)                                        Hyperpriors
     mu_b = pm.Normal('mu_beta', mu=0., sd=100**2)
     sigma_b = pm.Uniform('sigma_beta', lower=0,
     ➥ upper=100)

     a = pm.Normal('alpha', mu=mu_a, sd=sigma_a,
     ➥ shape=len(data.county.unique()))      ◁────── Intercept for each county
     b = pm.Normal('beta', mu=mu_b, sd=sigma_b,
     ➥ shape=len(data.county.unique()))      ◁────── Slope for each county

     eps = pm.Uniform('eps', lower=0, upper=100)      ◁────── Model error

     radon_est = a[county_idx] + b[county_idx] *
     ➥ data.floor.values        ◁───┐
                                     │ Expected value
     y_like = pm.Normal('y_like', mu=radon_est, sd=eps,
     ➥ observed=data.log_radon)      ◁───┐
                                          │ Data likelihood

 with hierarchical_model:
     # Use ADVI for initialization
     mu, sds, elbo = pm.variational.advi(n=100000)
     step = pm.NUTS(scaling=hierarchical_model.dict_to_array(sds)**2,
     ➥ is_cov=True)
     hierarchical_trace = pm.sample(5000, step, start=mu)

 pm.traceplot(hierarchical_trace[500:])
 plt.show()

if __name__ == "__main__":
 main()
```

From the trace plots in figure 6.5, we can see convergence in our posterior distributions for α_c and β_c, indicating different intercepts and slopes for different counties.

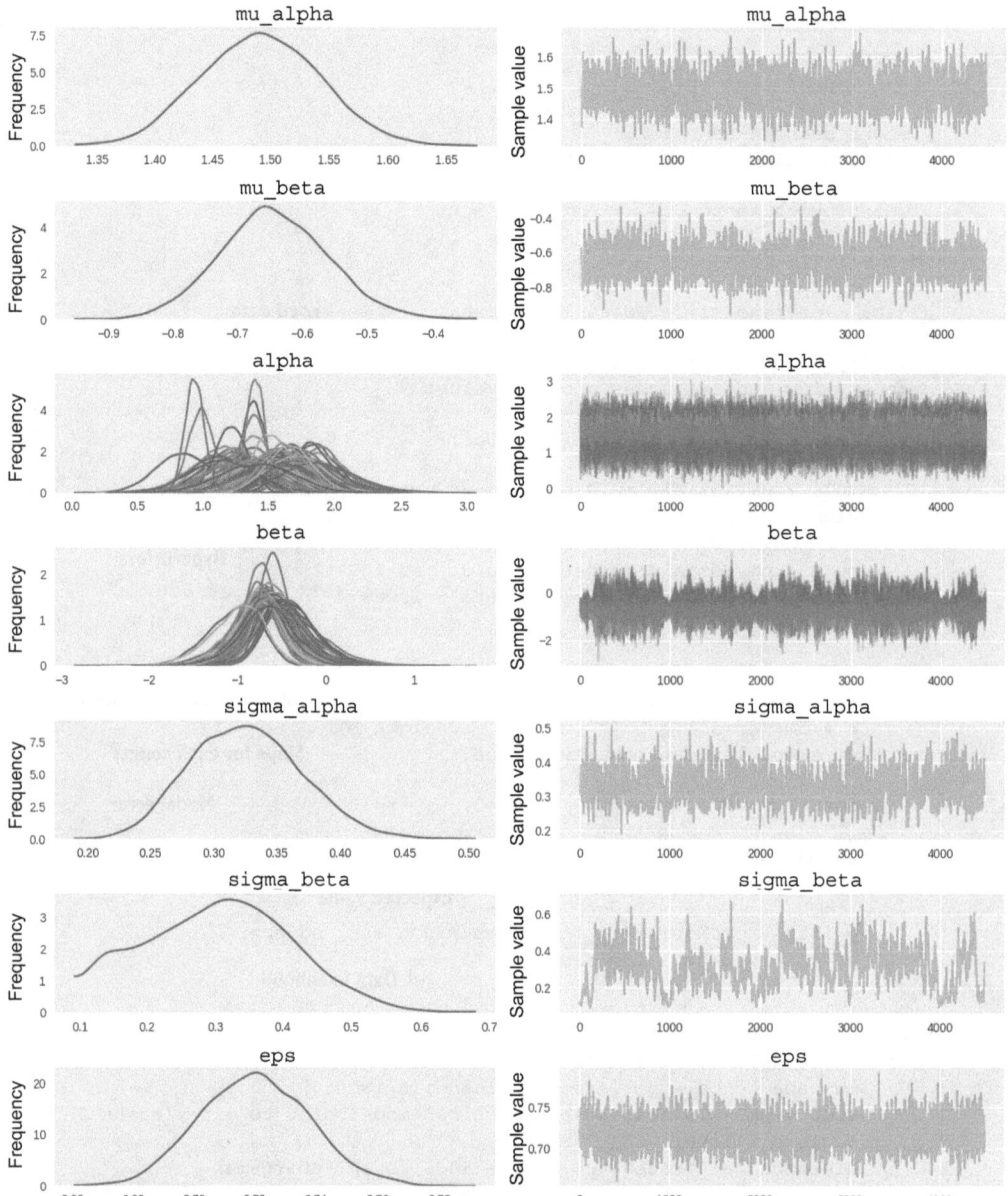

Figure 6.5   MCMC traceplots for hierarchical Bayesian regression

In addition, we also recover the posterior distribution of the shared parameters. μ_a means the group mean of log radon levels is close to 1.5, while μ_b means the slope is negative, with a mean of –0.65 and, therefore, having no basement decreases radon levels. In the next section, we will examine an algorithm suitable for nonlinear data.

6.4 KNN regression

K nearest neighbors (KNN) regression is an example of a nonparametric model, in which for a given query data point q, we find its k nearest neighbors in the training set and compute the average response variable y. In this section, we'll compute the average of KNN target labels for the iris dataset. The average is taken over the local neighborhood of K points that are closest to our query q.

$$y_q = \frac{1}{K} \sum_{i \in N_K(q,D)} y_i \tag{6.11}$$

Here, $N_K(q, D)$ denotes the local neighborhood of k nearest neighbors to query q from the training dataset D. To find the local neighborhood $N_K(q, D)$, we can compute a distance between the query point q and each of the training dataset points $x_i \in D$, sort these distances in ascending order, and take the top K data points. The runtime complexity of this approach is $O(n \log n)$, where n is the size of the training dataset due to the sort operation. We are now ready to implement a KNN regressor from scratch! In figure 6.6, KNN regression is computed by averaging the labels of K nearest neighbors based on Euclidean distance.

```
1: class KNN:
2:   function knn_search(K, X, y, Q)
3:     for query in Q:
4:       idx = argsort(euclidian_dist(query, X))[:K]  ← KNN IDs
5:       knn_labels = [y[i] for i in idx]  ← KNN labels
6:       y_pred = mean(knn_labels)  ← KNN regression
7:     end for
8:   return y_pred
```

Figure 6.6   KNN regression pseudo-code

The code consists of the `knn_search` function, in which for every K nearest neighbor query Q, we compute the Euclidean distance between the query and all of the data points, sort the results, and pick out K lowest distance IDs. We then form the KNN region by collecting the labels with KNN IDs. Finally, we compute our result by averaging over KNN labels.

Listing 6.3   K nearest neighbors regression

```
import numpy as np
import matplotlib.pyplot as plt

from sklearn import datasets
from sklearn.model_selection import train_test_split

np.random.seed(42)
```

```
class KNN():

    def __init__(self, K):
        self.K = K

    def euclidean_distance(self, x1, x2):
        dist = 0
        for i in range(len(x1)):
            dist += np.power((x1[i] - x2[i]), 2)
        return np.sqrt(dist)

    def knn_search(self, X_train, y_train, Q):
        y_pred = np.empty(Q.shape[0])

        for i, query in enumerate(Q):
            idx = np.argsort([self.euclidean_distance(
            ➡ query, x) for x in X_train])[:self.K]
            knn_labels = y_train[idx]
            y_pred[i] = np.mean(knn_labels)

        return y_pred
```

Gets K nearest neighbors to query the point ← (arrow pointing to `idx = np.argsort(...)[:self.K]` line)

Extracts KNN training labels → (arrow pointing to `knn_labels = y_train[idx]` line)

Computes the average of KNN training labels ← (arrow pointing to `y_pred[i] = np.mean(knn_labels)` line)

```
if __name__ == "__main__":

    plt.close('all')

    #iris dataset
    iris = datasets.load_iris()
    X = iris.data[:,:2]
    y = iris.target

    X_train, X_test, y_train, y_test = train_test_split(X, y,
    ➡ test_size=0.2, random_state=42)

    K = 4
    knn = KNN(K)
    y_pred = knn.knn_search(X_train, y_train, X_test)

    plt.figure(1)
    plt.scatter(X_train[:,0], X_train[:,1], s = 100, marker = 'x', color =
    ➡ 'r', label = 'data')
    plt.scatter(X_test[:,0], X_test[:,1], s = 100, marker = 'o', color =
    ➡ 'b', label = 'query')
    plt.title('K Nearest Neighbors (K=%d)'% K)
    plt.legend()
    plt.xlabel('X1')
    plt.ylabel('X2')
    plt.grid(True)
    plt.show()
```

Finding the exact nearest neighbors in high-dimensional space is often computationally intractable, and therefore, there exist approximate methods. There are two classes of approximate methods: those that partition the space into regions, such as k-d tree implemented in fast library for approximate nearest neighbors (FLANN), and hashing-based methods, such as locality-sensitive hashing (LSH). In the next section, we will discuss a different type of regression over functions.

6.5 *Gaussian process regression*

Gaussian processes (GPs) define a prior over functions that can be updated to a posterior once we have observed data (see C. E. Rasmussen and C. K. I. Williams's, *Gaussian Processes for Machine Learning*, The MIT Press, 2006). In a supervised setting, the function gives a mapping between the data points x_i and the target value y_i: $y_i = f(x_i)$. Gaussian processes infer a distribution over functions given the data $p(f|x, y)$ and then use it to make predictions given new data. A GP assumes that the function is defined at a finite and arbitrary chosen set of points $x_1, ..., x_n$, such that $p(f(x_1), ..., f(x_n))$ is jointly Gaussian with mean $\mu(x)$ and covariance $\Sigma(x)$, where $\Sigma_{ij} = \kappa(x_i, x_j)$ and κ is a positive definite kernel function. One example that can be solved by Gaussian Process regression is predicting the CO_2 level based on observed measurements. In code listing 6.4, we will assume a sinusoidal model and a radial basis function kernel.

Consider a simple regression problem.

$$f(x) = x^T w \quad y = f(x) + \epsilon \quad \epsilon \sim N\left(0, \sigma_n^2\right) \tag{6.12}$$

Assuming independent and identically distributed noise, we can write down the following likelihood function.

$$
\begin{aligned}
p(y|X, w) &= \prod_{i=1}^{n} p(y_i|x_i, w) = \prod_{i=1}^{n} \frac{1}{\sqrt{2\pi}\sigma_n} \exp\left\{-\frac{\left(y_i - x_i^T w\right)^2}{2\sigma_n^2}\right\} \\
&\sim N\left(Xw, \sigma_n^2 I\right)
\end{aligned}
\tag{6.13}
$$

In the Bayesian framework, we need to specify a prior over the parameters: $w \sim N(0, \Sigma_p)$. Writing only the terms of the likelihood and the prior, which depend on the weights, we get the following equation.

$$
\begin{aligned}
p(w|X, y) &\propto \exp\left\{-\frac{1}{2\sigma_n^2}||y - Xw||^2\right\} \exp\left\{-\frac{1}{2}w^T \Sigma_p^{-1} w\right\} \\
&\propto \exp\left\{-\frac{1}{2}(w - \bar{w})\left(\frac{1}{\sigma_n^2}XX^T + \Sigma_p^{-1}\right)(w - \bar{w})\right\} \\
&\sim N\left(\frac{1}{\sigma_n^2}A^{-1}Xy, A^{-1}\right)
\end{aligned}
\tag{6.14}
$$

Here, we assume the following.

$$A = \sigma_n^{-2} X X^T + \Sigma_p^{-1} \tag{6.15}$$

Thus, we have a closed-form posterior distribution over the parameters w. To make predictions using this equation, we need to invert the matrix A of size $p \times p$.

Assuming the observations are noiseless, we want to predict the function outputs $y^* = f(x^*)$, where x^* is our test data. Consider the following joint GP distribution.

$$\begin{pmatrix} f \\ f_* \end{pmatrix} \sim N \left(\begin{pmatrix} \mu \\ \mu_* \end{pmatrix}, \begin{pmatrix} K & K_* \\ K_*^T & K_{**} \end{pmatrix} \right) \tag{6.16}$$

Here, $K = \kappa(X, X)$, $K^* = \kappa(X, X^*)$ and $K^{**} = \kappa(X^*, X^*)$, where X is our training dataset, X^* is our test dataset, and κ is the kernel or covariance function. Using standard rules for conditioning Gaussians, the posterior has the following form.

$$\begin{aligned} p(f_* | X_*, X, f) &\sim N(f_* | \mu_*, \Sigma_*) \\ \mu_* &= \mu(X_*) + K_*^T K^{-1} (f - \mu(X)) \\ \Sigma_* &= K_{**} - K_*^T K^{-1} K_* \end{aligned} \tag{6.17}$$

In code listing 6.4, we use the radial basis function kernel as a measure of similarity defined in equation 6.18. We are now ready to implement GP regression from scratch (see figure 6.7)!

```
1: class GPreg:
2: function kernel_func(x, z)
3: Kfn = exp {-1/(2σ²) ||x − x||²}   ←| Radial basis function kernel
4: return Kfn
5: function compute_posterior(X)
6: K = kernel_func(X_train, X_train)
7: Ks = kernel_func(X_train, X_text)
8: Kss = kernel_func(X_test, X_test)
9: μ_post − μ(X_text) + K_s^T K^{-1} (f − μ(X_train))   ─| Gaussian
10: Σ_post = K_ss − K_s^T K^{-1} K_s                        ─→ process posterior
11: return μ_post, Σ_post
```

Figure 6.7   Gaussian process regression pseudo-code

The code consists of `kernel_func` and `compute_posterior` functions. The `kernel_func` returns a radial basis function (RBF) kernel, which measures the similarity between two inputs x and z. In the `computer_posterior` function, we first compute the ingredients required for posterior mean and covariance equations and then compute and return the posterior mean and covariance, as derived in the text.

Listing 6.4 Gaussian process regression

```python
import numpy as np
import matplotlib.pyplot as plt
from scipy.spatial.distance import cdist

np.random.seed(42)

class GPreg:

 def __init__(self, X_train, y_train, X_test):

     self.L = 1.0
     self.keps = 1e-8

     self.muFn = self.mean_func(X_test)
     self.Kfn = self.kernel_func(X_test, X_test) + 1e-15*np.eye(
     np.size(X_test))

     self.X_train = X_train
     self.y_train = y_train
     self.X_test = X_test

 def mean_func(self, x):
     muFn = np.zeros(len(x)).reshape(-1,1)
     return muFn

 def kernel_func(self, x, z):
     sq_dist = cdist(x/self.L, z/self.L, 'euclidean')**2
     Kfn = 1.0 * np.exp(-sq_dist/2)
     return Kfn

 def compute_posterior(self):
     K = self.kernel_func(self.X_train, self.X_train)
     Ks = self.kernel_func(self.X_train, self.X_test)
     Kss = self.kernel_func(self.X_test, self.X_test) + self
     .keps*np.eye(np.size(self.X_test))
     Ki = np.linalg.inv(K)            <------ O(N_train ^ 3)

     postMu = self.mean_func(self.X_test) + np.dot(np.transpose(Ks),
     np.dot(Ki, (self.y_train - self.mean_func(self.X_train))))
     postCov = Kss - np.dot(np.transpose(Ks), np.dot(Ki, Ks))

     self.muFn = postMu
     self.Kfn = postCov

     return None
```

```
    def generate_plots(self, X, num_samples=3):
        plt.figure()
        for i in range(num_samples):
            fs = self.gauss_sample(1)
            plt.plot(X, fs, '-k')
            #plt.plot(self.X_train, self.y_train, 'xk')

        mu = self.muFn.ravel()
        S2 = np.diag(self.Kfn)
        plt.fill(np.concatenate([X, X[::-1]]), np.concatenate([mu -
        ⮞ 2*np.sqrt(S2), (mu + 2*np.sqrt(S2))[::-1]]), alpha=0.2, fc='b')
        plt.show()
```

Returns n samples from the
multivariate Gaussian distribution

```
    def gauss_sample(self, n):
        A = np.linalg.cholesky(self.Kfn)
        Z = np.random.normal(loc=0, scale=1, size=(len(self.muFn),n))
        S = np.dot(A,Z) + self.muFn
        return S
```

S = AZ + mu

```
def main():

    # generate noise-less training data
    X_train = np.array([-4, -3, -2, -1, 1])
    X_train = X_train.reshape(-1,1)
    y_train = np.sin(X_train)

    # generate  test data
    X_test = np.linspace(-5, 5, 50)
    X_test = X_test.reshape(-1,1)

    gp = GPreg(X_train, y_train, X_test)
    gp.generate_plots(X_test,3)         ⬅—— Samples from the GP prior
    gp.compute_posterior()
    gp.generate_plots(X_test,3)         ⬅—— Samples from the GP posterior


if __name__ == "__main__":
    main()
```

Figure 6.8 shows three functions drawn at random from a GP prior (left) and GP posterior (right) after observing five data points in the case of noise-free observations. The shaded area corresponds to two times the standard deviation around the mean (95% confidence region). We can see that the model perfectly interpolates the training data and that the predictive uncertainty increases as we move further away from the observed data.

Since our algorithm is defined in terms of inner products in the input space, it can be lifted into feature space by replacing the inner products with $k(x, x')$; this is often referred to as the *kernel trick*.

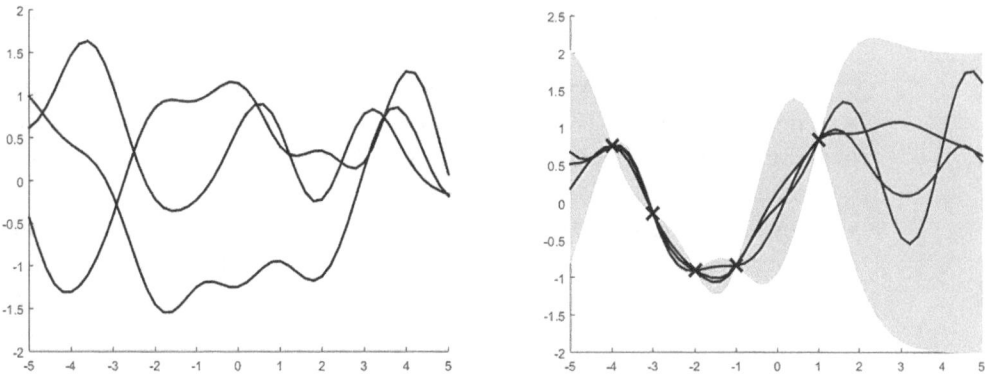

Figure 6.8   Gaussian process regression: Samples from the prior (left) and posterior (right)

The kernel measures similarity between objects, and it doesn't require pre-processing them into feature vector format. For example, a common kernel function is a *radial basis function.*

$$k(x, x') = \exp\left(-\frac{||x - x'||^2}{2\sigma^2}\right) \tag{6.18}$$

In the case of a Gaussian kernel, the feature map lives in an infinite dimensional space. In this case, it is clearly infeasible to explicitly represent the feature vectors.

Regression algorithms help us predict continuous quantities. Based on the nature of data (e.g., linear versus nonlinear relationship between the variables), we can choose either a linear algorithm, such as a Bayesian linear regression or nonlinear KNN regression. We may benefit from a hierarchical model in which certain features are shared among the population. Also, in the case of predicting functional relationships between variables, Gaussian process regression provides the answer to do so. In the following chapter, we will discuss more advanced supervised learning algorithms.

6.6   *Exercises*

6.1 Compute the runtime and memory complexity of a KNN regressor.
6.2 Derive the Gaussian process (GP) update equations based on the rules for conditioning of multivariate Gaussian random variables.

Summary

- The goal of a regression algorithm is to learn a mapping from inputs x to outputs y, where y is a continuous quantity.
- In Bayesian linear regression defined by $y(x) = w^\mathrm{T}x + \epsilon$, we assume the noise term is a zero-mean Gaussian random variable.

- Hierarchical models enable the sharing of features among groups. A hierarchical model assumes there is a common distribution from which individual parameters are sampled and, therefore, captures similarities between groups.
- K nearest neighbors (KNNs) regression is a nonparametric model, in which for a given query data point q, we find its KNN in the training set and compute the average response variable y.
- Gaussian processes (GPs) define a prior over functions that can be updated to a posterior once we have observed data. A GP assumes the function is defined at a finite and arbitrary chosen set of points $x_1, ..., x_n$, such that $p(f(x_1), ..., f(x_n))$ is jointly Gaussian with a mean of $\mu(x)$ and covariance of $\Sigma(x)$, where $\Sigma_{ij} = \kappa(x_i, x_j)$ and κ is a positive definite kernel function.

7
Selected supervised learning algorithms

This chapter covers

- Markov models: page rank and HMM
- Imbalanced learning, including undersampling and oversampling strategies
- Active learning, including uncertainty sampling and query by committee strategies
- Model selection, including hyperparameter tuning
- Ensemble methods, including bagging, boosting, and stacking
- ML research, including supervised learning algorithms

In the previous two chapters, we looked at supervised algorithms for classification and regression. In this chapter, we focus on a selected set of supervised learning algorithms. The algorithms are selected to give exposure to a variety of applications—from time series models used in computational finance to imbalanced learning used in fraud detection to active learning used to reduce the number of training labels to model selection and ensemble methods used in all data science competitions. Finally, we conclude with ML research and exercises. Let's begin by reviewing the fundamentals of Markov models.

7.1   Markov models

In this section, we discuss probabilistic models for a sequence of observations. Time series models have a wide range of applications, including in computational finance, speech recognition, and computational biology. We'll start by looking at two popular algorithms built upon the properties of Markov chains: the page rank algorithm and the EM algorithm for hidden Markov models (HMMs).

However, before we dive into individual algorithms, let's start with the fundamentals. A Markov model for a sequence of random variables $x_1, ..., x_T$ of order 1 is a joint probability model that can be factorized as follows.

$$
\begin{aligned}
p(x_1, ..., x_T) &= p(x_1)p(x_2|x_1)\cdots p(x_T|x_{T-1}) \\
&= p(x_1)\prod_{t=2}^{T} p(x_t|x_{t-1})
\end{aligned}
\tag{7.1}
$$

Notice that each factor is a conditional distribution conditioned by 1 random variable (i.e., each factor only depends on the previous state and, therefore, has a memory of 1). We can also say that X_{t-1} serves as a sufficient statistic for X_t. A *sufficient statistic* is a function of sample data (e.g., a summary of the data, such as a sum or a mean) that contains all the information needed to estimate an unknown parameter in a statistical model.

Let's look at the transition probability $p(x_t|x_{t-1})$ in more detail. For a discrete state sequence $x_t \in \{1, ..., K\}$, we can represent the transition probability as a $K \times K$ stochastic matrix (in which the rows sum to 1).

$$
A_{ij} = p(X_t = j|X_{t-1} = i), \text{ where } \sum_j A_{ij} = 1 \ \forall i
\tag{7.2}
$$

Figure 7.1 shows a simple Markov model with two states.

Here, α is the transition probability out of state 1 and $1 - \alpha$ is the probability of staying in state 1. Notice how the transition probabilities out of each state add up to 1. We can write down the corresponding transition probability matrix as follows.

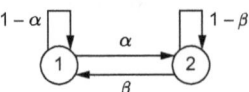

Figure 7.1   A two-state Markov model

$$
A = \begin{pmatrix} 1 - \alpha & \alpha \\ \beta & 1 - \beta \end{pmatrix}
\tag{7.3}
$$

If α and β do not vary over time; in other words, if the transition matrix A is independent of time, we call the Markov chain *stationary* or *time invariant*.

We are often interested in the long-term behavior of the Markov chain—namely, a distribution over states based on the frequency of visits to each state as time passes. Such distribution is known as *stationary distribution*. Let's compute it! Let π_0 be the initial distribution over the states. Then, after the first transition, we have the following.

$$\pi_1(j) = \sum_i \pi_0(i) A_{ij} \qquad (7.4)$$

Or in matrix notation, we have the following.

$$\pi_1 = \pi_0 A \qquad (7.5)$$

We can keep going and write down the second transition as follows.

$$\pi_2 = \pi_1 A = \pi_0 A^2 \qquad (7.6)$$

We see that raising the transition matrix A to a power of n is equivalent to modeling n hops (or transitions) of the Markov chain. After some time, we reach a state when left multiplying the row state vector π by the matrix A gives us the same vector π.

$$\pi = \pi A \qquad (7.7)$$

In the preceding case, we found the stationary distribution; it is equal to π, which is an eigenvector of A that corresponds to the eigenvalue of 1. We will also state here (with proof left as an exercise) that a stationary distribution exists if and only if the chain is *recurrent* (i.e., it can return to any state with probability 1) and *aperiodic* (i.e., it doesn't oscillate).

7.1.1 Page rank algorithm

Google uses a page rank algorithm to order search results from millions of web pages. We can formulate a collection of n web pages as a graph $G = (V, E)$. Let every node $v \in V$ represent a web page, and let every edge $e \in E$ represent a directed link from one page to another. Then, G is a sparse graph with $|V| = n$. Intuitively, a web page that receives a lot of incoming links from reputable sources should be promoted toward the top of the ranked list. Knowing how the pages are linked allows us to construct a giant transition matrix A, where A_{ij} is the probability of following a link from page i to page j. Given this formulation, we can interpret the entry π_j as the importance or rank of page j. Considering the Markov chain discussion in the previous section, the page rank is the stationary distribution π (i.e., the eigenvector of A corresponding to the eigenvalue of 1).

$$\pi_j = \sum_i A_{ij} \pi_i \qquad (7.8)$$

For the stationary distribution π (i.e., page rank) to exist, we need to guarantee that the Markov chain described by the transition matrix is recurrent and aperiodic. Let's look at how we can construct such transition matrix. Let's model the interaction with web pages as follows. If we have outgoing links for a specific page, then with probability $p > 0.5$ (p can be chosen using a simulation), we jump to one of the outgoing links (decided uniformly at random), and with probability $1-p$, we open a new page (also uniformly at random). If there are no outgoing links, we open a new page (decided uniformly at random). These two conditions ensure the Markov chain is recurrent and aperiodic, since random jumps can include self-transitions; thus, every state is reachable from every other state. Let G_{ij} be the adjacency matrix and $d_j = \sum_i G_{ij}$ represent the out-degree of page j. Then, if the out-degree is 0, we jump to a random page with probability $1/n$. With probability p we follow a link with probability equal to the out-degree $1/d_j$, and with probability $1-p$, we jump to a random page. Let's summarize our transition matrix in the following equation.

$$A_{ij} = \begin{cases} \frac{pG_{ij}}{d_j} + \frac{1-p}{n} & \text{if } d_j \neq 0 \\ \frac{1}{n} & \text{if } d_j = 0 \end{cases} \tag{7.9}$$

However, how do we find the eigenvector π given the enormous size of our transition matrix A? We will use an iterative algorithm called the *power method* for computing the page rank. Let v_0 be an arbitrary vector in the range of A—we can initialize v_0 at random. Consider now repeatedly multiplying v by A and renormalizing v.

$$\begin{aligned} v_t &= Av_{t-1} \\ v_t &= \frac{v_t}{\|v_t\|} \\ \lambda &= v_t^T A v_t \end{aligned} \tag{7.10}$$

If we repeat this algorithm until convergence ($\|v_t\| \approx \|v_{t-1}\|$) or until the maximum number of iterations T is reached, we get our stationary distribution $\pi = v_T$. The reason this works is that we can write out our matrix $A = U\lambda U^T$. Then, we get the following equation.

$$\begin{aligned} v_t &= Av_{t-1} = A^t v_0 = \left(U\Lambda U^T\right)^t v_0 = U\left(\Lambda^t U^T v_0\right) \\ &= a_1\lambda_1^t u_1 + a_2\lambda_2^t u_2 + \cdots + a_n\lambda_n^t u_n \\ &= \lambda_1^t\left(a_1 u_1 + a_2\left(\frac{\lambda_2}{\lambda_1}\right)^t u_2 + \cdots + a_n\left(\frac{\lambda_n}{\lambda_1}\right)^t u_n\right) \\ &\rightarrow \lambda_1^t a_1 u_1 \end{aligned} \tag{7.11}$$

Equation 7.11 is true for some coefficients a_i, and since U is an ortho-normal matrix (i.e., $U^T U = I$) and $|\lambda_k| / |\lambda_1| < 1$ for $k > 1$, v_t converges to u_1, which is equal to our stationary distribution! We can summarize the page rank algorithm in the pseudo-code in figure 7.2.

```
1: class page_rank
2: function power_iteration(A):
3: v_0 ~ Unif[0, 1]^d
4: while (not converged) and (iter ≤ max_iter):
5:     v_t = A v_{t-1}
6:     v_t = v_t / ||v_t||
7:     λ = v_t^T A v_t
8:     converged = ||v_t - v_{t-1}|| ≤ tolerance
9: end while
10: return λ, v_t
```

Figure 7.2   Page rank pseudo-code

We start by sampling the initial value of our vector v from a d-dimensional uniform distribution. Next, we iterate by multiplying A and v and renormalizing v. We repeat the process until we either converge or exceed the maximum number of iterations. We are now ready to implement the power method algorithm for computing page rank from scratch in the following listing.

Listing 7.1   Page rank algorithm

```python
import numpy as np
from numpy.linalg import norm

np.random.seed(42)

class page_rank():

    def __init__(self):
        self.max_iter = 100
        self.tolerance = 1e-5

    def power_iteration(self, A):
        n = np.shape(A)[0]
        v = np.random.rand(n)
        converged = False
        iter = 0

        while (not converged) and (iter < self.max_iter):
            old_v = v
            v = np.dot(A, v)
            v = v / norm(v)
            lambd = np.dot(v, np.dot(A, v))
            converged = norm(v - old_v) < self.tolerance
            iter += 1
        #end while
```

```
        return lambd, v

if __name__ == "__main__":

    X = np.random.rand(10,5)          Constructs a symmetric random
    A = np.dot(X.T, X)                real matrix for simplicity

    pr = page_rank()
    lambd, v = pr.power_iteration(A)

    print(lambd)
    print(v)

    #compare against np.linalg implementation
    eigval, eigvec = np.linalg.eig(A)
    idx = np.argsort(np.abs(eigval))[::-1]    Compares against
    top_lambd = eigval[idx][0]                np.linalg implementation
    top_v = eigvec[:,idx][0]
```

As we can see, our implementation successfully finds the eigenvector of A corresponding to the eigenvalue of 1, which is equal to the page rank.

7.1.2   Hidden Markov models

Hidden Markov models (HMMs) represent time-series data in applications ranging from stock market prediction to DNA sequencing. HMMs are based on a discrete-state Markov chain with latent states $z_t \in \{1, ..., K\}$, a transition matrix K, and an emission matrix E that models observed data X emitted from each state. An HMM graphical model is shown in figure 7.3.

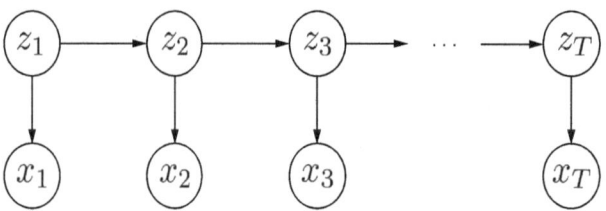

Figure 7.3   Hidden Markov model

We can write down the joint probability density as follows.

$$
\underbrace{p(z_{1:T}, x_{1:T}|\theta)}_{\text{Joint distribution}} = \underbrace{p(z_{1:T}|\theta)p(x_{1:T}|z_{1:T}, \theta)}_{\text{Factorization according to the HMM model}}
$$

$$
= \underbrace{p(z_1|\pi)}_{\substack{\text{Initial state} \\ \text{distribution}}} \left[\underbrace{\prod_{t=2}^{T} p(z_t|z_{t-1}, A)}_{\substack{\text{State transition} \\ \text{distribution}}} \right] \left[\underbrace{\prod_{t=1}^{T} p(x_t|z_t, E)}_{\substack{\text{State emission} \\ \text{distribution}}} \right] \quad (7.12)
$$

Here, $\theta = \{\pi, A, E\}$ are HMM parameters, with π being the initial state distribution. The number of states K is often determined by the application. For example, we can model the sleep–wake cycle using $K = 2$ states. The data itself can be either discrete or continuous. We are going to focus on the discrete case in which the emission matrix $E_{kl} = p(x_t = 1 \mid z_t = k)$. The transition matrix is assumed to be time invariant and equal to $A_{ij} = p(z_t = j \mid z_{t-1}) = i)$.

We are typically interested in predicting the unobserved latent state z based on emitted observations x at any given time. In mathematical notation, we are after $p(z_t = j \mid x_{1:t})$. Let's call this quantity $\alpha_t(j)$.

$$\alpha_t(j) = p(z_t = j \mid x_{1:t}) \tag{7.13}$$

Let's compute it! Notice the recurrent relationship between successive values of alpha. Let's develop this recurrence.

$$
\begin{aligned}
p(z_t = j \mid x_{1:t-1}) &= \sum_{z_{t-1}} p(z_t = j, z_{t-1} \mid x_{1:t-1}) \\
&= \sum_i p(z_t = j \mid z_{t-1} = i) p(z_{t-1} = i \mid x_{1:t-1}) \\
&= \sum_i A(i, j) \alpha_{t-1}(i) \tag{7.14}
\end{aligned}
$$

In the prediction step, we are summing over all possible i states and multiplying the alpha by the transition matrix into j state. Let's use the result of the prediction step in the update step.

$$
\begin{aligned}
\alpha_t(j) &= p(z_t = j \mid x_{1:t}) = p(z_t = j \mid x_t, x_{1:t-1}) \\
&= \frac{p(x_t \mid z_t = j, x_{1:t-1}) p(z_t = j \mid x_{1:t-1})}{p(x_t \mid x_{1:t-1})} \\
&= \frac{p(x_t \mid z_t = j) p(z_t = j \mid x_{1:t-1})}{\sum_{z_t} p(z_t, x_t \mid x_{1:t-1})} \\
&= \frac{p(x_t \mid z_t = j) p(z_t = j \mid x_{1:t-1})}{\sum_j p(x_t \mid z_t = j) p(z_t = j \mid x_{1:t-1})} \\
&= \frac{1}{Z_t} E_t(j) \sum_i A(i, j) \alpha_{t-1}(i) \tag{7.15}
\end{aligned}
$$

We can summarize our derivation in matrix notation as follows.

$$\alpha_t \propto E_t (A^T \alpha_{t-1}) \tag{7.16}$$

Given the recursion in alpha and the initial condition, we can compute the latent state marginals. This algorithm is referred to as the *forward algorithm*, due to its forward recursive pass to compute the alphas. It's a real-time algorithm suitable (with appropriate features) for applications such as handwriting or speech recognition. However, we can improve our estimates of the marginals by considering all the data up to time T. Let's figure out how we can do that by introducing the backward pass. The basic idea of the *forward–backward algorithm* is to partition the Markov chain into past and future by conditioning on z_t. Let T be the time our time series ends. Let's define the marginal probability over all observed data as the following.

$$
\begin{aligned}
\gamma_t(j) &= p(z_t = j | x_{1:T}) = p(z_t = j | x_{1:t}, x_{t+1:T}) \\
&= \frac{1}{Z_t} p(z_t = j | x_{1:t}) p(x_{t+1:T} | z_t = j) \\
&\propto \alpha_t(j) \beta_t(j)
\end{aligned}
\tag{7.17}
$$

Here, we defined $\beta_t(j) = p(x_{t+1:T} | z_t = j)$ and used conditional independence of the past and future chain conditioned on state z_t. But our question remains: how can we compute $\beta_t(j)$? We can use a similar recursion going backward from time $t = T$.

$$
\begin{aligned}
\beta_{t-1}(i) &= p(x_{t:T} | z_{t-1} = i) = \sum_j p(z_t = j, x_t, x_{t+1:T} | z_{t-1} = i) \\
&= \sum_j p(x_{t+1:T} | z_t = j, x_t, z_{t-1} = i) p(z_t = j, x_t | z_{t-1} = i) \\
&= \sum_j p(x_{t+1:T} | z_t = j) p(z_t = j, x_t | z_{t-1} = i) \\
&= \sum_j p(x_{t+1:T} | z_t = j) p(x_t | z_t = j, z_{t-1} = i) p(z_t = j | z_{t-1} = i) \\
&= \sum_j \beta_t(j) E_t(j) A(i, j)
\end{aligned}
\tag{7.18}
$$

We can summarize our derivation in the matrix notation as follows.

$$
\beta_{t-1} = A(E_t \beta_t)
\tag{7.19}
$$

Here, the base case is given by the following.

$$
\beta_T(i) = p(X_{T+1:T} | z_T = i) = 1
\tag{7.20}
$$

This is true since the sequence ends at time T and $X_{T+1:T}$ is a nonevent with probability 1. Having computed both alpha and beta messages, we can combine them to produce our smoothed marginals: $\gamma_t(j) \propto \alpha_t(j) \beta_t(j)$.

Let's now look at how we can decode the maximum likelihood sequence of transitions between the latent state variables z_t. In other words, we would like to find the following.

$$z^* = \arg\max_{z_{1:T}} p(z_{1:T}|x_{1:T}) \tag{7.21}$$

Let $\delta_t(j)$ be the probability of ending up in state j given the most probable path sequence $z_{1:t-1}*$.

$$\delta_t(j) = \max_{z_1,\ldots,z_{t-1}} p(z_t = j, z_{1:t-1}|x_{1:t}) \tag{7.22}$$

We can represent it recursively as the following.

$$\delta_t(j) = \max_i \delta_{t-1}(i)A(i,j)E_t(j) \tag{7.23}$$

This algorithm is known as the *Viterbi algorithm*. Let's summarize what we studied so far in the pseudo-code in figure 7.4.

```
1: class HMM
2: function forward_backward:
3: for t = 1 to n:
4:     α_t = normalize(E_t A^T α_{t-1})
5: end for
6: for t = n - 1 to 1:
7:     β_t = normalize(A (E_t β_{t+1}))
8: end for
9: γ = α · β
10: return γ, α, β
11: function viterbi:
12: for t = 1 to n:
13:     δ_t[j] = max_i(δ_{t-1}[i]A[i,j]E_t[j])
14: end for
```

Figure 7.4 Hidden Markov model pseudo-code

We have two main functions: `forward_backward` and `viterbi`. In the `forward_backward` function, we construct a sparse matrix X of emission indicators and compute the forward probabilities α, normalizing in every iteration. Similarly, we compute the backward probabilities β as previously derived. Finally, we compute the marginal probabilities γ by multiplying α and β. In the `viterbi` function, we apply the log scale for numerical stability and replace multiplication with addition, computing the expression for δ as derived earlier. We are now ready to implement the inference of the HMM from scratch!

Listing 7.2   Forward–backward HMM algorithm

```
import numpy as np
from scipy.sparse import coo_matrix
import matplotlib.pyplot as plt


np.random.seed(42)


class HMM():
    def __init__(self, d=3, k=2, n=10000):
        self.d = d
        self.k = k
        self.n = n

        self.A = np.zeros((k,k))
        self.E = np.zeros((k,d))
        self.s = np.zeros(k)

        self.x = np.zeros(self.n)

    def normalize_mat(self, X, dim=1):
        z = np.sum(X, axis=dim)
        Xnorm = X/z.reshape(-1,1)
        return Xnorm

    def normalize_vec(self, v):
        z = sum(v)
        u = v / z
        return u, z

    def init_hmm(self):

        #initialize matrices at random
        self.A = self.normalize_mat(np.random.rand(self.k,self.k))
        self.E = self.normalize_mat(np.random.rand(self.k,self.d))
        self.s, _ = self.normalize_vec(np.random.rand(self.k))

        #generate markov observations
        z = np.random.choice(self.k, size=1, p=self.s)
        self.x[0] = np.random.choice(self.d, size=1, p=self.E[z,:].ravel())
        for i in range(1, self.n):
            z = np.random.choice(self.k, size=1, p=self.A[z,:].ravel())
            self.x[i] = np.random.choice(self.d, size=1,
            ➥ p=self.E[z,:].ravel())
        #end for

    def forward_backward(self):

        #construct sparse matrix X of emission indicators
        data = np.ones(self.n)
        row = self.x
        col = np.arange(self.n)
        X = coo_matrix((data, (row, col)), shape=(self.d, self.n))

        M = self.E * X
```

Dimension of data ┌──▷ self.d = d

Dimension of latent state ◁─── self.k = k

Number of data points ◁─── self.n = n

Transition matrix ◁─── self.A = np.zeros((k,k))

Emission matrix ┌──▷ self.E = np.zeros((k,d))

Initial state vector ◁─── self.s = np.zeros(k)

Emitted observations ◁─── self.x = np.zeros(self.n)

```
        At = np.transpose(self.A)
        c = np.zeros(self.n)   #normalization constants
        alpha = np.zeros((self.k, self.n))   #alpha = p(z_t = j | x_{1:T})
        alpha[:,0], c[0] = self.normalize_vec(self.s * M[:,0])
        for t in range(1, self.n):
            alpha[:,t], c[t] = self.normalize_vec(np
            ➡ .dot(At, alpha[:,t-1]) * M[:,t])
        #end for

        beta = np.ones((self.k, self.n))
        for t in range(self.n-2, 0, -1):
            beta[:,t] = np.dot(self.A, beta[:,t+1] * M[:,t+1])/c[t+1]
        #end for
        gamma = alpha * beta

        return gamma, alpha, beta, c

    def viterbi(self):

        #construct sparse matrix X of emission indicators
        data = np.ones(self.n)
        row = self.x
        col = np.arange(self.n)
        X = coo_matrix((data, (row, col)), shape=(self.d, self.n))

        #log scale for numerical stability
        s = np.log(self.s)
        A = np.log(self.A)
        M = np.log(self.E * X)

        Z = np.zeros((self.k, self.n))
        Z[:,0] = np.arange(self.k)
        v = s + M[:,0]
        for t in range(1, self.n):
            Av = A + v.reshape(-1,1)
            v = np.max(Av, axis=0)
            idx = np.argmax(Av, axis=0)
            v = v.reshape(-1,1) + M[:,t].reshape(-1,1)
            Z = Z[idx,:]
            Z[:,t] = np.arange(self.k)
        #end for
        llh = np.max(v)
        idx = np.argmax(v)
        z = Z[idx,:]

        return z, llh


if __name__ == "__main__":

    hmm = HMM()
    hmm.init_hmm()

    gamma, alpha, beta, c = hmm.forward_backward()
    z, llh = hmm.viterbi()
```

After the code is executed, we return α, β, and γ parameters for a randomly initialized HMM model. After calling the viterbi decoder, we retrieve the maximum likelihood sequence of state transitions z.

In the following section, we will look at imbalanced learning. In particular, we will focus on undersampling and oversampling strategies for equalizing the number of samples among different classes.

7.2   Imbalanced learning

Most classification algorithms will only perform optimally when the number of samples in each class is roughly the same. Highly skewed datasets where the minority class is outnumbered by one or more classes commonly occur in fraud detection, medical diagnosis, and computational biology. One way of addressing this issue is by resampling the dataset to offset the imbalance and arrive at a more robust and accurate decision boundary. Resampling techniques can be broadly divided into four categories: undersampling the majority class, over-sampling the minority class, combining over and undersampling, and creating an ensemble of balanced datasets.

7.2.1   Undersampling strategies

Undersampling methods remove data from the majority class of the original dataset, as shown in figure 7.5. *Random undersampling* simply removes data points from the majority class uniformly at random. *Cluster centroids* is a method that replaces a cluster of samples by the cluster centroid of a K-means algorithm, where the number of clusters is set by the level of undersampling.

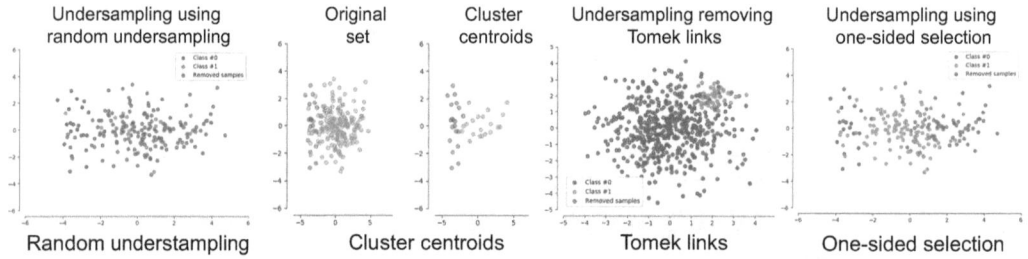

Figure 7.5   Undersampling strategies: Random, cluster centroids, Tomek links, and one-sided selection

Another effective undersampling method is *Tomek links*, which removes unwanted overlap between classes. Tomek links are removed until all minimally distanced nearest neighbor pairs are of the same class. A Tomek link is defined as follows: given an instance pair (x_i, x_j), where $x_i \in S_{min}$, $x_j \in S_{maj}$ and $d(x_i, x_j)$ is the distance between x_i and x_i, the (x_i, x_j) pair is called a Tomek link if there is no instance x_k such that $d(x_i, x_k) < d(x_i, x_k)$ or $d(x_j, x_k) < d(x_i, x_j)$. In this way, if two instances form a Tomek link, then either one of these instances is noise or both are near a border. Therefore, one can use Tomek links to clean up overlap between classes. By removing overlapping examples, one can establish well-defined clusters in the training set and lead to improved classification performance. The *one-sided selection* (OSS) method selects a representative subset of the majority class E and combines it with the set of all minority examples S_{min} to form $N = \{E \cup S_{min}\}$. The reduced set N is further processed to remove all majority class Tomek links. Let's experiment with Tomek links undersampling, using the imbalanced-learn library.

Listing 7.3   Tomek links algorithm

```python
import numpy as np
import seaborn as sns
import matplotlib.pyplot as plt

from sklearn.model_selection import train_test_split
from sklearn.utils import shuffle
from imblearn.under_sampling import TomekLinks

rng = np.random.RandomState(42)

def main():

    n_samples_1 = 500
    n_samples_2 = 50
    X_syn = np.r_[1.5 * rng.randn(n_samples_1, 2), 0.5 *
      rng.randn(n_samples_2, 2) + [2, 2]]                    ⟵——— Generates data
    y_syn = np.array([0] * (n_samples_1) + [1] * (n_samples_2))
    X_syn, y_syn = shuffle(X_syn, y_syn)
    X_syn_train, X_syn_test, y_syn_train, y_syn_test =
      train_test_split(X_syn, y_syn)

    tl = TomekLinks(sampling_strategy='auto')                        Removes
    X_resampled, y_resampled = tl.fit_resample(X_syn, y_syn)   ⟵——⏋ Tomek links
    idx_resampled = tl.sample_indices_
    idx_samples_removed =
     np.setdiff1d(np.arange(X_syn.shape[0]),idx_resampled)

    fig = plt.figure()          ⟵——— Generates plots
    ax = fig.add_subplot(1, 1, 1)

    idx_class_0 = y_resampled == 0
    plt.scatter(X_resampled[idx_class_0, 0], X_resampled[idx_class_0, 1],
      alpha=.8, label='Class #0')
    plt.scatter(X_resampled[~idx_class_0, 0], X_resampled[~idx_class_0, 1],
      alpha=.8, label='Class #1')
    plt.scatter(X_syn[idx_samples_removed, 0], X_syn[idx_samples_removed, 1],
      alpha=.8, label='Removed samples')
    plt.title('Undersampling: Tomek links')
    plt.legend()
    plt.show()

if __name__ == "__main__":
    main()
```

Figure 7.6 shows the resulting output. Thus, we can see that removing unwanted class overlap can increase the robustness of our decision boundary and improve classification accuracy.

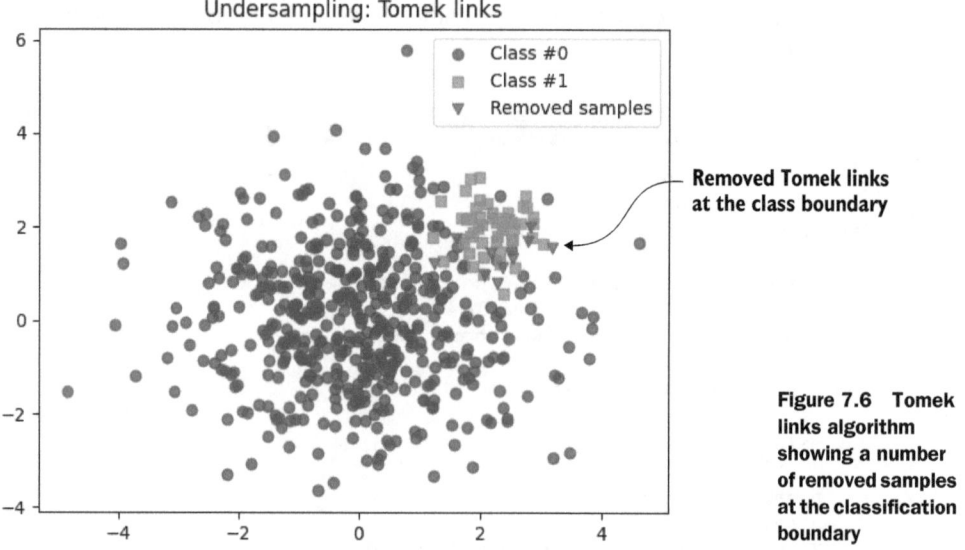

Figure 7.6   Tomek links algorithm showing a number of removed samples at the classification boundary

7.2.2   Oversampling strategies

Oversampling methods append data to the minority class of the original dataset, as shown in figure 7.7. *Random oversampling* simply adds data points to the minority class uniformly at random. The *synthetic minority oversampling technique* (SMOTE) generates synthetic examples by finding K-nearest neighbors in the feature space and generating a new data point along the line segments joining any of the K-minority class nearest neighbors. Synthetic samples are generated in the following way: take the difference between the feature vector (sample) under consideration and its nearest neighbor, multiply this difference by a random number between 0 and 1, and add it to the feature vector under consideration, augmenting the dataset with a new data point.

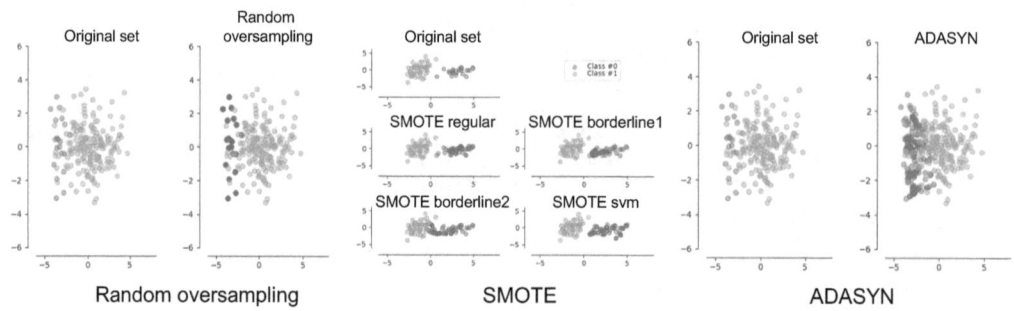

Figure 7.7   Oversampling strategies

Adaptive synthetic sampling (ADASYN) uses a weighted distribution for different minority class examples according to their level of difficulty in learning, where more synthetic data is generated for minority class examples that are harder to learn. As a result, the ADASYN approach improves learning of imbalanced datasets in two ways: reducing the bias introduced by class imbalance and adaptively shifting the classification decision boundary toward the difficult examples. Let's experiment with SMOTE oversampling using the imbalanced-learn library.

Listing 7.4 SMOTE algorithm

```
import seaborn as sns
import matplotlib.pyplot as plt

from sklearn.datasets import make_classification
from sklearn.decomposition import PCA

from imblearn.over_sampling import SMOTE

def plot_resampling(ax, X, y, title):
    c0 = ax.scatter(X[y == 0, 0], X[y == 0, 1], label="Class #0", alpha=0.5)
    c1 = ax.scatter(X[y == 1, 0], X[y == 1, 1], label="Class #1", alpha=0.5)
    ax.set_title(title)
    ax.spines['top'].set_visible(False)
    ax.spines['right'].set_visible(False)
    ax.get_xaxis().tick_bottom()
    ax.get_yaxis().tick_left()
    ax.spines['left'].set_position(('outward', 10))
    ax.spines['bottom'].set_position(('outward', 10))
    ax.set_xlim([-6, 8])
    ax.set_ylim([-6, 6])

    return c0, c1

def main():
    X, y = make_classification(n_classes=2, class_sep=2, weights=[0.3, 0.7],
                               n_informative=3, n_redundant=1, flip_y=0,
                               n_features=20, n_clusters_per_class=1,
                               n_samples=80,
                               random_state=10)    ⟵——— Generates the dataset

    pca = PCA(n_components=2)
    X_vis = pca.fit_transform(X)    ⟵——— Fits PCA for visualization

    method = SMOTE()
    X_res, y_res = method.fit_resample(X, y)    ⟵——— Applies regular SMOTE
    X_res_vis = pca.transform(X_res)

    f, (ax1, ax2) = plt.subplots(1, 2)    ⟵——— Generates plots
    c0, c1 = plot_resampling(ax1, X_vis, y, 'Original')
    plot_resampling(ax2, X_res_vis, y_res, 'SMOTE')
    ax1.legend((c0, c1), ('Class #0', 'Class #1'))
    plt.tight_layout()
```

```
    plt.show()

if __name__ == "__main__":
    main()
```

In listing 7.4, we generate a high dimensional dataset with two imbalanced classes. We apply a regular SMOTE oversampling algorithm and fit a two-component PCA to visualize the data in two dimensions. Figure 7.8 shows the resulting output.

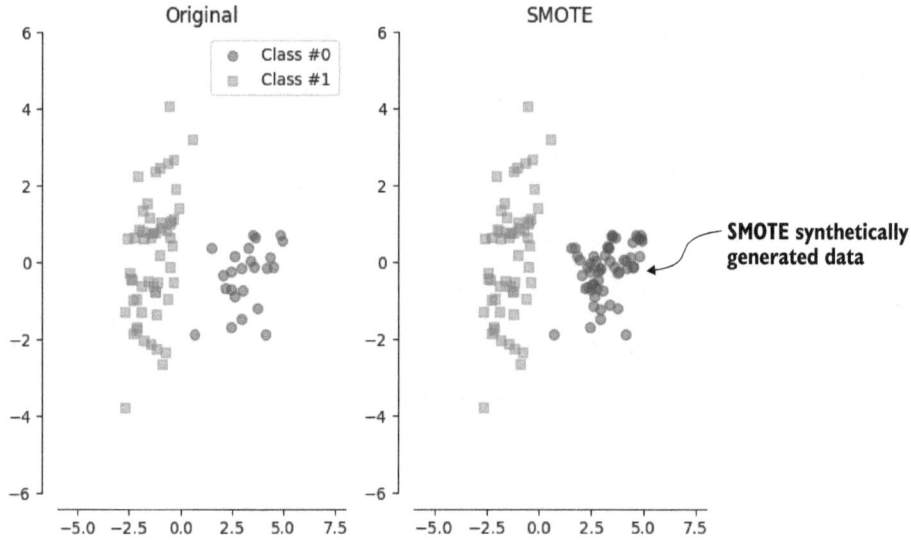

Figure 7.8   SMOTE algorithm

Thus, we can see that SMOTE densely populates the minority class with synthetic data. It's possible to combine oversampling and undersampling techniques into a hybrid strategy. Common examples include SMOTE and Tomek links or SMOTE and edited nearest neighbors (ENN). Additional ways of learning on imbalanced datasets include weighing training instances, introducing different misclassification costs for positive and negative examples, and bootstrapping. In the following section, we will focus on a very important principle in supervised ML that can reduce the number of required training examples: active learning.

7.3   *Active learning*

The key idea behind *active learning* is that a machine learning algorithm can achieve greater accuracy with fewer training labels if it is allowed to choose the data from which it learns. Active learning is well motivated in many modern machine learning problems where unlabeled data may be abundant, but labels are expensive to obtain. Active learning is sometimes called *query learning* or *optimal experimental design* because an active learner poses queries in the form of unlabeled data instances to be labeled by an oracle. In this way, the active learner seeks to achieve high accuracy using as few labeled instances as possible. For a review, see "Active Learning Literature Survey" by Burr Settles (University of Wisconsin-Madison, Department of Computer Sciences, 2009).

We focus on pool-based sampling that assumes that there is a small set of labeled data L and a large pool of unlabeled data U. Queries are selectively drawn from the pool according to an informativeness measure. Pool-based methods rank the entire collection of unlabeled data to select the best query. Therefore, for very large datasets, stream-based sampling, where the data is scanned sequentially and query decisions are evaluated individually, may be more appropriate. Figure 7.9 shows an example of pool-based active learning based on the binary classification of a synthetic dataset with two balanced classes using logistic regression (LR).

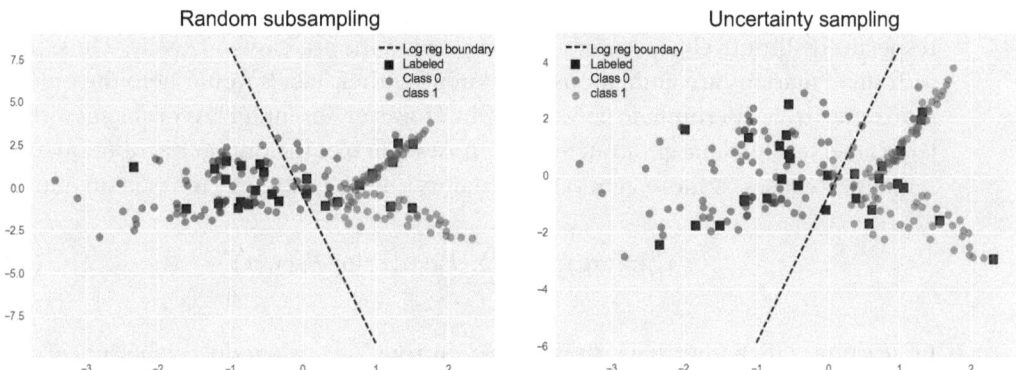

Figure 7.9   Active learning for logistic regression

On the left, we can see the LR decision boundary as a result of training on a randomly subsampled set of 30 labels that achieves a classification accuracy of 90% on held-out data. On the right, we can see the LR decision boundary as a result of training on 30 queries selected by uncertainty sampling based on entropy. Uncertainty sampling achieves a higher classification accuracy of 92.5% on the held-out set.

7.3.1   *Query strategies*

Query strategies refer to criteria we use to select a subset of the training examples as part of active learning. Here, we will look at two query strategies: uncertainty sampling and query by committee.

UNCERTAINTY SAMPLING

One of the simplest and most commonly used query frameworks is *uncertainty sampling*. In this framework, an active learner queries the label about which it is least certain. For example, in binary logistic regression, uncertainty sampling queries points near the boundary where the probability of being positive is close to ½. For multiclass problems, uncertainty sampling can query points that are least confident.

$$x_{LC}^* = \arg \max_x 1 - P_\theta(\hat{y}|x) \tag{7.24}$$

Here, $y \in \{1, ..., K\}$ is the class label with the highest posterior probability under the model θ. The criterion for the least confident strategy only considers information about the most probable label. We can use max margin sampling to preserve information about the remaining label distribution.

$$x_M^* = \arg \min_x P_\theta(\hat{y}_1|x) - P_\theta(\hat{y}_2|x) \tag{7.25}$$

Here, y_1 and y_2 are the first and second most probable class labels under the model, respectively. Intuitively, instances with large margins are easy to classify. Thus, points with small margins are ambiguous, and knowing their labels would help the model to more effectively discriminate between them. However, for multiclass problems with very large label sets, the margin strategy still ignores much of the output distribution for the remaining classes. A more general uncertainty sampling strategy is based on entropy.

$$x_H^* = \arg \max_x - \sum_i P_\theta(y_i|x) \log P_\theta(y_i|x) \tag{7.26}$$

By learning labels that have the highest entropy, we can reduce label uncertainty. Uncertainty sampling also works for regression problems, in which case the learner queries the point with the highest output variance in its prediction.

QUERY BY COMMITTEE

Another query selection framework is the query by committee (QBC) algorithm, which involves maintaining a committee $C = \{\theta^1, ..., \theta^C\}$ of models that are all trained on the current labeled set L but represent competing hypotheses. Each committee member is then allowed to vote on the labels of query candidates, and the most informative query is considered an instance about which they most disagree. The objective of QBC is to minimize a set of hypotheses that are consistent with the current labeled training data L. Two main approaches have been proposed for measuring the level of disagreement: vote entropy and KL divergence. Vote entropy is defined as follows.

$$x_{VE}^* = \arg \max_x - \sum_i \frac{V(y_i)}{C} \log \frac{V(y_i)}{C} \tag{7.27}$$

Here, $y_i \in \{1, ..., K\}$ is the class label, $V(y_i)$ is the number of votes a label received from the committee members, and C is the size of the committee. Notice the similarity to equation 7.26. The KL divergence for QBC voting is defined as follows.

$$x^*_{KL} = \arg\max_x \frac{1}{C} \sum_{c=1}^{C} KL(P_{\theta^{(c)}} \| P_C)$$

$$KL(P_{\theta^{(c)}} \| P_C) = \sum_i P_{\theta^{(c)}}(y_i|x) \log \frac{P_{\theta^{(c)}}(y_i|x)}{P_C(y_i|x)}$$

$$P_C(y_i|x) = \frac{1}{C} \sum_{c=1}^{C} P_{\theta^{(c)}}(y_i|x) \tag{7.28}$$

Here, θ_c represents a member model of the committee and $P_C(y_i|x)$ is the consensus probability that y_i is the predicted label. The KL divergence metric considers the most informative query to be the one with the largest average difference between the label distributions of any one committee member and the consensus distribution.

VARIANCE REDUCTION

We can reduce the generalization error by minimizing output variance. Consider a regression problem for which the learning objective is to minimize the mean squared error. Let $\bar{\theta} = [\hat{\theta}]$ be the expected value of the parameter estimate $\hat{\theta}$ and θ^* be the ground truth. Then, we get the following.

$$
\begin{aligned}
\text{MSE} &= E\left[(\hat{\theta} - \theta^*)^2\right] = E\left[[(\hat{\theta} - \bar{\theta}) + (\bar{\theta} - \theta^*)]^2\right] \\
&= E\left[(\hat{\theta} - \bar{\theta})^2\right] + 2(\bar{\theta} - \theta^*) E\left[\hat{\theta} - \bar{\theta}\right] + (\bar{\theta} - \theta^*)^2 \\
&= E\left[(\hat{\theta} - \bar{\theta})^2\right] + (\bar{\theta} - \theta^*)^2 \\
&= \text{VAR}\left[\hat{\theta}\right] + \text{bias}^2\left(\hat{\theta}\right)
\end{aligned}
\tag{7.29}
$$

This is called the *bias–variance tradeoff*. Thus, it is possible to achieve lower MSE with a biased estimator if it reduces the variance. We might then wonder how low the variance can be. The answer is given by the Cramer-Rao lower bound, which provides a lower bound on the variance of any unbiased estimator.

CRAMER-RAO LOWER BOUND

Assuming $p(x|\theta)$ satisfies the regularity condition, the variance of any unbiased estimator satisfies the following.

$$\text{VAR}(\hat{\theta}) \geq \frac{1}{-E\left[\frac{\partial^2 \log p(x|\theta)}{\partial \theta^2}\right]} = \frac{1}{I(\theta)} \tag{7.30}$$

Here, $I(\theta)$ is the Fisher information matrix. Thus, the minimum variance unbiased (MVU) estimator achieves the minimum variance equal to the inverse of the Fisher information matrix. To minimize the variance of parameter estimates, an active learner should select data that maximizes its Fisher information. For multivariate models with K parameters, Fisher information takes the form of a $K \times K$ matrix.

$$[I(\theta)]_{ij} = -E\left[\frac{\partial^2 \log p(x|\theta)}{\partial \theta_i \partial \theta_j}\right] \tag{7.31}$$

As a result, there are several options for minimizing the inverse information matrix: A-optimality minimizes the trace, $T_r(I^{-1}(\theta))$; D-optimality minimizes the determinant, $|I^{-1}(\theta)|$; and E-optimality minimizes the maximum eigenvalue, $\lambda_{max}[I^{-1}(\theta)]$.

However, there are some computational disadvantages to the variance reduction methods. Estimating output variance requires inverting a $K \times K$ matrix for each unlabeled instance, resulting in a time complexity of $O(UK^3)$, where U is the size of the query pool. As a result, variance reduction methods are empirically slower than simpler query strategies like uncertainty sampling. Let's look at some pseudo-code for active learner class in figure 7.10.

```
1: class ActiveLearner
2: function uncertainty_sampling(clf, X):
3:  Pθ(ŷ|x) = clf.predict_proba(X)
4:  if strategy = "least confident":
5:     return arg maxx 1 − Pθ(ŷ|x)
6:  else if strategy = "max margin":
7:     return arg minx Pθ(ŷ1|x) − Pθ(ŷ2|x)
8:  else if strategy = "entropy":
9:     return arg maxx − Σi Pθ(yi|x) log Pθ(yi|x)
10: end if
11: function query_by_committee(clf, X):
12: if strategy = "vote entropy":
13:    C = len(clf)
14:    for model in clf:
15:       yi = clf.predict
16:    end for
17:  V(yi) = 1/C Σi=1^C 1[[y1]]
18:    return arg maxx − Σi V(yi)/C log V(yi)/C
19: else if strategy = "average kl divergence":
20:    PC(yi|x) = 1/C Σc=1^C Pθ(c)(yi|x)
21:    KL(Pθ(c)||PC) = Σi Pθ(c)(yi|x) log Pθ(c)(yi|x)/PC(yi|x)
22:    return arg maxx 1/C Σc=1^C KL(Pθ(c)||PC)
23: end if
```

Figure 7.10   Active learner pseudo-code

We have two main functions: `uncertainty_sampling` and `query_by_committee`. In the `uncertainty_sampling` function, we pass in the classifier model `clf` and the unlabeled data `x` as inputs. We then predict the probability of the label, given the classifier model and the training data, and use this prediction to compute one of three uncertainty sampling strategies, as discussed in the text. In the `query_by_committee` function, we implement two committee methods: vote entropy and average KL divergence. However, we now pass a set of models `clf`—the predictions of which are used to vote on the predicted label, thus forming a distribution for evaluating the entropy. In the KL divergence case, we make use of averages of model predictions in the computation of KL divergence between each model and the average. We return the training sample that maximizes this KL divergence. We are now ready to review the following code listing.

Listing 7.5 Active learner class

```
from __future__ import unicode_literals, division
from scipy.sparse import csc_matrix, vstack
from scipy.stats import entropy
from collections import Counter
import numpy as np


class ActiveLearner(object):

    uncertainty_sampling_frameworks = [
        'entropy',                        #  Uncertainty sampling
        'max_margin',                     #  frameworks
        'least_confident',
    ]

    query_by_committee_frameworks = [
        'vote_entropy',                   #  Query by committee
        'average_kl_divergence',          #  frameworks
    ]

    def __init__(self, strategy='least_confident'):
        self.strategy = strategy

    def rank(self, clf, X_unlabeled, num_queries=None):

        if num_queries == None:
            num_queries = X_unlabeled.shape[0]

        elif type(num_queries) == float:
            num_queries = int(num_queries * X_unlabeled.shape[0])

        if self.strategy in self.uncertainty_sampling_frameworks:
            scores = self.uncertainty_sampling(clf, X_unlabeled)

        elif self.strategy in self.query_by_committee_frameworks:
            scores = self.query_by_committee(clf, X_unlabeled)

        else:
            raise ValueError("this strategy is not implemented.")

        rankings = np.argsort(-scores)[:num_queries]
        return rankings
```

```
    def uncertainty_sampling(self, clf, X_unlabeled):
        probs = clf.predict_proba(X_unlabeled)

        if self.strategy == 'least_confident':
            return 1 - np.amax(probs, axis=1)      ◁─── Least confident

        elif self.strategy == 'max_margin':
            margin = np.partition(-probs, 1, axis=1)
            return -np.abs(margin[:,0] - margin[:, 1])   ◁─── Max margin

        elif self.strategy == 'entropy':
            return np.apply_along_axis(entropy, 1,
            ➥ probs)                                ◁─── Entropy

    def query_by_committee(self, clf, X_unlabeled):
        num_classes = len(clf[0].classes_)
        C = len(clf)
        preds = []

        if self.strategy == 'vote_entropy':
            for model in clf:
                y_out = map(int, model.predict(X_unlabeled))
                preds.append(np.eye(num_classes)[y_out])

            votes = np.apply_along_axis(np.sum, 0, np.stack(preds)) / C
            return np.apply_along_axis(entropy, 1,
            ➥ votes)              ◁───┐
                                        │ Vote entropy
        elif self.strategy == 'average_kl_divergence':
            for model in clf:
                preds.append(model.predict_proba(X_unlabeled))

            consensus = np.mean(np.stack(preds), axis=0)
            divergence = []
            for y_out in preds:
                divergence.append(entropy(consensus.T, y_out.T))

            return np.apply_along_axis(np.mean, 0, np
            ➥ .stack(divergence))         ◁─── Average KL divergence
```

We apply our active learner to logistic regression example in the following listing.

Listing 7.6 Active learner for logistic regression

```
import numpy as np
import seaborn as sns
import matplotlib.pyplot as plt

from active_learning import ActiveLearner
from sklearn.metrics import accuracy_score
from sklearn.datasets import make_classification
from sklearn.linear_model import LogisticRegression
from sklearn.model_selection import train_test_split
```

```
np.random.seed(42)

def main():

    num_queries = 30   ◄──── Number of labeled points

    data, target = make_classification(n_samples=200, n_features=2,
    ➡ n_informative=2,\
                                  n_redundant=0,          ⎤ Generates
    ➡ n_classes=2, weights = [0.5, 0.5], random_state=0)  ◄──┘ data

    X_train, X_unlabeled, y_train, y_oracle = train_
    ➡ test_split(data, target, test_size=0.2, random_state=0)  ◄──┐ Splits into
                                                                    labeled and
    rnd_idx = np.random.randint(0, X_train.shape[0],                unlabeled
    ➡ num_queries)   ◄──────┐                                       pools
    X1 = X_train[rnd_idx,:]  │ Random subsampling
    y1 = y_train[rnd_idx]

    clf1 = LogisticRegression()
    clf1.fit(X1, y1)

    y1_preds = clf1.predict(X_unlabeled)
    score1 = accuracy_score(y_oracle, y1_preds)
    print("random subsampling accuracy: ", score1)

    #plot 2D decision boundary: w2x2 + w1x1 + w0 = 0
    w0 = clf1.intercept_
    w1, w2 = clf1.coef_[0]
    xx = np.linspace(-1, 1, 100)
    decision_boundary = -w0/float(w2) - (w1/float(w2))*xx

    plt.figure()
    plt.scatter(data[rnd_idx,0], data[rnd_idx,1], c='black', marker='s',
    ➡ s=64, label='labeled')
    plt.scatter(data[target==0,0], data[target==0,1], c='blue', marker='o',
    ➡ alpha=0.5, label='class 0')
    plt.scatter(data[target==1,0], data[target==1,1], c='red', marker='o',
    ➡ alpha=0.5, label='class 1')
    plt.plot(xx, decision_boundary, linewidth = 2.0, c='black', linestyle =
    ➡ '--', label='log reg boundary')
    plt.title("Random Subsampling")
    plt.legend()
    plt.show()
                                              ⎤ Active learning
    AL = ActiveLearner(strategy='entropy')    ◄──────┘
    al_idx = AL.rank(clf1, X_unlabeled, num_queries=num_queries)

    X2 = X_train[al_idx,:]
    y2 = y_train[al_idx]

    clf2 = LogisticRegression()
    clf2.fit(X2, y2)
```

```
y2_preds = clf2.predict(X_unlabeled)
score2 = accuracy_score(y_oracle, y2_preds)
print("active learning accuracy: ", score2)

#plot 2D decision boundary: w2x2 + w1x1 + w0 = 0
w0 = clf2.intercept_
w1, w2 = clf2.coef_[0]
xx = np.linspace(-1, 1, 100)
decision_boundary = -w0/float(w2) - (w1/float(w2))*xx

plt.figure()
plt.scatter(data[al_idx,0], data[al_idx,1], c='black', marker='s',
    s=64, label='labeled')
plt.scatter(data[target==0,0], data[target==0,1], c='blue', marker='o',
    alpha=0.5, label='class 0')
plt.scatter(data[target==1,0], data[target==1,1], c='red', marker='o',
    alpha=0.5, label='class 1')
plt.plot(xx, decision_boundary, linewidth = 2.0, c='black', linestyle =
    '--', label='log reg boundary')
plt.title("Uncertainty Sampling")
plt.legend()
plt.show()

if __name__ == "__main__":

    main()
```

Active learning and semi-supervised learning both attempt to make the most of unlabeled data. For example, a basic semi-supervised technique is self-training, in which the learner is first trained with a small amount of labeled data and then used to classify the unlabeled data. The most confident unlabeled instances together with their predicted labels are added to the training set, and the process repeats.

Figure 7.11 compares three uncertainty sampling techniques: least confident, max margin, and entropy with a random subsampling baseline on a dataset of 20 newsgroups classified with logistic regression.

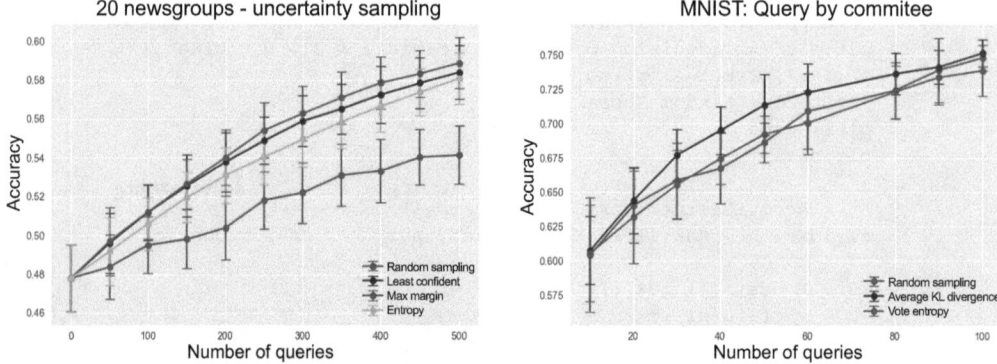

Figure 7.11   Uncertainty sampling techniques comparison. The left figure shows that active learning is better than random sampling. The right figure shows that average KL divergence is better than random sampling.

All three methods achieve higher accuracy in comparison to the baseline, which high-lights the benefit of active learning. On the right, we can see the performance of the query by committee strategy applied to the MNIST dataset. The committee consists of five instances of logistic regression. Two methods are compared against the random subsampling baseline: vote entropy and average KL divergence. We can see that aver-age KL divergence achieves the highest classification accuracy. All experiments were repeated 10 times.

7.4   Model selection: Hyperparameter tuning

In our machine learning journey, we are often faced with multiple models. Model selection is focused on choosing the optimal model (i.e., the model that has a suffi-cient number of parameters [degrees of freedom] so as to not underfit or overfit to training data). We can summarize model selection using the *Occam's razor* principle: choose the simplest model that explains the data well. In other words, we want to penalize model complexity out of all possible solutions.

In addition, we'd like to explain more than just the training data—we'd like to explain the future data. As a result, we want our model to generalize to new and unseen data. A model's behavior is often characterized by its hyperparameters (e.g., the number of nearest neighbors or the number of clusters in the K-means algo-rithm). Let's look at several ways in which we can find the optimum hyperparameters for model selection.

We often operate in a multidimensional hyperparameter space in which we would like to find an optimum point that leads to the highest-performing model on the vali-dation dataset. For example, in the case of support vector machines (SVMs), we may try different kernels, kernel parameters, and regularization constants.

There are several strategies we can use for hyperparameter tuning. The most straightforward strategy is called *grid search*, which is an exhaustive search over all pos-sible combinations of hyperparameters. When using grid search, we can set the hyper-parameter values using the log scale (e.g., 0.1, 1, 10, 100) to arrive at the right order of magnitude. Grid search works well for smaller hyperparameter spaces.

An alternative to grid search is a *random search*, which is based on sampling the hyperparameters from corresponding prior distributions. For example, in finding the number of clusters κ, we may sample κ from a discrete exponential distribution. The random search has the computational advantage of finding the optimum set faster than an exhaustive grid search. Moreover, for a random search, the number of iterations can be chosen independent of the number of parameters and adding parameters that do not influence performance does not decrease efficiency. A third, and most interesting, alternative we will look at in the following subsection is called *Bayesian optimization*.

7.4.1 *Bayesian optimization*

Rather than exploring the parameter space randomly (according to a chosen distribution), it would be great to adopt an active learning approach that selects continuous parameter values in a way that reduces uncertainty and provides a balance between exploration and exploitation. Bayesian optimization provides an automated Bayesian framework by utilizing Gaussian processes (GPs) to model the algorithm's generalization performance (see Jasper Snoek, Hugo Larochelle, and Ryan P. Adams's "Practical Bayesian Optimization of Machine Learning Algorithms," Conference and Workshop on Neural Information Processing Systems, 2012).

Bayesian optimization assumes that a suitable performance function was sampled from a GP and maintains a posterior distribution for this function as observations are made: $f(x) \sim \text{GP}(m(x), \kappa(x, x'))$. To choose which hyperparameters to explore next, one can optimize the expected improvement (EI) over the current best result or the Gaussian process upper confidence bound (UCB). EI and UCB have been shown to be efficient in the number of function evaluations required to find the global optimum of multimodal black-box functions.

Bayesian optimization uses all the information available from previous evaluations of the objective function, as opposed to relying on the local gradient and Hessian approximations. This results in an automated procedure that can find an optimum of non-convex functions with relatively few evaluations, at the cost of performing more computation to determine the next point to try. This is particularly useful when evaluations are expensive to perform, such as in selecting hyperparameters for deep neural networks. The Bayesian optimization algorithm is summarized in figure 7.12.

1: **for** $n = 1, 2, \ldots$ **do**
2:    select new x_{n+1} by optimizing acquisition function α
3:       $x_{n+1} = \arg\max_x \alpha(x; D_n, \theta)$
4:    query objective function to obtain $y_{n+1} = f(x_{n+1})$
5:    augment data $D_{n+1} = \{D_n, (x_{n+1}, y_{n+1})\}$
6:    update GP posterior and acquisition function
7: **end for**

Figure 7.12 Bayesian optimization algorithm

The following listing applies Bayesian Optimization for hyperparameter search in SVM and random forest classifier (RFC).

Listing 7.7 Bayesian optimization for SVM and RFC

```
import numpy as np
import pandas as pd

import seaborn as sns
import matplotlib.pyplot as plt

from sklearn.datasets import make_classification
from sklearn.model_selection import cross_val_score
```

```python
from sklearn.ensemble import RandomForestClassifier as RFC
from sklearn.svm import SVC

from bayes_opt import BayesianOptimization

np.random.seed(42)

# Load data set and target values
data, target = make_classification(
    n_samples=1000,
    n_features=45,
    n_informative=12,
    n_redundant=7
)
target = target.ravel()

def svccv(gamma):          # <——— SVM classifier
    val = cross_val_score(
        SVC(gamma=gamma, random_state=0),
        data, target, scoring='f1', cv=2
    ).mean()

    return val
                                                # Random forest
def rfccv(n_estimators, max_depth):    # <——| (RF) classifier
    val = cross_val_score(
        RFC(n_estimators=int(n_estimators),
            max_depth=int(max_depth),
            random_state=0
        ),
        data, target, scoring='f1', cv=2
    ).mean()
    return val

if __name__ == "__main__":

    gp_params = {"alpha": 1e-5}

    #SVM
    svcBO = BayesianOptimization(svccv,
        {'gamma': (0.00001, 0.1)})

    svcBO.maximize(init_points=3, n_iter=4, **gp_params)

    #Random Forest
    rfcBO = BayesianOptimization(
        rfccv,
        {'n_estimators': (10, 300),
         'max_depth': (2, 10)
        }
    )
    rfcBO.maximize(init_points=4, n_iter=4, **gp_params)

    print('Final Results')
    print(svcBO.max)
    print(rfcBO.max)
```

Figure 7.13 shows Bayesian optimization applied to SVM and RFC.

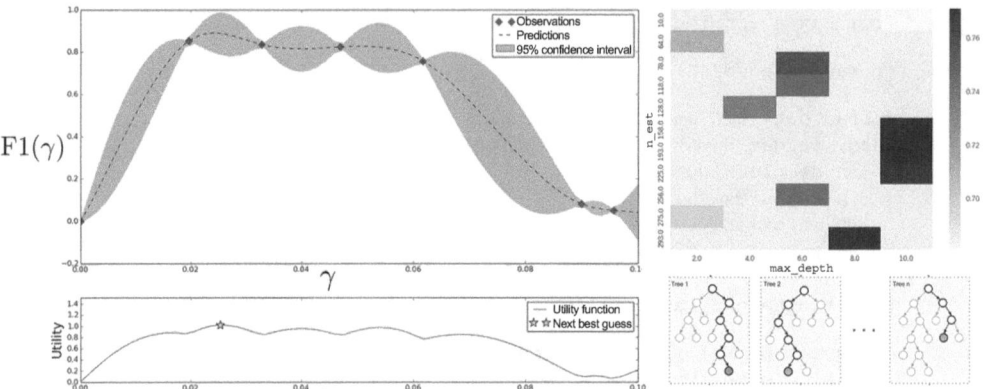

Figure 7.13   Bayesian optimization applied to SVM and RFC

The F1 score was used as a performance objective function for a classification task. The figure on the left shows the Bayesian optimization of the F1 score as a function of the gamma parameter of the SVM RBF kernel $K(x, x') = \exp\{-\gamma||x - x'||^2\}$, where gamma is the precision equal to the inverse variance. We can see that after only seven iterations, we have discovered the gamma parameter that gives the maximum F1 score. The peak of EI utility function at the bottom tells us which experiment to perform next. The figure on the right shows the Bayesian optimization of the F1 score as a function of maximum depth and the number of estimators of a Random Forest classifier. From the heatmap, we can tell that the maximum F1 score is achieved for 158 estimators with a depth equal to 10.

7.5   *Ensemble methods*

Ensemble methods are meta-algorithms that combine several ML techniques into one predictive model to decrease variance (bagging), decrease bias (boosting), or improve predictions (stacking). Ensemble methods can be divided into two groups: *sequential* ensemble methods, where the base learners are generated sequentially (e.g., AdaBoost), and *parallel* ensemble methods, where the base learners are generated in parallel (e.g., random forest). The basic motivation of sequential methods is to exploit the dependence between the base learners, since the overall performance can be boosted by weighing previously mislabeled examples with higher weight. The basic motivation of parallel methods is to exploit independence between the base learners, since the error can be reduced dramatically by averaging.

Most ensemble methods use a single base learning algorithm to produce homogeneous base learners (i.e., learners of the same type), leading to *homogeneous ensembles*. There are also some methods that use heterogeneous learners (i.e., learners of different types), leading to *heterogeneous ensembles*. To ensure ensemble methods are more accurate than any of their individual members, the base learners must be as accurate and diverse as possible.

7.5.1 Bagging

Bagging stands for *bootstrap aggregation*. One way to reduce the variance of an estimate is to average together multiple estimates. For example, we can train M different decision trees f_m on different subsets of the data (chosen randomly with replacement) and compute the ensemble.

$$f(x) = \frac{1}{M} \sum_{m=1}^{M} f_m(x) \qquad (7.32)$$

Bagging uses bootstrap sampling to obtain the data subsets for training the base learners. For aggregating the outputs of base learners, bagging uses voting for classification and averaging for regression. The following listing shows bagging ensemble experiments.

Listing 7.8 Bagging ensemble

```
import itertools
import numpy as np

import seaborn as sns
import matplotlib.pyplot as plt
import matplotlib.gridspec as gridspec

from sklearn import datasets

from sklearn.tree import DecisionTreeClassifier
from sklearn.neighbors import KNeighborsClassifier
from sklearn.linear_model import LogisticRegression
from sklearn.ensemble import RandomForestClassifier

from sklearn.ensemble import BaggingClassifier
from sklearn.model_selection import cross_val_score, train_test_split

from mlxtend.plotting import plot_learning_curves
from mlxtend.plotting import plot_decision_regions

def main():
    iris = datasets.load_iris()
    X, y = iris.data[:, 0:2], iris.target

    clf1 = DecisionTreeClassifier(criterion='entropy',
        max_depth=None)
    clf2 = KNeighborsClassifier(n_neighbors=1)

    bagging1 = BaggingClassifier(base_estimator=clf1, n_estimators=10,
        max_samples=0.8, max_features=0.8)
    bagging2 = BaggingClassifier(base_estimator=clf2, n_estimators=10,
```

KNN classifier ⟶ `clf2 = KNeighborsClassifier(n_neighbors=1)` | **Decision tree classifier**

```
↪   max_samples=0.8, max_features=0.8)

    label = ['Decision Tree', 'K-NN', 'Bagging Tree', 'Bagging K-NN']
    clf_list = [clf1, clf2, bagging1, bagging2]

    fig = plt.figure(figsize=(10, 8))
    gs = gridspec.GridSpec(2, 2)
    grid = itertools.product([0,1],repeat=2)

    for clf, label, grd in zip(clf_list, label, grid):
        scores = cross_val_score(clf, X, y, cv=3, scoring='accuracy')
        print("Accuracy: %.2f (+/- %.2f) [%s]" %(scores.mean(),
        ↪  scores.std(), label))

        clf.fit(X, y)
        ax = plt.subplot(gs[grd[0], grd[1]])
        fig = plot_decision_regions(X=X, y=y, clf=clf, legend=2)
        plt.title(label)

    plt.show()
    #plt.savefig('./figures/bagging_ensemble.png')

    #plot learning curves
    X_train, X_test, y_train, y_test = train_test_split(X, y,
    ↪  test_size=0.3, random_state=0)

    plt.figure()
    plot_learning_curves(X_train, y_train, X_test, y_test, bagging1,
    ↪  print_model=False, style='ggplot')
    plt.show()
    #plt.savefig('./figures/bagging_ensemble_learning_curve.png')

    #Ensemble Size
    num_est = list(map(int, np.linspace(1,100,20)))
    bg_clf_cv_mean = []
    bg_clf_cv_std = []
    for n_est in num_est:
        print("num_est: ", n_est)
        bg_clf = BaggingClassifier(base_estimator=clf1, n_estimators=n_est,
        ↪  max_samples=0.8, max_features=0.8)
        scores = cross_val_score(bg_clf, X, y, cv=3, scoring='accuracy')
        bg_clf_cv_mean.append(scores.mean())
        bg_clf_cv_std.append(scores.std())

    plt.figure()
    (_, caps, _) = plt.errorbar(num_est, bg_clf_cv_mean,
    ↪  yerr=bg_clf_cv_std, c='blue', fmt='-o', capsize=5)
    for cap in caps:
        cap.set_markeredgewidth(1)
plt.ylabel('Accuracy'); plt.xlabel('Ensemble Size'); plt.title('Bagging
↪  Tree Ensemble');
    plt.show()
    #plt.savefig('./figures/bagging_ensemble_size.png')

if __name__ == "__main__":
    main()
```

Figure 7.14 shows the decision boundary of a decision tree and KNN classifiers, along with their bagging ensembles applied to the iris dataset. The decision tree shows axes parallel boundaries, while the $k=1$ nearest neighbors fit closely to the data points. The bagging ensembles were trained using 10 base estimators with 0.8 subsampling of training data and 0.8 subsampling of features. The decision tree bagging ensemble achieved higher accuracy than the KNN bagging ensemble because KNN is less sensitive to perturbation on training samples; therefore, they are called *stable learners*. Combining stable learners is less advantageous, since the ensemble will not help improve generalization performance. Notice also that the decision boundary of the bagging KNN looks similar to the decision boundary of the bagging tree as a result of voting. The figure also shows how the test accuracy improves with the size of the ensemble. Based on cross-validation results, we can see the accuracy increases until approximately 20 base estimators and then plateaus afterward. Thus, adding base estimators beyond 20 only increases computational complexity, without accuracy gains for the iris dataset. The figure also shows learning curves for the bagging tree ensemble. We can see an average error of 0.15 on the training data and a *U*-shaped error curve for the testing data. The smallest gap between training and test errors occurs at around 80% of the training set size.

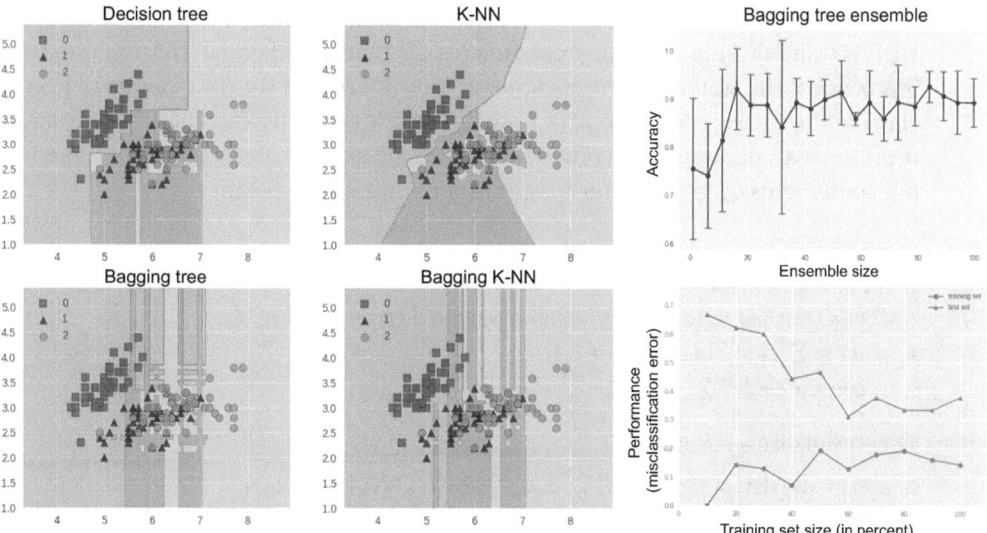

Figure 7.14   Bagging ensemble applied to the iris dataset, as generated by the code listing

A commonly used class of ensemble algorithms is forests of randomized trees. In a *random forest*, each tree in the ensemble is built from a sample drawn with replacement (i.e., a bootstrap sample) from the training set. In addition, instead of using all the features, a random subset of features is selected, further randomizing the tree. As a result, the bias of the forest increases slightly, but due to the averaging of less correlated trees, its variance decreases, resulting in an overall better model.

In the *extremely randomized trees*, algorithm randomness goes one step further: the splitting thresholds are randomized. Instead of looking for the most discriminative threshold, thresholds are drawn at random for each candidate feature and the best of these randomly generated thresholds is picked as the splitting rule. This usually allows the variance of the model to be reduced a bit more—at the expense of a slightly greater increase in bias.

7.5.2   Boosting

Boosting refers to a family of algorithms that can convert weak learners to strong learners. The main principle of boosting is to fit a sequence of weak learners (i.e., models that are only slightly better than random guessing, such as small decision trees) to weighted versions of the data, where more weight is given to examples that were misclassified by earlier rounds. The predictions are then combined through a weighted majority vote (classification) or a weighted sum (regression) to produce the final prediction. The principal difference between boosting and the committee methods, such as bagging, is that base learners are trained in sequence on a weighted version of the data.

The algorithm in figure 7.15 describes the most widely used form of boosting algorithm: *AdaBoost*, which stands for adaptive boosting. We see that the first base classifier $y_1(x)$ is trained using weighting coefficients w_n^1 that are all equal. In subsequent boosting rounds, the weighting coefficients w_n^m are increased for data points that are misclassified and decreased for data points that are correctly classified. The quantity ϵ_m represents a weighted error rate of each of the base classifiers. Therefore, the weighting coefficients α_m give greater weight to more accurate classifiers.

1: Init data weights $\{w_n\}$ to $\frac{1}{N}$
2: **for** $m = 1$ to M **do**
3:     fit a classifier $y_m(x)$ by minimizing weighted error function J_m:
4:     $J_m = \sum_{n=1}^{N} w_n^{(m)} 1[y_m(x_n) \neq t_n]$
5:     compute $\epsilon_m = \sum_{n=1}^{N} w_n^{(m)} \frac{1[y_m(x_n) \neq t_n]}{\sum_{n=1}^{N} w_n^{(m)}}$
6:     evalutate $\alpha_m = \log\left(\frac{1-\epsilon_m}{\epsilon_m}\right)$
7: update the data weights: $w_n^{(m+1)} = w_n^{(m)} \exp\{\alpha_m 1[y_m(x_n) \neq t_n]\}$
8: **end for**
9: Make predictions using the final model: $Y_M(x) = \text{sign}\left(\sum_{m=1}^{M} \alpha_m y_m(x)\right)$

Figure 7.15   AdaBoost algorithm pseudo-code

The following listing trains the AdaBoost classifier with different numbers of learners.

Listing 7.9   Boosting ensemble

```python
import itertools
import numpy as np

import seaborn as sns
import matplotlib.pyplot as plt
import matplotlib.gridspec as gridspec

from sklearn import datasets

from sklearn.tree import DecisionTreeClassifier
from sklearn.neighbors import KNeighborsClassifier
from sklearn.linear_model import LogisticRegression

from sklearn.ensemble import AdaBoostClassifier
from sklearn.model_selection import cross_val_score, train_test_split

from mlxtend.plotting import plot_learning_curves
from mlxtend.plotting import plot_decision_regions

def main():

    iris = datasets.load_iris()
    X, y = iris.data[:, 0:2], iris.target

    #XOR dataset
    #X = np.random.randn(200, 2)
    #y = np.array(map(int,np.logical_xor(X[:, 0] > 0, X[:, 1] > 0)))

    clf = DecisionTreeClassifier(criterion='entropy',
       max_depth=1)                        ⟵┐
                                            │ Base classifier
    num_est = [1, 2, 3, 10]
    label = ['AdaBoost (n_est=1)', 'AdaBoost (n_est=2)', 'AdaBoost
       (n_est=3)', 'AdaBoost (n_est=10)']

    fig = plt.figure(figsize=(10, 8))
    gs = gridspec.GridSpec(2, 2)
    grid = itertools.product([0,1],repeat=2)

    for n_est, label, grd in zip(num_est, label, grid):
        boosting = AdaBoostClassifier(base_estimator=clf, n_estimators=n_est)
        boosting.fit(X, y)
        ax = plt.subplot(gs[grd[0], grd[1]])
        fig = plot_decision_regions(X=X, y=y, clf=boosting, legend=2)
        plt.title(label)

    plt.show()
    #plt.savefig('./figures/boosting_ensemble.png')

    #plot learning curves
    X_train, X_test, y_train, y_test = train_test_split(X, y, test_size=0.3,
       random_state=0)
```

```
boosting = AdaBoostClassifier(base_estimator=clf, n_estimators=10)

plt.figure()
plot_learning_curves(X_train, y_train, X_test, y_test, boosting,
⇒ print_model=False, style='ggplot')
plt.show()
#plt.savefig('./figures/boosting_ensemble_learning_curve.png')

num_est = list(map(int, np.linspace(1,100,20)))    ←──── Ensemble size
bg_clf_cv_mean = []
bg_clf_cv_std = []
for n_est in num_est:
    print("num_est: ", n_est)
    ada_clf = AdaBoostClassifier(base_estimator=clf, n_estimators=n_est)
    scores = cross_val_score(ada_clf, X, y, cv=3, scoring='accuracy')
    bg_clf_cv_mean.append(scores.mean())
    bg_clf_cv_std.append(scores.std())

plt.figure()
(_, caps, _) = plt.errorbar(num_est, bg_clf_cv_mean,
⇒ yerr=bg_clf_cv_std, c='blue', fmt='-o', capsize=5)
for cap in caps:
    cap.set_markeredgewidth(1)
plt.ylabel('Accuracy'); plt.xlabel('Ensemble Size'); plt
⇒ .title('AdaBoost Ensemble');
plt.show()
#plt.savefig('./figures/boosting_ensemble_size.png')

if __name__ == "__main__":
    main()
```

The boosting ensemble is illustrated in figure 7.16. Each base learner consists of a decision tree with depth 1, thus classifying the data based on a feature threshold that partitions the space into two regions separated by a linear decision surface parallel to one of the axes. The figure also shows how the test accuracy improves with the size of the ensemble and the learning curves for training and testing data.

Gradient tree boosting is a generalization of boosting to arbitrary differentiable loss functions. It can be used for both regression and classification problems. Gradient boosting builds the model in a sequential way.

$$F_m(x) = F_{m-1}(x) + \gamma_m h_m(x) \qquad (7.33)$$

At each stage the decision tree, $h_m(x)$ is chosen to minimize a loss function L given the current model $F_{m-1}(x)$.

$$F_m(x) = F_{m-1}(x) + \arg\min_h \sum_{i=1}^{n} L(y_i, F_{m-1}(x_i) + h(x_i)) \qquad (7.34)$$

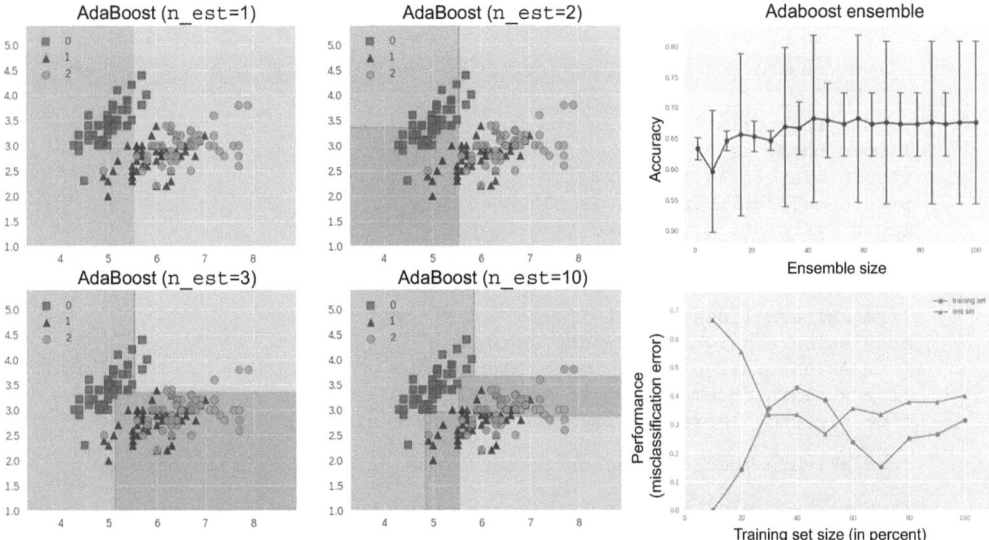

Figure 7.16   Boosting ensemble

Gradient boosting attempts to solve this minimization problem numerically via the steepest descent. The steepest descent direction is the negative gradient of the loss function evaluated at the current model F_{m-1}. The algorithms for regression and classification differ in the type of loss function used.

7.5.3   Stacking

Stacking is an ensemble learning technique that combines multiple classification or regression models via a meta-classifier or meta-regressor. The base level models are trained based on complete training set, and then the meta-model is trained on the outputs of base-level model as features. The base level often consists of different learning algorithms; therefore, stacking ensembles are often heterogeneous. The algorithm in figure 7.17 summarizes stacking.

1: Input: training data $D = \{x_i, y_i\}_{i=1}^{m}$
2: Output: ensemble classifier H
3: *Step 1: learn base-level classifiers*
4: **for** $t = 1$ to T **do**
5:      learn h_t based on D
6: **end for**
7: *Step 2: construct new data set of predictions*
8: **for** $i = 1$ to m **do**
9:      $D_h = \{x_i', y_i\}$, where $x_i' = \{h_1(x_i), \ldots, h_T(x_i)\}$
10: **end for**
11: *Step 3: learn a meta-classifier*
12: learn H based on D_h
13: **return** H

Figure 7.17   Stacking algorithm pseudo-code

The following listing shows the stacking classifier in action.

```python
import itertools
import numpy as np
import seaborn as sns
import matplotlib.pyplot as plt
import matplotlib.gridspec as gridspec

from sklearn import datasets

from sklearn.linear_model import LogisticRegression
from sklearn.neighbors import KNeighborsClassifier
from sklearn.naive_bayes import GaussianNB
from sklearn.ensemble import RandomForestClassifier
from mlxtend.classifier import StackingClassifier

from sklearn.model_selection import cross_val_score, train_test_split

from mlxtend.plotting import plot_learning_curves
from mlxtend.plotting import plot_decision_regions

def main():

    iris = datasets.load_iris()
    X, y = iris.data[:, 1:3], iris.target

    clf1 = KNeighborsClassifier(n_neighbors=1)
    clf2 = RandomForestClassifier(random_state=1)
    clf3 = GaussianNB()
    lr = LogisticRegression()
    sclf = StackingClassifier(classifiers=[clf1, clf2, clf3],
                              meta_classifier=lr)          #⟵——— Stacking classifier

    label = ['KNN', 'Random Forest', 'Naive Bayes', 'Stacking Classifier']
    clf_list = [clf1, clf2, clf3, sclf]

    fig = plt.figure(figsize=(10,8))
    gs = gridspec.GridSpec(2, 2)
    grid = itertools.product([0,1],repeat=2)

    clf_cv_mean = []
    clf_cv_std = []
    for clf, label, grd in zip(clf_list, label, grid):

        scores = cross_val_score(clf, X, y, cv=3, scoring='accuracy')
        print("Accuracy: %.2f (+/- %.2f) [%s]" %(scores.mean(),
        ↪ scores.std(), label))
        clf_cv_mean.append(scores.mean())
        clf_cv_std.append(scores.std())

        clf.fit(X, y)
        ax = plt.subplot(gs[grd[0], grd[1]])
        fig = plot_decision_regions(X=X, y=y, clf=clf)
        plt.title(label)

    plt.show()
    #plt.savefig("./figures/ensemble_stacking.png")
```

```
#plot classifier accuracy
plt.figure()
(_, caps, _) = plt.errorbar(range(4), clf_cv_mean, yerr=clf_cv_std,
➥ c='blue', fmt='-o', capsize=5)
for cap in caps:
    cap.set_markeredgewidth(1)
plt.xticks(range(4), ['KNN', 'RF', 'NB', 'Stacking'],
 rotation='vertical')
plt.ylabel('Accuracy'); plt.xlabel('Classifier');
➥ plt.title('Stacking Ensemble');
plt.show()
#plt.savefig('./figures/stacking_ensemble_size.png')

#plot learning curves
X_train, X_test, y_train, y_test = train_test_split(X, y,
➥ test_size=0.3, random_state=0)

plt.figure()
plot_learning_curves(X_train, y_train, X_test, y_test, sclf,
➥ print_model=False, style='ggplot')
plt.show()
#plt.savefig('./figures/stacking_ensemble_learning_curve.png')

if __name__ == "__main__":
    main()
```

The stacking ensemble is illustrated in figure 7.18. It consists of KNN, Random Forest, and naive Bayes base classifiers whose predictions are combined by logistic regression as a meta-classifier. We can see the blending of decision boundaries achieved by the stacking classifier. The figure also shows that stacking achieves higher accuracy than individual classifiers, and based on learning curves, it shows no signs of overfitting.

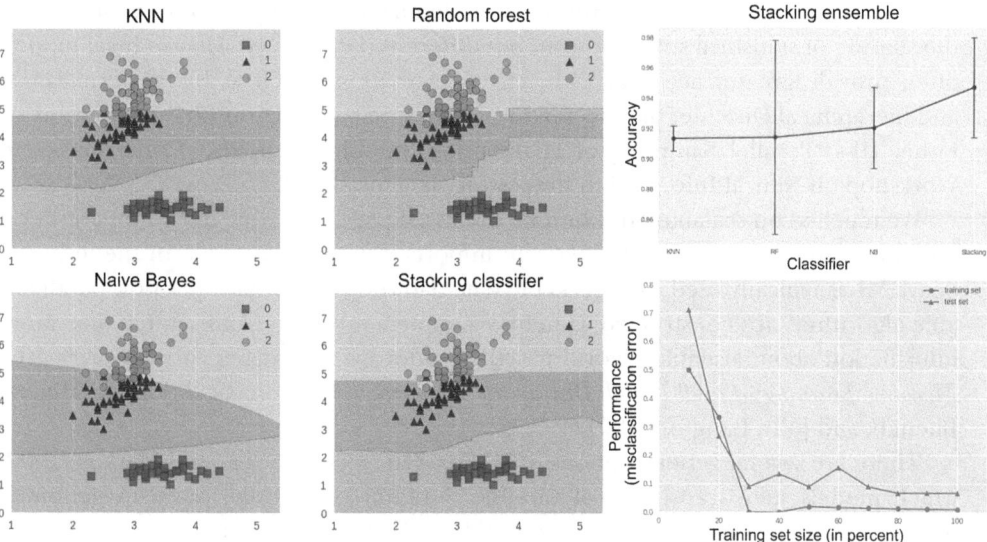

Figure 7.18   Stacking ensemble

7.6   *ML research: Supervised learning algorithms*

In this section, we cover additional insights and research related to the topics presented earlier in the chapter. In the classification section, we derived several classic algorithms and built a solid foundation for the design of new algorithms. For the perceptron algorithm, we saw how we can modularize the algorithm by introducing different loss functions, leading to slightly different update rules. Moreover, the loss function itself can be weighted to account for imbalanced datasets. Similarly, in the case of SVM, we have the flexibility of choosing the appropriate kernel function. We looked at multiclass SVM; however, a one-class SVM with an RBF kernel can be used for anomaly detection.

There are several extensions to solvers other than SGD for logistic regression, including liblinear (which uses coordinate descent), newton-cg (a second-order method that can lead to faster convergence), and LBFGS (a powerful optimization framework that is both memory and computation efficient). Similarly, there are several extensions to the Naive Bayes algorithm based on the type of data it models, such as multinomial naive Bayes and Gaussian naive Bayes. The derivations for these are very similar to the Bernoulli naive Bayes, which we looked at in detail.

In the section on regression, we had our first encounter with a nonparametric model—namely, the KNN regressor. We will explore this rich set of models in chapter 8, when we discuss Bayesian nonparametric models in which the number of parameters grows with data. For example, in the Dirichlet process (DP) HMM, we have a potentially infinite number of states, with probability mass concentrated on the few states supported by the data (e.g., see Emily B. Fox et al.'s "A Sticky HDP-HMM with Application to Speaker Diarization," *Annals of Applied Statistics*, 2011).

We observed the advantages of using hierarchical models. This technique can be used whenever different data groups have characteristics in common, which allows the sharing of statistical strength from the different data groups. Hierarchical models often provide greater accuracy with fewer observations, such as hierarchical HMM and hierarchical Dirichlet process mixture models (e.g., see Jason Chang and John W. Fisher III's "Parallel Sampling of HDPs using Sub-Cluster Splits," Conference and Workshop on Neural Information Processing Systems, 2014).

We touched on scalable ML when we discussed page rank, due to computations on millions of web pages. Scalable ML is an important area of research. In the industry, Spark ML is typically used to process big data. However, to understand how parallelizable algorithms are constructed, it helps to implement them from scratch. For more information about scalable algorithms, the reader is encouraged to read *Scaling Up Machine Learning: Parallel and Distributed Approaches* by Ron Bekkerman, Mikhail Bilenko, and John Langford (2011).

There are several generalizations of HMMs. One example is a semi-Markov HMM, which models state transitions of variable duration commonly found in genomics data. Another example is a hierarchical HMM, which models data with a hierarchical structure often present in speech applications. Finally, there are factorial HMMs, which consist of multiple interlinked Markov chains running in parallel to capture different aspects of the input signal.

There are several notable research areas within active learning. One such area is semi-supervised learning, which can be used, for example, in self-training. The learner is first trained on a small amount of labeled data and later augments their own dataset with the most confidently classified new training examples. Another are of research is the study of the exploration–exploitation tradeoff, which is commonly present in reinforcement learning. In particular, the active learner must be proactive and discerning when exploring examples of instances they are unsure how to label. Finally, submodular optimization is another important area of research (see Andreas Kraus's "Optimizing Sensing: Theory and Applications," Carnegie Mellon University, School of Computer Science, 2008). In problems with a fixed budget for gathering data, it is advantageous to formulate the objective function for data selection as a submodular function, which could then be optimized using greedy algorithms with performance guarantees.

In the area of model selection, reversible jump (RJ) Markov chain Monte Carlo (MCMC) is an interesting sampling-based method for selecting between models with different numbers of parameters. RJ-MCMC samples in parameter spaces of different dimensionality (e.g., when selecting the best Gaussian mixture model with a different number of clusters K). The interesting part arises in the Metropolis-Hastings sampling when we sample from distributions with different dimensions. RJ-MCMC augments the low dimensional space with extra random variables so that the two spaces have a common measure (see Peter J. Green's "Tutorial on Transdimensional MCMC," Highly Structured Stochastic Systems, 2003). Finally, ensemble methods coupled with model selection and hyperparameter tuning are the winning models in any data science competition!

7.7 Exercises

7.1 Explain how temperature softmax works for different values of the temperature parameter T.

7.2 In the forward–backward HMM algorithm, store the latent state variable z (as part of the HMM class) and compare the inferred z against the ground truth z.

Summary

- Markov models have the Markov property that conditioned on the present state—the future states are independent of the past. In other words, the present state serves as a sufficient statistic for the next state.
- Page rank is a stationary distribution of the Markov chain described by the transition matrix, which is recurrent and aperiodic. At scale, the page rank algorithm is computed using power iterations.
- Hidden Markov models model time series data and consist of a latent state Markov chain, a transition matrix between the latent states, and an emission matrix

that models observed data emitted from each state. Inference is carried out using either the EM algorithm or the forward–backward algorithm with a Viterbi maximum likelihood sequence decoder.

- There are two main strategies for imbalanced learning: undersampling the majority class and oversampling the minority class. An additional method includes introducing class weights in the loss function.

- In active learning, the ML algorithm chooses the data samples to train on in a way that maximizes learning and requires fewer training examples. There are two main query strategies: uncertainty sampling and query by committee.

- Bias–variance tradeoff necessitates that mean squared error is equal to bias squared plus variance. The minimum variance is given by the inverse of Fisher information, which measures the curvature of log likelihood.

- In model selection, we often want to follow the Occam's razor principle and choose the simplest model that explains the data well. In hyperparameter optimization, in addition to grid search and random search, Bayesian Optimization uses an active learning approach in a way that reduces uncertainty and provides a balance between exploration and exploitation.

- Ensemble methods are meta-algorithms that combine several machine learning techniques into one predictive model to decrease variance (bagging), decrease bias (boosting), or improve predictions (stacking).

Part 3

Unsupervised learning

In the third part of the book, we'll review unsupervised learning algorithms. Unsupervised learning takes place when no training labels are available. In the case of unsupervised learning, we are often interested in discovering patterns in data and learning data representations.

In chapter 8, we'll start by looking at the Bayesian nonparametric extension of the K-means algorithm followed by the EM algorithm for Gaussian mixture models. We will then look at two different dimensionality reduction techniques—namely, PCA and t-SNE applied to learning an image manifold.

In chapter 9, we'll continue the discussion on selected unsupervised learning algorithms. We'll start by looking at latent Dirichlet allocation for learning topic models, followed by density estimators and structure learning algorithms, and concluding with simulated annealing and genetic algorithms. Finally, we'll review ML research literature, focusing on unsupervised learning.

8

Fundamental unsupervised learning algorithms

This chapter covers

- Dirichlet process K-means
- Gaussian mixture models
- Dimensionality reduction

In previous chapters, we looked at supervised algorithms for classification and regression; in this chapter, we shift our focus to unsupervised learning algorithms. *Unsupervised learning* takes place when no training labels are available. In this case, we are interested in discovering patterns in data and learning data representations. Applications of unsupervised learning span from clustering customer segments in e-commerce to extracting features from image data. In this chapter, we'll start by looking at the Bayesian nonparametric extension of the K-means algorithm followed by the EM algorithm for Gaussian mixture models (GMMs). We will then look at two different dimensionality reduction techniques—namely, PCA and t-SNE—used to learn an image manifold. The algorithms in this chapter were selected for their mathematical depth and usefulness in real-world applications.

8.1   *Dirichlet process K-means*

Dirichlet process (DP) *K-means* is a Bayesian nonparametric extension of the *K*-Means algorithm. *K-means* is a clustering algorithm that can be applied, for instance, to customer segmentation, where customers are grouped by purchase history, interests, and geographical location. DP-means is similar to *K*-means except that new clusters are created whenever a data point is sufficiently far away from all existing cluster centroids; therefore, the number of clusters grows with the data. DP-means converges to a local optimum of a K-means-like objective that includes a penalty for the number of clusters.

We select the cluster K based on the smallest value of the following equation.

$$\arg\min_k\{||x_i - \mu_1||^2, ..., ||x_i - \mu_k||^2, \lambda\} \tag{8.1}$$

The resulting update is analogous to the *K*-means reassignment step, during which we reassign a point to the cluster corresponding to the closest mean or start a new cluster if the squared Euclidean distance is greater than λ. The DP means algorithm is summarized in figure 8.1.

1: Init. $K = 1, l_1 = \{x_1, \ldots, x_n\}$ and μ_1 the global mean
2: Init. labels $z_i = 1$ for all $i = 1, \ldots, n$
3: Init. $\lambda = \mathrm{kpp\_init}(X, \mathrm{K_{init}})$
4: Repeat until convergence:
5:    for each x_i:
6:        compute $d_{ic} = ||x_i - \mu_c||^2$ for $c = 1, \ldots, K$
7:        if $\min_c d_{ic} > \lambda$, set $K = K + 1$ and $\mu_k = x_i$
8:        otherwise, set $z_i = \arg\min_c d_{ic}$
9:    for each cluster $l_j = \{x_i | z_i = j\}$, compute $\mu_j = \frac{1}{|l_j|}\sum_{x \in l_j} x$
10:   Compute the objective: $\sum_{c=1}^K \sum_{x \in l_c} ||x - \mu_c||^2 + \lambda K$

Figure 8.1
DP-means algorithm
pseudo-code

To evaluate cluster performance, we can use the following metrics: normalized mutual information (NMI), variation of information (VI), and adjusted Rand index (ARI). The NMI is defined as follows.

$$\mathrm{NMI}(X, Y) = \frac{I(X;Y)}{\frac{H(X)+H(Y)}{2}} \tag{8.2}$$

Here, $H(X)$ is the entropy of X and $I(X; Y)$ is the mutual information between the ground truth label assignments X (when they are available) and the computed assignments Y. For a review of information measures, see *Elements of Information Theory* by Thomas M. Cover and Joy A. Thomas (Wiley, 2006) for details.

Let $p_{XY}(I, j) = |x_i \cap y_j| / N$ be the probability that a label belongs to cluster x_i in X and y_j in Y. Define $p_X(i) = |x_i| / N$ and $p_Y(j) = |y_j| / N$ similarly. Then, we get the following equation.

$$I(X;Y) = \sum_i \sum_j p_{XY}(i, j) \log \frac{p_{XY}(i, j)}{p_X(i) p_Y(j)} \tag{8.3}$$

Thus, NMI lies between 0 and 1, with higher values indicating more similar label assignments. The variation of information (*VI*) is defined as follows.

$$VI(X;Y) = H(X) + H(Y) - 2I(X;Y) = H(X|Y) + H(Y|X) \tag{8.4}$$

Thus, *VI* decreases as the overlap between label assignments X and Y increases. The ARI computes a similarity measure between two clusters by considering all pairs of samples and counting pairs assigned in the same or different clusters in the predicted and true clusters.

$$
\begin{aligned}
\text{ARI} &= \frac{RI - E[RI]}{\max RI - E[RI]} \\
RI &= \frac{TP + TN}{TP + FP + FN + TN}
\end{aligned}
\tag{8.5}
$$

Thus, ARI approaches 1 for cluster assignments that are similar to each other. Let's implement the Dirichlet process K-means algorithm from scratch!

Listing 8.1 Dirichlet process K-means

```python
import numpy as np
import matplotlib.pyplot as plt

import time
from sklearn import metrics
from sklearn.datasets import load_iris

np.random.seed(42)

class dpmeans:

    def __init__(self,X):          # Initializes parameters
        self.K = 1                 # for DP means
        self.K_init = 4
        self.d = X.shape[1]
        self.z = np.mod(np.random.permutation(X.shape[0]),self.K)+1
        self.mu = np.random.standard_normal((self.K, self.d))
        self.sigma = 1
```

```
        self.nk = np.zeros(self.K)
        self.pik = np.ones(self.K)/self.K

        self.mu = np.array([np.mean(X,0)])     ◄──── Initializes mean

        self.Lambda = self.kpp_init(X,self.K_init)   ◄──── Initializes lambda

        self.max_iter = 100
        self.obj = np.zeros(self.max_iter)
        self.em_time = np.zeros(self.max_iter)

    def kpp_init(self,X,k):        ◄──── K++ initialization

        [n,d] = np.shape(X)
        mu = np.zeros((k,d))
        dist = np.inf*np.ones(n)

        mu[0,:] = X[int(np.random.rand()*n-1),:]
        for i in range(1,k):
            D = X-np.tile(mu[i-1,:],(n,1))
            dist = np.minimum(dist, np.sum(D*D,1))
            idx = np.where(np.random.rand() <
    np.cumsum(dist/float(sum(dist))))
            mu[i,:] = X[idx[0][0],:]
            Lambda = np.max(dist)

        print "Lambda: ", Lambda

        return Lambda     ◄─┐ Lambda is the max
                            │ distance to k++ means
    def fit(self,X):

        obj_tol = 1e-3
        max_iter = self.max_iter
        [n,d] = np.shape(X)

        obj = np.zeros(max_iter)
        em_time = np.zeros(max_iter)
        print 'running dpmean I.')

        for iter in range(max_iter):
            tic = time.time()
            dist = np.zeros((n,self.K))

            for kk in range(self.K):                    Assignment
                Xm - X - np.tile(self.mu[kk,:],(n,1))   step
                dist[:,kk] = np.sum(Xm*Xm,1)

            dmin = np.min(dist,1)
            self.z = np.argmin(dist,1)                  Updates
            idx = np.where(dmin > self.Lambda)          labels

            if (np.size(idx) > 0):
                self.K = self.K + 1
                self.z[idx[0]] = self.K-1 #cluster labels in [0,...,K-1]
```

```
            self.mu = np.vstack([self.mu,np.mean(X[idx[0],:],0)])
            Xm - X - np.tile(self.mu[self.K-1,:],(n,1))
            dist = np.hstack([dist, np.array([np.sum(Xm*Xm,1)]).T])

        self.nk = np.zeros(self.K)
        for kk in range(self.K):                                Updates
            self.nk[kk] = self.z.tolist().count(kk)             the step
            idx = np.where(self.z == kk)
            self.mu[kk,:] = np.mean(X[idx[0],:],0)

        self.pik = self.nk/float(np.sum(self.nk))

        for kk in range(self.K):
            idx = np.where(self.z == kk)                        Computes the
            obj[iter] = obj[iter] + np.sum(dist[idx[0],         objective
        ➥ kk],0)
        obj[iter] = obj[iter] + self.Lambda * self.K

Checks the   if (iter > 0 and np.abs(obj[iter]-obj[iter-1]) <
convergence ➥ obj_tol*obj[iter]):
            print('converged in %d iterations\n'% iter)
            break
        em_time[iter] = time.time()-tic
    #end for
    self.obj = obj
    self.em_time = em_time
    return self.z, obj, em_time
                                        Computes the normalized
def compute_nmi(self, z1, z2):    ◄───── mutual information

    n = np.size(z1)
    k1 = np.size(np.unique(z1))
    k2 = np.size(np.unique(z2))

    nk1 = np.zeros((k1,1))
    nk2 = np.zeros((k2,1))

    for kk in range(k1):
        nk1[kk] = np.sum(z1==kk)
    for kk in range(k2):
        nk2[kk] = np.sum(z2==kk)

    pk1 = nk1/float(np.sum(nk1))
    pk2 = nk2/float(np.sum(nk2))

    nk12 = np.zeros((k1,k2))
    for ii in range(k1):
        for jj in range(k2):
            nk12[ii,jj] = np.sum((z1==ii)*(z2==jj))
    pk12 = nk12/float(n)

    Hx = -np.sum(pk1 * np.log(pk1 + np.finfo(float).eps))
    Hy = -np.sum(pk2 * np.log(pk2 + np.finfo(float).eps))

    Hxy = -np.sum(pk12 * np.log(pk12 + np.finfo(float).eps))
```

```
        MI = Hx +-Hy - Hxy;
        nmi = MI/float(0.5*(Hx+Hy))

        return nmi

    def generate_plots(self,X):

        plt.close('all')
        plt.figure(0)
        for kk in range(self.K):
            #idx = np.where(self.z == kk)
            plt.scatter(X[self.z == kk,0], X[self.z == kk,1], \
                        s = 100, marker= 'o', c = np.random.rand(3,),
                        label = str(kk))
        #end for
        plt.xlabel('X1')
        plt.ylabel('X2')
        plt.legend()
        plt.ti'le('DP-means clus'ers')
        plt.grid(True)
        plt.show()

        plt.figure(1)
        plt.plot(self.obj)
        plt.title('DP-means objective function')
        plt.xlabel('iterations')
        plt.ylalel('penalized 12 squared distance')
        plt.grid(True)
        plt.show()

if __name__ == "__main__":

    iris = load_iris()
    X = iris.data
    y = iris.target

    dp = dpmeans(X)
    labels, obj, em_time = dp.fit(X)
    dp.generate_plots(X)

    nmi = dp.compute_nmi(y,labels)
    ari = metrics.adjusted_rand_score(y,labels)

    print("NMI: %.4f" % nmi)
    print("ARI: %.4f" % ari)
```

The performance of DP-means algorithm is shown in figure 8.2. The performance of the DP-means algorithm was evaluated on the iris dataset. We can see good clustering results based on high NMI and ARI metrics. In the following section, we'll discuss a popular clustering algorithm that models each cluster as a Gaussian distribution, taking into account not just the mean but also the covariance information.

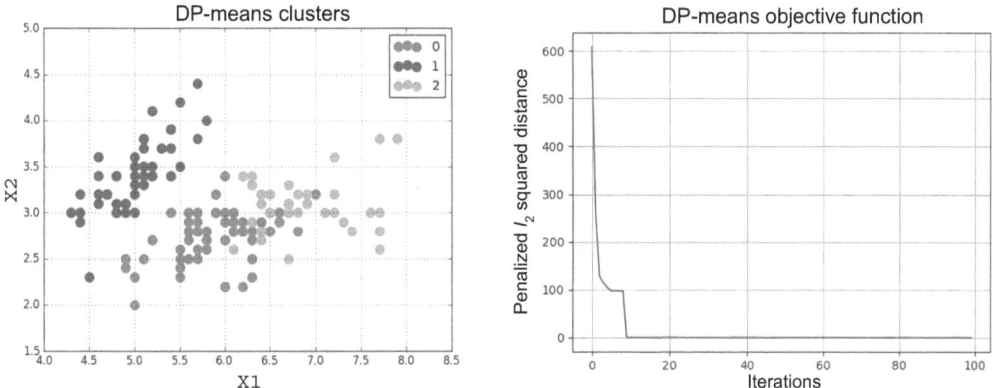

Figure 8.2 DP-means cluster centers (left) and objective (right) for the iris dataset

8.2   *Gaussian mixture models*

Mixture models are commonly used to model complex density distributions. For example, you may be interested in discovering patterns in census data consisting of information about the person's age, income, occupation, and other dimensions. If we plot the resulting data in high-dimensional space, we'll likely discover nonuniform density characterized by groups or clusters of data points. We can model each cluster using a base probability distribution. Mixture models consist of a convex combination of K base models. In the case of Gaussian mixture models, the base distribution is Gaussian and can be written as follows.

$$p(x_i|\theta) = \sum_{k=1}^{K} \pi_k p_k(x_i|\theta) = \sum_{k=1}^{K} \pi_k \mathcal{N}(x_i|\mu_k, \Sigma_k) \tag{8.6}$$

Here, π_k are the mixing proportions that satisfy $0 \leq \pi_k \leq 1$ and $\sum \pi_k = 1$. In contrast to K-means that only models cluster means, GMM models the cluster covariance as well. Thus, GMMs can capture the data more accurately.

8.2.1   *Expectation maximization (EM) algorithm*

The *expectation maximization* (EM) *algorithm* provides a way of computing ML/MAP estimates when we have unobserved latent variables or missing data. EM exploits the fact that if the data were fully observed, then the ML/MAP estimates would be easy to compute. In particular, EM is an iterative algorithm that alternates between inferring the latent variables, given the parameters (E step) and then optimizing the parameters given filled-in data (M step).

In the EM algorithm, we define the complete data log likelihood $l_c(\theta)$, where x_i are the observed random variables and z_i are unobserved. Since we don't know z_i, we can't compute $p(x_i, z_i | \theta)$, but we can compute an expectation of $l_c(\theta)$ wrt to parameters $\theta^{(k-1)}$ from the previous iteration.

$$l_c(\theta) = \sum_{i=1}^{N} \log p(x_i, z_i | \theta) \tag{8.7}$$

The goal of the E step is to compute $Q(\theta, \theta^{(k-1)})$, on which the ML/MAP estimates depend. The goal of the M step is to recompute θ by finding the ML/MAP estimates.

$$\text{E} - \text{step} \quad : \quad Q\left(\theta, \theta^{(k-1)}\right) = E_{\theta^{(k-1)}}\left[l_c(\theta) | D, \theta^{(k-1)}\right]$$

$$\text{M} - \text{step} \quad : \quad \theta^{(k)} = \arg\max_{\theta} Q\left(\theta, \theta^{(k-1)}\right) + \log p(\theta) \tag{8.8}$$

To derive the EM algorithm for GMM, we first need to compute the expected complete data log likelihood.

$$
\begin{aligned}
Q(\theta, \theta^{(k-1)}) &= E\left[\sum_i \log p(x_i, z_i | \theta)\right] \\
&= \sum_i E\left[\log\left[\prod_{k=1}^{K} (\pi_k p(x_i|\theta_k))^{1[z_i=k]}\right]\right] \\
&= \sum_i \sum_k E\left[1[z_i = k]\right] \log\left[\pi_k p(x_i|\theta_k)\right] \\
&= \sum_i \sum_k p\left(z_i = k | x_i, \theta^{(k-1)}\right) \log\left[\pi_k p(x_i|\theta_k)\right] \\
&= \sum_i \sum_k r_{ik} \log \pi_k + \sum_i \sum_k r_{ik} \log p(x_i|\theta_k) \tag{8.9}
\end{aligned}
$$

Here, $r_{ik} = p(z_i = k \mid x_i, \theta^{(k-1)})$ is the soft assignment of point x_i to cluster k.

We now start the E step. Given $\theta^{(k-1)}$, we want to compute the soft assignments.

$$
\begin{aligned}
r_{ik} &= p\left(z_i = k | x_i, \theta^{(k-1)}\right) \\
&= \frac{p\left(z_i = k, x_i | \theta^{(k-1)}\right)}{\sum_{k=1}^{K} p\left(z_i = k, x_i | \theta^{(k-1)}\right)} \\
&= \frac{p\left(x_i | z_i = k, \theta^{(k-1)}\right) \pi_k}{\sum_{k=1}^{K} p\left(x_i | z_i = k, \theta^{(k-1)}\right) \pi_k} \tag{8.10}
\end{aligned}
$$

In equation 8.10, $\pi_k = p(z_i = k)$ are the mixture proportions.

In the M step, we maximize Q with respect to model parameters π and θ_k. First, let's find π that maximizes the Lagrangian.

$$
\begin{aligned}
\frac{\partial Q}{\partial \pi_k} &= \frac{\partial}{\partial \pi_k}\left[\sum_i \sum_k r_{ik} \log \pi_k + \lambda\left(1 - \sum_k \pi_k\right)\right] \\
&= \sum_i r_{ik}\frac{1}{\pi_k} - \lambda = 0
\end{aligned}
\tag{8.11}
$$

Substituting th expression into the constraint, we get the following equation.

$$
\sum_k \pi_k = 1 \implies \sum_k \frac{1}{\lambda}\sum_i r_{ik} = 1 \implies \lambda = \sum_i \sum_k r_{ik} = \sum_i 1 = N
\tag{8.12}
$$

Therefore, $\pi_k = 1/\lambda \sum r_{ik} = 1/N \sum r_{ik}$. To find the optimum parameters $\theta_k = \{\mu_k, \Sigma_k\}$, we want to optimize the terms of Q that depend on θ_k.

$$
\begin{aligned}
l(\mu_k, \Sigma_k) &= \sum_i r_{ik} \log p(x_i | \theta_k) \\
&\propto -\frac{1}{2}\sum_i r_{ik}\left[\log |\Sigma_k| + (x_i - \mu_k)^T \Sigma_k^{-1}(x_i - \mu_k)\right]
\end{aligned}
\tag{8.13}
$$

To find the optimum μ_k, we differentiate this expression. First, focusing on the second term inside the sum, we can make a substitution $y_i = x_i - \mu_k$.

$$
\begin{aligned}
\frac{\partial}{\partial \mu_k}(x_i - \mu_k)^T \Sigma_k^{-1}(x_i - \mu_k) &= \frac{\partial}{\partial y_i}y_i^T \Sigma^{-1} y_i \frac{\partial y_i}{\partial \mu_k} \\
&= -1 \times \left(\Sigma^{-1} + \Sigma^{-T}\right)y_i
\end{aligned}
\tag{8.14}
$$

Substituting the expression in equation 8.14, we get the following equation.

$$
\begin{aligned}
\frac{\partial}{\partial \mu_k}l(\mu_k, \Sigma_k) &\propto -\frac{1}{2}\sum_i r_{ik}\left[-2\Sigma^{-1}(x_i - \mu_k)\right] \\
&= \Sigma^{-1}\sum_i r_{ik}(x_i - \mu_k) = 0
\end{aligned}
\tag{8.15}
$$

This implies the following equation.

$$\sum_i r_{ik}(x_i - \mu_k) = 0 \implies \mu_k = \frac{\sum_i r_{ik}x_i}{\sum_i r_{ik}} \tag{8.16}$$

To compute optimum Σ_k, we can use the trace identity.

$$x^T A x = \mathrm{tr}\left(x^T A x\right) = \mathrm{tr}\left(xx^T A\right) = \mathrm{tr}\left(Axx^T\right) \tag{8.17}$$

Using $\lambda = \Sigma - 1$ notation, we have the following.

$$\begin{aligned} l(\Lambda) \quad &\propto \quad -\frac{1}{2}\sum_i r_{ik}\log|\Lambda| - \frac{1}{2}\sum_i r_{ik}\mathrm{tr}\left[(x_i - \mu)(x_i - \mu)^T\Lambda\right] \\ &= \quad -\frac{1}{2}\sum_i r_{ik}\log|\Lambda| - \frac{1}{2}\mathrm{tr}(S_\mu\Lambda) \end{aligned} \tag{8.18}$$

Taking the matrix derivative, we get the following equation.

$$\begin{aligned} \frac{\partial l(\Lambda)}{\partial \Lambda} &= -\frac{1}{2}\sum_i r_{ik}\Lambda^{-T} - \frac{1}{2}S_\mu^T = 0 \\ \Lambda^{-1}\sum_i r_{ik} &= S_\mu^T \implies \Sigma = \frac{S_\mu^T}{\sum_i r_{ik}} \\ \Sigma &= \frac{\sum_i r_{ik}(x_i - \mu_k)(x_i - \mu_k)^T}{\sum_i r_{ik}} = \frac{\sum_i r_{ik}x_i x_i^T}{\sum_i r_{ik}} - \mu_k\mu_k^T \end{aligned} \tag{8.19}$$

These equations make intuitive sense; the mean of cluster k is weighted by r_{ik} average of all points assigned to cluster k, while the covariance is the weighted empirical scatter matrix. We are now ready to implement the EM algorithm for GMM from scratch! Let's start by looking at the pseudo-code in figure 8.3.

The GMM class consists of three main functions: gmm_em, estep, and mstep. In gmm_em, we initialize the means using the K-means algorithm and initialize covariances as identity matrices. Next, we iterate between the estep that computes responsibilities (aka soft assignments) of data point i to each of the k clusters and the mstep that takes the responsibilities as input and computes model parameters: mean, covariance, and mixture proportions for each cluster in the Gaussian mixture model (GMM). The code in the estep and mstep functions follows the derivations in the text. In the following code

```
1: class GMM
2: function gmm_em(X, k):
```
3: $\pi_{init} = \frac{1}{K}$
4: $\mu_{init} = $ KMeans(X, k) ← **Initializes with K-means**
5: $\Sigma_{init} = I_{d \times d}$
6: **for** iter = 1, 2, . . . , max_iter
7:     $r_{ik} = $ estep$(\pi_k, \mu_k, \Sigma_k, X)$ ← **Computes responsibilities**
8:     $\pi_k, \mu_k, \Sigma_k = $ mstep(r_{ik}, X) ← **Computes model parameters**
9: **end for**
10: **return** π_k, μ_k, Σ_k
11: **function** estep$(\pi_k, \mu_k, \Sigma_k, X)$:
12: $r_{ik} = \frac{N(x_i | \mu_k, \Sigma_k) \pi_k}{\sum_{k=1}^{K} N(x_i | \mu_k, \Sigma_k) \pi_k}$
13: **return** r_{ik}
14: **function** mstep(r_{ik}, X):
15: $\pi_k = \frac{1}{N} \sum_i r_{ik}$
16: $\mu_k = \frac{\sum_i r_{ik} x_i}{\sum_i r_{ik}}$
17: $\Sigma_k = \frac{\sum_i r_{ik} x_i x_i^T}{\sum_i r_{ik}} - \mu_k \mu_k^T$
18: **return** π_k, μ_k, Σ_k

Figure 8.3 **EM algorithm for Gaussian mixture model pseudo-code**

listing, we will use a synthetic dataset to compare our ground truth GMM parameters with the parameters inferred by the EM algorithm.

Listing 8.2   Expectation maximization for Gaussian mixture models

```python
import numpy as np
import matplotlib.pyplot as plt
import matplotlib as mpl

from sklearn.cluster import KMeans
from scipy.stats import multivariate_normal
from scipy.special import logsumexp
from scipy import linalg

np.random.seed(3)

class GMM:

    def __init__(self, n=1e3, d=2, K=4):    Number of
        self.n = int(n)              ◄──────┘ data points
        self.d = d          ◄──┐
        self.K = K             └── Data dimension
Number of ┌──► 
clusters  │
        self.X = np.zeros((self.n, self.d))

        self.mu = np.zeros((self.d, self.K))
        self.sigma = np.zeros((self.d, self.d, self.K))
        self.pik = np.ones(self.K)/K

    def generate_data(self):  ◄──── GMM generative model
```

```
    alpha0 = np.ones(self.K)
    pi = np.random.dirichlet(alpha0)

    #ground truth mu and sigma
    mu0 = np.random.randint(0, 10, size=(self.d, self.K)) -
    ➥ 5*np.ones((self.d, self.K))
    V0 = np.zeros((self.d, self.d, self.K))
    for k in range(self.K):
        eigen_mean = 0
        Q = np.random.normal(loc=0, scale=1, size=(self.d, self.d))
        D = np.diag(abs(eigen_mean + np.random.normal(loc=0, scale=1,
        ➥ size=self.d)))
        V0[:,:,k] = abs(np.transpose(Q)*D*Q)

    #sample data
    for i in range(self.n):
        z = np.random.multinomial(1,pi)
        k = np.nonzero(z)[0][0]
        self.X[i,:] = np.random.multivariate_normal(mean=mu0[:,k],
        ➥ cov=V0[:,:,k], size=1)

    plt.figure()
    plt.scatter(self.X[:,0], self.X[:,1], color='b', alpha=0.5)
    plt.title("Ground Truth Data"); plt.xlabel("X1"); plt.ylabel("X2")
    plt.show()

    return mu0, V0

def gmm_em(self):

    kmeans = KMeans(n_clusters=self.K,
    ➥ random_state=42).fit(self.X)            ◁──── Init mu with k-means
    self.mu = np.transpose(kmeans.cluster_centers_)

    #init sigma
    for k in range(self.K):
        self.sigma[:,:,k] = np.eye(self.d)

    #EM algorithm
    max_iter = 10
    tol = 1e-5
    obj = np.zeros(max_iter)
    for iter in range(max_iter):
        print("EM iter ", iter)
        #E-step
        resp, llh = self.estep()      ◁──── E step
        #M-step
        self.mstep(resp)   ◁──── M step
        #check convergence
        obj[iter] = llh
        if (iter > 1 and obj[iter] - obj[iter-1] < tol*abs(obj[iter])):
            break
        #end if
    #end for
    plt.figure()
```

```
        plt.plot(obj)
        plt.title('EM-GMM objective'); plt.xlabel("iter");
        ➡ plt.ylabel("log-likelihood")
        plt.show()

    def estep(self):

        log_r = np.zeros((self.n, self.K))
        for k in range(self.K):
            log_r[:,k] = multivariate_normal.logpdf(self.X,
            ➡ mean=self.mu[:,k], cov=self.sigma[:,:,k])
        #end for
        log_r = log_r + np.log(self.pik)
        L = logsumexp(log_r, axis=1)
        llh = np.sum(L)/self.n  #log likelihood
        log_r = log_r - L.reshape(-1,1) #normalize
        resp = np.exp(log_r)
        return resp, llh

    def mstep(self, resp):

        nk = np.sum(resp, axis=0)
        self.pik = nk/self.n
        sqrt_resp = np.sqrt(resp)
        for k in range(self.K):
            #update mu
            rx = np.multiply(resp[:,k].reshape(-1,1), self.X)
            self.mu[:,k] = np.sum(rx, axis=0) / nk[k]

            #update sigma
            Xm = self.X - self.mu[:,k]
            Xm = np.multiply(sqrt_resp[:,k].reshape(-1,1), Xm)
            self.sigma[:,:,k] = np.maximum(0, np.dot(np.transpose(Xm), Xm)
            ➡ / nk[k] + 1e-5 * np.eye(self.d))
        #end for

if __name__ == '__main__':

    gmm = GMM()
    mu0, V0 = gmm.generate_data()
    gmm.gmm_em()


    for k in range(mu0.shape[1]):
        print("cluster ", k)
        print("-----------")
        print("ground truth means:")
        print(mu0[:,k])
        print("ground truth covariance:")
        print(V0[:,:,k])
    #end for

    for k in range(mu0.shape[1]):
        print("cluster ", k)
        print("-----------")
```

```
    print("GMM-EM means:")
    print(gmm.mu[:,k])
    print("GMM-EM covariance:")
    print(gmm.sigma[:,:,k])

  plt.figure()
ax = plt.axes()
plt.scatter(gmm.X[:,0], gmm.X[:,1], color='b', alpha=0.5)

for k in range(mu0.shape[1]):

    v, w = linalg.eigh(gmm.sigma[:,:,k])
    v = 2.0 * np.sqrt(2.0) * np.sqrt(v)
    u = w[0] / linalg.norm(w[0])

    # plot an ellipse to show the Gaussian component
    angle = np.arctan(u[1] / u[0])
    angle = 180.0 * angle / np.pi  # convert to degrees
    ell = mpl.patches.Ellipse(gmm.mu[:,k], v[0], v[1], 180.0 + angle,
    ➥ color='r', alpha=0.5)
    ax.add_patch(ell)

    # plot cluster centroids
    plt.scatter(gmm.mu[0,k], gmm.mu[1,k], s=80, marker='x', color='k',
    ➥ alpha=1)
plt.title("Gaussian Mixture Model"); plt.xlabel("X1"); plt.ylabel("X2")
    plt.show()
```

As we can see from the output, the cluster means and covariances match closely to the ground truth.

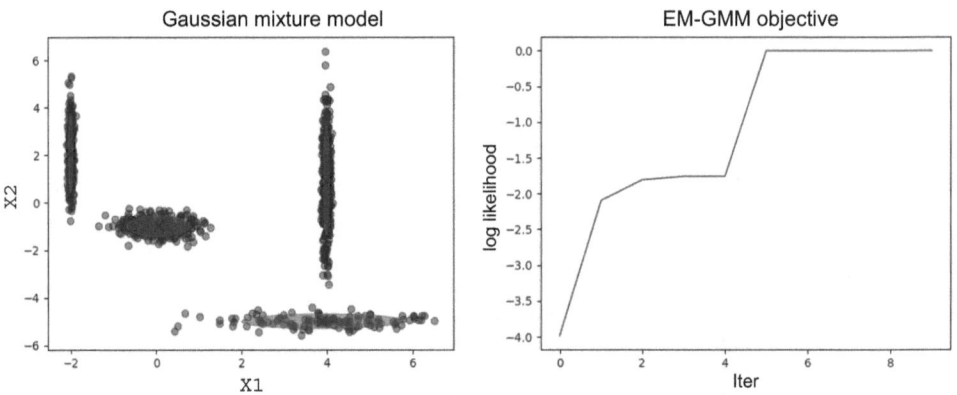

Figure 8.4   EM-GMM clustering results (left) and log likelihood objective function (right)

Figure 8.4 (left) shows the inferred Gaussian mixture overlayed with the data. We see that the Gaussian ellipses closely fit the data. This can also be confirmed by a monotonic increase of the log likelihood objective in figure 8.4 (right). In the next section, we will explore two popular dimensionality reduction techniques: principal component analysis and T-distributed stochastic neighbor embedding.

8.3   Dimensionality reduction

It is often useful to project high-dimensional data $x \in R^D$ onto lower-dimensional subspace $z \in R^L$ in a way that preserves the unique characteristics of the data. In other words, it is desirable to capture the essence of the data in the low dimensional projection. For example, if you were to train word embeddings on the Wikipedia corpus and you were trying to understand the relationships between different word vectors, it would be much easier to visualize the relationships in two dimensions by means of dimensionality reduction. In this section, we will examine two ML techniques for dimensionality reduction: principal component analysis (PCA) and t-SNE.

8.3.1   Principal component analysis

In principal component analysis (PCA), we would like to project our data vector $x \in R^D$ onto a lower dimensional vector $z \in R^L$ with $L < D$ such that the variance of the projected data is maximized. Maximizing the variance of the projected data is the core principle of PCA, and it allows us to preserve the unique characteristics of our data. We can measure the quality of our projection as a reconstruction error.

$$E = \frac{1}{N} \sum_{i=1}^{N} ||x_i - \hat{x}_i||^2 = ||X - WZ||_F^2 \qquad (8.20)$$

Here, $\hat{x}_i$ of size $D \times 1$ is the reconstructed vector lifted to the higher dimensional space, z_i of size $L \times 1$ is the lower dimensional principal component vector, and W is an orthonormal matrix of size $D \times L$. Recall that an orthonormal matrix is a real square matrix whose transpose is equal to its inverse (i.e., $W^T W = WW^T = I$). In other words, if our PCA projection is $z_i = W^T x_i$, then $\hat{x}_i = W z_i$. We will show that the optimal projection matrix W (one that maximizes the variance of projected data) is equal to a matrix of L eigenvectors corresponding to the largest eigenvalues of the empirical covariance matrix $\hat{\Sigma} = 1/N \sum x_i x_i^T$.

We can write down the variance of the projected data as follows.

$$\frac{1}{N} \sum_{i=1}^{N} z_i^2 = \frac{1}{N} \sum_{i=1}^{N} w^T x x^T w = w^T \hat{\Sigma} w \qquad (8.21)$$

We would like to maximize this quantity subject to orthonormal constraint (i.e., $||w||^2 = 1$). We can write down the Lagrangian as follows.

$$\max J(w) = w^T \hat{\Sigma} w + \lambda \left(w^T w - 1 \right) \qquad (8.22)$$

Taking the derivative and setting it to zero gives us the following expression.

$$\frac{\partial}{\partial w} J(w) = 2\hat{\Sigma}w - 2\lambda w = 0$$

$$\hat{\Sigma}w = \lambda w \qquad (8.23)$$

Thus, the direction that maximizes the variance is the eigenvector of the covariance matrix. Left multiplying by w and using orthonormality constraint, we get $w^T \hat{\Sigma} w = \lambda$. Therefore, to maximize the variance for the first principal component, we want to choose an eigenvector that corresponds to the largest eigenvalue. We can repeat the above procedure by subtracting the first principal component from x_i, and we'll discover that $\hat{\Sigma} w^2 = \lambda w^2$. By induction, we can show that the PCA matrix *WDL* consists of L eigenvectors corresponding to the largest eigenvalues of the empirical covariance matrix $\hat{\Sigma}$. We are now ready to implement the PCA algorithm from scratch! The pseudo-code in figure 8.5 summarizes the algorithm.

1: **class PCA**
2: **function** transform(X, K):
3: Σ = covariance_matrix(X) ←**Computes the empirical covariance**
4: V, λ = eig(Σ) ←**Eigenvalue decomposition**
5: idx = argsort(λ) ←**Sorts from largest to smallest**
6: $V_{pca} = V[\text{idx}][: K]$ | **Selects the top K eigen**
7: $\lambda_{pca} = \lambda[\text{idx}][: K]$ | **vectors and eigen values**
8: $X_{pca} = XV_{pca}$ ←**Projects the data onto principal components**
9: **return** X_{pca}

Figure 8.5   Principal component analysis pseudo-code

The main function in the PCA class is called transform. We first compute the empirical covariance matrix from the high dimensional data matrix *X*. Next, we compute the eigenvalue decomposition of the covariance matrix. We sort the eigenvalues from largest to smallest and use the sorted index to select the top *K* largest eigenvalues and their corresponding eigenvectors. Finally, we compute the PCA representation of our data by multiplying the data matrix with the matrix of top *K* eigenvalues. In the following code listing, we project a random d-dimensional matrix onto two principal components.

Listing 8.3   Principal component analysis

```
import numpy as np
import matplotlib.pyplot as plt

np.random.seed(42)

class PCA():

    def __init__(self, n_components = 2):
        self.n_components = n_components

    def covariance_matrix(self, X, Y=None):
```

```
    if Y is None:
        Y = X
    n_samples = np.shape(X)[0]
    covariance_matrix = (1 / (n_samples-1)) * (X - X.mean(axis=0))
    ↪ .T.dot(Y - Y.mean(axis=0))
    return covariance_matrix

def transform(self, X):
    Sigma = self.covariance_matrix(X)
    eig_vals, eig_vecs = np.linalg.eig(Sigma)

    idx = eig_vals.argsort()[::-1]
    eig_vals = eig_vals[idx][:self.n_components]
    eig_vecs = np.atleast_1d(eig_vecs[:,idx])[:, :self.n_components]

    X_transformed = X.dot(eig_vecs)

    return X_transformed

if __name__ == "__main__":

    n = 20
    d = 5
    X = np.random.rand(n,d)

    pca = PCA(n_components=2)
    X_pca = pca.transform(X)

    print(X_pca)

    plt.figure()
    plt.scatter(X_pca[:,0], X_pca[:,1], color='b', alpha=0.5)
    plt.title("Principal Component Analysis"); plt.xlabel("X1");
    ↪ plt.ylabel("X2")
    plt.show()
```

Sorts from largest to smallest eigenvalue (annotation for `idx = eig_vals.argsort()[::-1]`)

Projects the data onto principal components (annotation for `X_transformed = X.dot(eig_vecs)`)

Figure 8.6 shows a plot of the first two principal components applied to a random matrix. Recall that in PCA, the variance of the projected data is maximized; therefore, we can discover trends and patterns in the projected data.

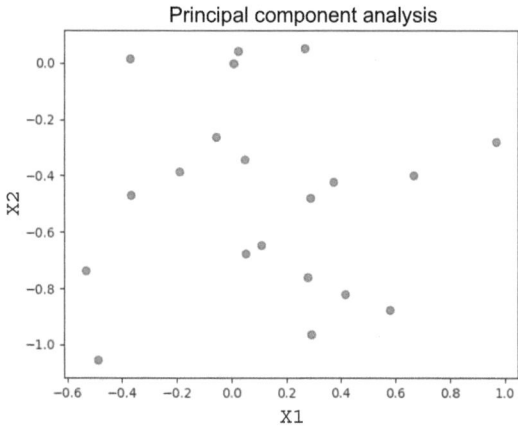

Figure 8.6 PCA projection of a random matrix

8.3.2   *t-SNE manifold learning on images*

Images are high dimensional objects that live on manifolds. A *manifold* is a topological space that locally resembles Euclidean space. By modeling image spaces as manifolds, we can study their geometric properties. We can visualize high dimensional objects with the help of an embedding. We consider two such embeddings: t-SNE and Isomap on the MNIST digits dataset.

Listing 8.4   t-SNE manifold on the MNIST digits dataset

```python
import numpy as np
import matplotlib.pyplot as plt

from time import time
from sklearn import manifold

from sklearn.datasets import load_digits
from sklearn.neighbors import KDTree

def plot_digits(X):

    n_img_per_row = np.amin((20, np.int(np.sqrt(X.shape[0]))))
    img = np.zeros((10 * n_img_per_row, 10 * n_img_per_row))
    for i in range(n_img_per_row):
        ix = 10 * i + 1
        for j in range(n_img_per_row):
            iy = 10 * j + 1
            img[ix:ix + 8, iy:iy + 8] = X[i * n_img_per_row +
            ➥ j].reshape((8, 8))

    plt.figure()
    plt.imshow(img, cmap=plt.cm.binary)
    plt.xticks([])
    plt.yticks([])
    plt.title('A selection from the 64-dimensional digits dataset')

def mnist_manifold():

    digits = load_digits()

    X = digits.data
    y = digits.target

    num_classes = np.unique(y).shape[0]

    plot_digits(X)

    #TSNE
    #Barnes-Hut: O(d NlogN) where d is dim and N is the number of samples
    #Exact: O(d N^2)
    t0 = time()
    tsne = manifold.TSNE(n_components = 2, init = 'pca', method =
    ➥ 'barnes_hut', verbose = 1)
```

```
X_tsne = tsne.fit_transform(X)
t1 = time()
print('t-SNE: %.2f sec' %(t1-t0))
tsne.get_params()

plt.figure()
for k in range(num_classes):
    plt.plot(X_tsne[y==k,0], X_tsne[y==k,1],'o')
plt.title('t-SNE embedding of digits dataset')
plt.xlabel('X1')
plt.ylabel('X2')
axes = plt.gca()
axes.set_xlim([X_tsne[:,0].min()-1,X_tsne[:,0].max()+1])
axes.set_ylim([X_tsne[:,1].min()-1,X_tsne[:,1].max()+1])
plt.show()

#ISOMAP
#1. Nearest neighbors search: O(d log k N log N)
#2. Shortest path graph search: O(N^2(k+log(N))
#3. Partial eigenvalue decomposition: O(dN^2)

t0 = time()
isomap = manifold.Isomap(n_neighbors = 5, n_components = 2)
X_isomap = isomap.fit_transform(X)
t1 = time()
print('Isomap: %.2f sec' %(t1-t0))
isomap.get_params()

plt.figure()
for k in range(num_classes):
    plt.plot(X_isomap[y==k,0], X_isomap[y==k,1], 'o', label=str(k),
    ⇨ linewidth = 2)
plt.title('Isomap embedding of the digits dataset')
plt.xlabel('X1')
plt.ylabel('X2')
plt.show()

#Use KD-tree to find k-nearest neighbors to a query image
kdt = KDTree(X_isomap)
Q = np.array([[-160, -30],[-102, 14]])
kdt_dist, kdt_idx = kdt.query(Q,k=20)
plot_digits(X[kdt_idx.ravel(),:])

if __name__ == "__main__":
    mnist_manifold()
```

Figure 8.7 shows a t-SNE embedding with 10 clusters in 2D, where each cluster corresponds to a digit from 0 to 9. We can see that without labels, we are able to discover 10 clusters that use t-SNE embedding in the two-dimensional space. Moreover, we expect adjacent clusters of digits to be similar to each other. The image on the right-hand side of figure 8.7 shows sample digits from two adjacent clusters (digit 0 and digit 6). We can visualize adjacent clusters by constructing a KD tree to find KNN to a query point.

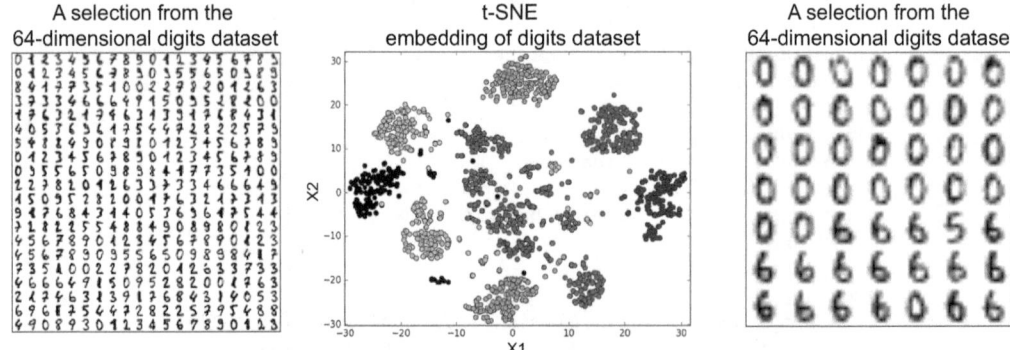

Figure 8.7   t-SNE embedding showing 10 clusters in 2D, where each cluster corresponds to a digit from 0 to 9

It's important to be aware of some of the pitfalls of t-SNE. For example, t-SNE results may vary based on the perplexity hyperparameter. The t-SNE algorithm also doesn't always produce similar outputs on successive runs and there are additional hyperparameters related to the optimization process. Moreover, the cluster sizes (as measured by standard deviation) and distances between clusters might not mean anything. Thus, the high flexibility of t-SNE also makes the results of the algorithm tricky to interpret.

8.4   Exercises

8.1 Show that the Dirichlet distribution $\mathrm{Dir}(\theta \mid \alpha)$ is a conjugate prior to the multinomial likelihood by computing the posterior. How does the shape of the posterior vary as a function of the posterior counts?

8.2 Explain the principle behind k-means++ initialization.

8.3 Prove the cyclic permutation property of the trace: $\mathrm{tr}(\mathrm{ABC}) = \mathrm{tr}(\mathrm{BCA}) = \mathrm{tr}(\mathrm{CAB})$.

8.4 Compute the runtime of the principal component analysis (PCA) algorithm.

Summary

- Unsupervised learning takes place when no training labels are available.
- The Dirichlet process K-means is a Bayesian nonparametric extension of the K-means algorithm, in which the number of clusters grows with data.
- Gaussian mixture models are commonly used to model complex density distributions. GMM parameters (means, covariances, and mixture proportions) can be inferred using the expectation maximization algorithm.
- Expectation-Maximization is an iterative algorithm that alternates between inferring the missing values given the parameters (E step) and then optimizing the parameters given filled-in data (M step).

- In dimensionality reduction, we project high dimensional data into a lower dimensional subspace in a way that preserves the unique characteristics of the data.
- In principal component analysis algorithm, the variance of the projected data is maximized.
- Common pitfalls of the t-SNE algorithm include variability of results due to the perplexity hyperparameter, dissimilar outputs on successive runs, a lack of interpretability of cluster sizes, and large distances between clusters.

Selected unsupervised learning algorithms

9

This chapter covers

- Latent Dirichlet allocation for topic discovery
- Density estimators in computational biology and finance
- Structure learning for relational data
- Simulated annealing for energy minimization
- Genetic algorithm in evolutionary biology
- ML research: unsupervised learning

In the previous chapter, we looked at unsupervised ML algorithms to help learn patterns in our data; this chapter continues that discussion, focusing on selected algorithms. The algorithms presented in this chapter have been included to cover the breadth of unsupervised learning, and they are important to learn because they cover a range of applications, from computational biology to physics to finance. We'll start by looking at latent Dirichlet allocation (LDA) for learning topic models, followed by density estimators and structure learning algorithms, and concluding with simulated annealing (SA) and genetic algorithms (GAs).

9.1 *Latent Dirichlet allocation*

A topic model is a latent variable model for discrete data, such as text documents. Latent dirichlet allocation (LDA) is a topic model that represents each document as a finite mixture of topics, where a topic is a distribution over words. The objective is to learn the shared topic distribution and topic proportions for each document. LDA assumes a bag of words model in which the words are exchangeable and, as a result, sentence structure is not preserved (i.e., only the word counts matter). Thus, each document is reduced to a vector of counts over the vocabulary v and the entire corpus of D documents is summarized in a *term-document* matrix A_{VD}. LDA can be seen as a nonnegative matrix factorization problem that takes the term-document matrix and factorizes it into a product of topics W_{VK} and topic proportions H_{KD}: $A = W_H$.

Term frequency–inverse document frequency (tf-idf) is a common method for adjusting the word counts, as it logarithmically drives down to zero word counts that occur frequently across documents: $A \log(D/n_t)$, where D is the total number of documents in the corpus and n_t is the number of documents where term t appears. The tf-idf smoothing of word counts identifies the sets of words that are discriminative for documents and leads to better model performance. The term-document matrix generalizes from counts of individual words (unigrams) to larger structural units, such as n-grams. In the case of n-grams, different techniques for smoothing word counts (e.g., Laplace smoothing) are used to address the lack of observations in a very large feature space. Figure 9.1 shows the graphical model for the LDA.

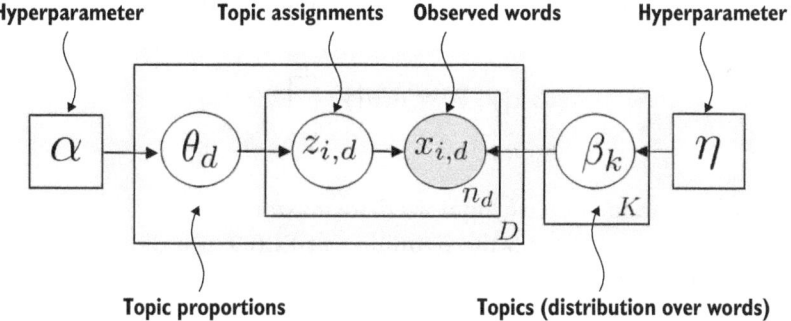

Figure 9.1 **Latent Dirichlet allocation graphical model**

The LDA topic model associates each word $x_{i,d}$ with a topic label $z_{i,d} \in \{1, 2, ..., K\}$. Each document is associated with topic proportions θ_d that could be used to measure document similarity. The topics β_k are shared across all documents. The hyperparameters α and η capture our prior knowledge of topic proportions and topics, respectively (e.g., from past online training of the model). The full generative model can be specified as follows.

$$
\begin{aligned}
\theta_d | \alpha &\sim \text{Dir}(\alpha) \\
z_{i,d} | \theta_d &\sim \text{Cat}(\theta_d) \\
\beta_k | \eta &\sim \text{Dir}(\eta) \\
x_{i,d} | z_{i,d} = k, \beta &\sim \text{Cat}(\beta_k)
\end{aligned}
\tag{9.1}
$$

The joint distribution for a single document d can be written as follows (as discussed in David M. Blei, Andrew Y. Ng, and Michael I. Jordan's "Latent Dirichlet Allocation," *Journal of Machine Learning Research*, 2003).

$$
p(x, z, \theta, |\alpha, \beta) = p(\theta_d|\alpha) \prod_{i=1}^{n_d} p(z_{i,d}|\theta_d)p(x_{i,d}|z_{i,d}, \beta)
\tag{9.2}
$$

The parameters α and β are corpus-level parameters, the variable θ_d is sampled once every document, and $z_{i,d}$ and $x_{i,d}$ are word-level variables sampled once for each word in each document. Unlike a multinomial clustering model, where each document is associated with a single topic, LDA represents each document as a mixture of topics.

9.1.1 Variational Bayes

The key inference problem we need to solve to use LDA is that of computing the posterior distribution of the latent variables for a given document: $p(\theta, z|x, \alpha, \beta)$. The posterior can be approximated with the following variational distribution.

$$
q(\theta, z|\gamma, \phi) = q(\theta|\gamma) \prod_{i=1}^{n} q(z_i|\phi_i)
\tag{9.3}
$$

The variational parameters are optimized to maximize the evidence lower bound (ELBO). Recall from chapter 3 the definition of ELBO as a difference between the energy term and the entropy term.

$$
\begin{aligned}
\log p(x|\alpha, \eta) &\geq L(x, \phi, \gamma, \lambda) \\
&= E_q[\log p(x, z, \theta, \beta|\alpha, \eta)] - E_q[\log q(z, \theta, \beta)]
\end{aligned}
\tag{9.4}
$$

We choose a fully factored distribution q of the form.

$$
q(z_{id} = k) = \phi_{dwk}; \quad q(\theta_d) \sim \text{Dir}(\theta_d|\gamma_d); \quad q(\beta_k) \sim \text{Dir}(\beta_k|\lambda_k)
\tag{9.5}
$$

We can expand the lower bound by using the factorizations of p and q (following David M. Blei, Andrew Y. Ng, and Michael I. Jordan's "Latent Dirichlet Allocation," *Journal of Machine Learning Research*, 2003) .

$$
\begin{aligned}
L(\gamma, \phi; \alpha, \beta) \;=\; & E_q[\log p(\theta|\alpha)] + E_q[\log p(z|\theta)] \\
& + E_q[\log p(x|z, \beta)] \\
& - E_q[\log q(\theta)] - E_q[\log q(z)]
\end{aligned}
\tag{9.6}
$$

Each of the five terms in $L(\gamma, \phi; \alpha, \beta)$ can be expanded as follows.

$$
\begin{aligned}
L(\gamma, \phi; \alpha, \beta) \;=\; & \log \Gamma\left(\sum_{j=1}^{k} \alpha_j\right) - \sum_{i=1}^{k} \log \Gamma(\alpha_i) \\
& + \sum_{i=1}^{k} (\alpha_i - 1)\left(\Psi(\gamma_i) - \Psi\left(\sum_{j=1}^{k} \gamma_j\right)\right) \\
& + \sum_{n=1}^{N}\sum_{i=1}^{k} \phi_{ni}\left(\Psi(\gamma_i) - \Psi\left(\sum_{j=1}^{k} \gamma_j\right)\right) \\
& + \sum_{n=1}^{N}\sum_{i=1}^{k}\sum_{j=1}^{V} \phi_{ni} x_n^{j} \log \beta_{ij} \\
& - \log \Gamma\left(\sum_{j=1}^{k} \gamma_j\right) + \sum_{i=1}^{k} \log \Gamma(\gamma_i) \\
& - \sum_{i=1}^{k} (\gamma_i - 1)\left(\Psi(\gamma_i) - \Psi\left(\sum_{j=1}^{k} \gamma_j\right)\right) \\
& - \sum_{n=1}^{N}\sum_{i=1}^{k} \phi_{ni} \log \phi_{ni}
\end{aligned}
\tag{9.7}
$$

Here, $\Psi(x) = d/dx \log \Gamma(x)$ is the digamma function. $L(\gamma, \phi; \alpha, \beta)$ can be maximized using coordinate ascent over the variational parameters ϕ, γ, α.

$$
\begin{aligned}
\phi_{dwk} &\propto \exp\{E_q[\log \theta_{dk}] + E_q[\log \beta_{kw}]\} \\
\gamma_{dk} &= \alpha + \sum_{w} n_{dw} \phi_{dwk} \\
\lambda_{kw} &= \eta + \sum_{d} n_{dw} \phi_{dwk}
\end{aligned}
\tag{9.8}
$$

Here, the expectations under q of $\log \theta$ and $\log \beta$ are as follows.

$$E_q[\log \theta_{dk}] = \Psi(\gamma_{dk}) - \Psi\left(\sum_{i=1}^{K} \gamma_{di}\right)$$

$$E_q[\log \beta_{kw}] = \Psi(\lambda_{kw}) - \Psi\left(\sum_{i=1}^{W} \lambda_{ki}\right) \tag{9.9}$$

The variational parameter updates can be used in an online setting that does not require a full pass through the entire corpus at each iteration. An online update of variational parameters enables topic analysis for very large datasets, including streaming data. Online variational Bayes (VB) for LDA is described in the algorithm in figure 9.2.

```
 1: Define ρt = (τ0 + t)⁻ᴷ
 2: Initialize λ randomly
 3: for t = 1 to ∞ do
 4:    E step:
 5:    Initialize γtk = 1
 6:    repeat
 7:       Set φtwk ∝ exp{Eq[log θtk] + Eq[log βkw]}  ←Topic assignments
 8:       Set γtk = α + Σw φtwk ntw  ←Topic proportions
 9:    until 1/K Σk |Δγtk| < ε
10:    M step:
11:    Compute λ̃kw = η + Dntw φtwk
12:    Set λ = (1 − ρt)λ + ρt λ̃
13: end for
```

Figure 9.2 LDA algorithm pseudo-code

As the t-th vector of word counts n_t is observed, we perform an E step to find locally optimal values of γ_t and ϕ_t, holding λ fixed. We then compute the $\tilde{\lambda}$ that would be optimal if our entire corpus consisted of the single document n repeated D times. We then update λ as a weighted average of its previous value and $\tilde{\lambda}$, where the weight is given by the learning parameter ρ_t for $\kappa \in (0.5, 1]$, controlling the rate at which old values of $\tilde{\lambda}$ are forgotten. We are now ready to implement variational Bayes for LDA from scratch in the following listing!

Listing 9.1 Variational Bayes for latent Dirichlet allocation

```python
import numpy as np
import matplotlib.pyplot as plt
from sklearn.datasets import fetch_20newsgroups
from sklearn.feature_extraction.text import TfidfVectorizer
from wordcloud import WordCloud
from scipy.special import digamma, gammaln
```

```
        np.random.seed(12)

        class LDA:
            def __init__(self, A, K):
                self.N = A.shape[0]     ⟵──── Word dictionary size
                self.D = A.shape[1]
                self.K = num_topics     ⟵──── Number of topics

                self.A = A      ⟵──── Term-document matrix

                #init word distribution beta
                self.eta = np.ones(self.N)
                self.beta = np.zeros((self.N, self.K))     ⟵──── NxK topic matrix
                for k in range(self.K):
                    self.beta[:,k] = np.random.dirichlet(self.eta)
                    self.beta[:,k] = self.beta[:,k] + 1e-6 #to avoid zero entries
                    self.beta[:,k] = self.beta[:,k]/np.sum(self.beta[:,k])
                #end for

                #init topic proportions theta and cluster assignments z
                self.alpha = np.ones(self.K)
                self.z = np.zeros((self.N, self.D))     ⟵──── Cluster assignments z
                for d in range(self.D):
                    theta = np.random.dirichlet(self.alpha)
                    wdn_idx = np.nonzero(self.A[:,d])[0]
                    for i in range(len(wdn_idx)):
                        z_idx = np.argmax(np.random.multinomial(1, theta))
                        self.z[wdn_idx[i],d] = z_idx  #topic id
                    #end for
                #end for

                #init variational parameters
                self.gamma = np.ones((self.D, self.K))     ⟵──── Topic proportions
                for d in range(self.D):
                    theta = np.random.dirichlet(self.alpha)
                    self.gamma[d,:] = theta
                #end for

                self.lmbda = np.transpose(self.beta)
            ⟹  #np.ones((self.K, self.N))/self.N     ⟵──── Word frequencies

                self.phi = np.zeros((self.D, self.N, self.K))     ⟵──── Assignments
                for d in range(self.D):
                    for w in range(self.N):
                        theta = np.random.dirichlet(self.alpha)
                        self.phi[d,w,:] = np.random.multinomial(1, theta)
                    #end for
                #end for

            def variational_inference(self, var_iter=10):

                llh = np.zeros(var_iter)
                llh_delta = np.zeros(var_iter)
```

Number of documents ┌─▷ (points to `self.D = A.shape[1]`)

Word dictionary size (points to `self.N = A.shape[0]`)

Uniform Dirichlet prior on words ┌─▷ (points to `self.eta = np.ones(self.N)`)

Uniform Dirichlet prior on topics ┌─▷ (points to `self.alpha = np.ones(self.K)`)

```
    for iter in range(var_iter):
        print("VI iter: ", iter)
        J_old = self.elbo_objective()
        self.mean_field_update()
        J_new = self.elbo_objective()

        llh[iter] = J_old
        llh_delta[iter] = J_new - J_old
    #end for

    #update alpha and beta
    for k in range(self.K):
        self.alpha[k] = np.sum(self.gamma[:,k])
        self.beta[:,k] = self.lmbda[k,:] / np.sum(self.lmbda[k,:])
    #end for

    #update topic assignments
    for d in range(self.D):
        wdn_idx = np.nonzero(self.A[:,d])[0]
        for i in range(len(wdn_idx)):
            z_idx = np.argmax(self.phi[d,wdn_idx[i],:])
            self.z[wdn_idx[i],d] = z_idx   #topic id
        #end for
    #end for

    plt.figure()
    plt.plot(llh); plt.title('LDA VI');
    plt.xlabel('mean field iterations'); plt.ylabel("ELBO")
    plt.show()

    return llh

def mean_field_update(self):

    ndw = np.zeros((self.D, self.N))        Word counts for
    for d in range(self.D):                 each document
        doc = self.A[:,d]
        wdn_idx = np.nonzero(doc)[0]

        for i in range(len(wdn_idx)):
            ndw[d,wdn_idx[i]] += 1
        #end for

        #update gamma
        for k in range(self.K):
            self.gamma[d,k] = self.alpha[k] + np.dot(ndw[d,:],
              self.phi[d,:,k])
        #end for

        #update phi
        for w in range(len(wdn_idx)):
            self.phi[d,wdn_idx[w],:] = np.exp(digamma(self.gamma[d,:])
 - digamma(np.sum(self.gamma[d,:])) + digamma(self.lmbda[:,wdn_idx[w]])
 - digamma(np.sum(self.lmbda, axis=1)))
            if (np.sum(self.phi[d,wdn_idx[w],:]) > 0): #to avoid 0/0
```

```
                self.phi[d,wdn_idx[w],:] = self.phi[d,wdn_idx[w],:] /
                ⮕ np.sum(self.phi[d,wdn_idx[w],:]) #normalize phi
            #end if
        #end for

    #end for

    #update lambda given ndw for all docs
    for k in range(self.K):
        self.lmbda[k,:] = self.eta
        for d in range(self.D):
            self.lmbda[k,:] += np.multiply(ndw[d,:], self.phi[d,:,k])
        #end for
    #end for

def elbo_objective(self):
    #see Blei 2003

    T1_A = gammaln(np.sum(self.alpha)) - np.sum(gammaln(self.alpha))
    T1_B = 0
    for k in range(self.K):
        T1_B +=  np.dot(self.alpha[k]-1, digamma(self.gamma[:,k]) -
        ⮕ digamma(np.sum(self.gamma, axis=1)))
    T1 = T1_A + T1_B

    T2 = 0
    for n in range(self.N):
        for k in range(self.K):
            T2 += self.phi[:,n,k] * (digamma(self.gamma[:,k]) -
            ⮕ digamma(np.sum(self.gamma, axis=1)))

    T3 = 0
    for n in range(self.N):
        for k in range(self.K):
            T3 += self.phi[:,n,k] * np.log(self.beta[n,k])

    T4 = 0
    T4_A = -gammaln(np.sum(self.gamma, axis=1)) +
    ⮕ np.sum(gammaln(self.gamma), axis=1)
    T4_B = 0
    for k in range(self.K):
        T4_B = -(self.gamma[:,k]-1) * (digamma(self.gamma[:,k]) -
        ⮕ digamma(np.sum(self.gamma, axis=1)))
    T4 = T4_A + T4_B

    T5 = 0
    for n in range(self.N):
        for k in range(self.K):
            T5 += -np.multiply(self.phi[:,n,k], np.log(self.phi[:,n,k]
            ⮕ + 1e-6))

    T15 = T1 + T2 + T3 + T4 + T5
    J = sum(T15)/self.D  #averaged over documents
    return J
```

```
if __name__ == "__main__":

    #LDA parameters
    num_features = 1000  #vocabulary size
    num_topics = 4       #fixed for LD

    #20 newsgroups dataset
    categories = ['sci.crypt', 'comp.graphics', 'sci.space',
    ➥ 'talk.religion.misc']

    newsgroups = fetch_20newsgroups(shuffle=True, random_state=42,
    ➥ subset='train',
                remove=('headers', 'footers', 'quotes'),
                    ➥ categories=categories)

    vectorizer = TfidfVectorizer(max_features = num_features, max_df=0.95,
    ➥ min_df=2, stop_words = 'english')
    dataset = vectorizer.fit_transform(newsgroups.data)
    A = np.transpose(dataset.toarray())  #term-document matrix

    lda = LDA(A=A, K=num_topics)
    llh = lda.variational_inference(var_iter=10)
    id2word = {v:k for k,v in vectorizer.vocabulary_.items()}

    #display topics
    for k in range(num_topics):
        print("topic: ", k)
        print("----------")
        topic_words = ""
        top_words = np.argsort(lda.lmbda[k,:])[-10:]
        for i in range(len(top_words)):
            topic_words += id2word[top_words[i]] + " "
            print(id2word[top_words[i]])

        wordcloud = WordCloud(width = 800, height = 800,
                    background_color ='white',
                    min_font_size = 10).generate(topic_words)

        plt.figure()
        plt.imshow(wordcloud)
        plt.axis("off")
        plt.tight_layout(pad = 0)
        plt.show()
```

Figure 9.3 shows the increase in ELBO as the number of mean-field iterations increases. Figure 9.4 shows the inferred topic distributions visualized as word clouds.

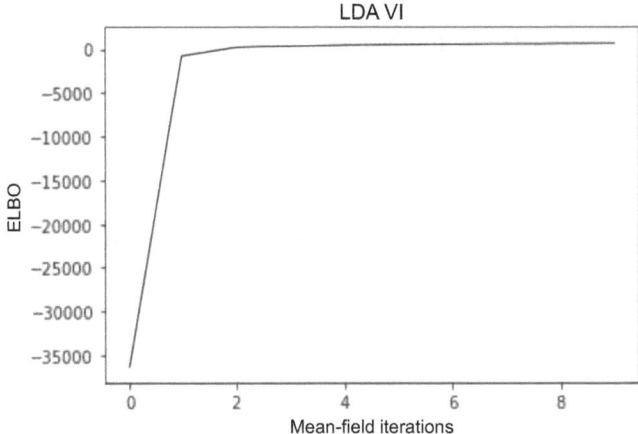

Figure 9.3 Increase in ELBO
vs. the number of mean-field
iterations

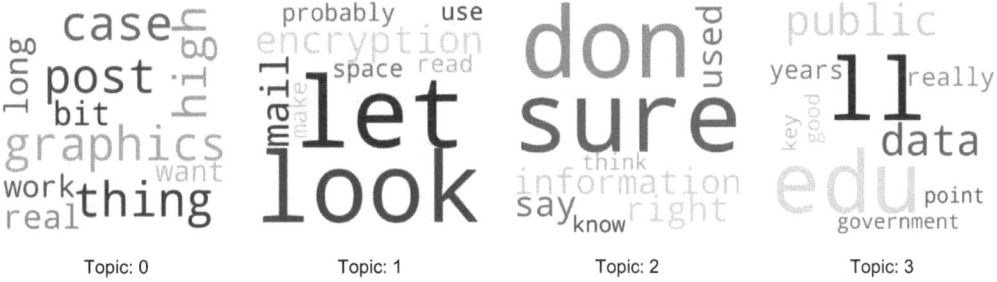

Topic: 0   Topic: 1   Topic: 2   Topic: 3

Figure 9.4 Inferred topic distributions via LDA mean-field variational inference

As we can see from the output, the top-K words for each topic match the categories in
the 20 newsgroups dataset. In the following section, we will explore several methods
to model the probability density of data for computational biology and finance.

9.2 Density estimators

The goal of *density estimation* is to model the probability density of data. In this section,
we will discuss kernel density estimators applied to computational biology and look at
how we can optimize a portfolio of stocks using tangent portfolio theory.

9.2.1 Kernel density estimator

An alternative approach to a K-component mixture model is a *kernel density estimator*
(KDE) that allocates one cluster center per data point. KDEs are an application of

kernel smoothing for probability density estimation that use kernels as weights. In the case of a Gaussian kernel, we have the following.

$$p(x|D) = \frac{1}{N} \sum_{i=1}^{N} \mathcal{N}(x|x_i, \sigma^2 I) \qquad (9.10)$$

Notice that we are averaging N Gaussians, with each Gaussian centered at the data point x_i. We can generalize the expression in equation 9.10 to any kernel $\kappa(x)$.

$$p(x|D) = \frac{1}{N} \sum_{i=1}^{N} \kappa_h(x - x_i) \qquad (9.11)$$

The advantage of KDEs over parametric models, such as density mixtures, is that no model fitting is required (except for fine-tuning the bandwidth parameter h) and there is no need to pick the number of mixtures K. The disadvantage is that the model takes a lot of memory to store as well as time to evaluate. In other words, KDE is suitable when an accurate density estimate is required for a relatively small dataset (small number of points N). Let's look at an example that analyzes RNA-seq data to estimate the flux of a T7 promoter.

Listing 9.2   Kernel density estimate

```
import numpy as np
import matplotlib.pyplot as plt

class KDE():

    def __init__(self):
        #Histogram and Gaussian Kernel Estimator used to
        #analyze RNA-seq data for flux estimation of a T7 promoter
        self.G = 1e9
        self.C = 1e3
        self.L = 100
        self.N = 1e6
        self.M = 1e4
        self.LN = 1000
        self.FDR = 0.05

        #uniform sampling (poisson model)
        self.lmbda = (self.N * self.L) / self.G
        self.C_est = self.M/(1-np.exp(-self.lmbda))
        self.C_cvrg = self.G - self.G *
          np.exp(-self.lmbda)
        self.N_gaps = self.N * np.exp(-self.lmbda)

        #gamma prior sampling (negative binomial model)
        #X = "number of failures before rth success"
```

Annotations (left):
- **Length of genome in base pairs (bp)** → `self.G = 1e9`
- **Number of unique read sequences, bp** → `self.N = 1e6`
- **False discovery rate** → `self.FDR = 0.05`

Annotations (right):
- `self.C = 1e3` ← **Number of unique molecules**
- `self.L = 100` ← **Length of a read, bp**
- `self.M = 1e4` ← **Number of reads, L bp long**
- `self.LN = 1000` ← **Total length of assembled/ mapped RNA-seq reads**
- `self.lmbda = (self.N * self.L) / self.G` ← **Expected number of bases covered**
- `self.C_est = self.M/(1-np.exp(-self.lmbda))` ← **Library size estimate**
- `self.C_cvrg = self.G - self.G * np.exp(-self.lmbda)` ← **Base coverage**
- `self.N_gaps = self.N * np.exp(-self.lmbda)` ← **Number of gaps (uncovered bases)**

Dispersion parameter (fit to data)

```
       self.k = 0.5
       self.p = self.lmbda/(self.lmbda + 1/self.k)   <——— Success probability
       self.r = 1/self.k              <—┐
                                        └── Number of successes
       #RNAP binding data (RNA-seq)
       self.data = np.random.negative_binomial(self.r, self.p, size=self.LN)

   def histogram(self):           ┌── Smoothing parameter
       self.bin_delta = 1   <——┘
       self.bin_range = np.arange(1, np.max(self.data), self.bin_delta)
       self.bin_counts, _ = np.histogram(self.data, bins=self.bin_range)

       #histogram density estimation
       #P = integral_R p(x) dx, where X is in R^3
       #p(x) = K/(NxV), where K=number of points in region R
       #N=total number of points, V=volume of region R

       rnap_density_est = self.bin_counts/(sum(self.bin_counts) *
       ⇒ self.bin_delta)
       return rnap_density_est

   def kernel(self):
       #Gaussian kernel density estimator with smoothing parameter h
       #sum N Guassians centered at each data point, parameterized by
       ⇒ common std dev h
```

Standard deviation

```
       x_dim = 1   <——— Dimension of x
       h = 10

       rnap_density_support = np.arange(np.max(self.data))
       rnap_density_est = 0
       for i in range(np.sum(self.bin_counts)):
           rnap_density_est += (1/(2*np.pi*h**2)**(x_dim/2.0))*np.exp(-
           ⇒ (rnap_density_support - self.data[i])**2 / (2.0*h**2))
       #end for

       rnap_density_est = rnap_density_est / np.sum(rnap_density_est)
       return rnap_density_est

if __name__ == "__main__":

   kde = KDE()
   est1 = kde.histogram()
   est2 = kde.kernel()

   plt.figure()
   plt.plot(est1, c='b', label='histogram')
   plt.plot(est2, c='r', label='gaussian kernel')
   plt.title("RNA-seq density estimate based on negative binomial sampling
   ⇒ model")
   plt.xlabel("read length, [base pairs]"); plt.ylabel("density");
   ⇒ plt.legend()
   plt.show()
```

Figure 9.5 shows the RNA-seq density estimate based on the negative binomial model. It shows two density estimates—one based on a histogram and the other based on Gaussian Kernel Density Estimator. We can see that the Gaussian density is much smoother and that we can further fine-tune bin size smoothing parameter in the histogram estimator.

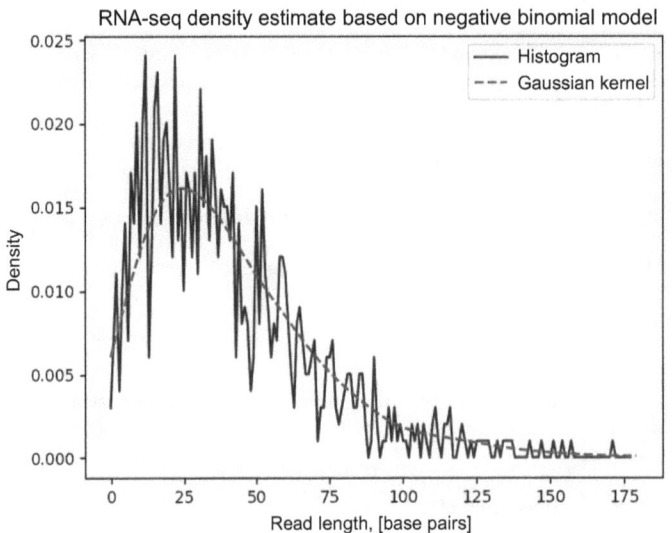

Figure 9.5 RNA-Seq density estimate via histogram and Gaussian KDE

9.2.2 *Tangent portfolio optimization*

The objective of mean-variance analysis is to maximize the expected return of a portfolio for a given level of risk, as measured by the standard deviation of past returns. By varying the mixing proportions of each asset, we can achieve different risk–return tradeoffs.

In listing 9.3, we first retrieve a data frame of closing prices for a list of stocks. We then examine stock price correlations via a scatter matrix plot. We then create a randomized portfolio and compute the portfolio risk. Next, we generate 1,000 randomly weighted portfolios and compute their value and risk. Finally, we choose the nearest neighbor portfolio weights in a way that minimizes standard deviation and maximizes portfolio value.

> **Listing 9.3 Tangent portfolio optimization**

```
import numpy as np
import pandas as pd
import matplotlib.pyplot as plt

from sklearn.neighbors import KDTree
from pandas.plotting import scatter_matrix
from scipy.spatial import ConvexHull
```

```
import pandas_datareader.data as web
from datetime import datetime
import pytz

STOCKS = ['SPY','LQD','TIP','GLD','MSFT']

np.random.seed(42)

if __name__ == "__main__":

    plt.close("all")

    #load data
    #year, month, day, hour, minute, second, microsecond
    start = datetime(2012, 1, 1, 0, 0, 0, 0, pytz.utc)
    end = datetime(2017, 1, 1, 0, 0, 0, 0, pytz.utc)

    data = pd.DataFrame()
    series = []
    for ticker in STOCKS:
        price = web.DataReader(ticker, 'stooq',
        ➥ start, end)                          ◄─────┐ Loads data
        series.append(price['Close'])                │

    data = pd.concat(series, axis=1)
    data.columns = STOCKS
    data = data.dropna()

    scatter_matrix(data, alpha=0.2, diagonal='kde')   ◄──── Plots data correlations
    plt.show()

    cash = 10000                              ◄───┐ Gets the current portfolio
    num_assets = np.size(STOCKS)              ◄───┘
    cur_value = (1e4-5e3)*np.random.rand(num_assets,1) + 5e3
    tot_value = np.sum(cur_value)
    weights = cur_value.ravel()/float(tot_value)

    Sigma = data.cov().values
    Corr = data.corr().values
    volatility = np.sqrt(np.dot(weights.T,
    ➥ np.dot(Sigma, weights)))               ◄──── Computes portfolio risk

    plt.figure()
    plt.title('Correlation Matrix')
    plt.imshow(Corr, cmap='gray')
    plt.xticks(range(len(STOCKS)),data.columns)
    plt.yticks(range(len(STOCKS)),data.columns)
    plt.colorbar()
    plt.show()
                                                      Generates random
                                                      portfolio weights
    num_trials = 1000
    W = np.random.rand(num_trials, np.size(weights))  ◄──┘
    W = W/np.sum(W,axis=1).reshape(num_trials,1)  ◄──┐ Normalizes
```

```
pv = np.zeros(num_trials)    ◄─── Portfolio value w'v
ps = np.zeros(num_trials)    ◄───┐
                                  │ Portfolio sigma: sqrt(w'Sw)
avg_price = data.mean().values
adj_price = avg_price

for i in range(num_trials):
    pv[i] = np.sum(adj_price * W[i,:])
    ps[i] = np.sqrt(np.dot(W[i,:].T, np.dot(Sigma, W[i,:])))

points = np.vstack((ps,pv)).T
hull = ConvexHull(points)

plt.figure()
plt.scatter(ps, pv, marker='o', color='b', linewidth = 3.0, label =
    'tangent portfolio')
plt.scatter(volatility, np.sum(adj_price * weights), marker = 's',
    color = 'r', linewidth = 3.0, label = 'current')
plt.plot(points[hull.vertices,0], points[hull.vertices,1], linewidth =
    2.0)
plt.title('expected return vs volatility')
plt.ylabel('expected price')
plt.xlabel('portfolio std dev')
plt.legend()
plt.grid(True)
plt.show()

#query for nearest neighbor portfolio
knn = 5
kdt = KDTree(points)
query_point = np.array([2, 115]).reshape(1,-1)
kdt_dist, kdt_idx = kdt.query(query_point,k=knn)
print("top-%d closest to query portfolios:" %knn)
print("values: ", pv[kdt_idx.ravel()])
print("sigmas: ", ps[kdt_idx.ravel()])
```

Figure 9.6 shows regression results between pairs of portfolio assets (left). Notice, for example, how SPY is uncorrelated with TIP and anticorrelated with GLD. Additionally, the diagonal densities are multimodal and show negative skewness for riskier assets (e.g., SPY versus LQD). Figure 9.6 also shows the expected return versus risk tradeoff for a set of randomly generated portfolios (right). The efficient frontier is defined by a set of portfolios at the top of the curve that corresponds to the maximum expected return for a given standard deviation. By adding a risk-free asset, we can choose a portfolio along a tangent line with the slope equal to the Sharpe ratio. In the following section, we will learn how to discover structure in relational data.

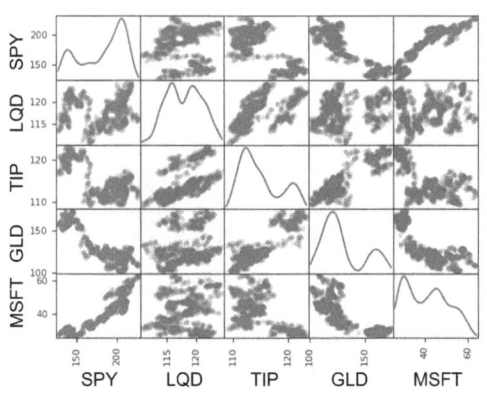 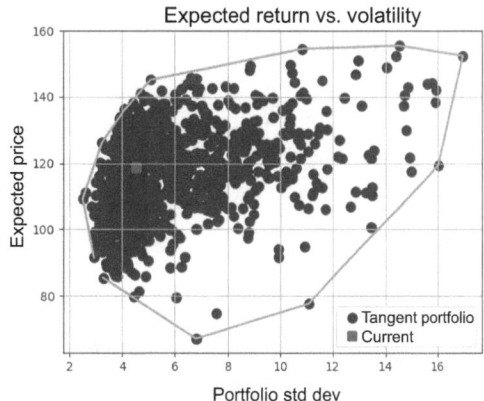

Figure 9.6   Pair plot (left) and tangent portfolio (right)

9.3   *Structure learning*

In this section, we will discover a graph's structure, given relational data. In other words, we would like to evaluate the probability of graph $G = (V, E)$, given observed data D. One challenge in inferring the graph structure is the exponential number of possible graphs. For example, in a directed graph G, we can have V choose 2 edges; since each edge has two possible directions, we have $O(2^{\wedge}V(V-1)/2)$ possible graphs. Since the problem of structure learning for general graphs is *NP*-hard, we will focus on approximate methods. Namely, we'll look at the Chow-Liu algorithm for tree-based graphs as well as inverse covariance estimation for general graphs.

9.3.1   *Chow-Liu algorithm*

We can define the joint probability model for a tree T as follows.

$$p(x|T) = \prod_{t \in V} p(x_t) \prod_{(s,t) \in E} \frac{p(x_s, x_t)}{p(x_s)p(x_t)} \tag{9.12}$$

Here, $p(x_t)$ is a node marginal and $p(x_s, x_t)$ is an edge marginal. For example, for a $|V| = 3$ node *V*-shaped undirected tree, we have the following.

$$\begin{aligned} p(x_1, x_2, x_3|T) &= p(x_1)p(x_2)p(x_3)\frac{p(x_1, x_2)p(x_2, x_3)}{p(x_1)p(x_2)p(x_2)p(x_3)} \\ &= \frac{p(x1, x2)p(x_2, x_3)}{p(x_2)} = p(x_2)p(x_1|x_2)p(x_3|x_2) \tag{9.13} \end{aligned}$$

To derive the Chow-Liu algorithm, we can use the tree decomposition in equation 9.13 to write down the likelihood.

$$
\begin{aligned}
\log P(D|\theta, T) \;=\; & \sum_t \sum_k N_{tk} \log p(x_t = k|\theta) \\
+ & \sum_{s,t} \sum_{j,k} N_{stjk} \log \frac{p(x_s = j, x_t = k|\theta)}{p(x_s = j|\theta)p(x_t = k|\theta)} \quad (9.14)
\end{aligned}
$$

Here, N_{stjk} is the number of times node s is in state j and node t is in state k and N_{tk} is the number of times node t is in state k. We can rewrite N_{tk} as $N \times p(x_t = k)$ and, similarly, N_{stjk} as $N \times p(x_s = j, x_t = k)$. If we plug this in to our expression for log likelihood, we get the following.

$$
\begin{aligned}
\frac{1}{N} \log P(D|\theta, T) \;=\; & \sum_{t \in V} \sum_k \hat{p}(x_t = k) \log \hat{p}(x_t = k) \\
+ & \sum_{(s,t) \in E} I(x_s, x_t | \hat{\theta}_{st}) \quad (9.15)
\end{aligned}
$$

Here, $I(x_s, x_t | \theta)$ is the mutual information between x_s and x_t. Therefore, the tree topology that maximizes the log likelihood can be computed via the maximum weight spanning tree, where the edge weights are pairwise mutual information $I(x_s, x_t | \theta)$. The algorithm in equation 9.15 is known as the *Chow-Liu algorithm*. Note that to compute the maximum spanning tree, we can use either Prim's algorithm or Kruskal's algorithms, which can be implemented in $O(E \log V)$ time. In the following section, we will examine how to infer the structure of a general graph based on inverse covariance estimation.

9.3.2   *Inverse covariance estimation*

Identifying stock clusters helps one discover similar companies, which can be useful for comparative analysis or a pairs trading strategy. We can find similar clusters by estimating the inverse covariance (precision) matrix that can be used to construct a graph network of dependencies, using the fact that zeros in the precision matrix correspond to the absence of edges in the constructed graph. Let's represent our unknown graph structure as a Gaussian graphical model. Let $\Lambda = \Sigma - 1$ represent the precision matrix of the multivariate normal. Then, the log likelihood of Λ can be derived as follows.

$$
l(\Lambda) = \log \det \Lambda - \mathrm{tr}[S\Lambda] \quad (9.16)
$$

Here, S is the empirical covariance matrix.

$$S = \frac{1}{N} \sum_{i=1}^{N} (x_i - \mu)(x_i - \mu)^T \tag{9.17}$$

To encourage sparse structure, we can add a penalty term for nonzero entries in the precision matrix. Thus, our graph lasso negative log likelihood objective becomes as follows.

$$\text{NLL}(\Lambda) = -\log \det \Lambda + \text{tr}[S\Lambda] + c||\Lambda||_1 \tag{9.18}$$

In listing 9.4, we'll be using the difference between opening and closing daily prices to compute empirical covariance, which is used to fit the graph lasso algorithm to estimate the sparse precision matrix. Affinity propagation is used to compute the stock clusters and a linear embedding is used to display high dimensional data in 2D.

Listing 9.4   Inverse covariance estimation

```
import numpy as np
import pandas as pd
from scipy import linalg

from datetime import datetime
import pytz

from sklearn.datasets import make_sparse_spd_matrix
from sklearn.covariance import GraphicalLassoCV, ledoit_wolf
from sklearn.preprocessing import StandardScaler
from sklearn import cluster, manifold

import seaborn as sns
import matplotlib.pyplot as plt
from matplotlib.collections import LineCollection

import pandas_datareader.data as web

np.random.seed(42)

def main():

    #generate data (synthetic)
    #num_samples = 60
    #num_features = 20
    #prec = make_sparse_spd_matrix(num_features, alpha=0.95,
    ⇒ smallest_coef=0.4, largest_coef=0.7)
    #cov = linalg.inv(prec)
    #X = np.random.multivariate_normal(np.zeros(num_features), cov,
    ⇒ size=num_samples)
```

```
#X = StandardScaler().fit_transform(X)

#generate data (actual)
STOCKS = {
    'SPY': 'S&P500',
    'LQD': 'Bond_Corp',
    'TIP': 'Bond_Treas',
    'GLD': 'Gold',
    'MSFT': 'Microsoft',
    'XOM': 'Exxon',
    'AMZN': 'Amazon',
    'BAC': 'BofA',
    'NVS': 'Novartis'}

symbols, names = np.array(list(STOCKS.items())).T

#load data
#year, month, day, hour, minute, second, microsecond
start = datetime(2015, 1, 1, 0, 0, 0, 0, pytz.utc)
end = datetime(2017, 1, 1, 0, 0, 0, 0, pytz.utc)

qopen, qclose = [], []
data_close, data_open = pd.DataFrame(), pd.DataFrame()
for ticker in symbols:
    price = web.DataReader(ticker, 'stooq', start, end)
    qopen.append(price['Open'])
    qclose.append(price['Close'])

data_open = pd.concat(qopen, axis=1)
data_open.columns = symbols
data_close = pd.concat(qclose, axis=1)
data_close.columns = symbols
```

```
variation = data_close - data_open    ←┐ Per day variation in
variation = variation.dropna()          └ price for each symbol
```

```
X = variation.values     ┐ Standardizes to use correlation
X /= X.std(axis=0)     ←─┘ rather than covariance
```

```
graph = GraphicalLassoCV()    ←┐
graph.fit(X)                    │ Estimates inverse
                                  covariance
```

```
gl_cov = graph.covariance_
gl_prec = graph.precision_
gl_alphas = graph.cv_alphas_
gl_scores = graph.cv_results_['mean_test_score']

plt.figure()
sns.heatmap(gl_prec, xticklabels=names, yticklabels=names)
plt.xticks(rotation=45)
plt.yticks(rotation=45)
plt.tight_layout()
plt.show()

plt.figure()
```

```
plt.plot(gl_alphas, gl_scores, marker='o', color='b', lw=2.0,
➥ label='GraphLassoCV')
plt.title("Graph Lasso Alpha Selection")
plt.xlabel("alpha")
plt.ylabel("score")
plt.legend()
plt.show()

_, labels = cluster.affinity_propagation(gl_cov)    ◄──┐ Clusters using
num_labels = np.max(labels)                              affinity propagation

for i in range(num_labels+1):
    print("Cluster %i: %s" %((i+1), ', '.join(names[labels==i])))

node_model = manifold.LocallyLinearEmbedding(
➥ n_components=2, n_neighbors=6, eigen_solver='dense')  ◄─┐ Finds a low
embedding = node_model.fit_transform(X.T).T                dimensional
                                                           embedding for
#generate plots                                            visualization
plt.figure()
plt.clf()
ax = plt.axes([0.,0.,1.,1.])
plt.axis('off')

partial_corr = gl_prec
d = 1 / np.sqrt(np.diag(partial_corr))
non_zero = (np.abs(np.triu(partial_corr, k=1)) >
➥ 0.02)    ◄────┐ Connectivity matrix

#plot the nodes
plt.scatter(embedding[0], embedding[1], s = 100*d**2, c = labels, cmap
➥ = plt.cm.Spectral)

#plot the edges
start_idx, end_idx = np.where(non_zero)
segments = [[embedding[:,start], embedding[:,stop]] for start, stop in
➥ zip(start_idx, end_idx)]
values = np.abs(partial_corr[non_zero])
lc = LineCollection(segments, zorder=0, cmap=plt.cm.hot_r,
➥ norm=plt.Normalize(0,0.7*values.max()))
lc.set_array(values)
lc.set_linewidths(2*values)
ax.add_collection(lc)

#plot the labels
for index, (name, label, (x,y)) in enumerate(zip(names, labels,
➥ embedding.T)):
    plt.text(x,y,name,size=12)

plt.show()

if __name__ == "__main__":
    main()
```

Figure 9.7 shows the sparse precision matrix estimated by the graph lasso algorithm.

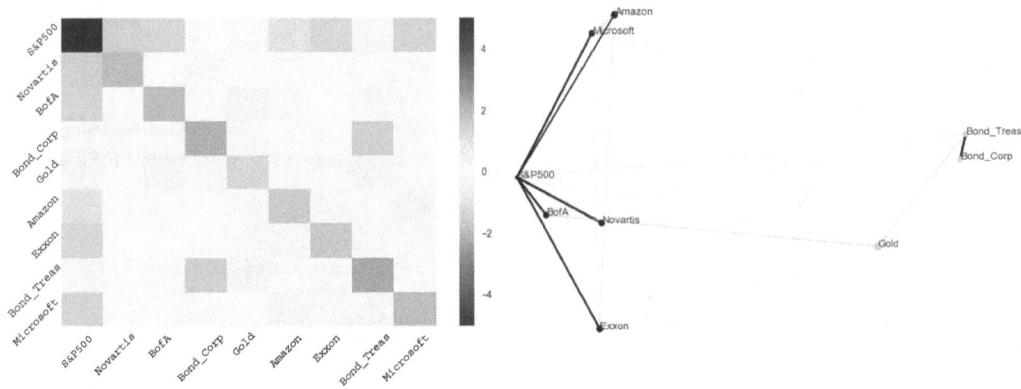

Figure 9.7   Graph lasso estimated precision matrix (left) and stock clusters (right)

The edge values in the precision matrix in figure 9.7 greater than a threshold corre-spond to connected components from which we can compute stock clusters, as visual-ized on the right-hand side of the figure. In the next section, we will learn about an energy minimization algorithm called simulated annealing.

9.4   *Simulated annealing*

Simulated annealing (SA) is a heuristic search method that allows for occasional transi-tions to less favorable states to escape local optima. We can formulate SA as an energy minimization problem with temperature parameter T as follows.

$$\alpha \;=\; \exp\left\{ \frac{E_{old} - E_{new}}{T} \right\}$$
$$p \;=\; \min(1, \alpha) \tag{9.19}$$

As we transition to a new state, we would like the energy in the new state to be lower—in which case, $\alpha > 1$ and $p = 1$—meaning we accept the state transition with the probabil-ity $p = 1$. On the other hand, if the energy of the new state is higher, this will cause $\alpha < 1$, and in that case, we accept the transition with probability $p = \alpha$. In other words, we accept unfavorable transitions with probability proportional to the difference in ener-gies between states and inversely proportional to the temperature parameter T. Ini-tially, the temperature T is high, allowing for many random transitions. As the temperature decreases (according to a cooling schedule), the difference in energy becomes more pronounced. The formulation in equation 9.19 allows simulated annealing to escape local optima. We are now ready to look at the pseudo-code in fig-ure 9.8.

```
1: class simulated_annealing
2: function run(x_init, y_init):
3: converged = False
4: T = 1
5: x_old, y_old = x_init, y_init
6: energy_old = target(x_init, y_init)
7: while not converged:
8:     x_new, y_new = proposal(x_old, y_old) ←Evaluates the proposal
9:     energy_new = target(x_new, y_new) ←Computes the energy
10:    converged = check_convergence()
11:    alpha = exp((energy_old – energy_new)/T)
12:    r = min(1, alpha) ←Transition probability
13:    u = Unif[0,1]
14:    if u < r
15:        x_old, y_old = x_new, y_new
16:        energy_old = energy_new      →Accepts the proposed state
17:    end if
18:    T = temperature_schedule()
19: end while
20: x_opt, y_opt = x_old, y_old
21: return x_opt, y_opt
```

Figure 9.8 Simulated annealing pseudo-code

The `simulated_annealing` class contains the main `run` function. We begin by initializing the annealing temperature `T` and evaluating our `target` function at the initial location. Recall that we are interested in finding a minimum point in a complex energy landscape represented by the target function. We sample from our proposal distribution to obtain a new set of coordinates and evaluate the energy of the proposed coordinates. We check for convergence to decide whether to break out of the loop or continue. Next, we compute the simulated annealing transition probability alpha as a difference between old and new energy states divided by the temperature T. In the case of $r > 1$, we accept the low energy state with a probability of 1, and in the case of $0 < r < 1$ (i.e., the energy of the new state is higher), we accept the transition with probability $r = \alpha$. Finally, we adjust the temperature according to a cooling schedule, and upon convergence, we return the optimal coordinates (those that achieve the minimum energy found by simulated annealing). We are now ready to implement the simulated annealing algorithm from scratch in the following listing.

Listing 9.5 Simulated annealing

```
import numpy as np
import matplotlib.pyplot as plt

np.random.seed(42)
```

```
class simulated_annealing():
    def __init__(self):
        self.max_iter = 1000
        self.conv_thresh = 1e-4
        self.conv_window = 10

        self.samples = np.zeros((self.max_iter, 2))
        self.energies = np.zeros(self.max_iter)
        self.temperatures = np.zeros(self.max_iter)

    def target(self, x, y):                     ⟵———— Energy landscape
        z = 3*(1-x)**2 * np.exp(-x**2 - (y+1)**2) \
            - 10*(x/5 -x**3 - y**5) * np.exp(-x**2 - y**2) \
            - (1/3)*np.exp(-(x+1)**2 - y**2)
        return z

    def proposal(self, x, y):
        mean = np.array([x, y])
        cov =  1.1 * np.eye(2)
        x_new, y_new = np.random.multivariate_normal(mean, cov)
        return x_new, y_new

    def temperature_schedule(self, T, iter):
        return 0.9 * T

    def run(self, x_init, y_init):

        converged = False
        T = 1
        self.temperatures[0] = T
        num_accepted = 0
        x_old, y_old = x_init, y_init
        energy_old = self.target(x_init, y_init)

        iter = 1
        while not converged:
            print("iter: {:4d}, temp: {:.4f}, energy = {:.6f}".format(iter,
            ➥ T, energy_old))
            x_new, y_new = self.proposal(x_old, y_old)
            energy_new = self.target(x_new, y_new)

            if iter > 2*self.conv_window:           ⟵———— Checks the convergence
                vals = self.energies[iter-self.conv_window : iter-1]
                if (np.std(vals) < self.conv_thresh):
                    converged = True
                #end if
            #end if

            alpha = np.exp((energy_old - energy_new)/T)
            r = np.minimum(1, alpha)
            u = np.random.uniform(0, 1)
            if u < r:
                x_old, y_old = x_new, y_new
                num_accepted += 1
```

```
            energy_old = energy_new
        #end if
        self.samples[iter, :] = np.array([x_old, y_old])
        self.energies[iter] = energy_old

        T = self.temperature_schedule(T, iter)
        self.temperatures[iter] = T

        iter = iter + 1

        if (iter > self.max_iter): converged = True
    #end while

    niter = iter - 1
    acceptance_rate = num_accepted / niter
    print("acceptance rate: ", acceptance_rate)

    x_opt, y_opt = x_old, y_old

    return x_opt, y_opt, self.samples[:niter,:], self.energies[:niter],
    ⇒ self.temperatures[:niter]

if __name__ == "__main__":

    SA = simulated_annealing()

    nx, ny = (1000, 1000)
    x = np.linspace(-2, 2, nx)
    y = np.linspace(-2, 2, ny)
    xv, yv = np.meshgrid(x, y)

    z = SA.target(xv, yv)
    plt.figure()
    plt.contourf(x, y, z)
    plt.title("energy landscape")
    plt.show()

    #find global minimum by exhaustive search
    min_search = np.min(z)
    argmin_search = np.argwhere(z == min_search)
    xmin, ymin = argmin_search[0][0], argmin_search[0][1]
    print("global minimum (exhaustive search): ", min_search)
    print("located at (x, y): ", x[xmin], y[ymin])

    #find global minimum by simulated annealing
    x_init, y_init = 0, 0
    x_opt, y_opt, samples, energies, temperatures = SA.run(x_init, y_init)
    print("global minimum (simulated annealing): ", energies[-1])
    print("located at (x, y): ", x_opt, y_opt)

    plt.figure()
    plt.plot(energies)
    plt.title("SA sampled energies")
    plt.show()
```

```
plt.figure()
plt.plot(temperatures)
plt.title("Temperature Schedule")
plt.show()
```

Figure 9.9 shows the target energy landscape (left) and SA sampled energies (right).

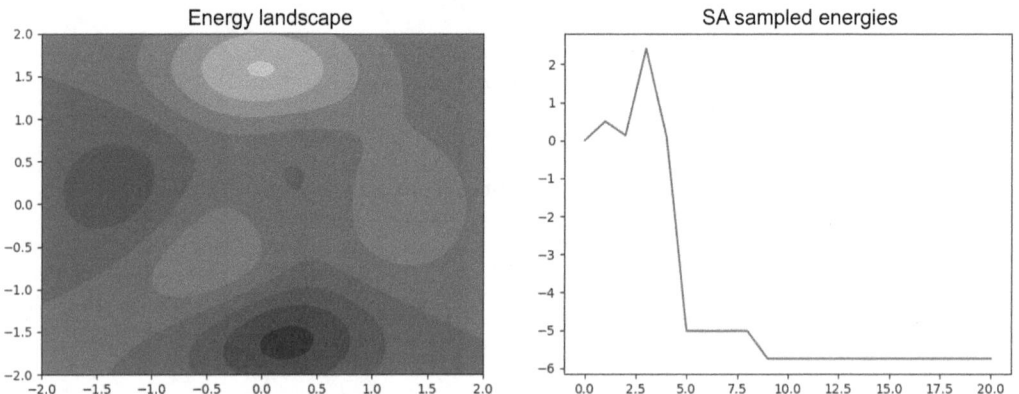

Figure 9.9   Energy landscape (left) and SA sampled energies (right)

In the example in figure 9.9, we were able to find the global minimum of an energy landscape using simulated annealing that matches the global minimum by exhaustive search. In the following section, we will study a genetic algorithm inspired by evolutionary biology.

9.5   Genetic algorithm

Genetic algorithms (GAs) are inspired by and modeled after evolutionary biology. They consists of a population of (randomly initialized) individual genomes that are evaluated for their fitness with respect to a target. Two individuals combine and cross over their genome to produce offspring. This crossover step is followed by a mutation, by which individual bases can change according to a mutation rate. These new individuals are added to the population and scored by the fitness function, which determines whether the individual survives in the population. Let's look at the pseudo-code in figure 9.10. In this example, we will evolve a random string to match a string target.

The GeneticAlgorithm class consists of the following functions: calculate_fitness, mutate, crossover, and run. In the calculate_fitness function, we compute the fitness score as 1/loss, where loss is defined as a distance between individual and target ASCII string characters. In the mutate function, we randomly change string characters of an individual according to a mutation rate. In the crossover function, we choose an index at which to cross the parents' genomes at random and then carry out the crossover of the parents' genomes at the chosen index producing two children. Finally, in the run function, we initialize the population and compute population fitness. After

```
 1: class GeneticAlgorithm
 2: function calculate_fitness(population, target):
 3: for individual in population:
 4:     compute loss as a distance between individual and target
 5:     compute fitness = 1 / (loss + epsilon)
 6: end for
 7: return population_fitness
 8: function mutate(individual, mutation_rate):
 9: randomly change characters with probability equal to mutation_rate
10: return new_individual
11: function crossover(parent1, parent2):
12: cross_idx = random_integer(0, len(parent1))
13: child1 = parent1[:cross_idx] + parent2[cross_idx:]
14: child2 = parent2[:cross_idx] + parent1[cross_idx:]
15: return child1, child2
16: function run(target, population_size, mutation_rate):
17: init_population()
18: for epoch in num_iter:
19:     population_fitness = calculate_fitness(population, target)
20:     fittest_individual = population(argmax(population_fitness))
21:     if fittest_individual == target
22:         return fittest_individual
23:     end if
24:     parent_probabilities = fitness / sum(population_fitness)
25:     new_population = []
26:     for i in population_size:
27:         parent1, parent2 = random_choice(population, p= parent_probabilities)
28:         child1, child2 = crossover(parent1, parent2)
29:         new_population += [mutate(child1), mutate(child2)]
30:     end for
31: end for
```

Figure 9.10   Genetic algorithm pseudo-code

that, we find the fittest individual in the population and compare it with the target. If the two match, we exit the algorithm and return the fittest individual. Otherwise, we select two parents according to parent probabilities, ranked by fitness; crossover to produce offspring; mutate each offspring; and then add the offspring back to the new population. We repeat this process a fixed number of times or until the target is found. Let's now look at genetic algorithm implementation in detail.

Listing 9.6   Genetic algorithm implmentation

```python
import numpy as np
import string

class GeneticAlgorithm():

    def __init__(self, target_string, population_size, mutation_rate):
```

```
        self.target = target_string
        self.population_size = population_size
        self.mutation_rate = mutation_rate
        self.letters = [" "] + list(string.ascii_letters)

    def initialize(self):        ◄───┤ Init population with
        self.population = []            random strings
        for _ in range(self.population_size):
            individual = "".join(np.random.choice(self.letters,
            ➡ size=len(self.target)))
            self.population.append(individual)

    def calculate_fitness(self):    ◄───┤ Calculates the fitness of each
        population_fitness = []             individual in the population
        for individual in self.population:
         ┌─► loss = 0
         │  for i in range(len(individual)):
         │      letter_i1 = self.letters.index(individual[i])
         │      letter_i2 = self.letters.index(self.target[i])
         │      loss += abs(letter_i1 - letter_i2)
         │  fitness = 1 / (loss + 1e-6)
         │  population_fitness.append(fitness)
        return population_fitness

    def mutate(self, individual):    ◄───┤ Randomly changes characters with a
        individual = list(individual)       probability equal to the mutation rate
        for j in range(len(individual)):
            if np.random.random() < self.mutation_rate:
                individual[j] = np.random.choice(self.letters)
        return "".join(individual)

    def crossover(self, parent1, parent2):    ◄───┤ Creates children from
        cross_i = np.random.randint(0, len(parent1))    parents by crossover
        child1 = parent1[:cross_i] + parent2[cross_i:]
        child2 = parent2[:cross_i] + parent1[cross_i:]
        return child1, child2

    def run(self, iterations):
        self.initialize()

        for epoch in range(iterations):
            population_fitness = self.calculate_fitness()

            fittest_individual =
            ➡ self.population[np.argmax(population_fitness)]
            highest_fitness = max(population_fitness)
            if fittest_individual == self.target:
                break
            parent_probabilities = [fitness / sum(population_fitness) for
            ➡ fitness in population_fitness]
            new_population = []        ◄──── Next generation
            for i in np.arange(0, self.population_size, 2):
                parent1, parent2 = np.random.choice(self.population,
                ➡ size=2, p=parent_probabilities, replace=False) ◄───┤
                child1, child2 = self.crossover(parent1, parent2)
```

Calculates the loss as the distance between characters → (points to `loss = 0` block)

Selects parents proportional to their fitness → (points to `parent_probabilities` line)

Crossover to produce offspring → (points to `child1, child2 = self.crossover` line)

Selects two parents → (points to `np.random.choice(self.population` line)

Keeps mutated offspring for the next generation

```
      ⌐→  new_population += [self.mutate(child1), self.mutate(child2)]
          print("iter %d, closest candidate: %s, fitness: %.4f" %(epoch,
          ⟜ fittest_individual, highest_fitness))
          self.population = new_population

          print("iter %d, final candidate: %s" %(epoch, fittest_individual))

if __name__ == "__main__":

    target_string = "Genome"
    population_size = 50
    mutation_rate = 0.1

    ga = GeneticAlgorithm(target_string, population_size, mutation_rate)
    ga.run(iterations = 1000)
```

As we can see from the output, we were able to produce the target sequence `"Genome"` by evolving randomly initialized letter sequences. In the next section, we will expand on the topics we've learned by reviewing the research literature on unsupervised learning.

9.6 *ML research: Unsupervised learning*

In this section, we cover additional insights and research related to the topics presented in this chapter. We had our first encounter with a Bayesian nonparametric model in the form of Dirichlet process *K*-means. The number of parameters in such models increases with data, and therefore, Bayesian nonparametric models are better able to model real-world scenarios. *DP*-means can be seen as a small variance asymptotics (SVA) approximation of the Dirichlet process mixture model. One of the main advantages of Bayesian nonparametric models is that they can be used for modeling infinite mixtures and hierarchical extensions can be utilized for sharing clusters across multiple data groups.

We looked at the EM algorithm, which is a powerful optimization framework used widely in machine learning. There are several extensions to the EM algorithm, such as online EM, which deals with online or streaming datasets; annealed EM, which uses the temperature parameter to smooth the energy landscape during optimization to track the global optimum; variational EM, which replaces exact inference in the E step with variational inference; Monte Carlo EM, which draws samples in the E step from the intractable distribution; and several others.

We looked at two ways to reduce dimensionality for the purpose of feature selection or data visualization. There are several other ways to learn the underlying data manifold, such as Isomap, which is an extension of Kernel PCA that seeks to maintain geodesic distances between all points; locally linear embedding (LLE), which can be thought of as a series of local PCA globally compared to find the best nonlinear embedding; spectral embedding based on the decomposition of the graph Laplacian; and multidimensional scaling (MDS) in which the distances in the embedding reflect the distances in the original high dimensional space well. Note that some of these methods can be combined, such as PCA, which can be used to preprocess the data and initialize t-SNE to reduce the computational complexity.

We looked at a powerful way to discover topics in text documents using the variational Bayes algorithm for latent Dirichlet allocation, for which there are several extensions as well. For example, the correlated topic model captures correlations between topics, the dynamic topic model tracks the evolution of topics over time, and the supervised LDA model can be used to grade or assign scores to documents to evaluate their quality.

We looked at the problem of density estimation using kernels and discovered the effect of the smoothing parameter on the resulting estimate. We can implement KDE more efficiently by using ball tree or KD tree to reduce the time complexity required to query the data.

Regarding structure learning, we discovered the exponential number of possible graph topologies and touched on the topic of causality. We looked at how we could construct simpler tree graphs using mutual information between nodes as edge weights in the maximum weight spanning tree. We also saw how regularizing the inverse covariance matrix for general graphs led to more interpretable topologies with fewer edges in the inferred graph.

Finally, we looked at two unsupervised algorithms inspired by statistical physics (simulated annealing) and evolutionary biology (the genetic algorithm). We saw how by using the temperature parameter and a cooling schedule, we can modify the energy landscape and how selecting unfavorable in the short-term moves can lead to better long-term optima. There are many NP-hard problems that can be approximated with simulated annealing, including the traveling salesman problem (TSP). We can often use several restarts and different initialization points to arrive at better optima. Genetic algorithms, on the other hand, although satisfying in their parallelism with nature, can take a long time to converge. However, they can lead to several interesting applications, such as neural network architecture search.

9.7   Exercises

9.1 Explain how latent Dirichlet allocation can be interpreted as nonnegative matrix factorization.

9.2 Explain why sparsity is desirable in inferring general graph structure.

9.3 List several NP-hard problems that can be approximated with the simulated annealing algorithm.

9.4 Brainstorm problems that can be efficiently solved by applying a genetic algorithm.

Summary

- Latent Dirichlet allocation (LDA) is a topic model that represents each document as a finite mixture of topics, where a topic is a distribution over words. The objective is to learn the shared topic distribution and topic proportions for each document.

- A common method for adjusting the word counts is tf-idf that logarithmically drives down to zero word counts that occur frequently across documents: $A \log (D / n_t)$, where D is the total number of documents in the corpus and n_t is the number of documents in which the term t appears.

- The goal of density estimation is to model the probability density of data. Kernel density estimation (KDE) allocates one cluster center per data point.

- The objective of mean-variance analysis is to maximize the expected return of a portfolio for a given level of risk, as measured by the standard deviation of past returns.

- Since the problem of structure learning for general graphs is NP-hard, we focused on approximate methods. Namely, we looked at the Chow-Liu algorithm for tree-based graphs as well as inverse covariance estimation for general graphs.

- Simulated annealing (SA) is a heuristic search method that allows for occasional transitions to less favorable states to escape local optima.

- We can formulate simulated annealing as an energy minimization problem with temperature parameter T, with which we can modify the energy landscape and select moves that are unfavorable in the short term but can lead to better long-term optima.

- Genetic algorithms (GA) are inspired by and modeled after evolutionary biology. They consist of a population of (randomly initialized) individual genomes that are evaluated for their fitness with respect to a target.

- In genetic algorithms, two individuals combine and cross over their genome to produce an offspring. This crossover step is followed by a mutation by which individual bases can change according to a mutation rate. The resulting offspring are added to the population and scored according to their fitness level.

Part 4

Deep learning

In the fourth part of the book, we'll introduce deep learning algorithms. Deep learning algorithms are part of supervised learning, which we encountered in part 2 of the book. Deep learning algorithms revolutionized the field of machine learning and enabled several research and business applications that were previously thought to be out of reach with classic ML algorithms.

In chapter 10, we'll begin with fundamentals, such as multilayer perceptron and LeNet convolutional models for MNIST digit classification followed by more advanced applications, such as image search based on the ResNet50 convolutional neural network. We will dive into recurrent neural networks applied to sequence classification using LSTMs and implement a multi-input model for sequence similarity, from scratch. Finally, we'll conduct a comparative study of different optimization algorithms used for training deep neural networks.

In chapter 11, we'll study more advanced deep learning algorithms. We will investigate generative models based on variational autoencoders and implement an anomaly detector for time series data, from scratch. We'll study an intriguing combination of neural networks and probabilistic graphical models and implement mixture density networks, from scratch. Next, we'll describe the powerful transformer architecture and apply it to text classification. Finally, we'll examine graph neural networks and use one to classify nodes in a citation graph. We'll conclude with ML research, focusing on deep learning.

10

Fundamental deep learning algorithms

This chapter covers

- Multilayer perceptron
- Convolutional neural nets: LeNet on MNIST and ResNet image search
- Recurrent neural nets: LSTM sequence classification and multi-input neural net
- Neural network optimizers

In the previous chapter, we discussed selected unsupervised ML algorithms to help discover patterns in our data. In this chapter, we introduce deep learning algorithms. Deep learning algorithms are part of supervised learning, which we encountered in chapters 5, 6, and 7. Deep learning algorithms revolutionized the industry and enabled many research and business applications previously thought to be out of reach by classic ML algorithms. We'll begin this chapter with the fundamentals, such as multilayer perceptron (MLP) and LeNet convolutional model for MNIST digit classification. We will follow these topics with more advanced applications, such as image search based on the ResNet50 convolutional neural network (CNN). We will delve into recurrent neural networks (RNNs) applied to sequence classification using long short-term memory (LSTM) and implement, from scratch, a multi-input model for sequence similarity. We'll then discuss different optimization algorithms used for training neural networks and conduct a comparative study. We will be using the Keras/TensorFlow deep learning library throughout this chapter.

10.1 Multilayer perceptron

Multilayer perceptron (MLP) is commonly used for classification and regression prediction tasks. An MLP consists of multiple densely connected layers that perform the following linear (affine) operation.

$$f(x; \theta) = Wx + b \tag{10.1}$$

Here, x is the input vector, W is the weight matrix, and b is the bias term. While the linearity of the operation makes it easy to compute, it is limiting when it comes to stacking multiple layers. Introducing nonlinearity between layers via activation functions enables the model to have greater expressive power. One common nonlinearity is ReLU, defined as follows.

$$\text{ReLU}(x) = \max(0, x) \tag{10.2}$$

We can define MLP with L layers as a composition of $f_l(x; \theta) = \text{ReLU}(W_{lx} + b_l)$ functions as follows.

$$\text{MLP}(x; \theta) = f_L(f_{L-1}(\cdots(f_1(x; \theta_1))\cdots)) \tag{10.3}$$

The activation of the last layer function f_L will depend on the task at hand: softmax for classification or identity for regression. The softmax activation computes class probabilities that sum to 1, based on real-valued input. It is defined as follows.

$$\text{softmax}(x) = \frac{e^x}{\sum_{i=1}^{K} e^{x_i}} \tag{10.4}$$

Here, K is the number of classes. Figure 10.1 shows an MLP architecture.

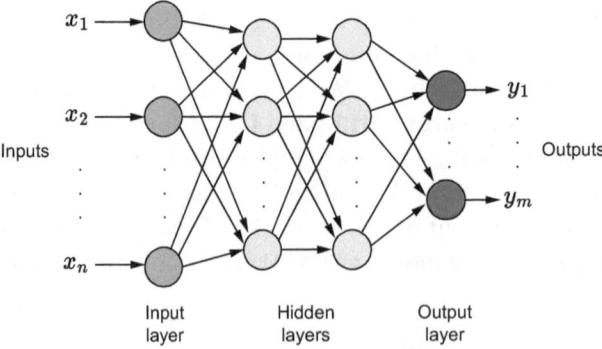

Figure 10.1   **MLP architecture**

To train the neural network, we need to introduce the loss function. A *loss function* tells us how far away the network output is from expected ground truth labels. The loss depends on the task we are optimizing for, and in the case of our MLP, it can be, for example, cross-entropy $H(p, q)$ loss for classification or mean squared error (MSE) loss for regression.

$$L_H(y, \hat{y}) \;=\; H(p, q) = -\sum_{x \in X} p(x) \log q(x) = -\sum_{k=1}^{K} y_k \log \hat{y}_k$$

$$L_{MSE}(y, \hat{y}) \;=\; \text{MSE}(y, \hat{y}) = \frac{1}{N} \sum_{i=1}^{N} (y_i - \hat{y}_i)^2 \tag{10.5}$$

Here, y is the true label and $p(x)$ is the true distribution; $\hat{y}$ is the predicted label and $q(x)$ is the predicted distribution.

MLPs are known as feed-forward networks because they have a direct computational graph from input to output. A neural network training consists of a forward and backward pass. During inference (forward pass), each layer produces a forward message $z = f(x; \theta)$ as the output (given the current weights of the network) followed by computation of the loss function. During the backward pass, each layer takes a backward message dL/dz of the next layer and produces two backward messages at the output dL/dx gradient wrt to the previous layer x and $dL/d\theta$ gradient wrt to parameters of the current layer.

This backpropagation algorithm is based on the chain rule and can be summarized as follows.

$$\frac{\partial L}{\partial x_i} \;=\; \sum_j \frac{\partial L}{\partial z_j} \frac{\partial z_j}{\partial x_i}$$

$$\frac{\partial L}{\partial \theta_i} \;=\; \sum_j \frac{\partial L}{\partial z_j} \frac{\partial z_j}{\partial \theta_i} \tag{10.6}$$

Once we know the gradient with respect to parameters for each layer, we can update the layer parameters as follows.

$$\theta_i^t = \theta_i^{t-1} - \lambda \frac{\partial L}{\partial \theta_i} \tag{10.7}$$

Here, λ is the learning rate. Note that the gradients are computed automatically by deep learning frameworks, such as TensorFlow/PyTorch.

During training, we may want to adopt a learning rate schedule to avoid local optima and converge on a solution. We typically start with the learning rate of some constant and reduce it according to a schedule over epochs, where one epoch is a single pass through the training dataset. Throughout this chapter, we'll be using an exponential learning rate schedule. Other alternatives include a piecewise linear schedule with successive halving, cosine annealing schedule, and one-cycle schedule.

Before we get to the implementation of MLP, it's advantageous to talk about model capacity, to avoid underfitting, and regularization, to prevent overfitting. Regularization can occur at multiple levels, such as weight decay, early stopping, and dropout. At a high level, we would like to increase model capacity by changing the architecture (e.g., increasing the number of layers and the number of hidden units per layer) if we find that the model is underfitting or not achieving high validation accuracy. On the other hand, to avoid overfitting, we can introduce weight decay or l2 regularization applied to nonbias weights (W but not b) of each layer. Weight decay encourages smaller weights and, therefore, simpler models. Another form of regularization is stopping the training early when we notice validation loss is starting to increase away from the training loss. This early stopping criterion can be used to save time and computational resources, while saving a checkpoint of the model. Finally, dropout is an effective regularization technique, where the dense connections are dropped or zeroed at random according to a fixed rate, as shown in figure 10.2. Dropout enables better generalization (see Nitish Srivastava et al.'s "Dropout: A Simple Way to Prevent Neural Networks from Overfitting," JMLR 2014).

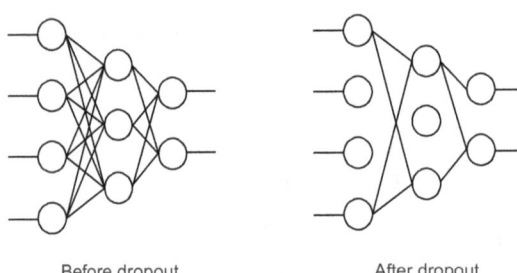

Before dropout   After dropout

Figure 10.2   Dropout applied to multilayer perceptron at one training epoch.

Let's combine the principles we learned so far in our first implementation of the multilayer perceptron (MLP) in Keras/TensorFlow! For more information regarding the Keras library, readers are encouraged to visit https://keras.io/ or review François Chollet's *Deep Learning with Python*, Manning, 2021.

Listing 10.1   Multilayer perceptron

```
import numpy as np
import tensorflow as tf
from tensorflow import keras
```

```
from keras.models import Sequential
from keras.layers import Dense, Dropout

from keras.callbacks import ModelCheckpoint
from keras.callbacks import TensorBoard          ◄──── For visualizing metrics
from keras.callbacks import LearningRateScheduler
from keras.callbacks import EarlyStopping

import math
import matplotlib.pyplot as plt

tf.keras.utils.set_random_seed(42)

SAVE_PATH = "/content/drive/MyDrive/Colab Notebooks/data/"

def scheduler(epoch, lr):      ◄──── Learning rate schedule
    if epoch < 4:
        return lr
    else:
        return lr * tf.math.exp(-0.1)

if __name__ == "__main__":

    (x_train, y_train), (x_test, y_test) = keras.datasets.mnist.load_data()
    x_train = x_train.reshape(x_train.shape[0], x_train.shape[1] *
    ➨ x_train.shape[2]).astype("float32") / 255
    x_test = x_test.reshape(x_test.shape[0], x_test.shape[1] *
    ➨ x_test.shape[2]).astype("float32") / 255

    y_train_label = keras.utils.to_categorical(y_train)
    y_test_label = keras.utils.to_categorical(y_test)
    num_classes = y_train_label.shape[1]

    batch_size = 64          │ Training params
    num_epochs = 16          │

    model = Sequential()
    model.add(Dense(128, input_shape=(784, ), activation='relu'))
    model.add(Dense(64, activation='relu'))
    model.add(Dropout(0.5))
    model.add(Dense(10, activation='softmax'))

    model.compile(
        loss=keras.losses.CategoricalCrossentropy(),
        optimizer=tf.keras.optimizers.RMSprop(),
        metrics=["accuracy"]
    )

    model.summary()

    #define callbacks
    file_name = SAVE_PATH + 'mlp-weights-checkpoint.h5'
    checkpoint = ModelCheckpoint(file_name, monitor='val_loss', verbose=1,
    ➨ save_best_only=True, mode='min')
    reduce_lr = LearningRateScheduler(scheduler, verbose=1)
```

```
early_stopping = EarlyStopping(monitor='val_loss', min_delta=0.01,
➥ patience=16, verbose=1)
#tensor_board = TensorBoard(log_dir='./logs', write_graph=True)
callbacks_list = [checkpoint, reduce_lr, early_stopping]

hist = model.fit(x_train, y_train_label,
➥ batch_size=batch_size, epochs=num_epochs,
➥ callbacks=callbacks_list, validation_split=0.2)    ◄──── Model training

test_scores = model.evaluate(x_test, y_test_label,
➥ verbose=2)                      ◄───┐
                                        │ Model evaluation
print("Test loss:", test_scores[0])
print("Test accuracy:", test_scores[1])

plt.figure()
plt.plot(hist.history['loss'], 'b', lw=2.0, label='train')
plt.plot(hist.history['val_loss'], '--r', lw=2.0, label='val')
plt.title('MLP model')
plt.xlabel('Epochs')
plt.ylabel('Cross-Entropy Loss')
plt.legend(loc='upper right')
plt.show()

plt.figure()
plt.plot(hist.history['accuracy'], 'b', lw=2.0, label='train')
plt.plot(hist.history['val_accuracy'], '--r', lw=2.0, label='val')
plt.title('MLP model')
plt.xlabel('Epochs')
plt.ylabel('Accuracy')
plt.legend(loc='upper left')
plt.show()

plt.figure()
plt.plot(hist.history['lr'], lw=2.0, label='learning rate')
plt.title('MLP model')
plt.xlabel('Epochs')
plt.ylabel('Learning Rate')
plt.legend()
plt.show()
```

Figure 10.3 shows the cross-entropy loss and accuracy for both training and validation datasets. The MLP model achieves 98% accuracy on the test dataset after only 16 training epochs. Notice how the training loss drops below the validation and, similarly, the accuracy on the training set is higher than the validation set. Since we are interested in how our model generalizes to unseen data, the validation set is the real indicator of performance. In the next section, we will examine a class of neural networks better suited for processing image data and, therefore, widely used in computer vision.

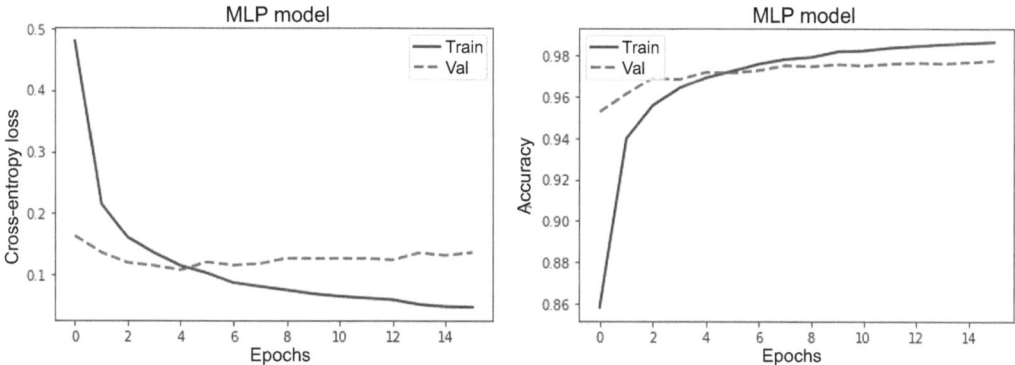

Figure 10.3   MLP cross-entropy loss and accuracy for training and validation datasets

10.2   *Convolutional neural nets*

Convolutional neural networks (CNNs) use convolution and pooling operations in place of vectorized matrix multiplications. In this section, we'll motivate the use of these operations and describe two architectures: LeNet, for MNIST digit classification, and ResNet50, applied to image search.

CNNs work exceptionally well for image data. Images are high dimensional objects of size $W \times H \times C$, where W is the width, H is the height, and C is the number of channels (e.g., $C=3$ for RGB image and $C=1$ for grayscale). CNNs consist of trainable filters or kernels that get convolved with the input to produce a feature map. This results in a vast reduction in the number of parameters and ensures invariance to translations of the input (since we would like to classify an object at any location of the image). The convolution operation is 2D in the case of images, 1D in the case of time series, and 3D in the case of volumetric data. A 2D convolution is defined as follows.

$$(f * g)(i, j) = \sum_a \sum_b f(a, b) g(i - a, i - b) \tag{10.8}$$

In other words, we slide the kernel across every possible position of the input matrix. At each position, we perform a dot-product operation and compute a scalar value. Finally, we gather these scalar values in a feature map output.

Convolutional layers can be stacked. Since convolutions are linear operators, we include nonlinear activation functions in between, just as we did in fully connected layers.

Many popular CNN architectures include a pooling layer. Pooling layers down-sample the feature maps by aggregating information. For example, max pooling computes a maximum over incoming input values, while average pooling replaces the max operation with the average. Similarly, global average pooling could be used to reduce a $W \times H \times D$ feature map into a $1 \times 1 \times D$ aggregate, which can then be reshaped to a D-dimensional vector for further processing. Let's look at a few applications of CNNs.

10.2.1 *LeNet on MNIST*

In this section, we will study the classic LeNet architecture (Yann LeCun et al.'s "Gradient-Based Learning Applied to Document Recognition," Proceedings of the IEEE, 1998) developed by Yann LeCun for handwritten digit classification trained on the MNIST dataset. It follows the design pattern of a convolutional layer, followed by ReLU activation, followed by max-pooling operation, as shown in figure 10.4.

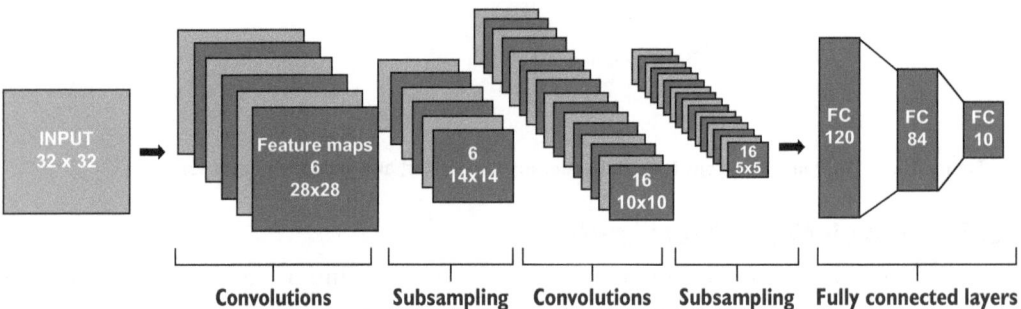

Figure 10.4   LeNet architecture for MNIST digits classification

This sequence is stacked, and the number of filters is increased as we go from the input to the output of the CNN. Notice, that we are both learning more features by increasing the number of filters and reducing the feature map dimensions through the max-pooling operations. In the last layer, we flatten the feature map and add a dense layer followed by a softmax classifier.

In the following code listing, we start off by loading the MNIST dataset and reshaping the images to the correct image size. We define our training parameters and model parameters, followed by the definition of CNN architecture. Notice a sequence of convolutional, ReLU, and max-pooling operations. We compile the model and define a set of callback functions that will be executed during model training. We record the training history and evaluate the model on the test dataset. Finally, we save the prediction results and generate accuracy and loss plots. We are now ready to implement a simple MNIST CNN architecture from scratch using Keras/TensorFlow!

Listing 10.2   Simple CNN for MNIST classification

```
import numpy as np
import pandas as pd
import tensorflow as tf
from tensorflow import keras

from keras.models import Sequential
from keras.layers import Dense, Dropout, Flatten
from keras.layers import Conv2D, MaxPooling2D, Activation

from keras.callbacks import ModelCheckpoint
```

```
from keras.callbacks import TensorBoard
from keras.callbacks import LearningRateScheduler
from keras.callbacks import EarlyStopping

import math
import matplotlib.pyplot as plt

tf.keras.utils.set_random_seed(42)

SAVE_PATH = "/content/drive/MyDrive/Colab Notebooks/data/"

def scheduler(epoch, lr):    ⟵──── Learning rate schedule
    if epoch < 4:
        return lr
    else:
        return lr * tf.math.exp(-0.1)


if __name__ == "__main__":

    img_rows, img_cols = 28, 28
    (x_train, y_train), (x_test, y_test) = keras.datasets.mnist.load_data()
    x_train = x_train.reshape(x_train.shape[0], img_rows, img_cols,
    ➥ 1).astype("float32") / 255
    x_test = x_test.reshape(x_test.shape[0], img_rows, img_cols,
    ➥ 1).astype("float32") / 255

    y_train_label = keras.utils.to_categorical(y_train)
    y_test_label = keras.utils.to_categorical(y_test)
    num_classes = y_train_label.shape[1]

    batch_size = 128      | Training
    num_epochs = 8        | parameters

    num_filters_l1 = 32   | Model
    num_filters_l2 = 64   | parameters

    #CNN architecture
    cnn = Sequential()
    cnn.add(Conv2D(num_filters_l1, kernel_size = (5, 5),
    ➥ input_shape=(img_rows, img_cols, 1), padding='same'))
    cnn.add(Activation('relu'))
    cnn.add(MaxPooling2D(pool_size=(2,2), strides=(2,2)))

    cnn.add(Conv2D(num_filters_l2, kernel_size = (5, 5), padding='same'))
    cnn.add(Activation('relu'))
    cnn.add(MaxPooling2D(pool_size=(2,2), strides=(2,2)))

    cnn.add(Flatten())
    cnn.add(Dense(128))
    cnn.add(Activation('relu'))

    cnn.add(Dense(num_classes))
    cnn.add(Activation('softmax'))
```

```
cnn.compile(
    loss=keras.losses.CategoricalCrossentropy(),
    optimizer=tf.keras.optimizers.Adam(),
    metrics=["accuracy"]
)

cnn.summary()

#define callbacks
file_name = SAVE_PATH + 'lenet-weights-checkpoint.h5'
checkpoint = ModelCheckpoint(file_name, monitor='val_loss', verbose=1,
    save_best_only=True, mode='min')
reduce_lr = LearningRateScheduler(scheduler, verbose=1)
early_stopping = EarlyStopping(monitor='val_loss', min_delta=0.01,
    patience=16, verbose=1)
#tensor_board = TensorBoard(log_dir='./logs', write_graph=True)
callbacks_list = [checkpoint, reduce_lr, early_stopping]

hist = cnn.fit(x_train, y_train_label, batch_size=batch_size,
    epochs=num_epochs, callbacks=callbacks_list,
    validation_split=0.2)                           ◁────── Model training

test_scores = cnn.evaluate(x_test, y_test_label,
    verbose=2)              ◁────── Model evaluation
print("Test loss:", test_scores[0])
print("Test accuracy:", test_scores[1])

y_prob = cnn.predict(x_test)
y_pred = y_prob.argmax(axis=-1)

submission = pd.DataFrame(index=pd.RangeIndex(start=1, stop=10001,
    step=1), columns=['Label'])
submission['Label'] = y_pred.reshape(-1,1)
submission.index.name = "ImageId"
submission.to_csv(SAVE_PATH + '/lenet_pred.csv', index=True, header=True)

plt.figure()
plt.plot(hist.history['loss'], 'b', lw=2.0, label='train')
plt.plot(hist.history['val_loss'], '--r', lw=2.0, label='val')
plt.title('LeNet model')
plt.xlabel('Epochs')
plt.ylabel('Cross-Entropy Loss')
plt.legend(loc='upper right')
plt.show()

plt.figure()
plt.plot(hist.history['accuracy'], 'b', lw=2.0, label='train')
plt.plot(hist.history['val_accuracy'], '--r', lw=2.0, label='val')
plt.title('LeNet model')
plt.xlabel('Epochs')
plt.ylabel('Accuracy')
plt.legend(loc='upper left')
plt.show()
```

```
plt.figure()
plt.plot(hist.history['lr'], lw=2.0, label='learning rate')
plt.title('LeNet model')
plt.xlabel('Epochs')
plt.ylabel('Learning Rate')
plt.legend()
plt.show()
```

With CNN architecture, we can achieve an impressive 99% accuracy on the test set!
Notice how the training and validation curves differ for both cross-entropy loss and
accuracy. Early stopping enables us to stop the training when the validation loss does
not improve over several epochs.

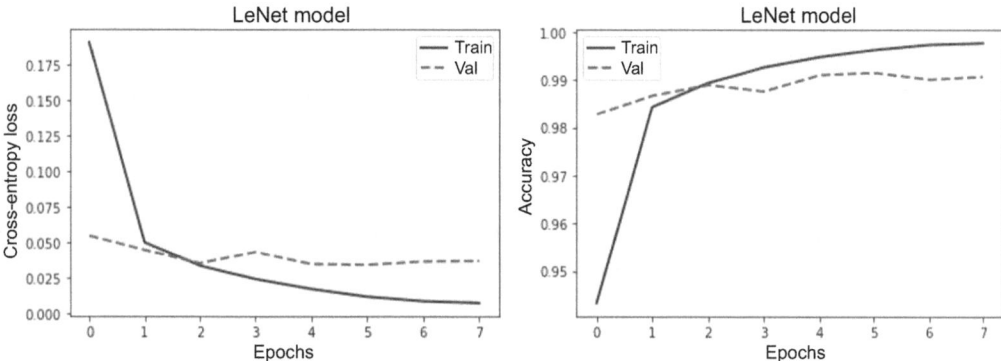

Figure 10.5   LeNet CNN loss and accuracy plots for training and validation datasets

10.2.2 ResNet image search

The goal of image search is to retrieve images from a database similar to the query
image. In this section, we'll be using a pretrained ResNet50 CNN to encode a collection of images into dense vectors. This allows us to find similar images by computing
distances between vectors.

The ResNet50 architecture (He et al.'s "Deep Residual Learning for Image Recognition," Conference on Computer Vision and Pattern Recognition, 2016) uses skip
connections to avoid the vanishing gradient problem. Skip connections skip some layers in the network, as shown in figure 10.6.

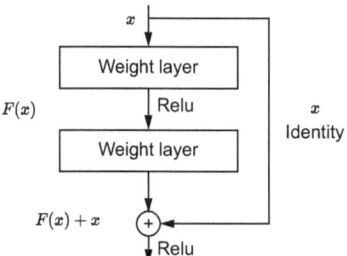

Figure 10.6   Skip connection

The core idea behind ResNet is to backpropagate through the identity function to preserve the gradient. The gradient is then multiplied by one and its value will be maintained in the earlier layers. This enables us to stack many of such layers and create very deep architectures. Let $H = F(x) + x$, and then we get the following equation.

$$\frac{\partial L}{\partial x} = \frac{\partial L}{\partial H}\frac{\partial H}{\partial x} = \frac{\partial L}{\partial H}\left(\frac{\partial F}{\partial x} + 1\right) = \frac{\partial L}{\partial H}\frac{\partial F}{\partial x} + \frac{\partial L}{\partial H} \qquad (10.9)$$

In this section, we'll be using the pretrained on the ImageNet convolutional base of ResNet50 CNN to encode every image in the Caltech 101 dataset. We start off by downloading the Caltech 101 dataset from http://www.vision.caltech.edu/datasets/. We select the model pretrained on ImageNet ResNet50 as our base model, and we set the output layer as the average pool layer, which effectively encodes an input image into a 2048-dimensional vector. We compute ResNet50 encoding of the dataset and store it in the activations list. To further save space, we compress the 2048-dimensional ResNet50 encoded vectors using principal component analysis (PCA) down to 300-dimensional vectors. We retrieve the nearest neighbor images by sorting vectors according to cosine similarity. We are now ready to implement our image search architecture from scratch using Keras/TensorFlow.

Listing 10.3   ResNet50 image search

```
import numpy as np
import pandas as pd
import tensorflow as tf
from tensorflow import keras

from keras import Model
from keras.applications.resnet50 import ResNet50
from keras.preprocessing import image
from keras.applications.resnet50 import preprocess_input

from keras.callbacks import ModelCheckpoint
from keras.callbacks import TensorBoard
from keras.callbacks import LearningRateScheduler
from keras.callbacks import EarlyStopping

import os
import random
from PIL import Image
from scipy.spatial import distance
from sklearn.decomposition import PCA

import matplotlib.pyplot as plt

tf.keras.utils.set_random_seed(42)

SAVE_PATH = "/content/drive/MyDrive/Colab Notebooks/data/"
```

```
DATA_PATH = "/content/drive/MyDrive/data/101_ObjectCategories/"

def get_closest_images(acts, query_image_idx, num_results=5):

    num_images, dim = acts.shape
    distances = []
    for image_idx in range(num_images):
        distances.append(distance.euclidean(acts[query_image_idx, :],
        ⇢ acts[image_idx, :]))
    #end for
    idx_closest  = sorted(range(len(distances)), key=lambda k:
    ⇢ distances[k])[1:num_results+1]

    return idx_closest

def get_concatenated_images(images, indexes, thumb_height):

    thumbs = []
    for idx in indexes:
        img = Image.open(images[idx])
        img = img.resize((int(img.width * thumb_height / img.height),
        ⇢ int(thumb_height)), Image.ANTIALIAS)
        if img.mode != "RGB":
            img = img.convert("RGB")
        thumbs.append(img)
    concat_image = np.concatenate([np.asarray(t) for t in thumbs], axis=1)

    return concat_image

if __name__ == "__main__":

    num_images = 5000
    images = [os.path.join(dp,f) for dp, dn, filenames in
    ⇢ os.walk(DATA_PATH) for f in filenames \
            if os.path.splitext(f)[1].lower() in ['.jpg','.png','.jpeg']]
    images = [images[i] for i in sorted(random.sample(range(len(images)),
    ⇢ num_images))]

    #CNN encodings                                     Pretrained on the
    base_model = ResNet50(weights='imagenet')   ◁──┘ ImageNet ResNet50 model
    model = Model(inputs=base_model.input,
     outputs=base_model.get_layer('avg_pool').output)

    activations = []
    for idx, image_path in enumerate(images):
        if idx % 100 == 0:
            print('getting activations for %d/%d image...'
            ⇢ %(idx,len(images)))
        img = image.load_img(image_path, target_size=(224, 224))
        x = image.img_to_array(img)
        x = np.expand_dims(x, axis=0)
        x = preprocess_input(x)
        features = model.predict(x)
        activations.append(features.flatten().reshape(1,-1))
```

```
print('computing PCA...')
acts = np.concatenate(activations, axis=0)
pca = PCA(n_components=300)
pca.fit(acts)
acts = pca.transform(acts)

print('image search...')
query_image_idx = int(num_images*random.random())
idx_closest = get_closest_images(acts, query_image_idx)
query_image = get_concatenated_images(images, [query_image_idx], 300)
results_image = get_concatenated_images(images, idx_closest, 300)

plt.figure()
plt.imshow(query_image)
plt.title("query image (%d)" %query_image_idx)
plt.show()

plt.figure()
plt.imshow(results_image)
plt.title("result images")
plt.show()
```

Reduces the activation dimension

Figure 10.7 shows the query image of a chair (left) and a retrieved nearest neighbor image (right). The retrieved images closely resemble the query image. In the next section, we will introduce neural networks for sequential data.

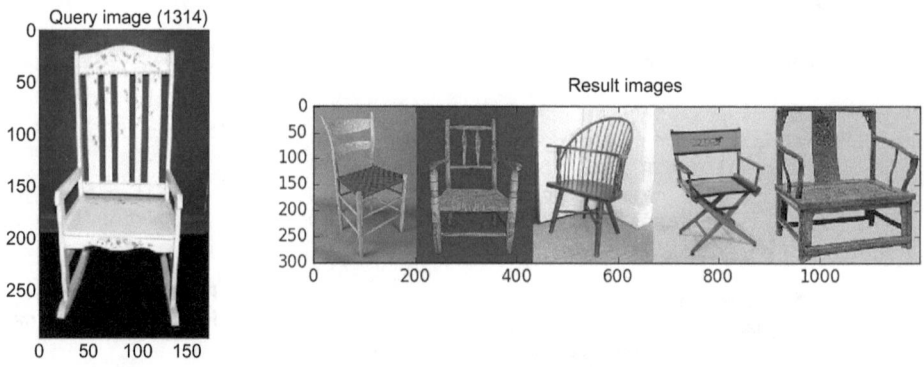

Figure 10.7 ResNet50 image search results

10.3 *Recurrent neural nets*

Recurrent neural nets (RNNs) are designed to process sequential data. RNNs maintain an internal state of the past and provide a natural way to encode a sequence (Seq) into a vector (Vec), and vice versa. Application of RNNs range from language generation (Vec2Seq) to sequence classification (Seq2Vec) to sequence translation (Seq2Seq). In this section, we'll focus on sequence classification using bidirectional LSTM and sequence similarity using pretrained word embeddings.

RNNs use a hidden layer that incorporates the current input x_t and prior state h_{t-1}.

$$h_t = f(W_{hh}h_{t-1} + W_{xh}x_t + b_h) \tag{10.10}$$

Here, W_{hh} are the hidden-to-hidden weights, W_{xh} are the input-to-hidden weights, and b_h is the bias term. Optionally, the outputs y_t can be produced at every step.

$$y_t = g(W_{hy}h_t + b_y) \tag{10.11}$$

The overall architecture is captured in figure 10.8. Let's look at a few applications of RNNs in the next subsection.

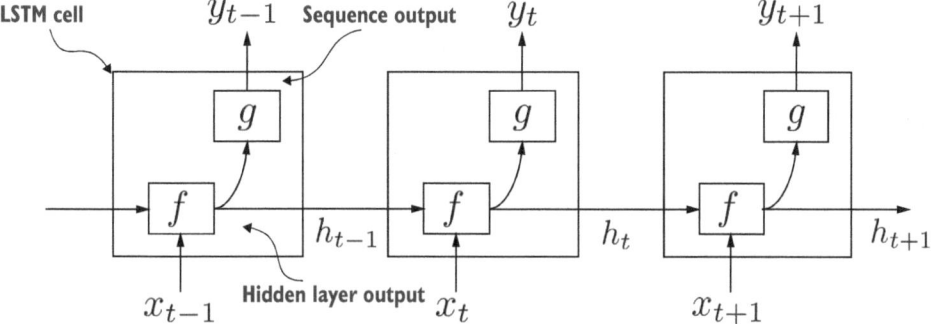

Figure 10.8   LSTM recurrent neural network architecture

10.3.1 *LSTM sequence classification*

In this section, our goal is to determine the sentiment of IMDb movie reviews. We start by tokenizing each word in the review and converting it into a vector via a trainable embedding layer. The sequence of word vectors forms the input to a forward LSTM model, which encodes the sequence into a vector. In parallel, we input our sequence into a backward LSTM model and concatenate its vector output with the forward model to produce a latent representation of the movie review.

$$
\begin{aligned}
\overrightarrow{h_t} &= f(W_{hh}^{\rightarrow}\overrightarrow{h_{t-1}} + W_{xh}^{\rightarrow}x_t + b_h^{\rightarrow}) \\
\overleftarrow{h_t} &= f(W_{hh}^{\leftarrow}\overleftarrow{h_{t-1}} + W_{xh}^{\leftarrow}x_t + b_h^{\leftarrow}) \\
h_t &= [\overrightarrow{h_t}, \overleftarrow{h_t}]
\end{aligned}
\tag{10.12}
$$

Here, h_t takes into account information from the past and the future. Combined, the two LSTMs are known as *bidirectional LSTM* and process input data as if time is running forward and backward. Figure 10.9 shows the architecture of bidirectional RNN.

Having encoded our review into a vector, we average several dense layers with l2 regularization and dropout to classify the sentiment as positive or negative via the sigmoid

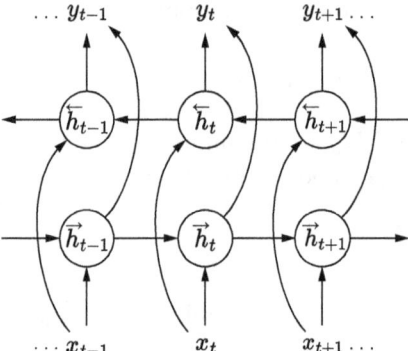

Figure 10.9   Bidirectional RNN architecture

activation function in the output layer. Let's take a look at the code for LSTM sequence classification based on the Keras/TensorFlow library.

Listing 10.4   Bidirectional LSTM for sentiment classification

```python
import numpy as np
import pandas as pd

import tensorflow as tf
from tensorflow import keras

from keras.models import Sequential
from keras.layers import LSTM, Bidirectional
from keras.layers import Dense, Dropout, Activation, Embedding

from keras import regularizers
from keras.preprocessing import sequence
from keras.utils import np_utils

from keras.callbacks import ModelCheckpoint
from keras.callbacks import TensorBoard
from keras.callbacks import LearningRateScheduler
from keras.callbacks import EarlyStopping

import matplotlib.pyplot as plt

tf.keras.utils.set_random_seed(42)

SAVE_PATH = "/content/drive/MyDrive/Colab Notebooks/data/"

def scheduler(epoch, lr):    ◁—— Learning rate schedule
    if epoch < 4:
        return lr
    else:
        return lr * tf.math.exp(-0.1)

if __name__ == "__main__":

    #load dataset
```

First 200 words of each movie review

```
max_words = 20000            ←——— Top 20K most frequent words
seq_len = 200
(x_train, y_train), (x_val, y_val) = keras.datasets.imdb.load_data(
➡ num_words=max_words)

x_train = keras.utils.pad_sequences(x_train, maxlen=seq_len)
x_val = keras.utils.pad_sequences(x_val, maxlen=seq_len)

batch_size = 256            │ Training
num_epochs = 8              │ paramaters

hidden_size = 64            │
embed_dim = 128             │
lstm_dropout = 0.2          │ Model
dense_dropout = 0.5         │ parameters
weight_decay = 1e-3         │

#LSTM architecture
model = Sequential()
model.add(Embedding(max_words, embed_dim, input_length=seq_len))
model.add(Bidirectional(LSTM(hidden_size, dropout=lstm_dropout,
➡ recurrent_dropout=lstm_dropout)))
model.add(Dense(hidden_size,
 kernel_regularizer=regularizers.l2(weight_decay),
  ➡ activation='relu'))
model.add(Dropout(dense_dropout))
model.add(Dense(hidden_size/4,
 kernel_regularizer=regularizers.l2(weight_decay), activation='relu'))
model.add(Dense(1, activation='sigmoid'))

model.compile(
    loss=keras.losses.BinaryCrossentropy(),
    optimizer=tf.keras.optimizers.Adam(),
    metrics=["accuracy"]
)

model.summary()

#define callbacks
file_name = SAVE_PATH + 'lstm-weights-checkpoint.h5'
checkpoint = ModelCheckpoint(file_name, monitor='val_loss', verbose=1,
➡ save_best_only=True, mode='min')
reduce_lr = LearningRateScheduler(scheduler, verbose=1)
early_stopping = EarlyStopping(monitor='val_loss', min_delta=0.01,
➡ patience=16, verbose=1)
#tensor_board = TensorBoard(log_dir='./logs', write_graph=True)
callbacks_list = [checkpoint, reduce_lr, early_stopping]

hist = model.fit(x_train, y_train, batch_size=
➡ batch_size, epochs=num_epochs, callbacks=
➡ callbacks_list, validation_data=(x_val, y_val))   ←——— Model training

test_scores = model.evaluate(x_val, y_val,
➡ verbose=2)              ←——┐
                              │ Model evaluation
```

```
print("Test loss:", test_scores[0])
print("Test accuracy:", test_scores[1])

plt.figure()
plt.plot(hist.history['loss'], 'b', lw=2.0, label='train')
plt.plot(hist.history['val_loss'], '--r', lw=2.0, label='val')
plt.title('LSTM model')
plt.xlabel('Epochs')
plt.ylabel('Cross-Entropy Loss')
plt.legend(loc='upper right')
plt.show()

plt.figure()
plt.plot(hist.history['accuracy'], 'b', lw=2.0, label='train')
plt.plot(hist.history['val_accuracy'], '--r', lw=2.0, label='val')
plt.title('LSTM model')
plt.xlabel('Epochs')
plt.ylabel('Accuracy')
plt.legend(loc='upper left')
plt.show()

plt.figure()
plt.plot(hist.history['lr'], lw=2.0, label='learning rate')
plt.title('LSTM model')
plt.xlabel('Epochs')
plt.ylabel('Learning Rate')
plt.legend()
plt.show()
```

As we can see from figure 10.10, we achieve a test classification accuracy of 85% on the IMDb movie review database. In the next section, we'll explore multiple-input neural network models.

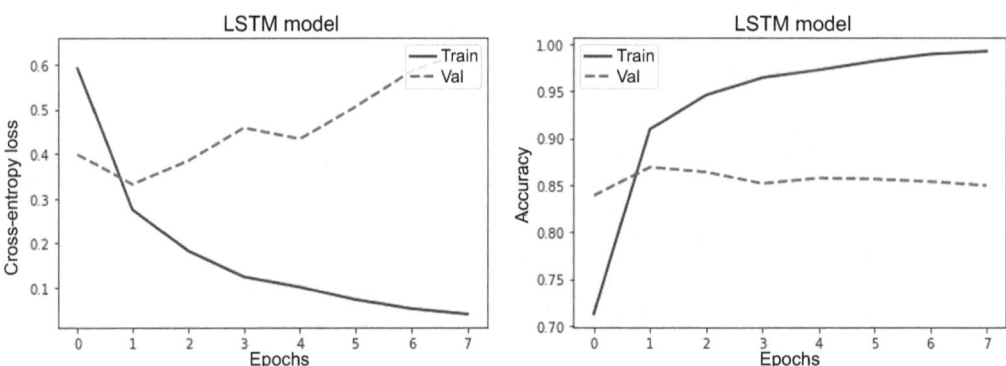

Figure 10.10   Bidirectional LSTM for sentiment classification loss and accuracy on training and validation datasets

10.3.2 *Multi-input model*

In this section, we will study a multi-input model as applied to sequence similarity, comparing two questions (one for each input branch) and deciding whether they have a similar meaning. This will help us determine whether the questions are redundant or duplicates of each other. This challenge appeared as part of the Quora Questions Pairs Kaggle data science competition, and the model we'll develop could be used as part of an ensemble leading to a high-performing solution.

In this case, we will use pretrained Glove word embeddings (Jeffrey Pennington, Richard Socher, Christopher Manning's "GloVe: Global Vectors for Word Representation", EMNLP, 2014) to encode each word into a 300-dimensional dense vector. We'll use 1D convolutions and max-pooling operations to process the sequence of data for each input branch and then concatenate the results into a single vector. After several dense layers, we will compute the probability of duplicate questions based on the sigmoid activation function.

The advantage of using 1D convolutions is that they are computationally faster and can be done in parallel (since there's no recurrent loop to unroll). Their accuracy will depend on whether the information in the recent past is more important than the distant past (in which case, LSTMs will be more accurate) or whether the information is equally important in different timeframes of the past (in which case, 1D convolution will be more accurate).

We'll be using the Quora question pairs dataset available for download from Kaggle: https://www.kaggle.com/datasets/quora/question-pairs-dataset. Let's examine how we can implement a multi-input sequence similarity model end-to-end in Keras/TensorFlow!

Listing 10.5 Multi-input neural network model for sequence similarity

```
import numpy as np
import pandas as pd

import tensorflow as tf
from tensorflow import keras

import os
import re
import csv
import codecs

from keras.models import Model
from keras.layers import Input, Flatten, Concatenate, LSTM, Lambda, Dropout
from keras.layers import Dense, Dropout, Activation, Embedding
from keras.layers import Conv1D, MaxPooling1D
from keras.layers import TimeDistributed, Bidirectional, BatchNormalization

from keras import backend as K
from keras.preprocessing.text import Tokenizer
from keras.preprocessing.sequence import pad_sequences
```

```
from nltk.corpus import stopwords
from nltk.stem import SnowballStemmer

from keras import regularizers
from keras.preprocessing import sequence
from keras.utils import np_utils

from keras.callbacks import ModelCheckpoint
from keras.callbacks import TensorBoard
from keras.callbacks import LearningRateScheduler
from keras.callbacks import EarlyStopping

import matplotlib.pyplot as plt

tf.keras.utils.set_random_seed(42)

SAVE_PATH = "/content/drive/MyDrive/Colab Notebooks/data/"
DATA_PATH = "/content/drive/MyDrive/data/"

GLOVE_DIR = DATA_PATH
TRAIN_DATA_FILE = DATA_PATH + 'quora_train.csv'
TEST_DATA_FILE = DATA_PATH + 'quora_test.csv'
MAX_SEQUENCE_LENGTH = 30
MAX_NB_WORDS = 200000
EMBEDDING_DIM = 300
VALIDATION_SPLIT = 0.01

def scheduler(epoch, lr):
    if epoch < 4:
        return lr
    else:
        return lr * tf.math.exp(-0.1)

def text_to_wordlist(row, remove_stopwords=False, stem_words=False):

    text = row['question']
    if type(text) is str:                              # Converts words to
        text = text.lower().split()           ◁────┘   lowercase and splits them
    else:
        return " "


    if remove_stopwords:
        stops = set(stopwords.words("english"))                # Removes
        text = [w for w in text if not w in stops]    ◁────┘   stop words

    text = " ".join(text)

    # Clean the text
    text = re.sub(r"[^A-Za-z0-9^,!.\/'+-=]", " ", text)

    if stem_words:
        text = text.split()
        stemmer = SnowballStemmer('english')
```

```
            stemmed_words = [stemmer.stem(word) for word in text]    ◁──┐ Shortens
            text = " ".join(stemmed_words)                                │ words to
                                                                          │ their stems
        return(text)


if __name__ == "__main__":


    print('Indexing word vectors...')
    embeddings_index = {}
    f = codecs.open(os.path.join(GLOVE_DIR, 'glove.6B.
    ➥ 300d.txt'), encoding='utf-8')          ◁──┐ Loads embeddings
    for line in f:
        values = line.split(' ')
        word = values[0]
        coefs = np.asarray(values[1:], dtype='float32')
        embeddings_index[word] = coefs
    f.close()
    print('Found %s word vectors.' % len(embeddings_index))


    train_df = pd.read_csv(TRAIN_DATA_FILE)   │ Loads the dataset
    test_df  = pd.read_csv(TEST_DATA_FILE)    │

    q1df = train_df['question1'].reset_index()
    q2df = train_df['question2'].reset_index()
    q1df.columns = ['index', 'question']
    q2df.columns = ['index', 'question']
    texts_1 = q1df.apply(text_to_wordlist, axis=1, raw=False).tolist()
    texts_2 = q2df.apply(text_to_wordlist, axis=1, raw=False).tolist()
    labels = train_df['is_duplicate'].astype(int).tolist()
    print('Found %s texts.' % len(texts_1))
    del q1df
    del q2df


    q1df = test_df['question1'].reset_index()
    q2df = test_df['question2'].reset_index()
    q1df.columns = ['index', 'question']
    q2df.columns = ['index', 'question']
    test_texts_1 = q1df.apply(text_to_wordlist, axis=1, raw=False).tolist()
    test_texts_2 = q2df.apply(text_to_wordlist, axis=1, raw=False).tolist()
    test_labels = np.arange(0, test_df.shape[0])
    print('Found %s texts.' % len(test_texts_1))
    del q1df
    del q2df


    tokenizer = Tokenizer(nb_words=MAX_NB_WORDS)
    tokenizer.fit_on_texts(texts_1 + texts_2 + test_texts_1 + test_texts_2)
    sequences_1 = tokenizer.texts_to_sequences(texts_1)
    sequences_2 = tokenizer.texts_to_sequences(texts_2)
    word_index = tokenizer.word_index
    print('Found %s unique tokens.' % len(word_index))


    test_sequences_1 = tokenizer.texts_to_sequences(test_texts_1)
    test_sequences_2 = tokenizer.texts_to_sequences(test_texts_2)
```

```
data_1 = pad_sequences(sequences_1, maxlen=MAX_SEQUENCE_LENGTH)
data_2 = pad_sequences(sequences_2, maxlen=MAX_SEQUENCE_LENGTH)
labels = np.array(labels)
print('Shape of data tensor:', data_1.shape)
print('Shape of label tensor:', labels.shape)

test_data_1 = pad_sequences(test_sequences_1, maxlen=MAX_SEQUENCE_LENGTH)
test_data_2 = pad_sequences(test_sequences_2, maxlen=MAX_SEQUENCE_LENGTH)
test_labels = np.array(test_labels)
del test_sequences_1
del test_sequences_2
del sequences_1
del sequences_2

print('Preparing embedding matrix...')
nb_words = min(MAX_NB_WORDS, len(word_index))

embedding_matrix = np.zeros((nb_words, EMBEDDING_DIM))
for word, i in word_index.items():
    if i >= nb_words:
        continue
    embedding_vector = embeddings_index.get(word)
    if embedding_vector is not None:
        # words not found in embedding index will be all-zeros.
        embedding_matrix[i] = embedding_vector
print('Null word embeddings: %d' % np.sum(np.sum(embedding_matrix,
➥ axis=1) == 0))

embedding_layer = Embedding(nb_words,
                            EMBEDDING_DIM,
                            weights=[embedding_matrix],
                            input_length=MAX_SEQUENCE_LENGTH,
                            trainable=False)

sequence_1_input = Input(shape=(MAX_SEQUENCE_LENGTH,), dtype='int32')
embedded_sequences_1 = embedding_layer(sequence_1_input)
x1 = Conv1D(128, 3, activation='relu')(embedded_sequences_1)
x1 = MaxPooling1D(10)(x1)
x1 = Flatten()(x1)
x1 = Dense(64, activation='relu')(x1)
x1 = Dropout(0.2)(x1)

sequence_2_input = Input(shape=(MAX_SEQUENCE_LENGTH,), dtype='int32')
embedded_sequences_2 = embedding_layer(sequence_2_input)
y1 = Conv1D(128, 3, activation='relu')(embedded_sequences_2)
y1 = MaxPooling1D(10)(y1)
y1 = Flatten()(y1)
y1 = Dense(64, activation='relu')(y1)
y1 = Dropout(0.2)(y1)

merged = Concatenate()([x1, y1])
merged = BatchNormalization()(merged)
merged = Dense(64, activation='relu')(merged)
merged = Dropout(0.2)(merged)
merged = BatchNormalization()(merged)
```

```
preds = Dense(1, activation='sigmoid')(merged)

model = Model(inputs=[sequence_1_input,sequence_2_input], outputs=preds)    ◁⌐
                                                    Multi-input architecture ⌐
model.compile(
    loss=keras.losses.BinaryCrossentropy(),
    optimizer=tf.keras.optimizers.Adam(),
    metrics=["accuracy"]
)

model.summary()

file_name = SAVE_PATH + 'multi-input-weights-checkpoint.h5'
checkpoint = ModelCheckpoint(file_name, monitor='val_loss', verbose=1,
➡  save_best_only=True, mode='min')
reduce_lr = LearningRateScheduler(scheduler, verbose=1)
early_stopping = EarlyStopping(monitor='val_loss', min_delta=0.01,
➡  patience=16, verbose=1)
#tensor_board = TensorBoard(log_dir='./logs', write_graph=True)
callbacks_list = [checkpoint, reduce_lr, early_stopping]

hist = model.fit([data_1, data_2], labels,
➡  batch_size=1024, epochs=10, callbacks=callbacks_list,
➡  validation_split=VALIDATION_SPLIT)    ◁⌐
                                         ⌐ Model training
num_test = 100000
preds = model.predict([test_data_1[:num_test,:],
➡  test_data_2[:num_test,:]])    ◁⌐
                                 ⌐ Model evaluation
quora_submission = pd.DataFrame({"test_id":test_labels[:num_test],
➡  "is_duplicate":preds.ravel()})
quora_submission.to_csv(SAVE_PATH + "quora_submission.csv", index=False)

plt.figure()
plt.plot(hist.history['loss'], 'b', lw=2.0, label='train')
plt.plot(hist.history['val_loss'], '--r', lw=2.0, label='val')
plt.title('Multi-Input model')
plt.xlabel('Epochs')
plt.ylabel('Cross-Entropy Loss')
plt.legend(loc='upper right')
plt.show()
#plt.savefig('./figures/lstm_loss.png')

plt.figure()
plt.plot(hist.history['accuracy'], 'b', lw=2.0, label='train')
plt.plot(hist.history['val_accuracy'], '--r', lw=2.0, label='val')
plt.title('Multi-Input model')
plt.xlabel('Epochs')
plt.ylabel('Accuracy')
plt.legend(loc='upper left')
plt.show()
#plt.savefig('./figures/lstm_acc.png')

plt.figure()
plt.plot(hist.history['lr'], lw=2.0, label='learning rate')
```

```
plt.title('Multi-Input model')
plt.xlabel('Epochs')
plt.ylabel('Learning Rate')
plt.legend()
plt.show()
#plt.savefig('./figures/lstm_learning_rate.png')
```

We can see the accuracy hovering around 69% on the validation dataset in figure 10.11, and we know there's room for improvement. We can potentially increase the capacity of our model or improve data representation.

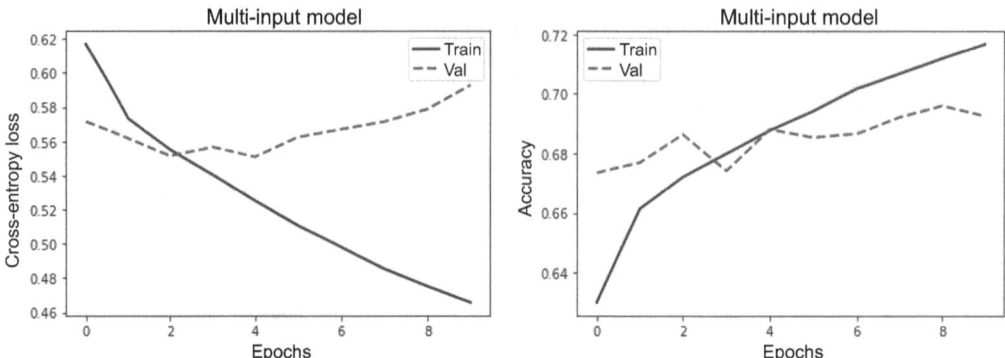

Figure 10.11   Multi-input model loss and accuracy for training and validation datasets

In this section, we focused on understanding an important class of neural nets: recurrent neural networks. We studied how they work and focused on two applications: sequence classification and sequence similarity. In the next section, we will examine different neural network optimizers.

10.4   *Neural network optimizers*

What are some of the most popular optimization algorithms used for training neural networks? We will attempt to answer this question using a convolutional neural network (CNN) trained on the CIFAR-100 dataset with Keras/TensorFlow.

Stochastic gradient descent (SGD) updates parameters θ in the negative direction of the gradient g by taking a subset or mini-batch of data of size m.

$$g = \frac{1}{m}\nabla_\theta \sum_i L\left(f\left(x^{(i)};\theta\right),y^{(i)}\right)$$

$$\theta = \theta - \epsilon_k \times g \tag{10.13}$$

Here, $f(x_i; \theta)$ is a neural network trained on examples x_i and labels y_i and L is the loss function. The gradient of loss L is computed with respect to model parameters θ. The learning rate ϵ_k determines the size of the step that the algorithm takes along the gradient (in the negative direction in the case of minimization and in the positive direction in the case of maximization).

The learning rate is a function of iteration k and is the single most important hyper-parameter. A lear ing rate that is too high (e.g., > 0.1) can lead to parameter updates that miss the optimum value; a learning rate that is too low (e.g., $< 1e{-}5$) will result in an unnecessarily long training time. A good strategy is to start with a learning rate of $1e{-}3$ and use a learning rate schedule that reduces the learning rate as a function of iterations. In general, we want the learning rate to satisfy the Robbins-Monroe conditions.

$$\sum_k \epsilon_k \; = \; \infty$$

$$\sum_k \epsilon_k^2 \; < \; \infty \tag{10.14}$$

The first condition ensures the algorithm will be able to find a locally optimal solution, regardless of the starting point, and the second one controls oscillations.

Momentum accumulates the exponentially decaying moving average of past gradients and continues to move in their direction; thus, the step size depends on how large and aligned the sequence of gradients are. Common values of momentum parameter α are 0.5 and 0.9.

$$v \; = \; \alpha v - \epsilon \nabla_\theta \left(\frac{1}{m} \sum_i L \left(f \left(x^{(i)}; \theta \right), y^{(i)} \right) \right)$$

$$\theta \; = \; \theta + v \tag{10.15}$$

Nesterov momentum is inspired by Nesterov's accelerated gradient method. The difference between Nesterov and standard momentum is where the gradient is evaluated, with the gradient being evaluated after the current velocity is applied in Nesterov momentum. Thus, Nesterov momentum adds a correction factor to the gradient.

$$v \; = \; \alpha v - \epsilon \nabla_\theta \left(\frac{1}{m} \sum_i L \left(f \left(x^{(i)}; \theta + \alpha \times v \right), y^{(i)} \right) \right)$$

$$\theta \; = \; \theta + v \tag{10.16}$$

AdaGrad is an adaptive method for setting the learning rate (John Duchi, Elad Hazan, and Yoram Singer's "Adaptive Subgradient Methods for Online Learning and Stochastic Optimization," *Journal of Machine Learning Research*, 2011). Consider the two scenarios in figure 10.12.

In the case of a slowly varying objective (left), the gradient would typically (at most points) have a small magnitude. As a result, we would need a large learning rate to

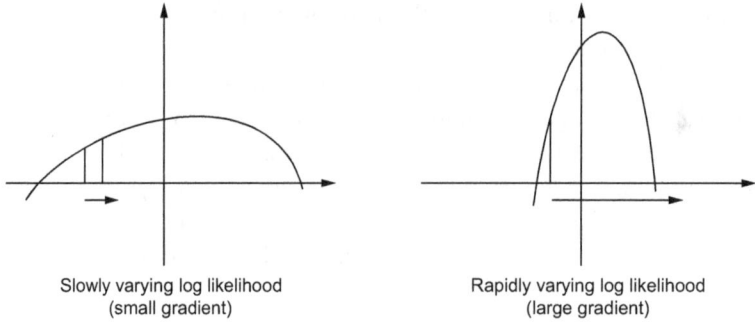

Slowly varying log likelihood
(small gradient)

Rapidly varying log likelihood
(large gradient)

Figure 10.12   Slowly varying (left) and rapidly varying (right) log likelihood

quickly reach the optimum. In the case of a rapidly varying objective (right), the gradient would typically be very large. Using a large learning rate would result in very large, steps, oscillating around but not reaching the optimum. These two situations occur because the learning rate is set independently of the gradient. AdaGrad solves this by accumulating squared norms of gradients seen so far and dividing the learning rate by the square root of the following sum.

$$g = \frac{1}{m}\nabla_\theta \sum_i L\left(f\left(x^{(i)};\theta\right),y^{(i)}\right)$$

$$s = s + g^T g$$

$$\theta = \theta - \epsilon_k \times \frac{g}{\sqrt{s+eps}} \tag{10.17}$$

As a result, parameters that receive high gradients have their effective learning rate reduced and parameters that receive small gradients have their effective learning rate increased. The net effect is greater progress in the more gently sloped directions of parameter space and more cautious updates in the presence of large gradients.

RMSProp modifies AdaGrad by changing the gradient accumulation into an exponentially weighted moving average (i.e., it discards history from the distant past).

$$g = \frac{1}{m}\nabla_\theta \sum_i L\left(f\left(x^{(i)};\theta\right),y^{(i)}\right)$$

$$s = \text{decay\_rate} \times s + (1 - \text{decay\_rate})g^T g$$

$$\theta = \theta - \epsilon_k \times \frac{g}{\sqrt{s+eps}} \tag{10.18}$$

Notice that AdaGrad implies a decreasing learning rate, even if the gradients remain constant, due to the accumulation of gradients from the beginning of training. By introducing an exponentially weighted moving average, we are weighing the recent past more heavily in comparison to the distant past. As a result, RMSProp has been shown to be an effective and practical optimization algorithm for deep neural networks.

Adam derives from *adaptive moments*. It can be seen as a variant on the combination of RMSProp and momentum, and the update looks like RMSProp, except a smooth version of the gradient is used instead of the raw stochastic gradient. The full Adam update also includes a bias correction mechanism (Diederik P. Kingma and Jimmy Ba, "Adam: A Method for Stochastic Optimization," *International Conference on Learning Representations*, 2015).

$$
\begin{aligned}
g &= \frac{1}{m}\nabla_\theta \sum_i L\left(\left(x^{(i)};\theta\right), y^{(i)}\right) \\
m &= \beta_1 m + (1 - \beta_1)g \\
s &= \beta_2 v + (1 - \beta_2)g^T g \\
\theta &= \theta - \epsilon_k \times \frac{m}{\sqrt{s + eps}}
\end{aligned}
\tag{10.19}
$$

The recommended values in the paper are $\epsilon = \text{1e--8}$, $\beta_1 = 0.9$, and $\beta_2 = 0.999$. Now, let's examine the performance of different optimizers using Keras/TensorFlow!

Listing 10.6 Neural network optimizers

```
import numpy as np
import pandas as pd
import tensorflow as tf
from tensorflow import keras

from keras import backend as K
from keras.models import Sequential
from keras.layers import Dense, Dropout, Flatten
from keras.layers import Conv2D, MaxPooling2D, Activation

from keras.callbacks import ModelCheckpoint
from keras.callbacks import TensorBoard
from keras.callbacks import LearningRateScheduler
from keras.callbacks import EarlyStopping

import math
import matplotlib.pyplot as plt

tf.keras.utils.set_random_seed(42)

SAVE_PATH = "/content/drive/MyDrive/Colab Notebooks/data/"

def scheduler(epoch, lr):
    if epoch < 4:
        return lr
    else:
        return lr * tf.math.exp(-0.1)
```

```
if __name__ == "__main__":

    img_rows, img_cols = 32, 32
    (x_train, y_train), (x_test, y_test) =
    ➡ keras.datasets.cifar100.load_data()        ⟵——————  cifar100 dataset
    x_train = x_train.reshape(x_train.shape[0], img_rows, img_cols,
    ➡ 3).astype("float32") / 255
    x_test = x_test.reshape(x_test.shape[0], img_rows, img_cols,
    ➡ 3).astype("float32") / 255

    y_train_label = keras.utils.to_categorical(y_train)
    y_test_label = keras.utils.to_categorical(y_test)
    num_classes = y_train_label.shape[1]

    batch_size = 256          | Training
    num_epochs = 32           | parameters

    num_filters_l1 = 64       | Model
    num_filters_l2 = 128      | parameters

    #CNN architecture
    cnn = Sequential()
    cnn.add(Conv2D(num_filters_l1, kernel_size = (5, 5),
    ➡ input_shape=(img_rows, img_cols, 3), padding='same'))
    cnn.add(Activation('relu'))
    cnn.add(MaxPooling2D(pool_size=(2,2), strides=(2,2)))

    cnn.add(Conv2D(num_filters_l2, kernel_size = (5, 5), padding='same'))
    cnn.add(Activation('relu'))
    cnn.add(MaxPooling2D(pool_size=(2,2), strides=(2,2)))

    cnn.add(Flatten())
    cnn.add(Dense(128))
    cnn.add(Activation('relu'))

    cnn.add(Dense(num_classes))
    cnn.add(Activation('softmax'))

    opt1 = tf.keras.optimizers.SGD()
    opt2 = tf.keras.optimizers.SGD(momentum=0.9,
    ➡ nesterov=True)                                        Optimizers
    opt3 = tf.keras.optimizers.RMSprop()
    opt4 = tf.keras.optimizers.Adam()

    optimizer_list = [opt1, opt2, opt3, opt4]

    history_list = []

    for idx in range(len(optimizer_list)):

        K.clear_session()

        opt = optimizer_list[idx]

        cnn.compile(
            loss=keras.losses.CategoricalCrossentropy(),
            optimizer=opt,
            metrics=["accuracy"]
```

```
    )

    #define callbacks
    reduce_lr = LearningRateScheduler(scheduler, verbose=1)
    callbacks_list = [reduce_lr]

    #training loop
    hist = cnn.fit(x_train, y_train_label, batch_size=batch_size,
    ➥ epochs=num_epochs, callbacks=callbacks_list, validation_split=0.2)
    history_list.append(hist)

#end for

plt.figure()
plt.plot(history_list[0].history['loss'], 'b', lw=2.0, label='SGD')
plt.plot(history_list[1].history['loss'], '--r', lw=2.0, label='SGD
➥ Nesterov')
plt.plot(history_list[2].history['loss'], ':g', lw=2.0, label='RMSProp')
plt.plot(history_list[3].history['loss'], '-.k', lw=2.0, label='ADAM')
plt.title('LeNet, CIFAR-100, Optimizers')
plt.xlabel('Epochs')
plt.ylabel('Cross-Entropy Training Loss')
plt.legend(loc='upper right')
plt.show()
#plt.savefig('./figures/lenet_loss.png')

plt.figure()
plt.plot(history_list[0].history['val_accuracy'], 'b', lw=2.0,
➥ label='SGD')
plt.plot(history_list[1].history['val_accuracy'], '--r', lw=2.0,
➥ label='SGD Nesterov')
plt.plot(history_list[2].history['val_accuracy'], ':g', lw=2.0,
➥ label='RMSProp')
plt.plot(history_list[3].history['val_accuracy'], '-.k', lw=2.0,
➥ label='ADAM')
plt.title('LeNet, CIFAR-100, Optimizers')
plt.xlabel('Epochs')
plt.ylabel('Validation Accuracy')
plt.legend(loc='upper right')
plt.show()
#plt.savefig('./figures/lenet_loss.png')

plt.figure()
plt.plot(history_list[0].history['lr'], 'b', lw=2.0, label='SGD')
plt.plot(history_list[1].history['lr'], '--r', lw=2.0, label='SGD
➥ Nesterov')
plt.plot(history_list[2].history['lr'], ':g', lw=2.0, label='RMSProp')
plt.plot(history_list[3].history['lr'], '-.k', lw=2.0, label='ADAM')
plt.title('LeNet, CIFAR-100, Optimizers')
plt.xlabel('Epochs')
plt.ylabel('Learning Rate Schedule')
plt.legend(loc='upper right')
plt.show()
#plt.savefig('./figures/lenet_loss.png')
```

Figure 10.13 shows the loss and validation dataset accuracy for a LeNet neural network trained on the cifar100 dataset using different optimizers.

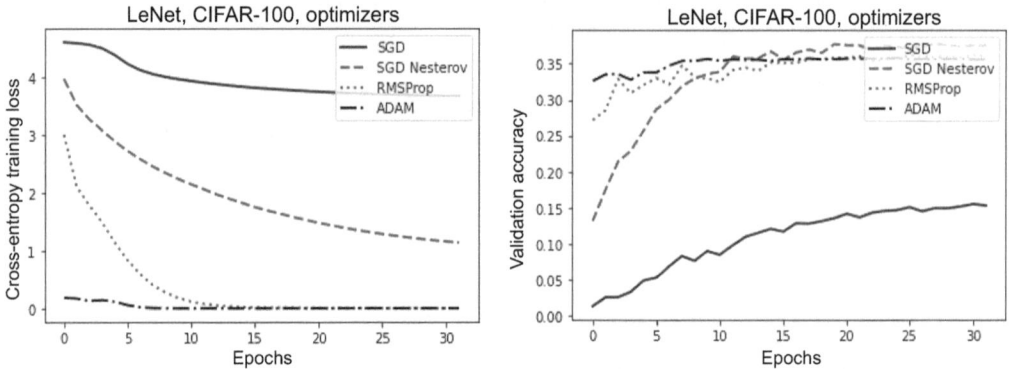

Figure 10.13   Cross-entropy loss and validation accuracy of LeNet trained on cifar100 using different optimizers

We can see that Adam and Nesterov Momentum optimizers experimentally produce the highest validation accuracy. In the following chapter, we will focus on advanced deep learning algorithms. We will learn to detect anomalies in time series data using a variational autoencoder (VAE), determine clusters using a mixture density network (MDN), learn to classify text with transformers, and classify citation graphs using a graph neural network (GNN).

10.5 Exercises

10.1 Explain the purpose of nonlinearities in neural networks.
10.2 Explain the vanishing/exploding gradient problem.
10.3 Describe some of the ways to increase neural model capacity and avoid overfitting.
10.4 Why does the number of filters increase in LeNet architecture as we go from input to output?
10.5 Explain how an Adam optimizer works.

Summary

- Multilayer perceptron consists of multiple densely connected layers followed by a nonlinearity.
- Cross-entropy loss is used in classification tasks, while mean squared error loss is used in regression tasks.
- Neural networks are optimized via a backpropagation algorithm, based on the chain rule.
- Increasing model capacity to avoid underfitting can be achieved by changing the model architecture (e.g., increasing the number of layers and hidden units per layer).

- Regularization to avoid overfitting can occur on multiple levels: weight decay, early stopping, and dropout.
- Convolutional neural nets work exceptionally well for image data and use convolution and pooling layers instead of vectorized matrix multiplications.
- Classic CNN architectures consist of a convolutional layer followed by ReLU nonlinear activation function and a max pooling layer.
- Pretrained CNNs can be used to extract feature vectors for images and used in applications such as image search.
- Recurrent neural nets are designed to process sequential data.
- Application of RNNs include language generation, sequence classification, and sequence translation.
- Multi-input neural nets can be constructed by concatenating the feature vector representations from individual input branches.
- Neural network optimizers include stochastic gradient descent, momentum, Nesterov momentum, AdaGrad, RMSProp, and Adam.

11

Advanced deep
learning algorithms

In the previous chapter, we looked at fundamental deep learning algorithms to help represent numerical, image, and text data. In this chapter, we will continue our discussion with advanced deep learning algorithms. The algorithms have been selected for their state-of-the-art performance architectures and a wide range of applications. We will investigate generative models based on variational autoencoders (VAEs) and implement, from scratch, an anomaly detector for time series data. We'll continue our journey with an intriguing combination of neural networks and classical Gaussian mixture models (GMMs) via amortized variational inference (VI) and implement mixture density networks (MDNs). We will then focus on the concept of attention and implement a transformer architecture from scratch for a classification task. Finally, we'll examine graph neural networks (GNNs) and use one to perform node classification for a citation graph. We will be using the Keras/TensorFlow deep learning library throughout this chapter.

11.1 Autoencoders

An *autoencoder* is an unsupervised neural network used for dimensionality reduction or feature extraction. They consist of an encoder followed by a hidden bottleneck layer followed by a decoder, where the encoder and decoder are both trainable neural networks, as shown in figure 11.1.

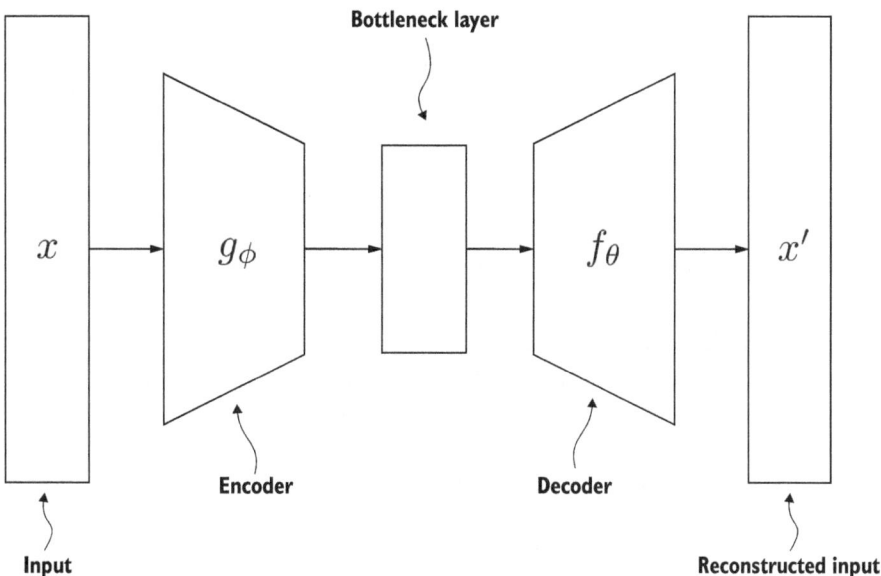

Figure 11.1 Autoencoder architecture, showing an encoder, a bottleneck layer, and a decoder

Autoencoders are trained to reconstruct their input. In other words, an autoencoder output should match the input as closely as possible. To prevent the neural network from learning a trivial identity function, the hidden layer in the middle is constrained to be a narrow bottleneck. Autoencoder training minimizes the reconstruction error by ensuring the hidden units capture the most relevant information in the input data.

In practice, autoencoders serve as feature extractors and do not lead to well-structured latent spaces. This is where VAEs come in (D. P. Kingma's "Variational Inference and Deep Learning: A New Synthesis," University of Amsterdam, 2017). A VAE also consists of an encoder and a decoder; however, instead of compressing its input image into a bottleneck layer, a VAE turns the image into parameters of statistical distribution (e.g., the mean and variance of a Gaussian random variable). The VAE then draws a sample from this distribution and uses it to decode the sample back to its original input. Figure 11.2 shows the architecture of the VAE.

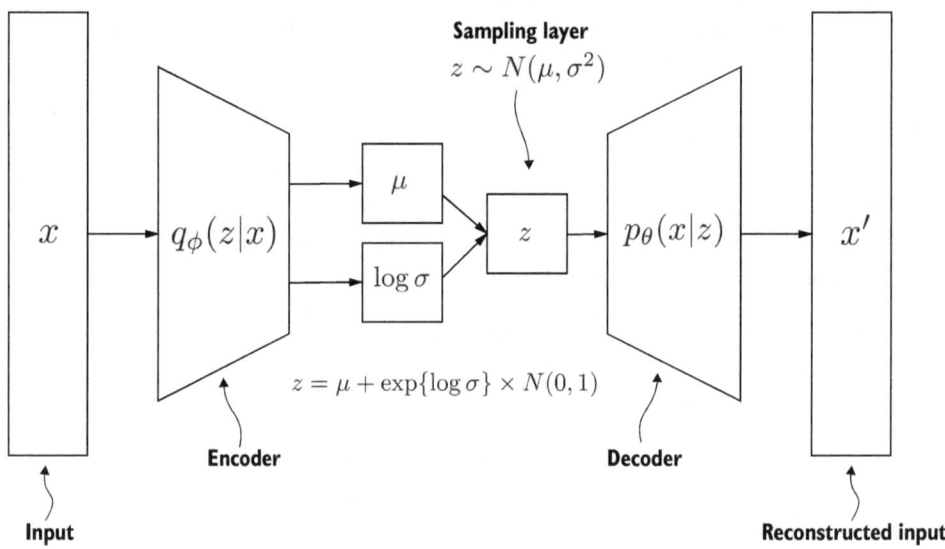

Figure 11.2   Variational autoencoder architecture, showing an encoder, a sampling layer, and a decoder

VAE training imposes a structure on the latent space such that every point can be decoded to a valid output. The optimization objective of the variational autoencoder is the evidence lower bound (ELBO). Let *x* represent the input space and *z* the latent space. Let $p(x|z)$ be the decoder distribution parameterized by θ that, conditioned on a sample *z* from the latent space, reconstructs the original input *x*. Similarly, let $q(z|x)$ be the encoder distribution parameterized by ϕ that takes the input x and encodes it into latent variable *z*. Note that both theta and phi parameters are trainable. Finally, let $p(z)$ be the prior distribution over the latent space. Since our goal for the variational posterior is to be as close as possible to the true posterior, the VAE is trained with the following loss function.

$$\min_{\theta,\phi} \text{Loss}(x; \theta, \phi) = E_{q_\phi(z|x)}\left[\log p_\theta(x|z)\right]$$
$$- D_{KL}\left(q_\phi(z|x)||p_\theta(z)\right) \qquad (11.1)$$

The first term controls how well the VAE reconstructs a data point *x* from a sample *z* of the variational posterior, while the second term controls how close the variational posterior $q(z|x)$ is to the prior $p(z)$. If we assume the prior distribution $p(z)$ is Gaussian, we can write the KL divergence term as follows. In the following section, we will examine how we can apply VAE to anomaly detection in time series.

$$D_{KL}(q_\phi(z|x)||p_\theta(z)) = -\frac{1}{2}\sum_{d=1}^{D}\left(1 + \log\sigma_d^2 - \mu_d^2 - \sigma_d^2\right) \tag{11.2}$$

11.1.1   VAE anomaly detection in time series

Let's look at a VAE model that operates on time series data with the goal of anomaly detection. The architecture is shown in figure 11.3.

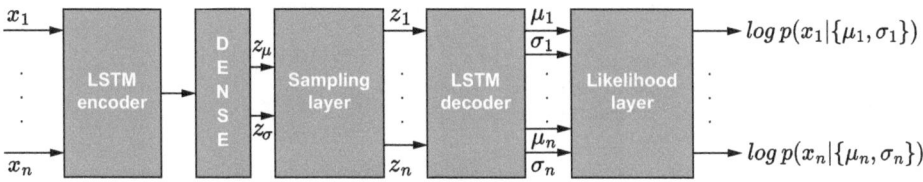

Figure 11.3   LSTM-VAE anomaly detector architecture

The input consists of n signals $x_1,..., x_n$, and the output is the log probability of observing input x_i under normal (nonanomalous) training parameters μ_i, σ_i. This means the model is trained on nonanomalous data in an unsupervised fashion and when an anomaly does occur on a given input x_i, the corresponding log likelihood $\log p(x_i|\{\mu_i, \sigma_i\})$ drops and we can threshold the resulting drop to signal an anomaly.

We assume a Gaussian likelihood; thus, every sensor has two degrees of freedom (μ, σ) to represent an anomaly. As a result, for n input sensors, we learn $2n$ output parameters (mean and variance) that can differentiate between anomalous and normal behavior.

While the input signals are independent, they are embedded in a joint latent space by the VAE in the sampling layer. The embedding is structured as a Gaussian that approximates standard normal $N(0,1)$ by minimizing *KL* divergence. The model is trained in an unsupervised fashion, with an objective function that achieves two goals: (1) maximizing the log likelihood output of the model, averaged over sensors and (2) structuring the embedding space to approximate $N(0,1)$.

$$\min_\theta \text{Loss}(\theta) = \min_\theta D_{KL}\left(N(z_\mu, z_\sigma)||N(0, 1)\right)$$
$$-\frac{1}{n}\sum_{i=1}^{n}\log p(x_i|\mu_i, \sigma_i) \tag{11.3}$$

We are now ready to implement the LSTM-VAE anomaly detector from scratch, using Keras/TensorFlow. In the following listing, we will load the NAB dataset (which can be found in the data folder of the code repo) and prepare the data for training. The Numenta Anomaly Benchmark (NAB) is a novel benchmark for evaluating algorithms for anomaly detection in streaming, online applications. Next, we define the anomaly detector architecture along with the custom loss function and train the model. You may want to run the code listing in a Google Colab notebook (accessible at https://colab.research.google.com/) to understand the code step by step and accelerate model training via GPU.

Listing 11.1   LSTM-VAE anomaly detector

```
import numpy as np
import pandas as pd

import tensorflow as tf
from tensorflow import keras
import tensorflow_probability as tfp

from keras.layers import Input, Dense, Lambda, Layer
from keras.layers import LSTM, RepeatVector
from keras.models import Model
from keras import backend as K
from keras import metrics
from keras import optimizers

import math
import json
from scipy.stats import norm
from sklearn.model_selection import train_test_split
from sklearn import preprocessing
from sklearn.metrics import confusion_matrix
from sklearn.preprocessing import StandardScaler

from keras.callbacks import ModelCheckpoint
from keras.callbacks import TensorBoard
from keras.callbacks import LearningRateScheduler
from keras.callbacks import EarlyStopping

import matplotlib.pyplot as plt

tf.keras.utils.set_random_seed(42)

SAVE_PATH = "/content/drive/MyDrive/Colab Notebooks/data/"
DATA_PATH = "/content/drive/MyDrive/data/"

def scheduler(epoch, lr):
    if epoch < 4:
        return lr
    else:
        return lr * tf.math.exp(-0.1)

nab_path = DATA_PATH + 'NAB/'
nab_data_path = nab_path

labels_filename = '/labels/combined_labels.json'
train_file_name = 'artificialNoAnomaly/art_daily_no_noise.csv'
test_file_name = 'artificialWithAnomaly/art_daily_jumpsup.csv'
```

```
#train_file_name = 'realAWSCloudwatch/rds_cpu_utilization_cc0c53.csv'
#test_file_name = 'realAWSCloudwatch/rds_cpu_utilization_e47b3b.csv'

labels_file = open(nab_path + labels_filename, 'r')
labels = json.loads(labels_file.read())
labels_file.close()

def load_data_frame_with_labels(file_name):
    data_frame = pd.read_csv(nab_data_path + file_name)
    data_frame['anomaly_label'] = data_frame['timestamp'].isin(
        labels[file_name]).astype(int)
    return data_frame

train_data_frame = load_data_frame_with_labels(train_file_name)
test_data_frame = load_data_frame_with_labels(test_file_name)

plt.plot(train_data_frame.loc[0:3000,'value'])
plt.plot(test_data_frame['value'])

train_data_frame_final = train_data_frame.loc[0:3000,:]
test_data_frame_final = test_data_frame

data_scaler = StandardScaler()
data_scaler.fit(train_data_frame_final[['value']].values)
train_data = data_scaler.transform(train_data_frame_final[['value']].values)
test_data = data_scaler.transform(test_data_frame_final[['value']].values)

def create_dataset(dataset, look_back=64):
    dataX, dataY = [], []
    for i in range(len(dataset)-look_back-1):
        dataX.append(dataset[i:(i+look_back),:])
        dataY.append(dataset[i+look_back,:])

    return np.array(dataX), np.array(dataY)

X_data, y_data = create_dataset(train_data, look_back=64) #look_back =
➡ window_size
X_train, X_val, y_train, y_val = train_test_split(X_data, y_data,
➡ test_size=0.1, random_state=42)
X_test, y_test = create_dataset(test_data, look_back=64)  #look_back =
➡ window_size
```

```
batch_size = 256          |  Training params
num_epochs = 32           |
timesteps = X_train.shape[1]
input_dim = X_train.shape[-1]
intermediate_dim = 16        Model params
latent_dim = 2
epsilon_std = 1.0         |

class Sampling(Layer):      ◄──── Sampling layer
    def call(self, inputs):
        z_mean, z_log_var = inputs
        batch = tf.shape(z_mean)[0]
```

```
        dim = tf.shape(z_mean)[1]
        epsilon = tf.keras.backend.random_normal(shape=(batch, dim))
        return z_mean + tf.exp(0.5 * z_log_var) * epsilon

class Likelihood(Layer):    ◁─── Likelihood layer
    def call(self, inputs):
        x, x_decoded_mean, x_decoded_scale = inputs
        dist = tfp.distributions.MultivariateNormalDiag(x_decoded_mean,
        ➥ x_decoded_scale)
        likelihood = dist.log_prob(x)
        return likelihood


#VAE architecture

#encoder
x = Input(shape=(timesteps, input_dim,))
h = LSTM(intermediate_dim)(x)

z_mean = Dense(latent_dim)(h)
z_log_sigma = Dense(latent_dim, activation='softplus')(h)

#sampling
z = Sampling()((z_mean, z_log_sigma))

#decoder
decoder_h = LSTM(intermediate_dim, return_sequences=True)
decoder_loc = LSTM(input_dim, return_sequences=True)
decoder_scale = LSTM(input_dim, activation='softplus', return_sequences=True)

h_decoded = RepeatVector(timesteps)(z)
h_decoded = decoder_h(h_decoded)

x_decoded_mean = decoder_loc(h_decoded)
x_decoded_scale = decoder_scale(h_decoded)

#log-likelihood
llh = Likelihood()([x, x_decoded_mean, x_decoded_scale])

vae = Model(inputs=x, outputs=llh)    ◁─── Defines the VAE model

# Add KL divergence regularization loss and likelihood loss
kl_loss = - 0.5 * K.mean(1 + z_log_sigma - K.square(z_mean) -
➥ K.exp(z_log_sigma))
tot_loss = -K.mean(llh - kl_loss)
vae.add_loss(tot_loss)

# Loss and optimizer.
loss_fn = tf.keras.losses.MeanSquaredError()
optimizer = tf.keras.optimizers.Adam()

@tf.function
def training_step(x):
    with tf.GradientTape() as tape:
        reconstructed = vae(x)  # Compute input reconstruction.
        # Compute loss.
```

```
            loss = 0 #loss_fn(x, reconstructed)
            loss += sum(vae.losses)
        # Update the weights of the VAE.
        grads = tape.gradient(loss, vae.trainable_weights)
        optimizer.apply_gradients(zip(grads, vae.trainable_weights))
        return loss

losses = []  # Keep track of the losses over time.
dataset = tf.data.Dataset.from_tensor_slices(X_train).batch(batch_size)
for epoch in range(num_epochs):
    for step, x in enumerate(dataset):
        loss = training_step(x)
        losses.append(float(loss))
    print("Epoch:", epoch, "Loss:", sum(losses) / len(losses))

plt.figure()
plt.plot(losses, c='b', lw=2.0, label='train')
plt.title('LSTM-VAE model')
plt.xlabel('Epochs')
plt.ylabel('Total Loss')
plt.legend(loc='upper right')
plt.show()

pred_test = vae.predict(X_test)

plt.plot(pred_test[:,0])

is_anomaly = pred_test[:,0] < -1e1
plt.figure()
plt.plot(test_data, color='b')
plt.figure()
plt.plot(is_anomaly, color='r')
```

We can see that for a simple square wave input in figure 11.4, we can detect a drop in log likelihood and threshold it to signal an anomaly. Figure 11.5 shows the decrease in total loss over epochs.

In the following section, we will explore amortized variational inference as applied to mixture density networks.

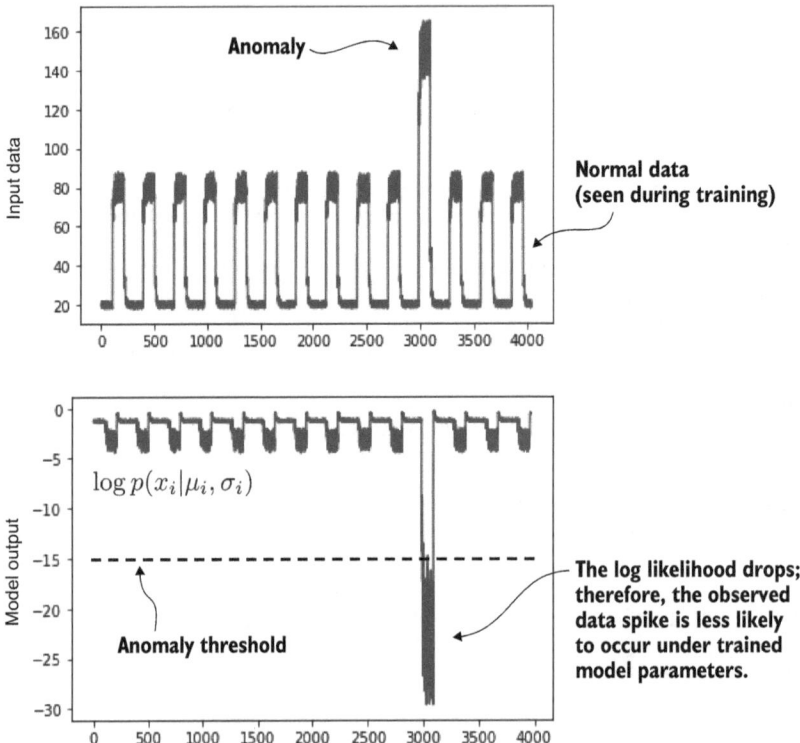

Figure 11.4   **LSTM-VAE anomaly detection result**

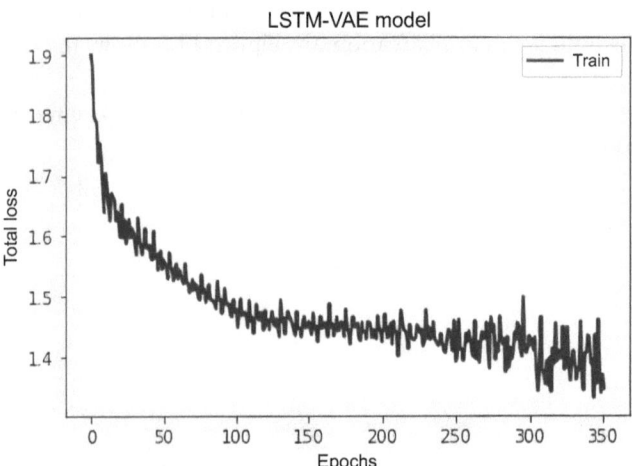

Figure 11.5   **LSTM-VAE training loss**

11.2   Amortized variational inference

Amortized *variational inference* (VI) is the idea that instead of optimizing a set of free parameters, we can introduce a parameterized function that maps from observation space to the parameters of the approximate posterior distribution. In practice, this could be a neural network that takes observations as input and outputs the mean and variance parameters for the latent variable associated with that observation (as we encountered in the VAE architecture). We can then optimize the parameters of this neural network instead of the individual parameters of each observation.

One advantage of amortized VI is memoized reuse of past inference, in a similar way to dynamic programming, in which we remember solutions to previously computed subproblems. For example, consider the following two queries in figure 11.6 (Samuel J. Gershman and Noah D. Goodman's "Amortized Inference in Probabilistic Reasoning," *Cognitive Science*, 2014).

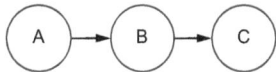

Query 1: $P(B|C) = P(C|B)P(B)/P(C)$

Query 2: $P(A|C) = \sum_B P(A|B)P(B|C)$

Figure 11.6   A simple Bayesian network. Query 1 is a subquery of query 2.

We can see that query 1 is a subquery of query 2. Thus, the conditional distribution computed for query 1 can be reused to answer query 2. Another advantage of amortized VI is that it omits the requirement to derive the ELBO analytically, since the optimization takes place via stochastic gradient descent (SGD). The limitation of amortized VI is that the generalization gap depends on the capacity of the chosen neural network as the stochastic function.

Let's look at one example of amortized VI—namely, the mixture density network (MDN), in which we'll be using a multilayer perceptron (MLP) neural network to parameterize a Gaussian mixture model (GMM).

11.2.1   Mixture density networks

Mixture density networks (MDNs) are mixture models in which the parameters, such as means, covariances, and mixture proportions, are learned by a neural network. MDNs combine a structured data representation (a density mixture) with unstructured parameter inference (an MLP neural network). MDNs learn the mixture parameters by maximizing the log likelihood or, equivalently, minimizing a negative log likelihood loss.

Assuming a Gaussian mixture model (GMM) with K components, we can write down the probability of a test data point y_i conditioned on training data x as follows.

$$p(y_i|x) = \sum_{k=1}^{K} \pi_k(x) N\left(y_i|\mu_k(x), \Sigma_k(x)\right) \tag{11.4}$$

Here, the parameters μ_k, σ_k, π_k are learned by a neural network (e.g., an MLP) parameterized by θ.

$$\mu_k, \sigma_k, \pi_k = NN(x; \theta) \tag{11.5}$$

The MDN architecture is captured in figure 11.7.

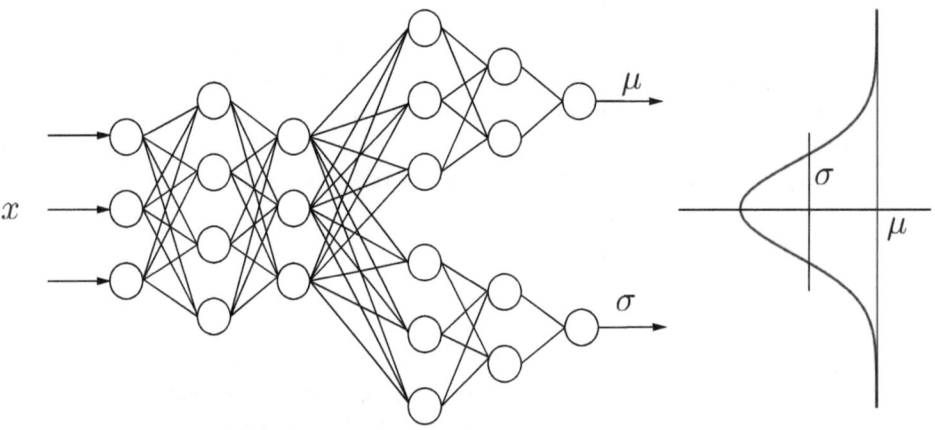

Figure 11.7   A multioutput neural network used to learn Gaussian parameters

As a result, the neural network (NN) is a multi-output model, subject to the following constraints on the output.

$$\begin{aligned} \forall k \ \sigma_k(x) &> 0 \\ \sum_{k=1}^{K} \pi_k(x) &= 1 \end{aligned} \tag{11.6}$$

In other words, we would like to enforce that the variance is strictly positive and the mixture weights add up to 1. The first constraint can be achieved using exponential activations, while the second constraint can be achieved using softmax activations. Finally, by making use of the iid assumption, we can attempt to minimize the following loss function.

$$\begin{aligned} \min_{\theta} L(\theta) &= NLLLoss(\theta) = -\log \prod_{i=1}^{n} p(y_i|x) = -\sum_{i=1}^{n} \log p(y_i|x) \\ &= -\sum_{i=1}^{n} \log \left[\sum_{k=1}^{K} \pi_k(x_i, \theta) N(y_i|\mu_k(x_i, \theta), \Sigma_k(x_i, \theta)) \right] \end{aligned} \tag{11.7}$$

In our example, we assume an isotropic covariance $\Sigma_k = \sigma_k^2 I$; thus, we can write a d-dimensional Gaussian as a product. Given the multivariate Gaussian, we get the following.

$$N(y_i|\mu_k, \Sigma_k) = \frac{1}{(2\pi)^{\frac{d}{2}}|\Sigma_k|^{\frac{1}{2}}} \exp\left(-\frac{1}{2}(y_i - \mu_k)^T \Sigma_k^{-1}(y_i - \mu_k)\right) \quad (11.8)$$

Since the covariance matrix is isotropic, we can rewrite equation 11.8 as follows.

$$
\begin{aligned}
N(y_i|\mu_k, \Sigma_k) &= \frac{1}{(2\pi\sigma_k^2)^{\frac{d}{2}}} \exp\left[-\frac{1}{2\sigma_k^2}\sum_{d=1}^{D}(y_{i,d} - \mu_{k,d})^2\right] \\
&= \prod_{d=1}^{D} \frac{1}{\sigma_k\sqrt{2\pi}} \exp\left[-\frac{1}{2\sigma_k^2}(y_{i,d} - \mu_{k,d})^2\right] \quad (11.9)
\end{aligned}
$$

Let's implement a Gaussian MDN using Keras/TensorFlow. We use synthetic data in our example with ground truth mean and covariance. We generate the data by sampling from a multivariate distribution. We then define the MDN multioutput architecture with constraints on mixing proportions and variance. Finally, we compute the negative log likelihood loss, train the model, and display the prediction results on test data. You may want to run the code listing in a Google Colab notebook (accessible at https://colab.research.google.com/) to understand the code step by step and accelerate model training via GPU.

Listing 11.2 Gaussian mixture density network

```
import numpy as np
import pandas as pd

import tensorflow as tf
from tensorflow import keras

from keras.models import Model
from keras.layers import concatenate, Input
from keras.layers import Dense, Activation, Dropout, Flatten
from keras.layers import BatchNormalization

from keras import regularizers
from keras import backend as K
from keras.utils import np_utils

from keras.callbacks import ModelCheckpoint
from keras.callbacks import TensorBoard
from keras.callbacks import LearningRateScheduler
from keras.callbacks import EarlyStopping
```



```
from sklearn.datasets import make_blobs
from sklearn.metrics import adjusted_rand_score
from sklearn.metrics import normalized_mutual_info_score
from sklearn.model_selection import train_test_split

import math
import matplotlib.pyplot as plt
import matplotlib.cm as cm

tf.keras.utils.set_random_seed(42)

SAVE_PATH = "/content/drive/MyDrive/Colab Notebooks/data/"

def scheduler(epoch, lr):        ◁──── Learning rate schedule
    if epoch < 4:
        return lr
    else:
        return lr * tf.math.exp(-0.1)
                                          Synthetic ground
def generate_data(N):            ◁────┘  truth data
    pi = np.array([0.2, 0.4, 0.3, 0.1])
    mu = [[2,2], [-2,2], [-2,-2], [2,-2]]
    std = [[0.5,0.5], [1.0,1.0], [0.5,0.5], [1.0,1.0]]
    x = np.zeros((N,2), dtype=np.float32)
    y = np.zeros((N,2), dtype=np.float32)
    z = np.zeros((N,1), dtype=np.int32)
    for n in range(N):
        k = np.argmax(np.random.multinomial(1, pi))
        x[n,:] = np.random.multivariate_normal(mu[k], np.diag(std[k]))
        y[n,:] = mu[k]
        z[n,:] = k
    #end for
    z = z.flatten()
    return x, y, z, pi, mu, std
                                      Isotropic multivariate
                                      Gaussian
def tf_normal(y, mu, sigma):     ◁────┘
    y_tile = K.stack([y]*num_clusters, axis=1) #[batch_size, K, D]
    result = y_tile - mu
    sigma_tile = K.stack([sigma]*data_dim, axis=-1) #[batch_size, K, D]
    result = result * 1.0/(sigma_tile+1e-8)
    result = -K.square(result)/2.0
    oneDivSqrtTwoPI = 1.0/math.sqrt(2*math.pi)
    result = K.exp(result) * (1.0/(sigma_tile + 1e-8))*oneDivSqrtTwoPI
    result = K.prod(result, axis=-1)    #[batch_size, K] iid Gaussians
    return result
                                     Negative log likelihood Loss
def NLLLoss(y_true, y_pred):     ◁────┘
    out_mu = y_pred[:,:num_clusters*data_dim]
    out_sigma = y_pred[:,num_clusters*data_dim : num_clusters*(data_dim+1)]
    out_pi = y_pred[:,num_clusters*(data_dim+1):]

    out_mu = K.reshape(out_mu, [-1, num_clusters, data_dim])

    result = tf_normal(y_true, out_mu, out_sigma)
```

```
      result = result * out_pi
      result = K.sum(result, axis=1, keepdims=True)
      result = -K.log(result + 1e-8)
      result = K.mean(result)
      return tf.maximum(result, 0)

#generate data
X_data, y_data, z_data, pi_true, mu_true, sigma_true = generate_data(4096)

data_dim = X_data.shape[1]
num_clusters = len(mu_true)

num_train = 3500
X_train, X_test, y_train, y_test = X_data[:num_train,:],
➡ X_data[num_train:,:], y_data[:num_train,:], y_data[num_train:,:]
z_train, z_test = z_data[:num_train], z_data[num_train:]

#visualize data
plt.figure()
plt.scatter(X_train[:,0], X_train[:,1], c=z_train, cmap=cm.bwr)
plt.title('training data')
plt.show()
#plt.savefig(SAVE_PATH + '/mdn_training_data.png')

batch_size = 128        │ Training params
num_epochs = 128        │

hidden_size = 32         │ Model params
weight_decay = 1e-4      │

#MDN architecture
input_data = Input(shape=(data_dim,))
x = Dense(32, activation='relu')(input_data)
x = Dropout(0.2)(x)
x = BatchNormalization()(x)
x = Dense(32, activation='relu')(x)
x = Dropout(0.2)(x)
x = BatchNormalization()(x)

mu = Dense(num_clusters * data_dim, activation    │ Cluster means
➡ ='linear')(x)                          ←
sigma = Dense(num_clusters, activation=K.exp)(x)   ←——— Diagonal covariance
pi = Dense(num_clusters, activation='softmax')(x)  ←
out = concatenate([mu, sigma, pi], axis=-1)         │ Mixture proportions

model = Model(input_data, out)

model.compile(
  loss=NLLLoss,
  optimizer=tf.keras.optimizers.Adam(),
  metrics=["accuracy"]
)

model.summary()
```

```
#define callbacks
file_name = SAVE_PATH + 'mdn-weights-checkpoint.h5'
checkpoint = ModelCheckpoint(file_name, monitor='val_loss', verbose=1,
➥ save_best_only=True, mode='min')
reduce_lr = LearningRateScheduler(scheduler, verbose=1)
early_stopping = EarlyStopping(monitor='val_loss', min_delta=0.01,
➥ patience=16, verbose=1)
#tensor_board = TensorBoard(log_dir='./logs', write_graph=True)
callbacks_list = [checkpoint, reduce_lr, early_stopping]

hist = model.fit(X_train, y_train, batch_size
➥ =batch_size, epochs=num_epochs, callbacks
➥ =callbacks_list, validation_split=0.2,
➥ shuffle=True, verbose=2)        ◄──── Model training

y_pred = model.predict(X_test)        ◄──── Model evaluation

mu_pred = y_pred[:,:num_clusters*data_dim]
mu_pred = np.reshape(mu_pred, [-1, num_clusters, data_dim])
sigma_pred = y_pred[:,num_clusters*data_dim : num_clusters*(data_dim+1)]
pi_pred = y_pred[:,num_clusters*(data_dim+1):]
z_pred = np.argmax(pi_pred, axis=-1)

rand_score = adjusted_rand_score(z_test, z_pred)
print("adjusted rand score: ", rand_score)

nmi_score = normalized_mutual_info_score(z_test, z_pred)
print("normalized MI score: ", nmi_score)

mu_pred_list = []
sigma_pred_list = []
for label in np.unique(z_pred):
    z_idx = np.where(z_pred == label)[0]
    mu_pred_lbl = np.mean(mu_pred[z_idx,label,:], axis=0)
    mu_pred_list.append(mu_pred_lbl)

    sigma_pred_lbl = np.mean(sigma_pred[z_idx,label], axis=0)
    sigma_pred_list.append(sigma_pred_lbl)
#end for

print("true means:")
print(np.array(mu_true))

print("predicted means:")
print(np.array(mu_pred_list))

print("true sigmas:")
print(np.array(sigma_true))

print("predicted sigmas:")
print(np.array(sigma_pred_list))

#generate plots
plt.figure()
plt.scatter(X_test[:,0], X_test[:,1], c=z_pred, cmap=cm.bwr)
```

```
plt.scatter(np.array(mu_pred_list)[:,0], np.array(mu_pred_list)[:,1],
    s=100, marker='x', lw=4.0, color='k')
plt.title('test data')

plt.figure()
plt.plot(hist.history['loss'], 'b', lw=2.0, label='train')
plt.plot(hist.history['val_loss'], '--r', lw=2.0, label='val')
plt.title('Mixture Density Network')
plt.xlabel('Epochs')
plt.ylabel('Negative Log Likelihood Loss')
plt.legend(loc='upper left')
```

Figure 11.8 shows the cluster centroids overlayed with test data in addition to training and validation loss.

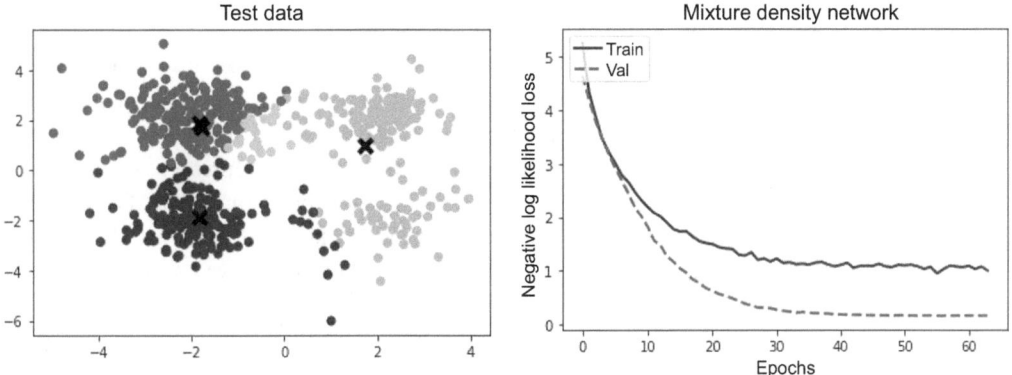

Figure 11.8   Mixture density network: cluster centroids and training and validation loss

We can see that inferred means are close to cluster centers. It's interesting to note that for this initialization, two of the cluster means coincide. Feel free to experiment with different seeds and numbers of training points to understand the behavior of the model. Also, we find that both training and validation loss are decreasing with the number of epochs. In the following section, we will look at a powerful transformer architecture based on self-supervised learning.

11.3   Attention and transformers

Attention allows a model to adaptively pay attention to different parts of the input by adjusting attention weights. Attention mechanisms can be applied to many kinds of neural networks but were first used in the context of recurrent neural networks (RNNs). In Seq2Seq RNN models, such as those used in machine translation, the output context vector that summarizes the input sentence does not have access to individual input words. This results in poor performance, as measured by the BLEU score. We can avoid this bottleneck by letting the output attend to input words directly, in a weighted fashion. In other words, we can compute the context vector as a weighted sum of input word vectors h_s^{enc}.

$$c_t = \sum_s a_{ts} h_s^{enc} \tag{11.10}$$

Here, a_{ts} are learned attention weights given by the following.

$$a_{ts} = \frac{\exp\left\{ \text{score}\left(h_{t-1}^{dec}, h_s^{enc} \right) \right\}}{\sum_{s'} \exp\left\{ \text{score}\left(h_{t-1}^{dec}, h_{s'}^{enc} \right) \right\}} \tag{11.11}$$

There are several ways to learn the scoring function (e.g., the multiplicative style).

$$\text{score}(a, b) = a^T W b \tag{11.12}$$

Here, W is an intermediate trainable matrix. We can generalize attention as a soft dictionary lookup. A soft dictionary lookup refers to a type of search in which an exact match is not found. This is useful when searching for words that may have been misspelled or are related to the search term. We can think of attention as comparing a set of target vectors or queries q_i with a set of candidate vectors or keys k_j. For each query, we compute how much the query is related to every key and then use these scores to weigh and sum the values v_j associated with every key. Thus, we can define the attention matrix A as follows.

$$A_{ij} = \text{score}(q_i, k_j) \tag{11.13}$$

Given the attention weights in A_{ij}, we compute a weighted combination of values v_j associated with each key. As a result, for the i-th query, we have the following.

$$r_i = \sum_j A_{ij} v_j = \sum_j \text{score}(q_i, k_j) v_j \tag{11.14}$$

Here, we can choose a normalized multiplicative score with $W=1$.

$$\text{score}(q_i, k_j) = \frac{q_i^T k_j}{\sqrt{D}} \tag{11.15}$$

In matrix notation, where we have N queries (Q of size $N \times D$) and N key–value pairs (K of size $N \times D$), we can write down the result (weighted set of values V, whose keys K most resemble the query Q).

$$
\begin{aligned}
R &= \text{attention}(Q, K, V) = AV \\
&= \text{score}(Q, K)V = \text{softmax}\left(\frac{QK^T}{\sqrt{D}} \right) V
\end{aligned}
\tag{11.16}
$$

The softmax part of the product ensures the distribution adds up to 1 and can be thought of as where to look in the value matrix *V*.

Figure 11.9 shows the attention matrix heatmap for neural machine translation (NMT). In NMT, the query is the target sequence, while the keys and values are the source sequence. We can see which source English words the model pays attention to when producing a target translated sequence in Spanish.

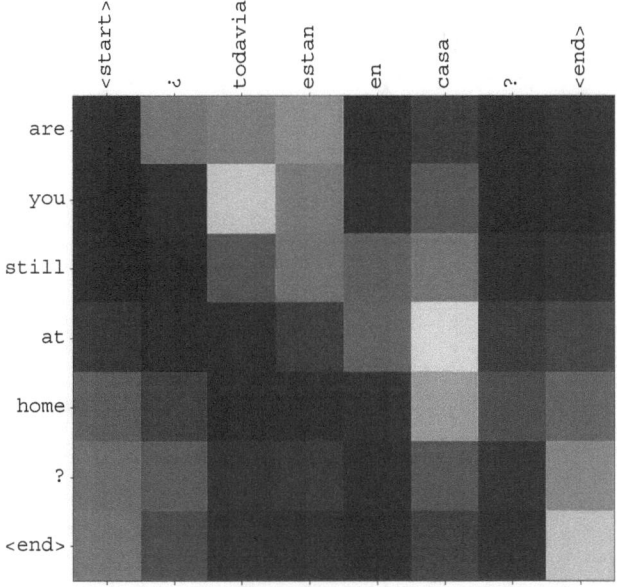

Figure 11.9   Attention matrix heatmap for neural machine translation

Self-attention is the key component of transformer architecture. A *transformer* is a Seq2Seq model that uses attention in the encoder as well as the decoder, thus eliminating the need for RNNs. Figure 11.10 shows the Transformer architecture (Vaswani et al.'s "Attention Is All You Need," NeurIPS, 2017). Let's look more closely at the building blocks of transfomers.

At a high level, we see an encoder–decoder architecture with inputs in the left branch and outputs in the right branch. We can identify multihead attention, positional encodings, dense and normalization layers, and residual connections for ease of gradient backpropagation.

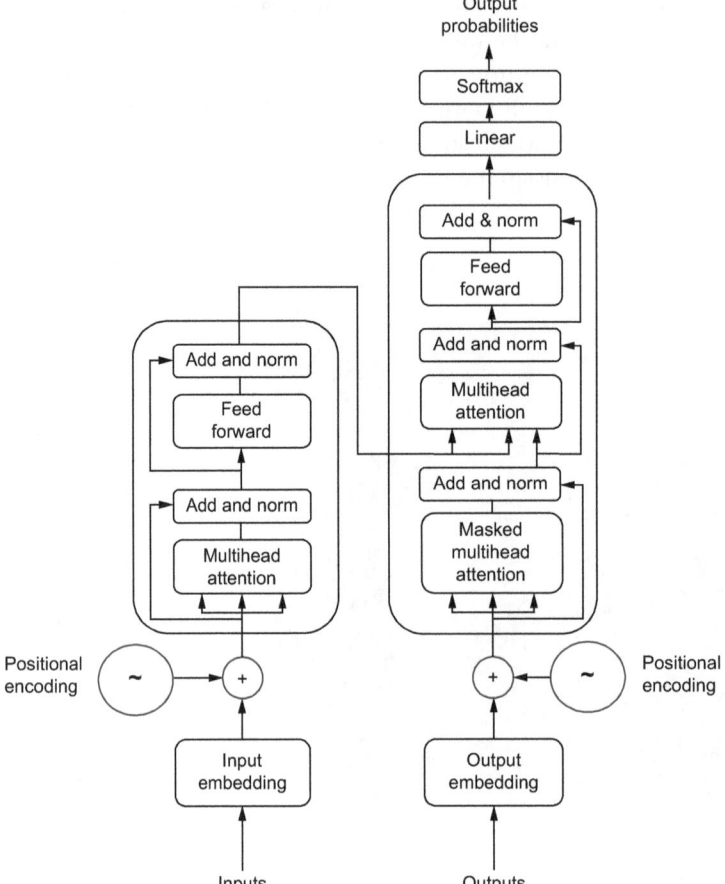

Figure 11.10
Transformer
architecture

The idea of self-attention can be expanded to multihead attention. In essence, we run the attention mechanism in parallel and form several output heads, as shown in figure 11.11. The heads are then concatenated and transformed using a dense layer. With multihead attention, the model has multiple independent ways to understand the input.

For the model to make use of the order of the sequence, we need to inject some information about the position of tokens in the sequence. This is precisely the purpose of positional encodings that get added to the input embeddings at the bottom of the encoder and decoder stacks. The positional encodings have the same dimensions as the embeddings so that the two can be summed. Thus,

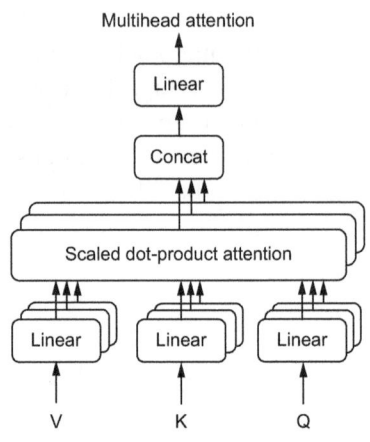

Figure 11.11 Multihead attention

if the same word appears in a different position, the actual word representation will be different, depending on where it appears in the sentence.

Finally, layer normalization is used to normalize the input by computing mean and variance across channels and spatial dimensions and a linear (dense) layer is added to complete the encoder. The linear layer comes after multihead self-attention to project the representation in higher dimensional space and then back to the original space. This helps solve stability issues and counters bad initializations.

If we look closely at the decoder, we'll notice it contains all of the earlier components, in addition to a masked multihead self-attention layer and a new multihead attention layer, known as *encoder-decoder attention*. The final output of the decoder is transformed through a final linear layer, and the output probabilities that predict the next token in the output sequence are calculated with the standard softmax function.

The purpose of masked attention is to respect causality when generating the output sentence. Since the entire sentence is not yet available and is generated one token at a time, we mask the output by introducing a mask matrix M that contains only two types of values: zero and negative infinity.

$$\text{MaskedAttention}(Q, K, V) = \text{softmax}\left(\frac{QK^T + M}{\sqrt{D}}\right)V \qquad (11.17)$$

Eventually, the zeros will be transformed into ones via softmax, while negative infinities will become zero, effectively removing the corresponding connection from the output.

The encoder–decoder attention is simply the multihead self-attention we are already familiar with, except the query Q comes from a different source than the keys K and values V. This attention is also known in the literature as *cross-attention*. Remember that in the machine translation example, our target sequence or query Q comes from the decoder, while the encoder acts like a database and provides us with keys K and values V. The intuition behind the encoder–decoder attention layer is to combine the input and output sentences. Thus, the encoder–decoder attention is trained to associate the input sentence with the corresponding output word, determining how related each target word is with respect to the input words.

And that's it! We are now ready to implement a transformer-based classifier from scratch! You may want to run the code listing in a Google Colab notebook (accessible at https://colab.research.google.com/) to understand the code step by step and accelerate model training via GPU.

Listing 11.3 Transformer for text classification

```
import numpy as np
import pandas as pd

import tensorflow as tf
from tensorflow import keras
```

```
from keras.models import Model, Sequential
from keras.layers import Layer, Dense, Dropout, Activation
from keras.layers import LayerNormalization, MultiHeadAttention
from keras.layers import Input, Embedding, GlobalAveragePooling1D

from keras import regularizers
from keras.preprocessing import sequence
from keras.utils import np_utils

from keras.callbacks import ModelCheckpoint
from keras.callbacks import TensorBoard
from keras.callbacks import LearningRateScheduler
from keras.callbacks import EarlyStopping

import matplotlib.pyplot as plt

tf.keras.utils.set_random_seed(42)

SAVE_PATH = "/content/drive/MyDrive/Colab Notebooks/data/"

def scheduler(epoch, lr):       ◄──── Learning rate schedule
    if epoch < 4:
        return lr
    else:
        return lr * tf.math.exp(-0.1)

#load dataset                       Top 20,000 most frequent words
max_words = 20000   ◄───────
seq_len = 200                                   First 200 words of
(x_train, y_train), (x_val, y_val) =            each movie review
➥ keras.datasets.imdb.load_data(num_words=max_words)

x_train = keras.utils.pad_sequences(x_train, maxlen=seq_len)
x_val = keras.utils.pad_sequences(x_val, maxlen=seq_len)

class TransformerBlock(Layer):
    def __init__(self, embed_dim, num_heads, ff_dim, rate=0.1):
        super(TransformerBlock, self).__init__()
        self.att = MultiHeadAttention(num_heads=num_heads, key_dim=embed_dim)
        self.ffn = Sequential(
            [Dense(ff_dim, activation="relu"), Dense(embed_dim)]
        )
        self.layernorm1 = LayerNormalization(epsilon=1e-6)
        self.layernorm2 = LayerNormalization(epsilon=1e-6)
        self.dropout1 = Dropout(rate)
        self.dropout2 = Dropout(rate)

    def call(self, inputs, training):
        attn_output = self.att(inputs, inputs)
        attn_output = self.dropout1(attn_output, training=training)
        out1 = self.layernorm1(inputs + attn_output)
        ffn_output = self.ffn(out1)
        ffn_output = self.dropout2(ffn_output, training=training)
        return self.layernorm2(out1 + ffn_output)

class TokenAndPositionEmbedding(Layer):
```

```
    def __init__(self, maxlen, vocab_size, embed_dim):
        super(TokenAndPositionEmbedding, self).__init__()
        self.token_emb = Embedding(input_dim=vocab_size,
        ➥ output_dim=embed_dim)
        self.pos_emb = Embedding(input_dim=maxlen, output_dim=embed_dim)

    def call(self, x):
        maxlen = tf.shape(x)[-1]
        positions = tf.range(start=0, limit=maxlen, delta=1)
        positions = self.pos_emb(positions)
        x = self.token_emb(x)
        return x + positions

batch_size = 32         | Training params
num_epochs = 8          |

embed_dim = 32          |
num_heads = 2           | Model parameters
ff_dim = 32             |

#transformer architecture
inputs = Input(shape=(seq_len,))
embedding_layer = TokenAndPositionEmbedding(seq_len, max_words, embed_dim)
x = embedding_layer(inputs)
transformer_block = TransformerBlock(embed_dim, num_heads, ff_dim)
x = transformer_block(x)
x = GlobalAveragePooling1D()(x)
x = Dropout(0.1)(x)
x = Dense(20, activation="relu")(x)
x = Dropout(0.1)(x)
outputs = Dense(2, activation="softmax")(x)

model = Model(inputs=inputs, outputs=outputs)

model.compile(
  loss=keras.losses.SparseCategoricalCrossentropy(),
  optimizer=tf.keras.optimizers.Adam(),
  metrics=["accuracy"]
)

#define callbacks
file_name = SAVE_PATH + 'transformer-weights-checkpoint.h5'
#checkpoint = ModelCheckpoint(file_name, monitor='val_loss', verbose=1,
➥ save_best_only=True, mode='min')
reduce_lr = LearningRateScheduler(scheduler, verbose=1)
early_stopping = EarlyStopping(monitor='val_loss', min_delta=0.01,
➥ patience=16, verbose=1)
#tensor_board = TensorBoard(log_dir='./logs', write_graph=True)
callbacks_list = [reduce_lr, early_stopping]

hist = model.fit(x_train, y_train, batch_size=batch_size,
➥ epochs=num_epochs, callbacks=callbacks_list, validation_data=(x_val,
➥ y_val))                              ⟵—— Model evaluation

test_scores = model.evaluate(x_val, y_val, verbose=2)   ⟵—— Model training
```

```
print("Test loss:", test_scores[0])
print("Test accuracy:", test_scores[1])

plt.figure()
plt.plot(hist.history['loss'], 'b', lw=2.0, label='train')
plt.plot(hist.history['val_loss'], '--r', lw=2.0, label='val')
plt.title('Transformer model')
plt.xlabel('Epochs')
plt.ylabel('Cross-Entropy Loss')
plt.legend(loc='upper right')
plt.show()

plt.figure()
plt.plot(hist.history['accuracy'], 'b', lw=2.0, label='train')
plt.plot(hist.history['val_accuracy'], '--r', lw=2.0, label='val')
plt.title('Transformer model')
plt.xlabel('Epochs')
plt.ylabel('Accuracy')
plt.legend(loc='upper left')
plt.show()

plt.figure()
plt.plot(hist.history['lr'], lw=2.0, label='learning rate')
plt.title('Transformer model')
plt.xlabel('Epochs')
plt.ylabel('Learning Rate')
plt.legend()
plt.show()
```

From figure 11.12, we can see early signs of overfitting. By preserving the model with lowest validation loss, we avoid the problem of overfitting.

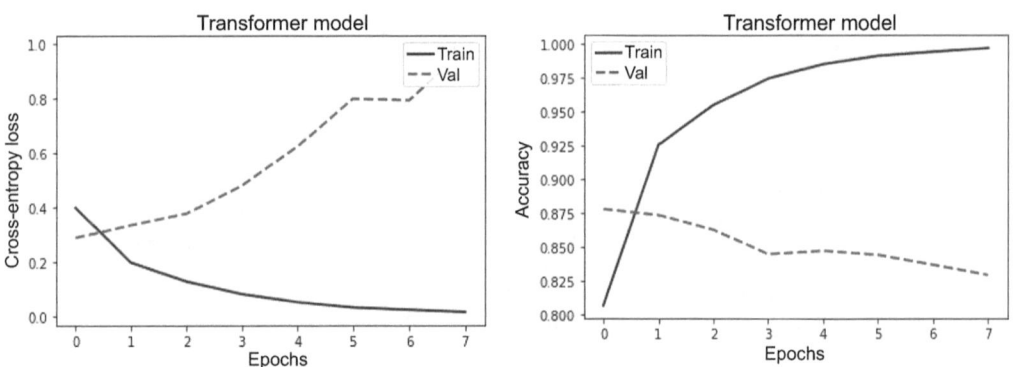

Figure 11.12 Transformer classifier loss (left) and accuracy (right) on training and validation datasets

In this section, we observed how self-attention can be used inside the transformer architecture to learn text sentiment. In the following section, we will study neural networks in application to graph data.

11.4   Graph neural networks

A wide variety of types of information can be represented by graphs. Some examples of graphs include knowledge graphs, social networks, molecular structures, and document citation networks. Graph neural networks (GNNs) operate on graphs and relational data. In this section, we'll study graph convolutional networks (GCNs) for classifying nodes in the CORA citation network dataset. But first, let's look at GNN fundamentals.

Let $G=(V,E)$ be our graph with vertices V and edges E. We can construct an adjacency matrix A to capture the interconnection of edges, such that $A_{ij} = 1$ if an edge exists between nodes i and j and 0 otherwise. For undirected graphs, we have a symmetric adjacency matrix such that $A = A^T$. Another matrix that will prove useful in training GNNs is the node feature matrix x. Assuming we have N nodes and F features per node, the size of X is $N{\times}F$.

As an example, in a CORA dataset, each node is a document and each edge is a citation that forms a directed edge between two nodes. We can capture the citation relationships in the adjacency matrix A. Since each document is a collection of words, we can introduce indicator features that tell us whether a particular dictionary word is present or absent from the document. In this case, N will be the number of documents and F will be the dictionary size. Thus, we can represent the text information in each document via a binary $N{\times}F$ matrix X.

It's important to note that edges can have their own features as well. In this case, if the size of edge features is S and the number of edges is M, we can construct an edge feature matrix E of size $M{\times}S$. It's also important to make a distinction between classifying the entire graph as a whole (e.g., as in molecule classification) and classifying nodes within a graph (e.g., as in the CORA citation network). The former method is called *batch mode classification*, while the latter is referred to as *single mode.*

It's interesting to draw a parallel between GCNs and CNNs. Images can also be seen as graphs, albeit with regular structure. For example, each node can represent a pixel, the node feature can represent the pixel value, and the edge feature can represent the Euclidean distance between each pixel in a complete graph. In this light, GCNs can be seen as a generalization of CNNs, since they operate on arbitrarily connected graphs.

We can think of information propagation in a spectral GCN as signal propagation along the nodes. Spectral GCN uses Eigen decomposition of a graph Laplacian matrix to propagate the signal with key forward equation as follows.

$$X' = D^{-\frac{1}{2}}(A + I)D^{-\frac{1}{2}}XW + b \tag{11.18}$$

Let's understand this equation step by step. If we take adjacency matrix A and multiply it by the feature matrix X, the product AX represents the sum of neighboring node features. However, this sum is over all the neighboring nodes except the node itself. To fix this, we add a self-loop in the adjacency matrix by summing it with an identity. This brings us to $(A + I) X$; however, this product is not normalized. To do so, we will divide by the degree of each node. Thus, we form a diagonal degree matrix D, pre and post multiplying our expression by the square root of D. Next, we add the familiar product by the learnable weight w and a bias term b. We wrap this in a nonlinearity, and voila! We have our forward GCN equation.

We are now ready to implement our graph neural network using the Spektral Keras/Tensorflow library. In listing 11.4, we begin by importing the dataset that can be found in the data folder of the code repository. We prepare the data for processing and define graph neural network architecture. We proceed by training the model and displaying the results. You may want to run the code listing in a Google Colab notebook (accessible at https://colab.research.google.com/) to understand the code step by step and accelerate model training via GPU.

Listing 11.4   Graph convolutional neural network for classifying citation graphs

```
import numpy as np
import pandas as pd

import tensorflow as tf
from tensorflow import keras

import networkx as nx
from tensorflow.keras.utils import to_categorical
from sklearn.preprocessing import LabelEncoder
from sklearn.utils import shuffle
from sklearn.metrics import classification_report
from sklearn.model_selection import train_test_split

from spektral.layers import GCNConv

from tensorflow.keras.models import Model
from tensorflow.keras.layers import Input, Dropout, Dense
from tensorflow.keras import Sequential
from tensorflow.keras.optimizers import Adam
from tensorflow.keras.callbacks import TensorBoard, EarlyStopping
from tensorflow.keras.regularizers import l2

import os
from collections import Counter
from sklearn.manifold import TSNE
import matplotlib.pyplot as plt

tf.keras.utils.set_random_seed(42)

SAVE_PATH = "/content/drive/MyDrive/Colab Notebooks/data/"
DATA_PATH = "/content/drive/MyDrive/data/cora/"

column_names = ["paper_id"] + [f"term_{idx}" for idx in range(1433)] +
➥ ["subject"]
node_df = pd.read_csv(DATA_PATH + "cora.content", sep="\t", header=None,
➥ names=column_names)
```

```
print("Node df shape:", node_df.shape)

edge_df = pd.read_csv(DATA_PATH + "cora.cites", sep="\t", header=None,
▶ names=["target", "source"])
print("Edge df shape:", edge_df.shape)

nodes = node_df.iloc[:,0].tolist()          Parses node
labels = node_df.iloc[:,-1].tolist()        data
X = node_df.iloc[:,1:-1].values

X = np.array(X,dtype=int)
N = X.shape[0] #the number of nodes
F = X.shape[1] #the size of node features

edge_list = [(x, y) for x, y in zip(edge_df['target'],
▶ edge_df['source'])]                    ◀───
                                              | Parses edge data
num_classes = len(set(labels))

print('Number of nodes:', N)
print('Number of features of each node:', F)
print('Labels:', set(labels))
print('Number of classes:', num_classes)

def sample_data(labels, limit=20, val_num=500, test_num=1000):
    label_counter = dict((l, 0) for l in labels)
    train_idx = []

    for i in range(len(labels)):
        label = labels[i]
        if label_counter[label]<limit:
            #add the example to the training data
            train_idx.append(i)
            label_counter[label]+=1

        #exit the loop once we found 20 examples for each class
        if all(count == limit for count in label_counter.values()):
            break

    #get the indices that do not go to traning data
    rest_idx = [x for x in range(len(labels)) if x not in train_idx]
    #get the first val_num
    val_idx = rest_idx[:val_num]
    test_idx = rest_idx[val_num:(val_num+test_num)]
    return train_idx, val_idx,test_idx


train_idx,val_idx,test_idx = sample_data(labels)

#set the mask
train_mask = np.zeros((N,),dtype=bool)
train_mask[train_idx] = True

val_mask = np.zeros((N,),dtype=bool)
val_mask[val_idx] = True
```

```
test_mask = np.zeros((N,),dtype=bool)
test_mask[test_idx] = True

print("Training data distribution:\n{}".format(Counter([labels[i] for i in
➥  train_idx])))
print("Validation data distribution:\n{}".format(Counter([labels[i] for i
➥  in val_idx])))

def encode_label(labels):
    label_encoder = LabelEncoder()
    labels = label_encoder.fit_transform(labels)
    labels = to_categorical(labels)
    return labels, label_encoder.classes_

labels_encoded, classes = encode_label(labels)

G = nx.Graph()                           Builds the
G.add_nodes_from(nodes)                  graph
G.add_edges_from(edge_list)

A = nx.adjacency_matrix(G)        ◁─── Obtains the adjacency matrix
print('Graph info: ', nx.info(G))

# Parameters                   Number of channels in the first layer
channels = 16         ◁────┘
dropout = 0.5        ◁──────── Dropout rate for the features
l2_reg = 5e-4          ◁──── L2 regularization rate
learning_rate = 1e-2
epochs = 200           ◁──── Number of training epochs
es_patience = 10      ◁─┐
                        Patience for early stopping

# Preprocessing operations
A = GCNConv.preprocess(A).astype('f4')

# Model definition
X_in = Input(shape=(F, ))
fltr_in = Input((N, ), sparse=True)

dropout_1 = Dropout(dropout)(X_in)
graph_conv_1 = GCNConv(channels,
                       activation='relu',
                       kernel_regularizer=l2(l2_reg),
                       use_bias=False)([dropout_1, fltr_in])

dropout_2 = Dropout(dropout)(graph_conv_1)
graph_conv_2 = GCNConv(num_classes,
                       activation='softmax',
                       use_bias=False)([dropout_2, fltr_in])

# Build model
model = Model(inputs=[X_in, fltr_in], outputs=graph_conv_2)
model.compile(optimizer=Adam(learning_rate=learning_rate),
              loss='categorical_crossentropy',
              weighted_metrics=['accuracy'])
```

Learning rate → learning_rate = 1e-2

```
model.summary()

# Train model
validation_data = ([X, A], labels_encoded, val_mask)
hist = model.fit([X, A],
            labels_encoded,
            sample_weight=train_mask,
            epochs=epochs,
            batch_size=N,
            validation_data=validation_data,
            shuffle=False,
            callbacks=[
                EarlyStopping(patience=es_patience,  restore_best_weights=True)
            ])
```

Model training

```
# Evaluate model
X_test = X
A_test = A
y_test = labels_encoded
```

Model evaluation

```
y_pred = model.predict([X_test, A_test], batch_size=N)
report = classification_report(np.argmax(y_test,axis=1),
    np.argmax(y_pred,axis=1), target_names=classes)
print('GCN Classification Report: \n {}'.format(report))

layer_outputs = [layer.output for layer in model.layers]
activation_model = Model(inputs=model.input, outputs=layer_outputs)
activations = activation_model.predict([X,A],batch_size=N)

#Get t-SNE Representation
#get the hidden layer representation after the first GCN layer
x_tsne = TSNE(n_components=2).fit_transform(activations[3])

def plot_tSNE(labels_encoded,x_tsne):
    color_map = np.argmax(labels_encoded, axis=1)
    plt.figure(figsize=(10,10))
    for cl in range(num_classes):
        indices = np.where(color_map==cl)
        indices = indices[0]
        plt.scatter(x_tsne[indices,0], x_tsne[indices, 1], label=cl)
    plt.legend()
    plt.show()

plot_tSNE(labels_encoded,x_tsne)

plt.figure()
plt.plot(hist.history['loss'], 'b', lw=2.0, label='train')
plt.plot(hist.history['val_loss'], '--r', lw=2.0, label='val')
plt.title('GNN model')
plt.xlabel('Epochs')
plt.ylabel('Cross-Entropy Loss')
plt.legend(loc='upper right')
plt.show()

plt.figure()
```

```
plt.plot(hist.history['accuracy'], 'b', lw=2.0, label='train')
plt.plot(hist.history['val_accuracy'], '--r', lw=2.0, label='val')
plt.title('GNN model')
plt.xlabel('Epochs')
plt.ylabel('Accuracy')
plt.legend(loc='upper left')
plt.show()
```

Figure 11.13 shows classification loss and accuracy for training and validation datasets.

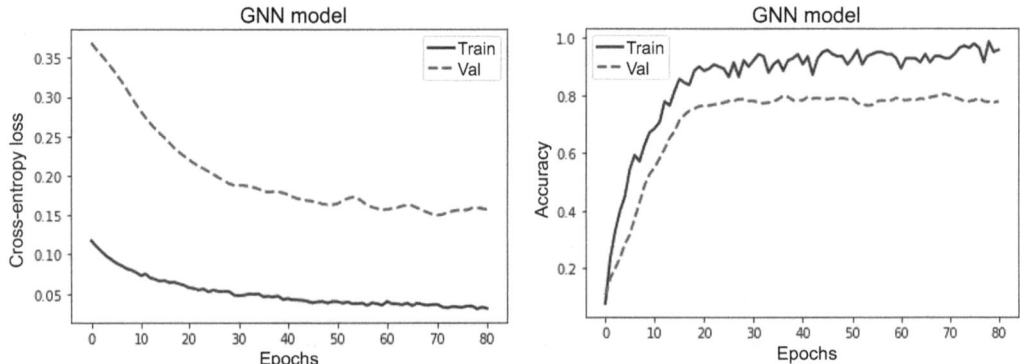

Figure 11.13   GNN model loss and accuracy for training and validation datasets

Figure 11.14 shows the t-SNE hidden layer representation of the CORA dataset embedding after the first GCN layer.

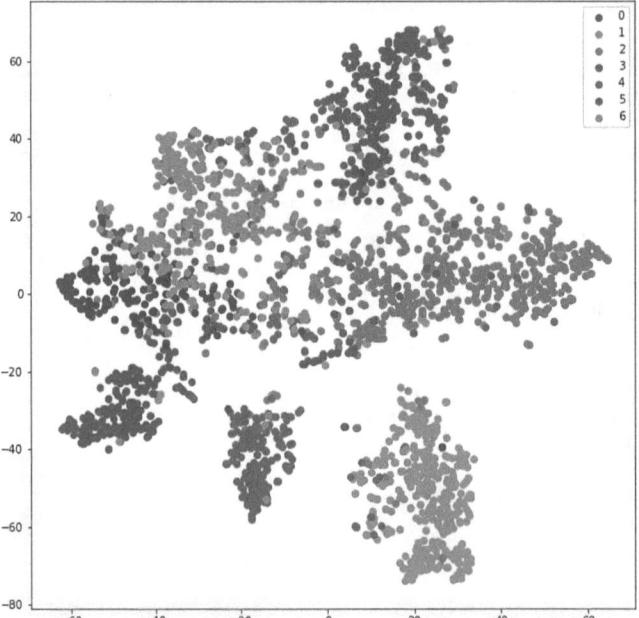

Figure 11.14   t-SNE hidden layer representation of the CORA dataset embedding after the first GCN layer

In the following section, we will review deep learning research in the area of computer vision and natural language processing.

11.5 *ML research: Deep learning*

In the area of computer vision (CV), the CNN architecture has evolved from convolutional, ReLU, and max pooling operations of LeNet (Yann LeCun et al.'s "Gradient-Based Learning Applied to Document Recognition," In Proceedings of the IEEE, 1998) to inception modules of GoogLeNet (Christian Szegedy et al.'s "Going Deeper with Convolutions," *Computer Vision and Pattern Recognition*, 2015). The inception module creates variable receptive fields by employing different kernel sizes. This, in turn, allows the capturing of sparse correlation patterns in the new feature map stack. GoogLeNet offers high accuracy on the ImageNet dataset with fewer parameters than AlexNet (Alex Krizhevsky, Ilya Sutskever, and Geoffrey E. Hinton's "ImageNet Classification with Deep Convolutional Neural Networks," Conference on Neural Information Processing Systems, 2012) or VGG (Karen Simonyan and Andrew Zisserman's "Very Deep Convolutional Networks for Large-Scale Image Recognition," International Conference on Learning Representations, 2015). We saw the introduction of residual connections in the ResNet model (Kaiming He et al.'s "Deep Residual Learning for Image Recognition," Conference on Computer Vision and Pattern Recognition, 2015), which became the standard architectural choice for modern neural networks of arbitrary depth. Fast-forwarding to ision transformer (ViT) model (Alexey Dosovitskiy et al.'s "An Image is Worth 16x16 Words: Transformers for Image Recognition at Scale," International Conference on Learning Representations, 2021) employs a transformer-like architecture over patches of the image. The image is divided into fixed-size patches, each of which being linearly and positionally embedded and the resulting sequence of vectors fed to a standard transformer encoder followed by a MLP head for classification.

In the area of generative models, generative adversarial networks (GANs), introduced by Ian Goodfellow et al in "Generative Adversarial Networks" (Conference and Workshop on Neural Information Processing Systems, 2014), draw on the ideas from game theory and use two networks trained to approximate the distribution of the data: a generator to generate images and a discriminator to discriminate between real and fake images. On the other hand, likelihood-based generative models model the distribution of the data, using a likelihood function. The most popular subclass of likelihood-based generative models is the variational autoencoder (VAE), introduced by Diederik P. Kingma and Max Welling in "Auto-Encoding Variational Bayes" (International Conference on Learning Representations, 2014). A VAE consists of an encoder that takes in data as input, transforming it into a latent representation, and a decoder that takes a latent representation and returns a reconstruction. A beta-VAE is a modification of VAE with a special emphasis on discovering disentangled latent factors (Irina Higgins et al.'s "beta-VAE: Learning Basic Visual Concepts with a Constrained Variational Framework," International Conference on Learning Representations, 2017).

Shifting the spotlight to diffusion models, which gained popularity for their ability to generate high resolution images, are parametrized Markov chains trained using variational inference to produce samples matching the input data. Diffusion models consist of a forward pass, in which an image gets progressively noisier via additive Gaussian noise, and a reverse pass, in which the noise is transformed back into a sample from the target distribution (Jonathan Ho, Ajay Jain, and Pieter Abbeel's "Denoising Diffusion Probabilistic Models," Conference and Workshop on Neural Information Processing Systems, 2020).

In the area of natural language processing (NLP), the architecture for machine translation, for example, has evolved from Seq2Seq LSTM models to transformer-based models, such as BERT (Jacob Devlin et al.'s "BERT: Pre-training of Deep Bidirectional Transformers for Language Understanding," North American Chapter of the Association for Computational Linguistics, 2019). The pretrained BERT model can be fine-tuned with just one additional output layer to create state-of-the-art models for a wide range of tasks, such as question answering and language inference, without substantial task-specific architectural modifications. Zero-shot and few-shot learning gained popularity with large Transformer models, such as GPT-3, introduced by Tom B. Brown et al. in "Language Models are Few-Shot Learners" (Conference and Workshop on Neural Information Processing Systems, 2020). The applications of GPT-3 range from text completion to code completion. For example, OpenAI's codex model, which is a descendant of the GPT-3 series that's trained on natural language as well as billions of lines of code, serves as an AI pair programmer that can turn comments into code and complete the next line or function in context.

A number of learning tasks require processing graph data that contains rich relational information, from modeling social networks to predicting protein structure calls for a model that can work with graph data. Graph neural networks (GNNs) are neural models that capture dependence relationships via message passing between the nodes of the graph (Thomas N. Kipf and Max Welling's "Semi-Supervised Classification with Graph Convolutional Networks," International Conference on Learning Representations, 2017). In recent years, variants of GNNs, such as graph convolutional networks (GCNs), graph attention networks (GATs), and graph recurrent networks (GRNs), have demonstrated groundbreaking performance on many deep learning tasks.

Finally, amortized variational inference (D. P. Kingma's "Variational Inference and Deep Learning: A New Synthesis," University of Amsterdam, 2017) is an interesting research area, as it combines the expressive power and representation learning of deep neural networks with domain knowledge of probabilistic graphical models. We saw one such application of MDNs when we used a neural network to map from the observation space to the parameters of the approximate posterior distribution.

Deep learning research is a very active field. For state-of-the-art developments and applications, the reader is encouraged to review the Conference and Workshop on Neural Information Processing Systems, the International Conference on Learning Representations, and the research conferences mentioned in appendix A.

11.6 Exercises

11.1 What is a receptive field in a CNN?

11.2 Explain the benefit of residual connections by deriving the backward pass.

11.3 Compare the pros and cons of using CNNs, RNNs, and transformer neural networks.

11.4 Give an example of a neural network that uses amortized variational inference.

11.5 Show via an example the intuition behind the GCN forward equation: $D^{-1/2}(A+I)D^{-1/2}XW+b$.

Summary

- Autoencoders are unsupervised neural networks trained to reconstruct the input. The bottleneck layer of the autoencoder can be used for dimensionality reduction or feature extraction.

- A variational autoencoder consists of an encoder that takes in data as input, transforming it into a latent representation, and a decoder that takes a latent representation, returning a reconstruction.

- Amortized variational inference is the idea that instead of optimizing a set of free parameters, we can introduce a parameterized function that maps from observation space to the parameters of the approximate posterior distribution.

- Mixture density networks are mixture models in which the parameters, such as means, covariances, and mixture proportions, are learned by a neural network.

- Attention allows a model to adaptively focus on different parts of the input by adjusting the attention weights.

- A transformer is a Seq2Seq model that uses attention in the encoder as well as the decoder. Self-attention is the key component of transformer architecture.

- Graph neural networks are neural models that capture dependence relationships via passing messages between the nodes of the graph.

appendix A
Further reading
and resources

A.1   Competitive programming

There are a number of great resources available for learning algorithms. I highly recommend Steven Halim's *Competitive Programming* book, in addition to the classic *Algorithm Design Manual* by Steven Skiena and *Introduction to Algorithms* by Thomas H. Cormen et al.

There are a number of great coding challenge websites some of which are listed here:

- LeetCode: https://leetcode.com
- TopCoder: https://www.topcoder.com
- CodeForces: https://codeforces.com
- HackerRank: https://www.hackerrank.com
- GeeksForGeeks: https://www.geeksforgeeks.org
- uVAOnlineJudge: https://onlinejudge.org

I hope you find these resources helpful in your journey to becoming a competitive programmer.

A.2   Recommended books

Machine learning mastery requires a solid understanding of fundamentals. New ML algorithms are designed by building on the fundamentals or combining new trends with classical results. This section highlights some of the key machine learning books that anyone who strives to get better in the field must read. The books summarized in figure A.1 range from theoretical to applied and span the topics of statistics, machine learning, optimization, information theory, algorithms, and data structures.

Figure A.1   Recommended books

I highly recommend the following books, as shown in figure A.1, on your journey to machine learning mastery:

- Kevin Murphy, *Machine Learning: A Probabilistic Perspective*, MIT Press, 2012
- Christopher Bishop, *Patter Recognition and Machine Learning*, Springer, 2011
- David MacKay, *Information Theory, Inference, and Learning Algorithms*, Cambridge University Press, 2003
- Steven Skiena, *Algorithm Design Manual*, Springer, 2011
- Thomas Cormen, Charles Leiserson, Ronald Rivest, and Clifford Stein, *Introduction to Algorithms*, MIT Press, 2009
- Steven Halim, *Competitive Programming*, lulu, 2013
- Francois Chollet, *Deep Learning with Python*, Manning Publications, 2017
- Trevor Hastie, Robert Tibshirani, and Jerome Friedman, *The Elements of Statistical Learning: Data Mining, Inference, and Prediction*, Springer, 2016
- Stephen Boyd and Lieven Vandenberghe, *Convex Optimization*, Cambridge University Press, 2004
- Thomas Cover and Joy A. Thomas, *Elements of Information Theory*, Wiley, 1991

A.3   *Research conferences*

The field of machine learning is rapidly evolving, and the best way to stay on top of latest research is by reviewing conference papers. This section summarizes the top conferences in the area of machine learning, computer vision, natural language processing, and theoretical computer science.

A.3.1   *Machine learning*

- NeurIPS: Neural Information Processing Systems: https://nips.cc/
- ICLR: International Conference on Learning Representations: https://iclr.cc/
- ICML: International Conference on Machine Learning: https://icml.cc/
- AISTATS: Artificial Intelligence and Statistics: https://www.aistats.org/
- UAI: Uncertainty in Artificial Intelligence: https://www.auai.org/

A.3.2   *Computer vision*

- CVPR: Computer Vision and Pattern Recognition
- ICCV: International Conference on Computer Vision
- ECCV: European Conference on Computer Vision

A.3.3   *Natural language processing*

- EMNLP: Empirical Methods in Natural Language Processing
- NAACL: North American chapter of the ACL

A.3.4   *Theoretical computer science*

- STOC: ACM Symposium on Theory of Computing: http://acm-stoc.org/
- FOCS: IEEE Symposium on Foundations of Computer Science: http://ieee-focs.org/

To be an expert in your area, it's important to stay current with latest research. All conference proceedings are available online on their official websites as well as on arxiv.org. To make the volume of research papers manageable and to more easily track latest arXiv papers, readers can visit http://www.arxiv-sanity.com/. For a quick overview and AI conference deadlines, visit https://aideadlin.es/?sub=ML,CV,NLP,RO,SP. Finally, reproducible state-of-the-art machine learning results can be found at https://paperswithcode.com/.

appendix B
Answers to exercises

2.1 Derive full conditionals $p(x_A|x_B)$ for multivariate Gaussian distribution, where A and B are subsets of x_1, x_2, ..., x_n of jointly Gaussian random variables.

Let's partition our vector x into two subsets, x_A and x_B, and then we can write down the mean and covariance matrices in block form:

$$\mu = \begin{pmatrix} \mu_A \\ \mu_B \end{pmatrix}$$

$$\Sigma = \begin{pmatrix} \Sigma_{AA} & \Sigma_{AB} \\ \Sigma_{BA} & \Sigma_{BB} \end{pmatrix}$$

To compute the conditional distributions, we get the following result:

$$p(x_A|x_B) = N\left(x_A|\mu_A + \Sigma_{AB}\Sigma_{BB}^{-1}(x_B - \mu_B), \Sigma_{AA} - \Sigma_{AB}\Sigma_{BB}^{-1}\Sigma_{BA}\right)$$

$$p(x_B|x_A) = N\left(x_B|\mu_B + \Sigma_{BA}\Sigma_{AA}^{-1}(x_A - \mu_A), \Sigma_{BB} - \Sigma_{BA}\Sigma_{AA}^{-1}\Sigma_{AB}\right)$$

2.2 Derive marginals $p(x_A)$ and $p(x_B)$ for multivariate Gaussian distribution, where A and B are subsets of x_1, x_2, ..., x_n of jointly Gaussian random variables.

Let's partition our vector x into two subsets, x_A and x_B, and then we can write down the mean and covariance matrices in block form:

$$\mu = \begin{pmatrix} \mu_A \\ \mu_B \end{pmatrix}$$

$$\Sigma = \begin{pmatrix} \Sigma_{AA} & \Sigma_{AB} \\ \Sigma_{BA} & \Sigma_{BB} \end{pmatrix}$$

To compute the marginals, we simply read off corresponding rows and columns from mean and covariance:

$$p(x_A) = \int N(x|\mu, \Sigma)dx_B = N(x_A|\mu_A, \Sigma_{AA})$$

$$p(x_B) = \int N(x|\mu, \Sigma)dx_B = N(x_B|\mu_B, \Sigma_{BB})$$

2.3 Let $y \sim N(\mu, \Sigma)$, where $\Sigma = LL^T$. Show that you can get samples y as follows: $x \sim N(0, I)$; $y = Lx + \mu$.

Let $y = Lx + \mu$. Then, $E[y] = LE[x] + \mu = 0 + \mu = \mu$. Similarly, $cov(y) = L\ cov(x)L^T + 0 = LIL^T = LL^T = \Sigma$. Since y is an affine transformation of a Gaussian RV, y is also Gaussian distributed as $y \sim N(\mu, \Sigma)$.

3.1 Compute KL divergence between two univariate Guassians: $p(x) \sim N(\mu_1, \sigma_1^2)$ and $q(x) \sim N(\mu_2, \sigma_2^2)$.

$$
\begin{aligned}
KL(p||q) &= -\int p(x) \log q(x)dx + \int p(x) \log p(x)dx \\
&= \frac{1}{2} \log\left(2\pi\sigma_2^2\right) + \frac{\sigma_1^2 + (\mu_1 - \mu_2)^2}{2\sigma_2^2} \\
&\quad - \frac{1}{2}\left(1 + \log 2\pi\sigma_1^2\right) \\
&= \log\frac{\sigma_2}{\sigma_1} + \frac{\sigma_1^2 + (\mu_1 - \mu_2)^2}{2\sigma_2^2} - \frac{1}{2}
\end{aligned}
$$

3.2 Compute $E[X], \mathrm{Var}(X)$, and $H(X)$ for a Bernoulli distribution.

A Bernoulli distribution is defined as $p(x) = p^x(1-p)^{1-x}$, where $x \in \{0,1\}$. By the definitions of mean, variance, and entropy, we can compute the following quantities:

$$E[X] = \sum_{x \in \{0,1\}} p_x(x)x = p_x(0) \times 0 + p_x(1) \times 1 = p$$

$$
\begin{aligned}
var(X) &= E[X^2] - E[X]^2 = \sum_{x \in \{0,1\}} p_x(x)x^2 - p^2 \\
&= p_x(0) \times 0^2 + p_x(1) \times 1^2 - p^2 = p(1-p)
\end{aligned}
$$

$$
\begin{aligned}
H(X) &= -\sum_{x \in \{0,1\}} p_x(x) \log p_x(x) \\
&= -p_x(0) \log p_x(0) - p_x(1) \log p_x(1) \\
&= -(1-p) \log(1-p) - p \log p
\end{aligned}
$$

3.3 Derive the mean, mode, and variance of a Beta(a,b) distribution.

The beta distribution has support over the interval $[0, 1]$ and is defined as follows:

$$\text{Beta}(x|a, b) = \frac{\Gamma(a+b)}{\Gamma(a)\Gamma(b)} x^{a-1}(1-x)^{b-1}$$

We have the following expressions for the mean, mode, and variance of the Beta distribution:

$$E[X] = \frac{a}{a+b} \qquad \text{mode}[X] = \frac{a-1}{a+b-2} \qquad \text{VAR}(X) = \frac{ab}{(a+b)^2(a+b+1)}$$

4.1 Prove the following binomial identity: $C(n, k) = C(n-1, k-1) + C(n-1, k)$.

We'll be using an algebraic proof. By definition, expanding the left-hand side, we have the following:

$$\binom{n-1}{k-1} + \binom{n-1}{k} = \frac{(n-1)!}{(n-k)! \cdot (k-1)!} + \frac{(n-1)!}{(n-k-1)! \cdot (k)!}$$

$$= \frac{(n-1)!}{(n-k-1)! \cdot (k-1)!} \cdot \left(\frac{1}{n-k} + \frac{1}{k} \right)$$

$$= \frac{n!}{(n-k)! \cdot k!}$$

$$= \binom{n}{k}$$

4.2 Derive the Gibbs inequality $H(p, q) \geq H(q)$, where $H(p, q) = -\sum p(x) \log q(x)$ is the cross-entropy and $H(q) = -\sum q(x) \log q(x)$ is the entropy.

First, we show that KL divergence is nonnegative:

$$-KL(p\|q) = -\sum_x p(x) \log \frac{p(x)}{q(x)} dx = \sum_x p(x) \log \frac{q(x)}{p(x)} dx$$

$$\leq \log \sum_x p(x) \frac{q(x)}{p(x)} dx = \log \sum_x q(x)$$

$$\leq \log 1 = 0$$

Using the previously derived property, we can write down the Gibbs inequality as follows:

$$KL(p\|q) \geq 0$$

$$\sum_x p(x) \log p(x) - \sum_x p(x) \log q(x) \geq 0$$

$$-H(p) + H(p, q) \geq 0$$

$$H(p, q) \geq H(p)$$

4.3 Use Jensen's inequality with $f(x) = \log(x)$ to prove the AM $\geq$ GM inequality.

Since $f(x) = \log(x)$ is a concave function, we can write the Jensen's inequality as follows:

$$
\begin{aligned}
f(E[x]) &\geq E[f(x)] \\
\log(E[x]) &\geq E[\log(x)] \\
\log(\frac{x_1 + \cdots + x_n}{n}) &\geq \frac{\log x_1 + \cdots + \log x_n}{n} \\
\log(\frac{x_1 + \cdots + x_n}{n}) &\geq \log(x_1 \times \cdots \times x_n)^{\frac{1}{n}} \\
AM &\geq GM
\end{aligned}
$$

4.4 Prove that $I(x;y) = H(x) - H(x|y) = H(y) - H(y|x)$.

By the definition of mutual information, we have the following:

$$
\begin{aligned}
I(X;Y) &= \sum_x \sum_y p(x,y) \log \frac{p(x,y)}{p(x)p(y)} \\
&= E_{p(x,y)}\left[\log \frac{p(x|y)}{p(x)}\right] = E_{p(x,y)}\left[\log \frac{p(y|x)}{p(y)}\right] \\
&= H(X) - H(X|Y) \\
&= H(Y) - H(Y|X)
\end{aligned}
$$

5.1 Given a data point $y \in R^d$ and a hyperplane $\theta \cdot x + \theta_0 = 0$, compute the Euclidean distance from the point to the hyperplane.

Let x be a point on the hyperplane—in other words, ensure it satisfies the equation $\theta \cdot x + \theta_0 = 0$. To find the Euclidean distance from the point to the hyperplane, we construct a vector $y - x$ and project it onto the unique vector perpendicular to the plane. Thus, we have the following:

$$
\begin{aligned}
d &= \|\text{proj}_\theta(y - x)\| \\
&= \left\|\frac{(y-x) \cdot \theta}{\theta \cdot \theta}\theta\right\| = |y \cdot \theta - x \cdot \theta| \frac{\|\theta\|}{\|\theta\|^2} \\
&= \frac{|y \cdot \theta - x \cdot \theta|}{\|\theta\|} = \frac{|y \cdot \theta + \theta_0|}{\|\theta\|}
\end{aligned}
$$

5.2 Given a primal linear program (LP) min $c^T x$ subject to $Ax <= b$, x >= 0, write down the dual version of the LP.

Each variable in the primal LP corresponds to a constraint in the dual LP, and vice versa. The primal is a minimization problem, so the dual is a maximization problem. The primal constraints are less than or equal, so the dual variables are greater than or equal. The primal variables are nonnegative, so the dual constraints are nonnegative. In other words, the dual is the following:

$$\max b^T w$$
$$\text{s.t. } A^T w \geq c$$
$$w \geq 0$$

5.3 Show that the radial basis function kernel is equivalent to the computing similarity between two infinite dimensional feature vectors.

The radial basis function kernel can be expanded using the multinomial theorem, as follows. Assuming the sigma is equal to 1, we have the following:

$$
\begin{aligned}
\kappa(x, x') &= \exp\left(-\frac{1}{2}||x - x'||^2\right) \\
&= \exp\left(x^T x' - \frac{1}{2}||x||^2 - \frac{1}{2}||x'||^2\right) \\
&= \exp\left(x^T x'\right)\exp\left(-\frac{1}{2}||x||^2\right)\exp\left(-\frac{1}{2}||x'||^2\right) \\
&= \sum_{k=0}^{\infty} \frac{(x^T x')^k}{k!}\exp\left(-\frac{1}{2}||x||^2\right)\exp\left(-\frac{1}{2}||x'||^2\right)
\end{aligned}
$$

This implies that RBF expansion has an infinite number of dimensions.

5.4 Verify that the learning rate schedule $\eta_k = (\tau_0 + k)^{-\kappa}$ satisfies Robbins-Monro conditions.

To show that the learning rate satisfies Robbins-Monro conditions, we need to show the following for nonnegative τ_0 and κ in $(0.5, 1]$:

$$\sum_{k=1}^{\infty} \eta_k = \sum_{k=1}^{\infty} \frac{1}{(\tau_0 + k)^{\kappa}} = \infty$$

$$\sum_{k=1}^{\infty} \eta_k^2 = \sum_{k=1}^{\infty} \frac{1}{(\tau_0 + k)^{2\kappa}} < \infty$$

This is true according to power series convergence.

5.5 Compute the derivative of the sigmoid function $\sigma(a) = [1 + \exp(-a)]^{-1}$.

We can compute the derivative as follows:

$$
\begin{aligned}
\frac{d}{dx}\sigma(x) &= \frac{d}{dx}(1+e^{-x})^{-1} \\
&= -(1+e^{-x})^{-2}(-e^{-x}) \\
&= \frac{e^{-x}}{(1+e^{-x})^2} \\
&= \frac{1}{1+e^{-x}}\frac{e^{-x}}{1+e^{-x}} \\
&= \sigma(x)(1-\sigma(x))
\end{aligned}
$$

5.6 Compute the runtime and memory complexity of the Bernoulli naive Bayes algorithm. The following pseudo-code captures the Bernoulli naive Bayes algorithm:

```
1:  Training:
2:  N_c = 0, N_jc = 0
3:  for i = 1, 2, ..., n do
4:      c = y_i // class label for ith example
5:      N_c = N_c + 1
6:      for j = 1, ..., D do
7:          if x_ij = 1 then
8:              N_jc = N_jc + 1
9:      end for
10: end for
11: π̂_c = N_c/N, θ̂_jc = N_jc/N
12: return π̂_c, θ̂_jc
13: Testing (for a single test document):
14: for c = 1, 2, ..., C do
15:     log p[c] = log π_c
16:     for j = 1, 2, ..., D do
17:         if x_j = 1 then
18:             log p[c]+ = log θ̂_jc
19:         else
20:             log p[c]+ = log(1 - θ̂_jc)
21:     end for
22: end for
23: c = arg max_c log p[c]
24: return c
```

Given that we have two nested for loops, the runtime complexity is $O(ND)$, where N is the number of training documents and D is the dictionary size. The runtime complexity during test time is $O(TCD)$, where T is the number of test documents, T is the number of classes, and D is the dictionary size. Similarly, space complexity is the size of arrays required to store model parameters that grow as $O(DC)$.

6.1 Compute the runtime and memory complexity of a KNN regressor.

The following pseudo-code captures the KNN regression algorithm:

```
1: class KNN:
2: function knn_search(K, X, y, Q)
3:   for query in Q:
4:     idx = argsort(euclidean_dist(query, X))[:K]
5:     knn_labels = [y[i] for i in idx]
6:     y_pred = mean(knn_labels)
7:   end for
8:   return y_pred
```

As we can see, we have a sorting operation that takes $O(N \log N)$ time, where N is the number of training data points. Thus, the runtime complexity is $O(N \log N + K) = O(N \log N)$ for each query q in Q. The KNN regressor is a nonparametric model; therefore, it has $O(1)$ parameter space complexity.

6.2 Derive the Gaussian process update equations based on the rules for conditioning multivariate Gaussian random variables.

Consider the following joint GP distribution:

$$\begin{pmatrix} f \\ f_* \end{pmatrix} \sim \left(\begin{pmatrix} \mu \\ \mu_* \end{pmatrix}, \begin{pmatrix} K & K_* \\ K_*^T & K_{**} \end{pmatrix} \right)$$

Here, we want to predict the function outputs $y^* = f(x^*)$ (i.e., starred variables represent a prediction on test data X^* and $K = \kappa(X,X)$, $K^* = \kappa(X,X^*)$ and $K^{**} = \kappa(X^*,X^*)$). Using the following rules for conditional distributions, we have the following:

$$p(x_A | x_B) = N\left(x_A | \mu_A + \Sigma_{AB}\Sigma_{BB}^{-1}(x_B - \mu_B), \Sigma_{AA} - \Sigma_{AB}\Sigma_{BB}^{-1}\Sigma_{BA} \right)$$

$$p(x_B | x_A) = N\left(x_B | \mu_B + \Sigma_{BA}\Sigma_{AA}^{-1}(x_A - \mu_A), \Sigma_{BB} - \Sigma_{BA}\Sigma_{AA}^{-1}\Sigma_{AB} \right)$$

Here, set A corresponds to X and set B corresponds to X^*. We get the Gaussian process update equations:

$$\begin{aligned} p(f_* | X_*, X, f) &\sim N(f_* | \mu_*, \Sigma_*) \\ \mu_* &= \mu(X_*) + K_*^T K^{-1}(f - \mu(X)) \\ \Sigma_* &= K_{**} - K_*^T K^{-1} K_* \end{aligned}$$

7.1 Explain how temperature softmax works for different values of the temperature parameter T.

Temperature softmax is defined as follows:

$$p_i = \text{softmax}(x, T) = \frac{\exp\left(\frac{x_i}{T}\right)}{\sum_{j=1}^{N} \exp\left(\frac{x_j}{T}\right)}$$

When $T=1$, we get the regular soft-max function. As T approaches infinity, the output distribution becomes more uniform (all outcomes are more equally likely). Thus, heating the distribution increases its entropy. As T approaches 0, we are decreasing the entropy of the output distribution, thereby accentuating high probability outputs.

7.2 In the forward–backward HMM algorithm, store the latent state variable z (as part of the HMM class) and compare the inferred z against the ground truth z.

To store the latent state variable z, initialize it as part of HMM class constructor: `self.z=np.zeros(self.n)` and modify the subsequent code to use `self.z[idx]` instead of `z[idx]`.

8.1 Show that the Dirichlet distribution $\text{Dir}(\theta|\alpha)$ is a conjugate prior to the multinomial likelihood by computing the posterior. How does the shape of the posterior vary as a function of the posterior counts?

Suppose we observe N dice rolls $D=\{x_1,\ldots,x_n\}$, where x_i in $\{1,\ldots,K\}$. If we assume the data is independent and identically distributed, the likelihood has the following form:

$$p(\mathcal{D}|\theta) = \prod_{k=1}^{K} \theta_k^{N_k}$$

Here, N_k is the number of times event k occurred. Since the parameter vector lives on a K-dimensional probability simplex, we need a prior that has support over this simplex. The Dirichlet distribution satisfies this criterion:

$$\text{Dir}(\theta|\alpha) = \frac{1}{B(\alpha)} \prod_{k=1}^{K} \theta_k^{\alpha_k-1}$$

Multiplying the likelihood and the prior, we see that the posterior is also Dirichlet:

$$
\begin{aligned}
p(\theta|\mathcal{D}) \quad &\propto \quad p(\mathcal{D}|\theta)p(\theta) \\
&\propto \quad \prod_{k=1}^{K} \theta_k^{N} \theta_k^{\alpha_k-1} = \prod_{k=1}^{K} \theta_k^{\alpha_k+N_k-1} \\
&= \quad \text{Dir}(\theta|\alpha_1 + N_1, \ldots, \alpha_K + N_K)
\end{aligned}
$$

We can see that the posterior counts are obtained by adding the prior counts and the observed counts. Since the posterior distribution has the same form as the prior, Dirichlet is said to be conjugate prior to the multinomial likelihood. As the observed counts increase, the Dirichlet posterior becomes more concentrated.

8.2 Explain the principle behind K-means++ initialization.

K-means++ initialization addresses the problem of poor centroid initialization that leads to poor clustering results. The basic idea is that the initial cluster centroids should be far away from each other. The principle behind K-means++ initialization is to first sample a cluster centroid at random and then sample the subsequent centroids with probability proportional to the distance away from the existing centroids. This ensures the centroids are spread out and provides a better initialization strategy.

8.3 Prove the cyclic permutation property of the trace: $tr(ABC) = tr(BCA) = tr(CAB)$.

Using the definition of trace, we can expand the product as follows:

$$tr(ABC) = \sum_i (ABC)_{ii} = \sum_i \sum_j A_{ij}(BC)_{ji} = \sum_i \sum_j \sum_k A_{ij}B_{jk}C_{ki};$$

Now, we can exchange the product of matrices and prove the permutation property:

$$tr(ABC) = \sum_i \sum_j \sum_k A_{ij}B_{jk}C_{ki} = \sum_i \sum_j \sum_k B_{jk}C_{ki}A_{ij} = tr(BCA)$$

8.4 Compute the runtime of the principal component analysis algorithm.

The pseudo-code for principal component analysis is as follows:

```
1: class PCA
2: function transform(X, K):
3:   Σ = covariance_matrix(X)
4:   V, λ = eig(Σ)
5:   idx = argsort(λ)
6:   V_pca = V[idx][ :K]
7:   λ_pca = λ [idx][: K]
8:   X_pca = XV_pca
9:   return X_pca
```

The PCA algorithm has three computationally expensive steps: covariance matrix computation, eigenvalue decomposition, and sorting. Let N be the number of data points, each represented with D features, and the covariance matrix computation is $O(ND^2)$, where we assume $D < N$. The eigenvalue decomposition complexity is $O(D^3)$, while the sorting operation takes $O(D \log D)$ time. Therefore, the runtime of the PCA algorithm is $O(ND^2 + D^3 + D \log D) = O(ND^2 + D^3)$.

9.1 Explain how latent Dirichlet allocation can be interpreted as nonnegative matrix factorization.

Recall the term–document matrix A_{vd}, where V is the vocabulary and D is the number of documents. Since we are interested in finding the number of topics K, LDA can be interpreted as a matrix factorization problem that takes the term–document matrix A_{vd} and factorizes it into a product of topics W_{vk} and topic proportions H_{kd}: $A=WH$. Since topics and topic proportions are probability distributions, the resulting matrices are constrained to be nonnegative:

$$\min_{W \geq 0, H \geq 0} \quad ||A - WH||_F$$

Therefore, LDA can be interpreted as nonnegative matrix factorization that can be solved using the alternating least squares (ALS) algorithm.

9.2 Explain why sparsity is desirable in inferring general graph structure.

Sparsity is a desirable property in graph structure inference because we want to be able to interpret our results. A fully connected graph does not provide much insight; therefore, we would like to adjust the threshold in the inverse covariance matrix estimator until we achieve a sparse graph structure we can draw meaningful conclusions from.

9.3 List several NP-hard problems that can be approximated with the simulated annealing algorithm.

Several applications of simulated annealing include the traveling salesman problem (TSP), maximum cut, independent set, and many others.

9.4 Brainstorm problems that can be efficiently solved by applying a genetic algorithm.

Some examples of problems that can be solved using genetic algorithms are the 8 queens problem, the traveling salesman problem, the feature selection problem, neural network topology, and many others.

10.1 Explain the purpose of nonlinearities in neural networks.

The purpose of nonlinearities in neural networks is to model nonlinear relationships between the input and output of a network layer. Without nonlinearities, the neural network will behave as a single-layer perceptron.

10.2 Explain the vanishing/exploding gradient problem.

Exploding gradients occur when the gradients get larger and larger with every layer during backpropagation. The vanishing gradient problem occurs when the gradients approach zero during backpropagation.

10.3 Describe some of the ways to increase neural model capacity and avoid overfitting.

To increase neural model capacity, we can increase the size and the number of layers. This can potentially lead to overfitting. To combat overfitting, we can use weight decay, dropout, and early stopping.

10.4 Why does the number of filters increase in LeNet architecture as we go from input to output?

The number of filters increases to capture more complex patterns in the image data. The earlier layers are used to extract geometric features, like edges, corners, and so on, while subsequent layers combine these patterns into more complex shapes.

10.5 Explain how an Adam optimizer works.

Adam can be seen as a variant on the combination of RMSProp and momentum optimizers. The update looks like RMSProp, except a smooth version of the gradient is used instead of the raw stochastic gradient. The full Adam update also includes a bias correction mechanism:

$$g \;=\; \frac{1}{m}\nabla_\theta \sum_i L\left(\left(x^{(i)};\theta\right),y^{(i)}\right)$$

$$m \;=\; \beta_1 m + (1 - \beta_1)g$$

$$s \;=\; \beta_2 v + (1 - \beta_2)g^T g$$

$$\theta \;=\; \theta - \epsilon_k \times \frac{m}{\sqrt{s + eps}}$$

11.1 What is a receptive field in a CNN?

A receptive field is the number of input pixels that produce a feature map. It is a measure of association of an output feature (of any layer) to the input region.

11.2 Explain the benefit of residual connections by deriving the backward pass.

The benefit of residual connections is that they allow gradients to flow through the network directly, without passing through nonlinear activation functions that cause the gradients to explode or vanish (depending on the weights).

Let $H = F(x) + x$. Then, we get the following.

$$\frac{\partial L}{\partial x} = \frac{\partial L}{\partial H}\frac{\partial H}{\partial x} = \frac{\partial L}{\partial H}\left(\frac{\partial F}{\partial x} + 1\right) = \frac{\partial L}{\partial H}\frac{\partial F}{\partial x} + \frac{\partial L}{\partial H}$$

11.3 Compare the pros and cons of using CNNs, RNNs, and transformer neural networks.

CNNs are highly parallelizable and, therefore, computationally fast. They are great at learning and detecting patterns in signals; however, they don't account for signal history. RNNs maintain an internal model of the past; however, they are restricted in parallel computation. Transformers have a high model capacity for learning; however, they may result in overfitting.

11.4 Give an example of a neural network that uses amortized variational inference.

In the example we looked at in this book, we used a multilayer perceptron to learn the mixture model parameters. Thus, MLP is one example of a neural network that can amortize variational inference computations over multiple data points.

11.5 Show via an example the intuition behind the GCN forward equation: $D^{(-1/2)}(A+I)D^{(-1/2)}XW+b$.

The product AX in the equation represents a summation of neighboring node features in matrix X. By adding identity to A, we now have a summation that includes the node itself: $(A+I)X$. To normalize this product, we form a diagonal degree matrix D and pre and post multiply our product by the square root of D. Finally, we multiply our expression by the weight matrix W and add a bias term b.

index

MANNING

The Manning Early Access Program

Don't wait to start learning! In MEAP, the Manning Early Access Program, you can read books as they're being created and long before they're available in stores.

Here's how MEAP works.

- **Start now.** Buy a MEAP and you'll get all available chapters in PDF, ePub, Kindle, and liveBook formats.

- **Regular updates.** New chapters are released as soon as they're written. We'll let you know when fresh content is available.

- **Finish faster.** MEAP customers are the first to get final versions of all books! Pre-order the print book, and it'll ship as soon as it's off the press.

- **Contribute to the process.** The feedback you share with authors makes the end product better.

- **No risk.** You get a full refund or exchange if we ever have to cancel a MEAP.

Explore dozens of titles in MEAP at www.manning.com.